GAZETTEER OF CHANDA DISTRICT IN CENTRAL PROVINCES

CITY WALL, CHANDA, SHOWING ACHALESHWAR TEMPLE AND GOND RAJA'S TOMB.

GAZETTEER OF CHANDA DISTRICT IN CENTRAL PROVINCES

L.F. Begbie

Gian Publishing House

GIAN PUBLISHING HOUSE
PUBLISHERS OF BOOKS ON HUMAN CIVILIZATION
29/6 SHAKTI NAGAR, DELHI-110007

First Reprint in India, 1986

*Printed at Goyal Offset Printers, Delhi-110035
and published by Smt. Gayatri Garg
for Gian Publishing House, Delhi-110007*

PREFATORY NOTE.

The Chānda District with a population composed of three main elements Marāthās, Telugus and Gonds, each speaking more or less an impure variety of their natural language, is of peculiar interest from a linguistic and ethnological point of view. It has also many other claims to distinction. In mineral wealth it is remarkably rich; it possesses vast forests and the area of its Government forest alone surpasses that of many entire Districts; its archæological remains are of unwonted interest for this part of the country; its systems of agriculture are unusually varied and in some respects unique in the Province; its irrigation system, already very extensive, is now attracting considerable attention on the part of Government, while its sporting possibilities, although no longer what they were in the not distant past, are still surpassed in few parts of India. The major portion of the Gazetteer has been written by Mr. L. F. Begbie, I.C.S., who possesses in a very special measure the knowledge, enthusiasm and literary gifts required for the task. Unfortunately his health broke down before he could complete the work and he was compelled to leave India. The book has thus lacked the finishing touches of its author and would no doubt have been greatly improved had Mr. Begbie been able to see it through the press. Chapter II, History and Archæology and the sections on Religion, Caste and Social Life and Customs have been written by the Rev. A. Wood, who gratefully acknowledges his indebtedness to the notes supplied by Mr. Hīrā Lāl and to Major Lucie Smith's records in the preparation of all these sections. Some of the Gazetteer articles have also been written by Mr. Wood, who has in addition read the whole book through in proof. Mr. Wood's intimate knowledge of the District gives a peculiar value to his suggestions and criticisms and I cannot be sufficiently grateful for his assistance. Chapter IX, General Administration, has been written by Mr. J. T. Marten, Deputy Commissioner, who also supplied some notes on the Leading Families. Mr. Begbie acknowledges his great indebtedness to Colonel Lucie Smith's Settlement Report of 1869, which is a work of considerable distinction and a veritable mine of information. Captain Glasfurd's Settlement Report of the Upper Godāvari District (1868), Mr. P. Hemingway's Settlement Report of 1905, and Mr. J. T. Chamberlain's Report on the Settlement of the Zamīndāris (1908) have also been freely utilised. The article on Geology was written by Mr. Begbie from notes supplied by Mr. P. N. Datta of the Geological Survey, and has been read and corrected by Mr. L. L. Fermor of the same Department. Mr. F. J. Langhorne of the Forest Department supplied Mr. Begbie with notes for the Botany and Forest sections which have also been read by Mr. J. Donald, I.F.S., and for the article on the Ahīri zamīndāri. The Chapters on Agriculture and Land Revenue have been read by Mr. P. Hemingway. The reports of the Archæological Survey of India have been freely borrowed from. The whole book has been read in proof by Mr. J. T. Marten.

A. E. N.

NAGPUR:
30th March 1909.

CHANDA DISTRICT GAZETTEER.

CONTENTS.

Chapter V.—LOANS, PRICES, WAGES, MANUFACTURES, TRADE AND COMMUNICATIONS.

Chapter VI.—FORESTS AND MINERALS.

Gian Publishing House
DELHI-110007

LIST OF MAPS AND PHOTOGRAPHS.

PARAGRAPH INDEX.

CHAPTER I.—GENERAL DESCRIPTION.

CHAPTER III.—POPULATION.

CHAPTER IV.—AGRICULTURE.

Chapter VI.—FORESTS AND MINERALS.

List of Deputy Commissioners who have held charge of the District since its constitution.

Name of Deputy Commissioner.	Period.	
	From	To
Captain R. S. Ellis ...	18-12-1854	...
Major W. H. Crichton ...	1857	30-9-63
Mr. H. J. MacGeorge ...	1-10-63	13-12-63
Captain H. F. Waddington ...	14-12-63	28-1-64
Captain L. B. Lucie Smith ...	29-1-64	6-5-70
Mr. J. F. Beddy ...	7-5-70	6-7-70
Captain M. P. Ricketts ...	7-7-70	31-12-71
Captain L. B. Lucie Smith ...	1-1-72	28-5-72
Mr. S. H Hennessy ...	29-5-72	15-6-72
Lieutenant-Colonel C. L. R. Glasfurd.	16-6-72	9-10-73
Mr. T. Drysdale ...	10-10-73	24-12-73
Lieutenant-Colonel C. L. R. Glasfurd.	25-12-73	10-4-75
Major W. Vertue ...	11-4-75	6-6-77
Mr. E. W. C. H. Miller ...	7-6-77	6-9-77
Major W. Vertue ...	7-9-77	9-1-78
Major A. Bloomfield ...	10-1-78	11-4-78
Mr. G. Pemberton ...	12-4-78	11-7-78
Major A. Bloomfield ...	12-7-78	24-3-79
Mr. J. F. Beddy ...	25-3-79	6-4-79
Mr. A. M. Russell ...	7-4-79	17-12-79
Mr. J. P. Goodridge ...	18-12-79	19-1-80
Major W. S. Brooke ...	20-1-80	16-3-80
Mr. J. P. Goodridge ...	17-3-80	11-3-81
Mr. T. E. Ellison ...	12-3-81	8-3-83
Colonel W. B. Thomson ...	9-3-83	27-6-83
Mr. E. W. C. H Miller ...	28-6-83	4-1-84
Mr. H. J. MacGeorge ...	5-1-84	11-3-85
Mr. L. Gordon ...	12-3-85	11-6-85
Mr. H. J. MacGeorge ...	12-6-85	1-3-89
Mr. L. Gordon ...	2-3-89	30-4-89
Mr. H. J. MacGeorge ...	1-5-89	1-1-90
Mr. C. W. McMinn ...	2-1-90	2-4-91
Mr. J. A. C. Skinner ...	3-4-91	21-6-91
Mr. F. G. Sly ...	22-6-91	6-7-91
Colonel R. M. B. Thomas ...	7-7-91	19-4-92
Mr. J. A. C. Skinner ...	20-4-92	23-7-94

List of Deputy Commissioners who have held charge of the District since its constitution.

Name of Deputy Commissioner.		Period.	
		From	To
Mr. A. B. Napier	...	24-7-94	14-9-94
Mr. H. F. Mayes	...	15-9-94	16-10-94
Mr. J. A. C. Skinner	...	17-10-94	28-6-95
Mr. S. W. Coxon	...	29-6-95	19-4-96
Mr. E. R. K. Blenkinsop	...	20-4-96	20-5-96
Mr. S. W. Coxon	...	21-5-96	5-5-98
Mr. R. F. Grimley	...	6-5-98	9-8-98
Mr. S. W. Coxon	...	10-8-98	12-9-99
Mr. A. B. Napier	...	13-9-99	1-12-99
Mr. S. W. Coxon	...	2-12-99	27-3-01
Mr. P. Hemingway	...	28-3-01	7-4-01
Mr. H. F. Hallifax	...	8-4-01	28-12-01
Mr. E. A. DeBrett	...	29-12-01	23-7-02
Mr. L. A. G. Clarke	...	24-7-02	20-10-02
Mr. W. N. Maw	...	21-10-02	26-7-03
Mr. J. T. Marten	...	27-7-03	14-7-04
Mr. P. S. Patuck	...	15-7-04	17-8-04
Mr. J. T. Marten	...	18-8-04	8-9-04
Mr. P. Hemingway	...	9-9-04	3-10-04
Mr. P. S. Patuck	...	4-10-04	8-11-04
Mr. W. N. Maw	...	9-11-04	31-1-06
Mr. J. W. E. Poynting	...	1-2-06	9-3-06
Mr. J. T. Chamberlain	...	10-3-06	17-12-06
Mr. H. F. Mayes	...	18-12-06	2-5-07
Mr. J. T. Marten	...	3-5-07	To date.

DISTRICT
CHANDA
Scale 1 Inch = 20 Miles
Miles.
REFERENCES TO ZAMINDARIS
1...Ahiri
2...Paimuranda
3...Gilgaon
4...Potegaon
5...Chandala
6...Palasgarh
7...Gewarda
8...Rangi
9...Dhanora
10...Khutgaon
11...Sonsari
12...Jharapapra
13...Kotgal
14...Muramgaon
15...Sirsundi
16...Dudhmala
BHANDARA
NAGPUR
WARDHA
DRUG
to Umrer
from Hinganghat
to Chauki
to Mohali
TIPAGARH HILL
Palasgarh
Gewarda
Kotgal
Sonsari
Sirsundi
Muramgaon
Rangi
Dhanora
Dudhmala
GARHCHIROLI
BRAMHAPURI
Deotek
Nagbhir
Talodhi
Amgaon
Arher Nawargaon
Pipalgaon Makta
Bhisi
Bandar
Pipalneri
Chimur
Govindpur
Neri
Mahadwadi
Wadhona
Ratnapur
Khatoda
Kesalbori
Segaon
Bhatala
Kosarsar
Nagri
Waghnak
Kharwad
Panjurni
Chandankheda
Chicholi
WARORA
Wunna R.
Erai N.
Gadbori
Sindewahi
Palebarsa
Mendha
Porla
Narot
Dewalgaon
Ingada
Thanegaon
Armori
Sathnala
Bokurdon
Ratoli
Barsaga
Khutgaon
Chandala

Prepared specially for the Superintendent Gazetteer Revision. C. P. from an Original supplied by him.

Helio., S. I O., Calcutta

CHANDA DISTRICT.

CHAPTER I.
GENERAL DESCRIPTION.

BOUNDARIES AND PHYSICAL FEATURES.

Position and boundaries.

1. Chānda, the most southerly District of the Central Provinces, is situated between 20° 50′ and 17° 56′ north latitude and 80° 59′ and 78° 48′ east longitude. The main body of the District is roughly triangular in shape, its north boundary forming the base of the triangle which gradually tapers towards its apex in the south. South of this main body and completely separated from it by a stretch of foreign territory some 15 miles in length lies a tract of 593 square miles known as the Lower Tāluks of Sironchā, which forms a kind of pendant to the rest of the District.[1] In fact, the shapes and relative position of these two divisions of the District roughly reproduce those of the Indian Peninsula and Ceylon on a small scale. The District has undergone numerous changes of area since its formation, but as at present constituted comprises an area of 9911 square miles, and is thus the largest District in the Province. It forms part of the Nāgpur Division, and is bounded on the north by the Wardhā, Nāgpur and Bhandāra Districts of that Division, on the west by the Yeotmāl District of Berār and territories of the Nizām of Hyderābād, and on the east by the Feudatory States of Kānker and Bastar and Drug District of Chhattīsgarh. The space between the main body of the District and the Lower Tāluks of Sironchā is occupied by the Nizām's Dominions and Bastar, which also bound the Lower Tāluks on the west and east respectively, while the Upper Godāvari District of

[1] The Lower Tāluks have since been transferred to Madras from 1st July 1909.

the Madras Presidency bounds them to the south. Some idea of the great size of the District may be obtained from the following measurements. From either the north-west or the north-east corner of the District to the confluence of the Godāvari and Indrāvati rivers which forms the apex of the main body of the District the distance is as the crow flies about 150 miles. From the latter point to the southernmost point of the Lower Tāluks of Sironchā is an additional 66 miles. From east to west the greatest breadth is in the extreme north, and the distance is almost 120 miles as the crow flies. The total area of the District exceeds that of Wales by one-third, and is slightly larger than the combined areas of Kent, Surrey, Sussex, Hampshire, Berks, Bucks, Bedfordshire, Hertfordshire, Essex and Middlesex.

Administrative divisions.

2. For administrative purposes the District is divided into five tahsīls, Warorā with an area of 1282 square miles occupying the north-west, Bramhapurī (897 square miles) lying in the centre of the northern half, Chānda (1174 square miles) in the west and centre, Garhchirolī (2883 square miles) east of the Waingangā, and Sironchā (3675 square miles) forming the whole of the tapering portion to the south. Besides these administrative divisions, there is an important distinction between the *khālsa* and the zamīndāri area; the latter of these occupies 4011 square miles of the country east of the Waingangā and consists of an undeveloped and hitherto somewhat under-administered tract in the possession of the hereditary petty chiefs known as zamīndārs.

Rivers.

3. On the first glance at the map of the District, the eye is at once arrested by a prominent river system. The whole of the western border of the District is uninterruptedly bounded by the Wardhā, Prānhita and Godāvari rivers, while the Indrāvati runs for a considerable distance along the south-east corner of the main body of the District. But even more striking to the eye is the bold north and south line of the Waingangā which

enters the District near the centre of the northern boundary, and slices it into two unequal halves, the western half containing the Warorā, Chānda and Bramhapurī tahsīls and representing a stage of comparatively high development, and the eastern half being composed of the Garhchirolī tahsīl with its numerous zamīndāris and the Ahīri zamīndāri of the Sironchā tahsīl, a tract which may be fairly described as on the whole one of the most backward parts of the Province. A detailed description of each of these rivers will be found in the Gazetteer appendix; it will be sufficient here to characterise them broadly. The Wardhā is a sluggish stream which flows in a south-easterly direction through fertile country where the soil is mostly black cotton. During its course in this District, the principal affluents which it receives are the Pengangā on the right bank, and the Erai on its left. Of these the Erai pursues its whole course of 50 miles within this District, rising in the north of the Warorā tahsīl and flowing almost due south till it joins the Wardhā, a short distance below Chānda. At about 19° 35′ north latitude the Wardhā forms a confluence with the Waingangā, and the combined streams continue to flow in a southerly direction under the name of Prānhita. Near Sironchā, the Prānhita joins the Godavari and takes its name, while yet further south at the southern corner of the Upper Tāluk of Sironchā the volume of the combined rivers is still further swelled by the influx of the Indrāvati. The only other important tributary of the Godavari running through this District is the Tālpir, which, rising in Bastar, falls into the Godāvari in the Cherlā tāluk after a total course of 70 miles. So far, in spite of elaborate navigation schemes, rocky barriers have prevented the navigation of the Godāvari on any large scale within its course through this District. Save in the extreme south the Waingangā is the recipient of numerous tributaries on either bank, and ultimately receives the drainage of the entire central portion of the District. On its left bank, the majority of its tributaries flow in almost at right angles to its course after pursuing a line almost due east and west. The chief affluents on this bank are from north to south the Gārhvi, the Kophrāgarhi and the Katnī. Of these the Kophrāgarhi is a very considerable stream 50 miles in length draining, with the aid of its large affluent the Sātnāla, a wide area of the northern zamīndāris. On its right bank the Waingangā is joined by a river called the Andhāri, 63 miles in length. This river with its numerous tributaries, the chief of which is known as the Mūl river, drains nearly the whole tract between the Erai and Waingangā rivers. The Waingangā is a slightly more rapid river than the Wardhā. A certain amount of traffic is carried upon it during the rains from Paunī in Bhandāra to Armorī, but it is not strictly speaking a navigable river. All the tributaries, both of the Wardhā and Waingangā, have an inconsiderable volume of water in the dry season, and as a rule are then reduced to a mere chain of pools. The Indrāvati rises in the highlands of Tohamāl in the Eastern Ghāts and, entering this District in the east of the Ahīri zamīndāri, at first flows due west, but later in its course it turns south and falls into the Godāvari after a total course of about 275 miles. Its largest tributary is the Bāndia river which rises in the Aundhī zamīndāri just outside this District, and flows south, draining a very large tract of country in its course of 80 miles. The Indrāvati is a true mountain torrent, with long deep pools joined by rocky rapids and, although used to some extent for floating timber, makes more appeal to the sportsman and the artist than to the merchant. It will thus be seen that as means of communication the rivers of the District are of practically no value; nor have they so far been utilised on any large scale for purposes of irrigation. But besides these main streams and rivers, the country is covered with a perfect network of small streams and nullahs, which are of the greatest service in ensuring an unfailing water-supply even in the worst seasons of drought and giving scope for the construction of numberless tanks for rice cultivation.

Hills.

4. The Waingangā and Wardhā rivers are separated by a watershed composed of two main ranges, the Chimūr and the Mūl hills. The general elevation of these valleys is some 600 to 800 feet above sea-level, and besides the ranges about to be described they are interspersed with numerous small isolated hills which do not require particularisation. The Chimūr hills commence east of Chimūr in the north of the Warorā tahsīl and run down southwards with one break of about five miles as far as Moharlī, gradually diminishing in size from north to south. The range is 20 miles in length and six in breadth, with an average elevation of 450 feet above the surrounding plain. In a basin of these hills lies the famous Tāroba lake, one of the beauty-spots of the District. The Mūl hills lie further to the south passing three miles west of the village from which they take their name; they measure 18 miles from north to south, and 13 from east to west, with a height above the plain of 400 feet. East of and parallel to the Chimūr hills runs a range known as the Pharsāgarh hills which forms part of the boundary between the Warorā and Bramhapurī tahsīls. This range extends for 13 miles with an average height of 600 feet above the plain, and terminates in a scarped cliff named Sāt Bahinī, 1508 feet above sea-level, which is a conspicuous feature of the landscape for forty miles southwards.

East of the Waingangā stretches a tangle of highlands, forming a table-land which runs the entire length of the northern division of the District. Numerous hills rise out of this table-land, and in fact in this part of the country one is seldom out of sight of a hill but there is no regular range in the northern zamīndāris. Two blocks of hills, however, deserve special mention. The more northerly lies in Palāsgarh and the Bedgaon pargana of Gewardhā, and is known as the Sātnāla hills, taking its name from the Sāt river which rises there and flows into the Kophrāgarhi and eventually into the Waingangā. To the south-east of this in the Kotgal and Muramgaon zamīndāris and stretching into the

Drug District, there is another block of hills rising to an elevation of 2000 feet. This is the Tīpagarh range, so called from the stronghold of that name now in ruins and hidden in almost impenetrable jungle. Travelling southwards to the Ahiri zamīndāri, we at length come to a regular range, occupying nearly the whole of the almost circular excrescence which projects on the eastern side of that zamīndāri into Bastar. Here the hills attain a height of 2000 or 3000 feet and beyond Lahir there is scarcely a mile of level land; the country is so rugged that travelling is impossible except on foot. Westward towards Sironchā the land is interspersed with hill ranges, the most notable of which is the Sirkondā range near Sironchā, rising to a height of some 1800 feet above sea-level. These hills are only some 18 miles from Sironchā, and were once used as a sanitarium with some success. Hills run southward from Sironchā with one or two small breaks as far as the junction of the Godāvari and Indrāvati. The highest peaks in the District occur in the Lower Tāluks of Sironchā. Here the Gādulgutta hills, which are a continuation of the Eastern Ghāts, run parallel to the Godāvari from the Indrāvati to the Tālpir, a distance of about 70 miles, forming a boundary between the Tāluks and Bastar. The highest peak here attains a height of 3174 feet. These mountains are extremely picturesque, and so rugged that rough sheafs of bamboos with projecting pieces to serve as steps are erected at frequent intervals on the footpaths which are the only means of communication with the plain along the river. The elevation of the Sironchā plain country is somewhat lower than that of the rest of the District, an increasingly nearer approach to the sea-level naturally marking the downward progress of the Godāvari. At Sironchā the height above sea-level is only 406 feet as compared with 643 at Chānda.

General conformation and scenery.

5. The foregoing review of the hill and river system of Chānda should now enable the reader to comprehend the broad and general features of the physical conformation

of the District. It is, to put the matter briefly, arranged in a dual series of valleys and watersheds running from north to south. The western halves of the Warorā and Chānda tahsīls lie in the valley of the Wardhā; they are separated from the central valley of the Waingangā by the watershed which is formed by the Mūl and Chimūr hills. Beyond this watershed the broad valley of the Waingangā stretches to the east until it meets and is lost in the highlands and plateaux of the zamīndāri area. The basins of the Wardhā and Waingangā are further subdivided into more or less numerous smaller valleys which are formed by their tributaries. Sironchā in both its divisions repeats the arrangement of valley to the west and highland to the east, but in this case the valley is a comparatively narrow strip, and there is only one valley and one range of hills.

The broad characteristics of the scenery of the District follow the varieties of its conformation. The riverain tract of the Wardhā valley in general reproduce the features of the country made familiar to the traveller by rail from Bhusāwal to Nāgpur; a bare, almost treeless, monotony most depressing to look upon, and only redeemed from positive ugliness during the few short weeks while the crops are approaching maturity. But even here occasional patches of jungle lend some variety to the scene and at the worst this type of country is limited to a comparatively small area in the extreme west. Far more pleasant to the eye is the valley of the Waingangā. Here between adjacent villages fairly extensive stretches of jungle almost always occur, and the alternation of jungle and cultivation makes a pleasant variety in the morning ride. The open country, too, is here diversified by numerous fine trees such as the mahuā, the tamarind, the pīpal and the mango, and nearly every village has its tank of brilliant blue water. Perhaps the worst fault that can be found with this type of scenery is that like most Indian plain scenery it repeats itself continually until robbed of much of its charm. Turning to the scenery of the hilly tracts, there are in these many spots of great beauty: Tāroba, with its sanctuary and lake whither all manner of beasts of the jungle come fearlessly to quench their thirst, 'the glittering heights of Surjāgarh,' the meeting of three mountain rivers at remote Bhamrāgarh, a scene extolled by those who have visited it as being unrivalled throughout the length and breadth of the Provinces--these are but a few of many beautiful spots that might be named or are nameless. At times it must be admitted that the interminable stretches of gloomy forest oppress the imagination, and the traveller is glad to emerge for a space into the more open haunts of men, and welcomes the uninterrupted view even of an Indian sun. In such a mood, it is a pleasant and fairly frequent sight to see the clearings made by the Gonds for the purposes of their *gātā* cultivation, where some little brook has been dammed with a descending series of stockades and the pool above each stockade has been sown with rice. These chosen plots of fertile land, amongst wide wastes set like a little nest, are among the most grateful memories of those who have camped through the forest country of Chānda.

GEOLOGY.

Geological formations.

6. Chānda offers a field of unusual interest to the geologist in that its structure is very varied and embraces almost all the formations which occur in the Central Provinces. To Messrs. Hislop and Hunter belongs the credit of having acted as pioneers of geological research in this District, and they were also the discoverers of several localities from which a rich harvest of fossils was collected.

The geological formations observed in this District are as follows:—

Archæan ...	Granites and Gneisses Dhārwars
Purāna ...	Vindhyans

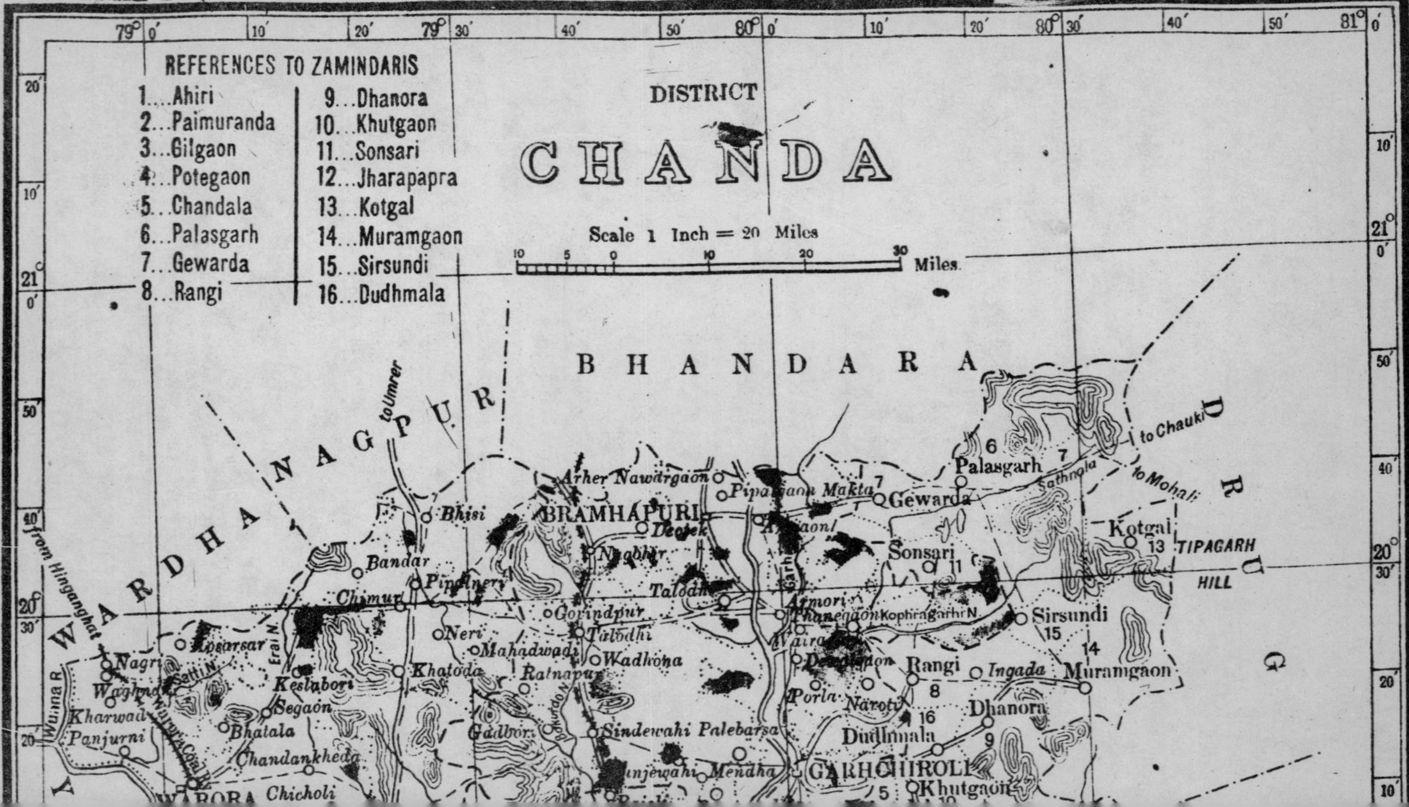
DISTRICT
CHANDA
REFERENCES TO ZAMINDARIS
1...Ahiri
2...Paimuranda
3...Gilgaon
4...Potegaon
5...Chandala
6...Palasgarh
7...Gewarda
8...Rangi
9...Dhanora
10...Khutgaon
11...Sonsari
12...Jharapapra
13...Kotgal
14...Muramgaon
15...Sirsundi
16...Dudhmala
Scale 1 Inch = 20 Miles
Miles
BHANDARA
NAGPUR
WARDHA
DRUG
to Umrer
to Chauki
to Mohali
from Hinganghat
TIPAGARH
HILL
Palasgarh
Gewarda
Kotgal
Sonsari
Sirsundi
Muramgaon
Rangi
Ingada
Dhanora
Dudhmala
GARHCHIROLI
Khutgaon
Mendha
Sindewahi
Palebarsa
BRAMHAPURI
Arher Nawargaon
Bhisi
Bandar
Chimur
Neri
Mahadwadi
Ratnapur
Wadhona
Talodhi
Gorindpur
Armori
Khatoda
Keslabori
Segaon
Bhatala
Chandankheda
Chicholi
Nagri
Kharwad
Panjurni
Wunna R.
Erai N.
Porla
Naroti

Prepared specially for the Superintendent Gazetteer Revision. C. P. from an Original supplied by him.

Helio, S. I. O. Calcutta

Aryan ...	Gondwānas	Tālchir group Barākar group Kāmthi group Kotā-Malerī group	Carboniferous to Jurassic.
	Deccan Trap series—Cretaceous.		
	Laterite.		
	Alluvium.		

I.—Archæan Formations.

Granites are holocrystalline rocks typically composed of quartz, felspar, and mica or hornblende, and are of very varying grain; in this District they are also associated with diorites and other holocrystalline basic rocks. *Gneisses* consist of gneiss proper—a foliated crystalline rock having much the same constituents as a granite—with schists of hornblende, mica, and quartz, and with much vein quartz. *Dhārwārs*, as they occur in this District, are highly altered shales (argillites) with some quartzites, sometimes ferruginous, and with some micaceous schists.

II.—Purāna Formations.

Resting unconformably on the gneisses occur the *Vindhyans* consisting mostly of sandstones, quartzitic sandstones, and quartzites, with some shales and limestones. The Vindhyans of this District belong to the Lower Vindhyan series.

III.—Aryan Formations.

The rocks of the *Tālchir* group, the lowest member of the Gondwāna series, are generally fine buff sandstones, greenish-gray silty shales and sandstones, underlaid by a bed containing boulders polished and striated, this striation or scratching being supposed to be due to glacial action. The *Barākar* group is notable as containing all the workable beds of coal. Beginning from the top the arrangement of layers is (1) coal, (2) sandstones and shales, (3) carbonaceous beds, and (4) sandstones and shales. The *Kāmthi* group is found resting unconformably on the Barākars. The rocks composing it are (1) grits, more or less compact,

(2) sandstones, coarse or fine-grained, with red blotchy streaks, with some conglomerate, and (3) sandstones, argillaceous and ferruginous. Clays, usually red and green, and shales of various colours occur intercalated among the sandstones. The rocks constituting the *Kotā-Malerī* group are mainly red and green clays and argillaceous sandstones, the basal sandstones containing green clay-galls; limestone beds are found in association with the clays.

The *Deccan Trap* series is composed of volcanic lavas and has been classified into upper, middle and lower traps; beneath it lie basal sedimentary beds, known as Lametā or Infratrappean, consisting of sandstones, sometimes calcareous, with limestones, which are generally cherty and impure and some clays. Intercalated among the lava-flows occur volcanic ash beds and also some sedimentary beds; these latter are known as intertrappean beds. The only traps found in Chānda belong to the Lower Trap group.

Laterites are next in succession to the trappean rocks, and later still are the various deposits which include all the soils of the present area. In the river valleys ossiferous gravels often cemented into a conglomerate of tolerable hardness are of frequent occurrence.

Topographical distribution.

7. East of the Waingangā the formation is almost entirely of the Archæan series, granite, gneiss, massive quartz and hornblende, mica, talc and chlorite, schists being the typical rocks. Large areas of this formation are concealed by overlying laterite. Fossiliferous strata are but sparingly represented. A band of gneiss is found west of the Waingangā, which practically bisects the Ghātkul pargana and forms the watershed between the Waingangā and Wardhā rivers. Granite may be seen exposed at many points in the zamīndāris, while gneiss is rarely exposed in comparison with the area actually occupied by it. Abutting on the gneiss area west of the Waingangā and running airly parallel to the course of the Wardhā lies the Gondwāna

area which forms part of the Wardhā Valley Coalfield. This extends, as far as this District is concerned, from Kirmiri, 9 miles above the junction of the Wardhā with the Waingangā to a little above the village of Aikonā north of Warorā. This belt is 75 miles in length, from 8 to 22 miles in breadth, and comprises an area of about 1000 square miles: the coal deposits in it will be found fully described in the chapter on Minerals. The Tālchir beds are usually concealed by the younger Gondwāna rocks but between Chānda and Bhāndak Tālchirs are found extensively exposed. The varieties of sandstones found in the Barākar division are very numerous, the strata in some places being extremely thick-bedded, in others thin bands of flagstone, and in others again mere laminæ, many of which would go to an inch, while the texture ranges from coarse conglomerate to a stone of the finest grain, and the colours shade from white to purple and from yellow to red. Fireclay and other valuable clays are interstratified in the system, and in the boulder and conglomerate beds of the underlying Tālchirs limestone occurs in great abundance. The Barākar rocks are frequently overlaid by Kāmthis; the most notable outcrop of this latter group is that which extends from the town of Chānda eastwards to Keljhar, and from the Wardhā near Lāthi north-westwards as far as Bhatāla. Chānda itself and the cave temples of Bhāndak stand on the lower and basal sandstones of this group respectively. A white argillaceous band which stretches for miles in the vicinity of Chānda is very even in texture but rather soft, and can be carved into very minute forms of ornaments. Other outcrops of Kāmthi occur about Bhatāla, Mangli and Salori in the Warorā tahsīl. North of the carboniferous Barākar sandstones lie sandstones of an older age, belonging to the Lower Vindhyan series. The most important outcrop of these extends in a broad band from

---

[1] See *Mem. Geol. Survey, India*, Vol. XIII, Pt. 1, pages 24-28

the neighbourhood of Chimūr in a south-easterly direction to a point four miles west of Mūl. Other outcrops occur in the hilly ground between Nāgbhīr and Sankarpur, in the low tract extending north-east from Kānpa as far as the Waingangā, and in the parts about Bramhapurī and Adar. In the extreme north-west of the District is a very small area of trap; this series is not represented elsewhere in the District. Lametās are found near Segaon and Dongargaon and also at Pisdurā, all in the Warorā tahsīl. Kotā-Malerī rocks crop out along the left bank of the Wardhā at Porsā and Sakmūr (south of Dābha), at Chikiāla in the north of the Sironchā tāluk, and both at Sironchā itself and in its neighbourhood at Kotā. Between Porsā and Sironchā outcrops are to be observed along the right bank of the river in Hyderābād territory as well as the left. Laterite, in addition to the area covered by it east of the Waingangā, occupies a large portion of the Bramhapurī, Garborī and Rājgarh parganas; its thickness must once have been great, as is testified by the height of the laterite hills scattered about.

Geology of Sironchā.

8. The southern portion of the District, the Sironchā tahsīl, forms a southward-pointing projection between the Nizām's territory on the west and Bastar State on the east, being separated from the former by the Prānhita and Godāvari rivers, and from the latter by the Indrāvati.[1] The northern portion of the tahsīl is made up of crystalline rocks, whilst the southern portion is crossed by younger formations arranged in bands, having a general N. N. W. to S. S. E. strike. These younger formations are, in descending order:—

Chikiāla Series ...	Upper Gondwānas.
Kotā Series ...	Upper Gondwānas.
Kāmthi Series ...	Lower Gondwānas.
Sullavai Series ...	Lower Vindhyans.
Pākāl Series ...	Upper Kadapahs.

[1] See King, W. *Mem. Geol. Survey, India*, XVIII, Pt. 2 (1881).

The *Pākāls* consist of quartzites and slates, with subordinate limestones, and form the Sirkondā range of hills, rising to 1751 feet above sea-level. The *Sullavai* series is made up of sandstones and quartzites, and forms a mass of hills to the S. E. of Devalmarri, rising to perhaps 2000 feet. The *Kāmthi* are found as a S. E. running strip, at the N. W end of which, by the Prānhita river, stands the town of Sironchā. They consist of sandstones, conglomerates and clays. The *Kotā* group takes its name from the village of Kotā, situated some 5 miles to the north of Sironchā. It consists of a series of sandstones, with red clay bands and well developed limestones, and occurs as a strip immediately to the N. E. of the Kāmthi band. It has yielded fossil remains of fish, ferns, cycads and conifers, and is regarded as partly of Rājmahal and partly of Jabalpur age. The *Chikiāla* series forms a band to the N. E. of the Kotā strip, stretching from Darsiāra on the Prānhita, past Chikiāla, to the Godāvari, giving rise to a low flat-topped range of hills some 8 or 10 miles N. E. of Sironchā. It consists of ferruginous sandstones and conglomerates.

Fossils.

9. From the Kāmthi rocks at Mangli some miles north of Warorā, Mr. Hislop obtained the fossil remains of a remarkable Labyrinthodont reptile, *Brachyops laticeps*, the scales and jaws of fish, *Estheriæ* (a kind of bivalved crutacean) and vegetable remains. *Glossopteris Browniana* and *Indica*, species common in the coal-bearing rocks of Bengal and in Australia, and *Glossopteris musæfolia* have been obtained from similar rocks at Isāpur near Chānda, while *Actinopteris* and seeds have also been found at Charwat, three miles south of Chānda. Among fossil-plants derived from the Kotā-Malerī group are a *Palissya conferta*, *Palissya Jabalpurensis* and *Araucarites Kachensis*, while among the fauna are *Estheria*, *Lepidotus*, *Aechmodus*, *Ceratodus*, *Parasuchus* and *Hyperodapedon*. The Lametā area at Pisdurā yielded to the researches of Mr. Hislop[1] the bones

[1] Quarterly Journal, *Geol. Society of London*, XVI, page 163.

of large denosaurs, coprolites, saurian teeth, fish vertebræ, and fragments of the plastron of a freshwater turtle. A femur upwards of a foot broad at the condyles and one vertebra about seven inches across are among the further discoveries[1] made at this place. In the similar formation at Dongargaon, Mr. Hislop found a specimen of a fish consisting of a head with a long muzzle armed with formidable sauroid teeth and rows of smaller ones; this was supposed by Sir P. Egerton to be allied to *Sphyrœnoaus* of the London clay.[2] Mr. Fedden of the Geological Survey found some fish remains at Dhamni, south of Segaon, but they were injured in transit and never identified. Mr. Hislop also found some intertrappean shells at Pisdurā such as *Paludina normalis*, *Paludina wapsharei*, *Limnœa oviformis*, *Physa Prinsepii* or *inflata*.

BOTANY.

Shrubs.

10. The flora of the District bear many evidences of the proximity of the more luxuriant forest of Southern India. This is most strikingly exemplified in the case of river bed shrubs, for of the nine most common species three are recorded as being found only from Chānda southwards. These are *Vitex leucoxylon* locally called *rāwan bel*, *Homonoia retusa*, a red-petioled blunt-leafed shrub of the same family and habit as the well known willow-like *taniki* (*Homonoia riparia*) and the *khatwat* (*Ficus asperrima*). The other river bed shrubs of most frequent occurrence such as the *jhau* (*Tamarix dioica*), *Phyllanthus Lawii* and *Rhabdia lycioides* are found commonly in other parts of the Province. Of shrubs which are met with in village and forest lands, the *chhota ber* (*Zizyphus nummularia*) is exceptionally common in cultivated areas; it is a small thorny shrub resembling the common *ber*, but with very crooked branches. The *kharāsni* (*Nyctanthes arbor-tristis*), the *adura* (*Adhatoda Vasica*), the gaudy-flowered *ghogurli* (*Grewia sapida*), the *lokhandi* (*Ixora parviflora*) from

[1] Quarterly Journal, *Geol. Society of London*, XVI, page 282.

[2] *Ibidem*, page 163.

which postal runners obtain their torches, are a few of the other shrubs which most frequently occur. The *burangi* (*Streblus asper*) is common throughout and its small rough dark green leaves make it easily recognisable.

Weeds and grasses.

11. Turning to weeds and grasses, their name is legion, and it is a matter of some difficulty to review even the chief species within the space at command. *Bhendā* (*Urena lobata*) may prove to be one of economic importance as it possesses a fibre which is stronger but unfortunately shorter than jute fibre. It is at present little known but the market value is said to be approximately that of "Medium" jute or about Rs. 225 per ton.[1] The *mundi* or *Sphæranthus Indicus* abounds in fallow fields in the western half of the District; while in black soil fields in the same tract occurs the Indian spurge or *dudhai* (*Euphorbia pilulifera*), the milk of which is commonly used in tattooing. *Nāgarmotha* or *Cyperus scariosus* is another familiar weed which infests black soils. Very common too is the *gokarnī* or *Clitoria Ternatea*, whose twining stems, large solitary bright blue blossom and graceful pinnate leaves are very noticeable in the rains and the early cold weather. In the Bramhapurī tahsīl the *kacherī* or *Cucumis maderaspatanus* is common, and is easily to be recognised by its creeping stems, lobed hairy leaves, and long ellipsoid fruit. Grateful to horses is the succulent *dūb* grass or *Cynodon dactylon*, common on black soil throughout the District. *Achyranthus aspera*, the prickly chaff flower or *aghāra*, haunts the skirts of villages west of the Waingangā; *Amaranthus viridis*, called in the vernacular *chaolai*, is everywhere found in fields, *bāris* and places where refuse is stacked. *Ocimum sanctum*, the *tulsī* or sacred basil, is cultivated in many Hindu households. The *wāgnakhi* or tiger claw (*Martynia diandra*) is found chiefly in the Chānda and Bramhapurī tahsīls; it has a double clawed fruit, which finds favour among children for

[1] Agricultural Ledger, 1908-09, No. 4.

their games. The deadly *dhatūra* (*Datura Stramonium*) is found in all parts. The *ghol* or Indian purslane (*Portulaca oleracea*) is another common weed; its small clusters of yellow flowers may often be seen during the rains. The *kānte dhotra* or prickly poppy (*Argemone mexicana*), the *akowā* (*Calotropis gigantea*), the *tarotā* or negro coffee (*Cassia occidentalis*), the *bhatkataiyā* (*Solanum indicum*), the *pitpāpra* (*Fumaria parviflora*), the *baochī* (*Psoralea corylifolia*) and the *katsuruiyā* (*Barleria Prionitis*) are other weeds of frequent occurrence which must be dismissed with the mere mention of their names; the two last named abound on waste lands. Among weeds which haunt watery and marshy places may be mentioned the *god* (*Ischæmum rugosum*), the *tālimakhāna* (*Hygrophila spinosa*), and the *pasai* or *deodhān* (*Hygrorhiza aristata*).

Nearly all the plants mentioned and many others too numerous to mention find a place in the villager's pharmacopœia if not in his mess of pottage. They are decocted into potions, philtres, hair-washes, pain-killers, and endless other varieties of nostrums; the neglected wife has only to go a few paces from her door to gather either the friendly herb that will restore her husband's affection to her, or the decisive *dhatūra* which will cut him short in his career of unfaithfulness.

Principal timber trees.

12. The chief high-class timber trees of the District are teak (*Tectona grandis*), *bijasāl*, often known as the bastard teak (*Pterocarpus Marsupium*), and *shīsham*, the black wood or rosewood tree (*Dalbergia latifolia*), which all yield timber of extreme value as building wood and for the manufacture of furniture. The celebrated teak of the Ahīri and Alāpalli forests attains large dimensions and is freely exported to Rājahmundry in Madras, where it is preferred to Burma teak. *Bijasāl* labours under the disadvantage of not floating unless supported by lighter woods, two teak logs being required to float one *bija*, while it takes years to season and is full of gum resin which

exudes an unpleasant and most tenacious rusty stain when the wood is exposed to damp. The tree is sometimes tapped for this gum resin which yields the true kino of commerce, and is used medicinally. *Shīsham* grows to a large size in the forests of Ahīri, Alāpalli and Moharlī, but its weight prevents it from being exported at a profit. Next in importance is the *sāj* or *yen* (*Terminalia tomentosa*) whose merits are not so fully recognised by the traders of this Province as they are in Madras where it finds a ready sale at the same rate as *bijasāl.* The tree attains a girth of 8 to 12 feet in Ahīri, Alāpalli and Moharlī. It is the principal house-building material of the District, and is the chief tree used locally for rearing the tasar silk worms. *Haldū* (*Adina cordifolia*) is a large sized tree which is found scattered throughout the forests; the trunks are sometimes hollowed out to form *dongās* or canoes which ply up and down the Prānhita and Indrāvati rivers. The export of this timber to Rājahmundry is steadily increasing, its value being placed slightly below that of *bijasāl* and *sāj.* Nearly akin to *haldū* is *kalam* or *kaini* (*Mitragyna parvifolia*) from which native combs are made. It has almost no sale as large timber although it is an excellent turning wood and polishes well. Its leaves are eaten by cattle and both bison and deer strip off the bark for fodder. *Anjan* (*Hardwickia binata*) is a useful tree found at its best in the forests of Ahīri and Sironchā; its heavy and durable timber is largely employed for the naves of cart-wheels; the bark yields a good and strong fibre out of which the natives make ropes, while its leaves afford fodder for cattle. Both *anjan* and *shīsham* have been found suitable for the construction of gun-carriages, but are unfortunately too heavy to export for this purpose. The smooth white bark of the *dhaurā* (*Anogeissus latifolia*) renders it a prominent object in the forest landscape. Its tough, elastic close grained wood possesses great transverse strength, and hence is employed universally for the axles of carts; there is a large demand for the wood from Berār. It makes a fairly good charcoal which is freely used for lime-burning and boiling down sugarcane juice; its bark when incised exudes a clear white crystalline gum which is used medicinally and also for other purposes such as calico-printing, while the leaves are sometimes utilised for tanning. The satinwood tree or *bhīra* (*Chloroxylon Swietenia*) is found throughout the District on poor soils and flourishes to the south of the Dābha range; it is easily recognised by its soft yellow corky bark which protects it from injury by fire. The heartwood displays a beautiful satin-like sheen whence the tree derives its name, and, when water-seasoned for six months, makes excellent furniture which takes a fine polish. There is a good demand for it for cabinet-maker's work. Locally it is fashioned into agricultural implements, as also is the *lendia* (*Lagerstrœmia parviflora*) the timber of which is also useful in construction work. Poles of this species come next in value to the teak in the southern markets. The bark yields a sweet chewing gum, while both bark and leaves are used in tanning. The ironwood tree (*Xylia dolabriformis*) is found in small numbers and inferior size in the forests of Dābha, Ahīri and Alāpalli. Its vernacular name is *suria*; it is but sparingly used as it is unworkable with the ordinary country tools. The *beherā* (*Terminalia belerica*) and the *hirdā* or *harrā* (*Terminalia Chebula*) yield fruits commercially known as myrobalans in which there is a fair export trade. The former is a very large tree attaining a height growth of 80 to 100 feet and a girth of 10 to 16 feet; it is fairly common throughout the District. Its dirty grey coloured flowers emit an offensive smell, and the wood having little durability is seldom used. Native ink is extracted from the fruit; the kernel of the seed is eaten and also produces oil. *Harrā* fruit is freely used for dyeing and as a country medicine. The *anjan* (*Terminalia Arjuna*), found almost invariably growing on the banks of nullahs, and the *rohan* (*Soymida febrifuga*) are in demand for well-curbs and for stakes in making tank embankments; the bark of the former has medicinal properties, while that of the latter is used in dyeing and tanning. From the *khair* (*Acacia Catechu*) is obtained heavy charcoal of the best quality; its wood is durable and immune from white-ants, and is therefore useful for house-poles and fencing, plough-shares, cane and oil-presses and excellent rice pounders are made from it; it also yields the catechu of commerce. The bark is astringent and is used medicinally. *Kosam* (*Schleichera trijuga*) by its pleasant habit of shooting a new head of foliage in March, just when all other trees are more or less leafless, and so affording a grateful shade to the traveller, has earned the *sobriquet* of the 'Forester's friend'. Commercially it is of considerable importance, as it produces the finest and most valuable lac. *Semal* (*Bombax malabaricum*) is used for door-panels and packing cases and is also hollowed out into dug-outs. It has a large scarlet flower, the calyx of which is eaten as a vegetable when it is in the bud; the fruit yields a soft silky cotton with which quilts and pillows are often stuffed. The common and well-known mahuā (*Bassia latifolia*) is of the highest importance as furnishing meat and drink for the aboriginal tribes; country liquor is prepared by distilling the succulent fleshy corolla which is eaten either green or dried in a mess of juāri or rice. The fruit yields an oil which is used both as a food and for lighting purposes. Common also is the *chār* (*Buchanania latifolia*), whose fruit is a valuable diet especially in days of famine. The kernel of the seed goes by the name of *chironjī* and sells at the rate of R. 1-8-0 per seer; it yields an oil, but its more general use is as an ingredient in native sweetmeats. The evergreen *khirnī* (*Mimusops indica*) is very common in the Dābha range; its wood is converted into walking sticks, and it has a sickly sweet fruit which appeals to the native palate. The *tendū* (*Diospyros Melanoxylon*) is the Indian ebony, but as a matter of fact it is only the older trees which in this District sometimes contain the black heartwood from which the latter name is derived. The wood is not extensively used, as the fruit finds much favour as an article of diet. The *tiwas* (*Ougeinia dalbergioides*) gives a tough and durable timber, while its bark is pounded and used to poison fish. It also produces a red gum which acts as an excellent styptic for cuts. The brilliant red blossoms of the *palās* (*Butea frondosa*) are the most conspicuous points of colour in the forests during the early hot weather, but ordinarily it is a dreary and woe-begone looking tree. From the flower is extracted a dye which is scattered about freely at the Holi festival; its leaves are made into plates and platters, and are employed in thatching houses; its bark yields a gum called 'Bengal kino' which is used medicinally, and the bark of the roots is transformed into an excellent fibre which is worked up into ropes; it is the species on which the lac insect is most commonly cultivated; its gregarious habit on black cotton soils makes the tending and the collection of the lac exceptionally easy. Another fibre-yielding tree is the *dhāmin* (*Grewia tiliæfolia*); it has a tough and elastic wood which is worked up into oars, shafts, and handles of implements and into *kāwars* for carrying goods. The *gongal* (*Cochlospermum gossypium*) is common; it is a small tree with large handsome yellow flowers. Most of the trees are found in other Districts. The *suria* (*Xylia dolabriformis*) is only found in these Provinces in Chānda, Bhandāra and Bālāghāt; the *polgu* or *polki* (*Givotia rottleriformis*), another southern species, is peculiar to the District. On the other hand, the *sāl* (*Shorea robusta*) so common in the Sātpurā tract and to the east of Chānda in the Raipur District is entirely absent; and the *harrā* (*Terminalia Chebula*) is not nearly so common as in the more northerly forests of the Province.

Among bamboos, *Dendrocalamus strictus*, the common bamboo of this Province, holds a practical monopoly save in Moharlī, in the east of the Sironchā tāluk and in Cherla where the large thorny *katang* forms brakes which are often well nigh impenetrable; the common *rattan* or *bent* (*Calamus Rotang*) is also found gregariously in the Ahīri zamīndāri below the Surjāgarh hills.

13. The foremost place among the fruit trees of the District is taken by the mango or *ām* (*Mangifera indica*), which is common in avenues and groves and also occurs as an "escape" in forests. The fruit is usually too stringy and redolent of turpentine to appeal to the European palate. The best mangoes come from a tree called *ambyabahār* about three miles from Chānda. A striking feature in the flora of the District is the large number of tamarind trees (*Tamarindus indica*). The succulent pulp of the fruit holds a high place in the native menu. The custard apple or *sītāphal* (*Anona squamosa*) is also cultivated for its fruit. The *jāmun* (*Eugenia Jambolana*) bears an acid and astringent fruit which finds some favour. Other trees bearing edible fruit are the *kawīth* (*Feronia Elephantum*) and *bel* (*Aegle Marmelos*) the fruit of which is a useful remedy in diarrhœa and dysentery, a refreshing sherbet being prepared from it, the *nīm* (*Melia azadirach*), the *ber* (*Zizyphus Jujuba* and *Z. nummularia*) and the *soanjua* (*Moringa pterygosperma*), also known as the horse-radish tree from the flavour of its root. Plantains and oranges are cultivated in a few places.

Fruit trees.

14. The most common creepers are the *kukudranj* (*Calycopteris floribunda*) whose dense round heads of pale green flowers may often be seen along the roadside, the much-to-be-avoided *yerun* (*Zizyphus Œnoplia*) whose straggling armed stems render some parts along the Prānhita river almost impenetrable, and the *belia palās* (*Butea superba*), a gigantic climber which in spring crowns the tops of the highest trees with wreaths of brilliant red blossoms. *Loranthus longiflorus* is the chief parasite ; it has thick and somewhat fleshy leaves, and slender red flowers. It is doing a great deal of damage to the *chār* (*Buchanania latifolia*) and to the mahuā, and to a lesser extent to several other trees.

Creepers.

WILD ANIMALS, ETC.

Wild animals.

15. The District has always enjoyed a considerable reputation as a resort for sportsmen, and most of the larger animals of the chase are to be found in it. Elephants have long been extinct, but, according to tradition, they once roamed the Chānda wastes, and under the Mūl hills is to be seen a large excavation into which it is said that they used to be driven. The tiger (*Felis tigris*) ranges throughout the District, but is most abundant in the forests of Moharlī, Dābha, Ghot and Ahīri, and also in the northern zamīndāris. It is very destructive both to game and cattle. During the hot weather it subsists mainly on the former, lying in ambush near one of the few pools that retain water at that season, and pouncing upon any animal that comes thither to quench its thirst. In the cold weather it roams far and wide over large tracts of forest and preys on both game and cattle, whichever come in its way. It is in the rains that its depredations on cattle become most frequent. Driven out of the depths of the jungles by the swarms of flies which infest them at this period, it emerges into the more open forests on the border of cultivation, and makes a business of dogging and taking toll, as opportunity affords, of the herds which graze there. In this way it accounts for some member of the herds marked down by it every third or fourth day, and should there be, as sometimes happens, a family of tigers on the prowl, they are terribly destructive and two or three head of cattle may be killed in a single day. Buffaloes, however, when attacked frequently combine to defend themselves and baffle their assailant. The tiger, as a rule, fears man and makes himself scarce when there is a human being in the neighbourhood. An unarmed herdsman, even a small boy, will generally tackle a tiger which attacks his herd, and frequently succeeds in driving it away. Man-eaters, which were once so common that Major Lucie Smith wrote that no ten miles of country could be traversed without some token being seen to attest

their ravages, are now few and far between. So much have things changed in the forty years since 1867-68, when one tigress killed 135 men and women along a forest cart-track. The panther (*Felis pardus*) known in the vernacular as *tendua* is fairly common in the District, and attains to a length of about eight feet. It generally keeps to the forests and is very destructive to game; when it takes to cattle-lifting or man-eating it is far more to be dreaded than the tiger, as it is almost devoid of fear, not infrequently having been known to drag people out of their houses or carts. *Felis leopardis*, the true leopard, locally called *borbachchā*, has sometimes been regarded as a distinct species, but the generally accepted view now is that it is a mere variety with no very hard and fast line between it and the *Felis pardus*. It is much the smaller of the two varieties, never measuring more than seven feet, its skin is the more densely marked generally with a design of horse-shoes or crescents, its habitat is the more open country or the borders of the forest, and its prey is more or less limited to sheep, goats, dogs, the smaller species of deer and monkeys. These latter it regards as particularly toothsome dainties, while its partiality for dogs frequently gives touring officials cause for lamentation. Of the smaller cats, *Felis bengalensis* and *Felis chaus*, both called by the native *jangli billi*, are found, but whereas the latter is common, the former is rarely met with and then only in forests. Both species prey freely on game birds such as peafowl, green pigeon and quail. *Felis caracal*, the Indian lynx, is extremely rare, but has been killed near Wairāgarh. The common civet (*Viverra Malaccensis*) is common in the precincts of villages or towns and does much damage to poultry. A case has been known in which a member of this species bit off the heads of a dozen pigeons in one night. *Paradoxurus laniger*, the tree civet, is of more retiring habits. It keeps to the jungles and preys on birds of all kinds. *Herpestes pallidus* the mongoose, locally called *neolā*, is common everywhere.

It is destructive to both poultry and wild birds, but can be easily tamed. The common striped hyæna (*Hyæna striata*), called *lagarbagar*, conspicuous by its bony crest and awkward gait, indulges in a diet of carrion diversified by an occasional pariah, and is of more or less nocturnal habits. *Cyon Dukhunensis*, the wild dog, is found in all the jungly parts of the District, travelling in packs, which roam over very extensive tracts of country, but seldom stay in one locality for more than a couple of days, as their arrival is the signal for a *sauve qui peut* among all the other animals. Even tigers and panthers desert their kills when these are appropriated by the wild dog. The packs average about a dozen and hunt both by sight and by scent, and once on the track of their victims, they never relax the chase until it has ended in a kill. Major Lucie Smith says: 'The Gonds 'have it that when wild dogs meet a tiger they never leave it 'alive but course round and round in wide circles until at 'length the tiger becomes blinded by the effluvium of their 'urine, and being blind eventually perishes from starvation.' This is a variant of a somewhat similar belief referred to in the Gazetteer of the Bālāghāt District. Whatever the foundation for this belief, there is no doubt that wild dogs have developed a very deadly form of co-operative attack, by which part of the pack keep the victim (if a male) in play by demonstrations in front while one or more of the remainder steal round behind and emasculate him. It is on record that a tiger has been seen surrounded by wild dogs, and standing with his haunches glued to a tree, not daring to budge for fear of being subjected to an attack of this nature The Government reward for the skins of wild dogs has been raised within the last few years to Rs. 15, but this has not had much effect in thinning them out. Fortunately disease has greatly reduced their numbers recently, packs of 40 being reduced to 5 or 6 in some cases. *Canis aureus*, the omnivorous jackal, is found everywhere in the neighbourhood of villages. *Vulpes Bengalensis*, the Indian fox, occurs in open plains. The Indian ratel or honey-badger (*Mellivora Indica*) also occurs and is regarded by the native with a good deal of awe. The black bear (*Ursus labiatus*), called *rīchh* or *aswal*, is common throughout most of the District. It lives in caves which as a rule it does not leave before sunset, although during the rains and cold weather it may not infrequently be seen lumbering about in the forests. Its diet consists mainly of forest fruits, roots, honey and insects; it has a particular partiality for white ants. Its attitude towards man is uncertain; at one time it will move off at his approach, at another will bar the way, or even charge. If taken by surprise, it invariably attacks and many people, whose occupation lies in the forests, get mauled in this way. *Sus cristatus*, the Indian boar, is one of the chief enemies of cultivation and does enormous damage to the crops almost everywhere.

Monkeys.

16. Of monkeys two species are found, *Macacus rhesus*, called in the vernacular *bandar*, and the *langūr*, (*Semnopithecus entellus*). The former is the small common red-faced monkey of Northern India, where it is held sacred. In this District it occurs only on the southern and eastern borders of the Sironchā tahsīl in the proximity of the Godāvari and Indrāvati rivers, and is not regarded with any such feeling. The *langūr* is very common throughout the District both in the open and in forests and does much harm to crops and fruit trees.

Bats.

17. Among bats it is sufficient to mention *Megaderma legra*, the Indian vampire, which is fairly common in Ahīri, and preys on small frogs and sparrows, and *Pteropus*, the flying-fox, whose noisy tree colonies cause a light sleeper many a wakeful night, and whose appetite for fruit is a marvel of voracity.

Rodents.

18. In the order of rodents the most familiar member is the grey or palm squirrel (*Sciurus palmaram*). The Malābār squirrel

(*Sciurus malabaricus*) is fairly common in the Sironchā tahsīl, *Pteromys petaurista*, the flying squirrel, also occurs in Ahīri. It has a membrane extending from the fore to the hind feet which it spreads during its flight. It cannot fly more than about 50 feet, nor can it change its course once it has launched itself into the air. Its habits are nocturnal. A passing mention is sufficient for the porcupine (*Hystrix leucura*) which is fairly, and the hare (*Lepus ruficaudatus*) which is very, common in most parts of the District.

Deer and antelope.

19. Among deer, sāmbhar (*Rusa Aristotelis*) and *chītal* (*Axis maculatus*) are found throughout the District in abundance. The horns of the former average about 36, and of the latter about 28 to 30 inches. But Mr. Langhorne once picked up the horns of a sāmbhar which had been killed by a tiger, and found them to measure 47¾ inches. *Bārāsinghā* only occurs in Ahīri in small herds, and it is matter for curious speculation how it ever found its way down to those parts. The mouse deer (*Memimna Indica*) is found in parts of Ahīri and Ghot, while the barking deer (*Cervulus muntjac*) inhabits parts of the District, but is rare. The black buck (*Antilope Cervicapra*) is common in the open country, and the horns attain an average length of 20 inches The four-horned antelope (*Tetracerus quadricornis*) and *chinkāra* (*Gazelle Bennetti*) are widely distributed and fairly common. The stupid and clumsy *nilgai* (*Bos Elephas Iragocamelus*) keeps to the more or less open forest, and finds his favourite haunt in the sites of deserted villages.

Bison and buffalo.

20. Noblest among the beasts of sport in the District is *Gavæus Gaurus*, the Gaur popularly, although incorrectly known as the Indian bison, whose range is confined to thick forest, but which still survives in fair numbers. The bull is a mighty beast of a dull black colour, while the cows are light brown picked out with white below the knees and hocks. Efforts are being made to restrict the destruction of this animal,

but the native *shikāri* is thinning his numbers woefully; recently the remains of no fewer than four bison were simultaneously discovered in one forest who had thus fallen victims to the poacher's gun. *Bubalus Arni*, the wild buffalo, frequents the Ahīri zamīndāri and parts of the Ghot range. The bull is a huge ungainly brute about twice the size of the domestic buffalo. Buffaloes occasionally mingle with village herds, and bulls have been known to leave their own kind and join the domesticated animals for months together.

Game birds.

21. The District has the usual land game birds of this part of India, while the prevalence of tanks in the rice tract to the west of the Waingangā river renders that part an excellent resort for duck and snipe shooting. Almost every village possesses its tank, and every tank possesses its quota of ducks, if not of snipe. Sand grouse (*Pteloclurus exustus*) are fairly common and frequent rocky ground, where they are usually to be seen in pairs, though also very often in large flocks. The peacock (*Pavo cristatus*) is ubiquitous along the banks of nullahs, and may be shot without fear of wounding the religious susceptibilities of the people. The grey or Madras jungle cock (*Gallus sonnerati*) pervades all the jungle; the cock is a handsome bird with grey and orange markings on the wings and with golden-yellow neck-feathers. *Galloperdix spadiceus*, the red spur fowl, is found in parts, generally where there are hills. He is a shy bird and not much of a flier, but trusts to the swiftness of his feet to escape from danger. The grey partridge (*Francolinus Pondicerinus*) exists everywhere, and more particularly haunts the skirts of villages, where it plays the part of a scavenger. It is easily tamed and is a favourite bird with the natives; often it may be seen following its master. The fighting proclivities of these birds are great, and they are kept for sporting purposes. The painted partridge (*Francolinus pictus*) occurs sporadically. It has an unmistakable call. The grey quail (*Coturnix communis*) visits the District in small numbers in the cold weather.

The rain quail (*Coturnix coromandelicus*), which exists everywhere, is generally found in flocks, but goes about in pairs during the mating season. The common jungle or bush quail (*Perdicula Asiatica*) is another favourite cage-bird with the native. *Grus antigone*, the *sāras*, or red-headed crane, is common, and *Oedicnemus Indicus*, the goggle-eye or bustard florican, fairly so. The former is as a rule met with in pairs and is the Hindu type of conjugal fidelity; it is also a recognised totem of a sect of Gonds, and enjoys immunity from the gun.

Gallinago cœlestis, the common snipe, is fairly common in parts during the season. *Gallinago Stenura*, the pintail, occurs everywhere, but is not common. *Gallinago gallinula*, the jack snipe, is a larger bird, and is met with all over the District. *Numenius arquatus*, the common curlew, inhabits most rivers, while *Geronticus papillosus*, the black king curlew, is everywhere common.

Of the duck tribe the most familiar species are *Nyroca filigula*, the tufted pochard, *Dendrocyena Javanica*, the whistling teal, *Casarca rutila*, the Brahminy duck, which frequents rivers and fields, the crops of which have been cut, *Nettopus coromandelianus*, the cotton or goose teal, *Anas Boscas*, the mallard, *Chaulelasmus streperus*, the gadwall, *Dafila acuta*, the pintail, *Querquedula circia*, the gerganey or blue-winged teal. The red-crested, the red-headed and the white-eyed pochard, the comb duck, the shoveller, the spotted bill, and the common teal are also found but not in such great numbers.

Deaths from wild animals.

22. During the 16 years ending 1906 a total of 549 persons and 10,095 cattle were killed by tigers giving an annual average of 34 and 631 respectively, while panthers killed a total of 198 persons and 4205 cattle. During the same period a total of 517 tigers and 889 panthers were destroyed, the annual average being 32 and 56 respectively; and the total amount paid in rewards was Rs. 42,701. The number of persons dying from snake bite was 1227 or more than twice the number killed by tigers.

RAINFALL AND CLIMATE.

Rainfall.

23. Rainfall is at present registered for general purposes at ten stations, *viz.*, the five tahsīl headquarters, and also at Mūl, Armorī, Chimūr, Muramgaon and Alāpalli. Besides these seven more stations of fairly recent origin are maintained by the Public Works Department in connection with the more important State tanks. The stations at Chānda, Warorā, Bramhapurī, Sironchā and Mūl date from the sixties, and it is the returns of these only that are taken into account in giving the average rainfall of past years. During the 39 years ending with 1905-06, the average annual rainfall of the whole District has been 49 inches, the heaviest falls being recorded at Brahmapurī which has an annual rainfall of 54½ inches, and the lightest at Warorā with an average of 45¼ inches. During the same period the District rainfall has in 18 years exceeded 50, and in nine years fallen short of 40 inches. The highest recorded annual fall was 69·94 inches in 1887-88 and the lowest 19·28 inches in the famine year 1899-1900. In 1868-69, another year of famine, only 27·78 inches were recorded. The monsoon usually breaks about the second or third week in June, and, if it follows a normal course, should increase in intensity through July, somewhat abating in August and continuing to slacken through September, disappearing about the middle of October. The actual average monthly figures for the 33 years ending in 1899-1900 are 7¼ inches in June, 15¾ in July, 11¾ in August, 8½ in September and 2 inches in October. In the remaining portion of the year the average rainfall is only 3¾ inches. The rainfall is heaviest in the hilly and jungly rice tracts of Bramhapurī and also in the thickly wooded Ahīri zamīndāri, and lightest in the cotton country of the Warorā tahsīl. From the agricultural point of view the distribution of the monsoon is quite as important as its amount, and it is the irregularity that seems to have come over the course of the monsoon of recent years rather than any deficiency in the total moisture received that has been

the cause of the late cycle of misfortune. In this respect, the Sironchā tahsīl enjoys greater latitude than the rest of the District, and even if the rain holds off as late as the beginning of August the cultivator need not despair of securing a fair juāri harvest should rain subsequently arrive.

Temperature and climate.

24. Chānda enjoys the reputation of being the hottest District in the Central Provinces. At headquarters it is usually about one degree warmer than Nāgpur in the hot weather, and about the middle of May a maximum of at least 115° may be confidently expected. In the cold weather when under canvas a fire is sometimes acceptable in December and January, but as a rule it is a luxury rather than a necessity. Ice in thin films has been occasionally seen in the north of the District in years of exceptional severity, as for instance in the great frosts of February 1905.[1] The term cold weather is in fact somewhat of a misnomer when applied to this District, merely denoting that short period of the year during which the heat is not at some part of the day oppressive. This period usually does not begin before November has set in, and the end of it is well in sight when about the middle of February violent winds begin to herald the approaching hot weather. Even at the height of summer, however, the nights are usually sufficiently bearable to allow of a tolerably comfortable rest in the open without the

---

[1] An extraordinary discovery of a block of ice some three feet square was made at the Warorā Water-works Reservoir on the 23rd February 1870. Although its formation was certainly not due to climatic causes, the weather at that time being warm, the general interest of the occurrence must be the excuse for mentioning the matter here. The block of ice was found in the horizontal duct of the escape sluice, which it completely filled preventing the egress of the water. Connection with the tank had been shut off for some months previously, and the water transformed into ice had been standing undisturbed in an earthen pipe bound round with cotton steeped in linseed oil and plastered with mortar. The theory favoured at the time was that the freezing must have been brought about by chemical action in the salts of the surrounding soil, although it was not exactly known what the chemical explanation of the phenomenon was, but the more probable explanation is that the ice was due to the creation of an exhaust. In appearance the ice was an opaque white resembling machine made ice, and took long to melt. The occurrence was reported to the Asiatic Society of Calcutta at the time.

aid of a *pankhā*, and on the eastern plateau the air at this season is clear and bright, and the nights pleasant. The average monthly maximum and minimum temperatures as recorded at the observatory established at Chānda in 1870 are 85·5° and 54° in January, 109·5° and 82° in May, and 88·5° and 76° in July. The highest temperature on record is 119·2° on the 18th May 1897, and the lowest 37·1° on the 10th January 1899. Chānda has usually the reputation of being an unhealthy District, but this belief is not borne out by figures. Undoubtedly the prevalence of jungle and the extensive areas under rice cultivation tend to propagate malarial fever during the rains and early cold weather, but the rate of mortality from this cause as compared with other Districts is not such as to excite remark within the District itself; the climate of the Sironchā tahsīl is given a very bad name, but this opinion again appears to be founded on a misconception, or rather upon the tendency to regard *omne ignotum pro horrifico.*

CHAPTER II.

HISTORY AND ARCHÆOLOGY.

HISTORY.

Local traditions.

25. The early history of Chānda, previous to the rule of the Gond kings, has to be pieced together from such inscriptions belonging to the District as have hitherto been deciphered by the Archæological Survey and from somewhat vague references to the District in the records of neighbouring States. A number of inscriptions fiom the ruined temples of Bhāndak and Mārkanda have not yet been deciphered. When these are interpreted they may bring new facts to light. Local tradition carries the history back to the creation of the world and even a little farther. A popular local legend, which is partly derived from the Jaimini Ashwamedha, runs as follows :—'During the Krita Yuga the city of Lokapur extended over a wide expanse, including the site where the 'modern Chānda now stands. Here resided the goddess 'Mahākāli and here she created her son, the beautiful Bhūtnāth. The gods, however, enraged at his intriguing with 'their wives, complained to Mahākāli, who changed his name 'from Bhūtnāth to Achaleshwar (the immovable), and sealing 'him with the print of the cow's hoof, fixed him for ever on 'the banks of the Jharpat. During this age Rāma passed 'through the land and rested beneath the Chimūr hills, and 'near Ballālpur on the Wardhā river. In the Tretā Yuga, 'Lokapur was governed by a king of the race of moon, who 'altered its designation to Indupur (city of the moon). Indupur 'afterwards became desolate, but about the end of the Dwāpar 'and commencement of the Kali Yuga we see the great city of 'Bhadrāvati (the modern Bhāndak) stretching from Bhatāla 'on the north, to the Jharpat on the south and east, beautiful 'with lakes and stately palaces, and guarded by a vast host

'with horses, chariots and elephants. Here reigned the 'mighty Yauvanāshva, having in his possession the Shyām-'karna steed, to obtain which came the demi-god Bhīm and his 'two companions Meghavarna and Vrishaketu. Then ensued 'a battle of heroes and the horse was borne away by the 'demi-god to Hastināpur for sacrifice by Dharm the king. 'About this time ruled east of the Waingangā Wairochan, a 'prince of the family of the moon, and founded a city which 'is called Wairāgarh. Later in the Kali Yuga came the 'famous physician Hemādpanth, and built the Mārkanda tem-'ple by the waters of the Waingangā.'

The city of Bhadrāvati.

26. In this legend the important point is the identification of the modern Bhāndak with the ancient city of Bhadrāvati. General Cunningham rejects this hypothesis and holds that Bhāndak was the capital of the Vākātaka dynasty and that the present name of that village is merely a corruption of the dynastic name Vākātaka. This has been however disallowed by Drs. Bühler and Fleet on philological grounds. No such objection arises in identifying Bhāndak with Bhadrāvati or Bhadrikāvati. There are further cogent reasons for this identification. Bhadrāvati literally means the city of Bhadra (an epithet of Siva). To this day the oldest and most important temple in Bhāndak is called Bhadranāth or Bhadranāg, and probably in ancient times the city grew up round this famous shrine and was called, from the name of the god, Bhadra's city or Bhadrāwati. Local legend also strongly holds that the ancient city of Bhadrāvati had its north gate at Bhatāla and its southern extremity at Chānda, a distance of 28 miles, and was 16 miles wide. This is probably an exaggeration but all over the area indicated, even where it is now covered with jungle, the ruins of ancient temples and deep rock-cut wells with stairs down to the water, similar to the ancient wells at Bhāndak, are met with. These ruins may have caused the legends but the impression is forced on any one who examines the ground that it once was covered with large

villages or towns, of which these traces alone remain. Just as to-day Chānda city, within its extensive walls, is really a collection of villages with gardens and tanks between, so the ancient Bhadrāvati may have been a confederation of smaller towns welded into one, as modern great cities annex their suburbs.

The Vākātaka kings.

27. The identification of Bhāndak with Bhadrāvati however does not preclude the possibility of the Vākātaka domination there. True, the Vākātakas are not mentioned in Sanskrit classical literature, but several inscriptions have been found to prove that their rule extended over a large area in which Chānda was included. According to General Cunningham their boundaries were approximately the Mahādeo range of hills on the north and the Godāvari river on the south with the Ajantā hills on the west and the hills at the sources of the Mahānadi on the east. But his identifications from inscriptions are, Dr. Fleet states, of doubtful authority.[1] Since he wrote, other inscriptions have been found in Berār and elsewhere. One inscription found in the Jasso State in the heart of Bundelkhand shows that the influence of the Vākātakas extended much farther north. At any rate it is clear that a great portion of Berār and at least some portion of Chānda were included in the Vākātaka dominions. This dynasty came into power in the third century A.D., the name of the perhaps semi-mythical hero who founded it being given as Vindhya Sakti. Nine successors of this king are mentioned, and taking 25 years as an average for their rule, they must have come to an end by the close of the 6th century. Dr. Fleet dating the marriage of Rudrasena, the 5th prince of the line, with the daughter of Deva Gupta, king of Magadha, in 675 A.D., places the dynasty about two hundred years later. But if that be so there is strong evidence that long before they ceased to rule, the Chānda portion of their realm had passed over to the kings of Kosala.

[1] Gupta Inscriptions, p. 234, Note 5.

Buddhist kings.

28. It is in connection with Kosala that we arrive at the first authentic historical record in the history of the District. Hiuen Tsiang, the Chinese pilgrim, records that he visited the capital of Kosala in the year 639 A.D. and thus writes of it:—'The 'king is of the Kshattriya caste. He deeply reverences the 'law of Buddha and is well affected towards learning and the 'arts. There are one hundred Sanghārams (Buddhist mon-'asteries) here and ten thousand priests (monks). There 'are a great number of heretics who have intermixed with 'the population and also Deva temples.' Three identifications of the capital of Kosala have been suggested, Chānda by General Cunningham, and Wairāgarh and Bhāndak between which Dr. Fergusson long wavered. The founding of Chānda by Khandkia Ballāl Shāh about 1450 A.D. seems sufficiently authentic to put that place out of the question. None of its buildings are older than that date, save the shrine of Achaleshwar which appears to have been always a Hindu shrine. Wairāgarh has no trace of Buddhist remains at all, nor is there any record to show that it was ever of such size as would accommodate one hundred monasteries. Bhāndak both has the Buddhistic remains in its cave temples to this day, and the legend of its wide bounds. It seems practically certain that Bhāndak was the city visited by the pilgrim and his account goes far to justify the legends of the vast extent of prehistoric Bhadrāvati. A city which contained 100 Buddhist monasteries with 10,000 monks besides a large number of heretics, or Hindus who had not changed their faith, could not be a small or unimportant place. Be that as it may, it seems clear that in 639 A.D. Chānda was ruled by Buddhist kings, and from the inscription found in Bhāndak (now in the Nāgpur Museum) it appears that they ruled at least till the 9th century A.D. How much longer Buddhist rule continued there are no records to show, and though Buddhism lingered here longer than in most parts of India, it never quite succeeded in

winning the allegiance of the common people but remained the faith of the upper classes. Its complete disappearance is therefore less mysterious.

Haihaya kings of Kosala.

29. The next notice in the scanty annals of the period is the Ratanpur inscription of the Haihaya king, Jājalladeva, 1114 A.D. which states that the chiefs of Wairāgarh, Lānjika (Lānji) and Bhānāra (Bhandāra) paid tribute to the king. Who the chiefs of Wairāgarh were can only be conjectured. Major Lucie Smith mentions the local tradition of the line of Māna kings who ruled there, and were subdued by the Gonds. The Māna princes whose names he recorded were Kurumpruhoda, the first of the line, who ruled in Wairāgarh which he fortified along with Garbori and Rajoli ; Surjāt Badwaik who fortified Surjāgarh, and Gahilu who built the fortress of Mānikgarh in Hyderābād State. Mr. Hīra Lāl taking Mānikgarh to be a corruption of Mānikyagarh suggests that Gahilu named his fort after the tutelary deity of his race. Mānikyadevi was also the tutelary goddess of the Nāgvansi kings of Bastar who ruled about the 11th century A.D. He is therefore of opinion that the Māna or Māni kings were not of the Māna caste, but Kshattriyas, and a branch of these Nāgvânsi kings, and suggests that it was they who succeeded the Buddhist kings, and restored the ancient temple of Bhadranāth at Bhāndak, changing its name to Bhadranāg. It is noteworthy that it is the only temple in the District dedicated to snake worship.

Gond kings.

30. The Māna or Nāgvansi kings of Wairāgarh were superseded by the Gond dynasty. Major Lucie Smith in his Settlement Report of 1869 compiled from oral and written traditions, and from genealogies no longer available, an interesting sketch of the romantic history of this dynasty. This is reproduced below with some necessary corrections of dates which later research demands. According to Gond tradition there arose among them a man Kol Bhīl, great in wisdom and strength.

GOND KING'S TOMB, CHANDA.

He welded the scattered tribes of Gonds into one nation, taught them to extract iron from the ore, and led them against the Mānas. After a troubled supremacy of 200 years the Wairāgarh kings fell before the Gonds. Then Bhīm Ballāl Singh is seen subduing his fellow chiefs and ruling over a wide dominion. The succession of the Gond kings as given by Major Lucie Smith is as follows :—

1.	Bhīm Ballāl Singh	... 870–895	A.D.
2.	Khurjā Ballāl Singh	... 895—935	"
3.	Hīr Singh ...	... 935—970	"
4.	Andia Ballāl Singh	... 970—995	"
5.	Talwār Singh ...	... 995—1027	"
6.	Keshar Singh ...	... 1027—1072	"
7.	Dinkar Singh ...	... 1072—1142	"
8.	Rām Singh ...	... 1142—1207	"
9.	Surjā Ballāl Singh or Sher Shāh Ballāl Shāh	... 1207—1242	"
10.	Khandkia Ballāl Shāh	... 1242—1282	"
11.	Hīr Shāh ...	... 1282—1342	"
12.	Bhūma and Lokbā, jointly	... 1342—1402	"
13.	Kondia Shāh ..	... 1402—1442	"
14.	Bābājī Ballāl Shāh	... 1442—1522	"
15.	Dhundia Rām Shāh	... 1522—1597	"
16.	Krishna Shāh ...	... 1597—1647	"
17.	Bīr Shāh ...	... 1647—1672	"
18.	Rām Shāh ...	... 1672—1735	"
19.	Nīlkanth Shāh	... 1735—1751	"

When the line of kings is examined apart from the narrative of their history, the first thing that strikes the reader is the extraordinary length of the reigns. No less than six kings rule for 60 years and over, one rules for 75 years, while Bābājī Ballāl Shāh reigns for the extraordinary period of 80 years. In all, nineteen reigns cover a period of 881 years, or an average of nearly 46½ years for each reign. It is possible that some names may have been omitted, but in most cases the kingdom is represented as descending from father to son, or as in the case of Rām Shāh, when an adoption occurs, it is recorded. It is self-evident that the first king is dated some 400 years too early, as taking the average of 25 years to a reign, there are only names sufficient to carry us back to 1276 A.D. instead of 870 A.D. The dates of the later kings of the line are probably correct enough. Rām Shāh is represented as having been adopted in infancy in 1672 and his long reign of 63 years seems reasonable. Taking 1672 as a starting point the 25 years' average for the other reigns carries the line back to 1247, which agrees well enough with the history compiled from inscriptions. Two external dates tend to establish the accuracy of this estimate. (1) The Ain-i-Akbarī records that when the list of the territories of Akbar (1556—1603) was compiled a Gond prince named Bābjī, evidently Bābājī Ballāl Shāh, was ruling in Chānda. He is dated in the list 1442—1522 and is therefore placed nearly a century too soon. On the suggested computation his reign would be 1572—97 which would make him contemporary with Akbar. (2) On this computation the reign of Khandkia Ballāl Shāh, the founder of the present city of Chānda, would be 1437—62 which agrees well enough with Cunningham's computation of 1450 for the date of founding the city. The genealogy of the kings appears to have been collected from so many concurrent sources that it may be accepted as a fairly correct list of the princes of the line, though some names are probably omitted, but in this account Major Lucie Smith's dates previous to the reign of Rām Shāh are discarded. The only early dates that may be accepted as approximately correct are—

1.	Bhīm Ballāl Singh approximately	1240	A.D.
10.	Khandkia Ballāl Shāh ...	... 1437—62	„
	Founding of Chānda	... 1450	„
14	Bābājī Ballāl Shāh	... 1572—97	„
18.	Rām Shāh ...	... 1672—1735	„

All the subsequent dates in Major Lucie Smith's narrative are historically accurate.

The first eight Gond kings.

31. The first king, Bhīm Ballāl Singh, on completing his conquest made Sirpur on the right bank of the river Wardhā his capital; while his chief stronghold was the Māna fortress of Mānikgarh, in the high range of hills which rise beyond Sirpur. He was succeeded by his son Khurjā Ballāl Singh. This prince was of a gentle and unwarlike nature, but in the shadow of his father's fame he reigned unmolested. On his death his son Hīr Singh came to the throne. Unlike his predecessors, he delighted in war, and being also wise and prudent he made his rule respected throughout the kingdom. Previous to his accession land had been like air, untaxed and free to all, but Hīr Singh, for the first time in the history of the nation, levied an impost on occupied ground. He, however, claimed for himself no right of ownership in the soil, and such right was possessed by none. All lands were in common, and the absence of any recognised partition bred constant disputes among the people. He was succeeded by his son Andia Ballāl Singh who proved a cruel and tyrannical prince. Frequent rebellions occurred during his reign, and a conspiracy was on foot for dethroning him, when he died. His son Talwār Singh had not the vices of his father; but as a king he showed himself fickle and vacillating, and thus brought his name into contempt. He had two sons, the youngest of whom named Keshar Singh he dearly loved, and to him he relinquished the throne. Keshar Singh was an able and successful ruler. He subdued rebellion throughout the land, and then carried his arms to the boundary of the Bhīl country. There his progress was stayed, and he had to retire; but large tracts beyond his former frontier were permanently conquered and added to his dominions. In wealth he exceeded any of his predecessors and he possessed horses and oxen. Keshar Singh was succeeded by his son Dinkar Singh. This prince devoted himself to peaceful pursuits; and the one shadow on his name is that of excessive voluptuousness. He invited to

his court great numbers of the Gond bards and studied the religion not only of his own people but of other nations. The visits of foreigners he encouraged, and he was the first to induce persons acquainted with Marāthī literature to reside at his capital. The legend runs that he possessed the philosopher's stone, by whose aid he amassed large treasures, and this tradition may be taken to show that his revenues were flourishing. On his death his son Rām Singh mounted the throne. Just and truthful in his intercourse with his subjects and daring and successful as a soldier, Rām Singh governed the kingdom righteously and enlarged its bounds. To increase its security he erected several hill forts in the south-west and maintained a chosen band of warriors called Tarvels. These men had eaten the *tāru* (a rare orchid occasionally found on the bamboo) with certain ceremonial observances and were supposed to be invulnerable, and to each the king granted a tract of forest varying in length from two to fifty miles.

Surjā Ballāl Singh and his interview with the Delhi Emperor.

32. Rām Singh was succeeded by his son Surjā Ballāl Singh. This prince who was of very comely person, proceeded to Upper India and resided for some time at Benāres and Lucknow, where he devoted himself to learning the arts of war and of song. His escort, however, took to plundering the country, and the Emperor of Delhi gave orders for his capture. In the skirmishes which ensued the Gonds were victorious, but Surjā Ballāl Singh while wandering alone in the vicinity of the camp was seized by the Emperor's soldiers and carried to Delhi, where he was placed in confinement. About this time Mohan Singh, the Rājput chief of Kaibur, had refused to give his daughter, who was of great beauty, to the Emperor and a force was despatched to bring him to submission. The expedition failed, but the Emperor did not relinquish his project. Contemporaneously with these events Surjā Ballāl Singh's followers returned to Sirpur, and acquainted the regent Jarbā and the

Gond king's family with what had happened to their lord. Jarbā immediately raised the standard of war, and having collected an army of 70,000 men, of whom 10,000 were Tarvels, set out for Delhi. Whilst this force was on its march the admiration of the Emperor's daughter was excited by hearing Surjā's frequent songs, and she begged her father to send for the captive. The Emperor did so, and being pleased with the appearance of the Gond King enquired whether he were willing to fight for Delhi. Surjā replied by asking to be assigned an achievement of difficulty and the Emperor allotted to him the attack on the Kaibur fort. While Surjā was preparing to return to Gondwāna, with a view to mustering his forces for the enterprise, Jarbā and his army arrived in the vicinity of Delhi. Surjā went out to meet them and presented Jarbā to the Emperor who directed Surjā to take any further troops he required from the imperial host. A contingent of 10,000 men was selected, and the combined army moved against Kaibur. The siege lasted for eleven days, and ended in the death of Mohan Singh, and the capture of his stronghold. Among the spoil was found a sacred sword, which has been preserved to the present day in the family of the Gond kings. On Mohan Singh's death his widow fell at Surjā's feet and implored him to save her daughter and herself from the Emperor. Surjā assured her that he would protect both to his utmost power, and that if all else failed he would slay them with his own sword rather than deliver them to the Emperor. He then posted a garrison in the fortress, and having proclaimed it to be the Emperor's, marched back to Delhi, accompanied by the Rājput princess and her daughter, the latter a girl of eleven. On approaching the city a rumour was spread through the army that Surjā's young son had arrived, and next morning Surjā, attiring the Rājput maiden as a boy, placed her on the elephant of State, the king and Jarbā sitting behind. In this manner they proceeded to the imperial palace, where they were received with all honour.

The Emperor seeing the pretended prince said 'Come in dear child,' and seated her on his knee; then turning to Surjā he asked 'Where is the fruit of your victory?' Surjā replied 'Your Majesty holds her in your lap, and as you have called her your dear child, she can be nothing else to you.' The Emperor, although chagrined at the strategem, relinquished his claim with a good grace and conferred a dress of honour on the Gond king. The latter then prayed that as his ancestor had reigned over Khundal and Mandlā, and the country from Bengal to Bundelkhand, and as far south as Rājahmundry that the same kingdom be granted to him. The Emperor decreed the whole to be his, and conferred upon him the title of Sher Shāh. Shortly afterwards Surjā returned to Gondwāna, taking with him the two Rājput ladies, and the experience gained by the king in Hindustān is said to have told beneficially on the subsequent government of the kingdom. After Surjā's visit to Delhi he was known as Sher Shāh Ballāl Shāh, and his descendants have since substituted Shāh for Singh in their names. The change seems, however, to have been made without the sanction of the paramount power, for in the two seals that are extant, granted by the Emperor of Delhi to the Gond kings, the word is Singh and not Shāh.

Khandkia Ballāl Shāh, the founder of Chānda.

33. On the death of Sher Shāh his son Khandkia Ballāl Shāh reigned in his stead. This prince was covered with tumours, and all the tender care of his wife, a wise, beautiful and virtuous woman, was unavailing to effect his cure. At last she induced him to leave Sirpur and reside on the opposite bank of the Wardhā, where he erected a fort called Ballālpur. One day, says the legend, while the king was hunting north-west of Ballālpur he grew thirsty, and rode up to the dry bed of the Jharpat, looking for water. Some was soon discovered in a hole, and the king after drinking washed his face, hands and feet. That night he slept soundly, the first time for many years; and next

morning the queen was gladdened by seeing that many of the ulcers had disappeared, for all parts touched by the water of the previous day had become whole. On ascertaining what had occurred during the king's ride she ascribed his partial cure to the virtue of the water then used, and entreated him to take her to the spot where he had quenched his thirst. Accordingly both proceeded to the Jharpat and in a little while the hole was found. On clearing away the grass and sand there were seen five footprints of a cow in the solid rock, each filled with water, and the strange thing was that take how much one would, the water would not diminish. Thus was discovered the Tīrth of Achaleshwar who had been fixed to the spot in the Tretā Yuga. The king was bathed with the water, which had hardly been done when every tumour vanished. That night the royal party encamped near the place, and in the visions of sleep Achaleshwar appeared to the king, and spoke comforting words. On hearing the dream the queen advised the erection of a temple over the healing waters, and the king approving of the idea sent his officers to collect skilled artificers for the work. He took a great interest in its progress, and one morning, after his daily visit, was riding away when a hare darted out of a bush and pursued his dog, which fled. Astonished at the sight, he followed; the dog ran in a wide circle while the hare took zig-zag cuts to catch it. At one point it closed with the dog which however shook it off and continued its flight. On nearing the point where the chase had commenced, the dog turned on and killed the hare and the king then saw that on the forehead of the latter was marked a white spot. Pondering what this might mean, he rode home and recounted to his wife all that he had seen. That wise woman counselled that the occurrence was of good omen, and that a fortified city should be built within the circuit of the chase, with walls following the hare's track. She further advised that special bastions should be erected, both where the hare had closed with the dog and where the dog had killed the hare, expressing her belief that the latter point would prove the point of danger to the future city. The king lost no time in giving effect to her suggestions; a trench was run along the hare's track, which was easily discernible by the footprints of the king's horse; then gates and bastions were planned, the whole marked out, and the foundations commenced; the work being under the management of the Rājput officers of the king, called Tel Thākurs. Thus began the building of the city of Chānda or Chandrapur. The learned derive the name from Indupur (city of the moon), which stood near the Jharpat in the Tretā Yuga, but the common people see its origin in the white spot (*chandar*) which marked the forehead of the wondrous hare.

Hīr Shāh, an independent ruler.

34. Khandkia Ballāl Shāh was succeeded by his son Hīr Shāh, in whose reign the country made rapid progress. He called to a solemn banquet all the Tarvels and others whom his ancestor Rām Shāh had rewarded with forest lands, and on the conclusion of the feast proposed to them that whoever cleared and peopled his land should become its chief, and that he who did not should forfeit his right thereto. The Rājās (or zamīndārs as they are now called) agreed to the terms and to the best of their ability began cutting down the forest and founding villages. In due time Hīr Shāh visited each zamīndāri, and caused the boundaries to be marked out in his own presence, bestowing on each a *sanad*. He also proclaimed that to every one who constructed a tank, as much land would be given as the tank watered. Many did so and received grants accordingly, in each case by a deed under the seal of the king; and this is the origin of the present tukumdārs. Hīr Shāh further cleared large tracts from jungle and induced numbers from every quarter to settle on them, fixing a small rent on each holding. A legend states that the people paid their rent not in money but in their field implements which were yearly taken to the king, and changed by him into gold, and this story doubtless refers

Bemrose, Collo., Derby.

PATHANPURA GATE. CHANDA.

to some annual muster of agricultural gear on which the year's assessment was based. Hīr Shāh completed the Chānda gates, filled in the foundations of the walls, and cleared the area enclosed. He also built the citadel, and erected within it a palace, which was taken possession of with great pomp and rejoicings. It is specially mentioned of this king that he paid tribute to no one, which implies that his predecessors were paying tribute to some overlord. There is however nothing in Firishta to show that the dominions of the Bahmani kings whose power collapsed when Hīr Shāh's is supposed to have risen extended east of the Wardhā. In none of the descriptions of their territories is any place on this side of the river mentioned. It therefore Hīr Shāh's predecessors really paid a tribute to any king it may have been to the Haihayas of Ratanpur to whom the Mānas were subordinate. The Gonds may have been practically independent, but out of policy might have recognised the sovereignty which Hīr Shāh possibly was the first to throw off.

His successors and Gond dances.

35. On the latter's death his two sons Bhūma or Agbā and Lokbā jointly held the throne, the former being the elder. They ruled according to the system inaugurated by their father, and were faithfully served by their officers. On an appointed day in the summer of each year all the Gond chiefs of the kingdom attended at Chānda, and having painted their persons with various colours, and adorned themselves with peacock's feathers, beetles' wings, and red and black berries, they came singing and dancing to the two princes, and laid before them specimens of every useful animal and vegetable product found on their estates; and the ceremony concluded with a great banquet at the palace. During this reign an Elma (Velamā) chief of Amrāvati, near Guntūr, obtained the cession of a large portion of the southern part of the kingdom, in return for a valuable gift of diamonds.

Karn Shāh and dispensation of justice.

36. On the death of the two brothers the son of one of them named Kondia Shāh, or as he was generally called Karn Shāh, came to the throne. This prince was attached to the Hindu religion, and delighted in hearing the narratives of its sacred books. Large numbers of Telugu and other Brāhmans thronged to his kingdom and he conferred upon them pensions and rent-free fields and villages. He set up *lingas* of Mahādeo in various places, and built numerous temples, assigning to the attendants grants of land. All the ancient temples and caves he caused to be cleared from vegetation and kept in repair. He also proved himself a valiant soldier, and no chief who disobeyed his commands long remained unpunished. In the meanwhile the oppression of the neighbouring kings, especially in Telingāna, had induced thousands to flock to Chānda, where they were kindly treated; and soon, there being no building room within the city walls, outlying suburbs were commenced. Up to this time the Gond kings had not interfered in the disputes of their subjects. If a man complained, for instance, that another had murdered his father, 'then,' would say the king, 'kill his'. Karn Shāh however established the following system. When a complaint was made he called both parties before him, and heard their stories; if the accused spoke falsely he was banished the kingdom, but if he told the truth he was cautioned and released. If a second complaint came up against the same man a similar course was pursued; but in the event of a third offence being committed, the offender was expelled from the country; and a like fate awaited him who thrice preferred false charges. During this reign the city walls reached more than half their destined height.

Bābāji Ballāl Shāh mentioned in the Ain-i Akbari.

37. Karn Shāh was succeeded by his son Bābāji Ballāl Shāh, a sensual and ignorant but harmless prince. He left the affairs of the kingdom entirely to his officers, who fortunately administered the trust faith-

fully and well. This prince is mentioned in the Ain-i-Akbarī as independent, paying no tribute to Delhi and having an army of 10,000 cavalry and 40,000 infantry. He is stated to have wrested Birāgarh (Wairāgarh) in which was a diamond mine, from another chief, which shows that Wairāgarh had passed out of the hands of this family probably during the joint rule of Bhūma and Lokbā who had allowed the southern portion of their country to go to an Elmā in exchange for a gift of diamonds.

His successors.

38. On Bābāji's death his son Dhundia Rām Shāh was enthroned. This king was foolish, drunken, untruthful and treacherous; but to him fell the honour of inaugurating the city walls, which were completed in his reign; in the ceremonies which took place many thousand Brāhmans were fed, and numerous grants of land were made; amongst others the Ghātkul pargana was bestowed on a Rājur Brāhman and the parganas of Kelāpur, Bhori, Yeotmāl, Kalam and Haveli (the first four being now included in Berār) on a Lingāyat Baniā. He was succeeded by his son Krishna Shāh, who governed the people well, and reduced the army, giving many of the leaders tracts of land in the east and south. The Gond princes of Deogarh had hitherto been subject to the Chānda kings, but in this reign a treaty was concluded by which Deogarh was declared independent of Chānda. This was probably a formal recognition of Deogarh's independence, as the latter in Jātba's times was much stronger than Chānda; Abul Fazl gave its strength as 2000 cavalry, 50,000 foot and more than 100 elephants. Up to this time the Gond kings were wont to sacrifice two cows yearly to Pharsā Pen, but Krishna Shāh substituted goats, and the sacrifice of cows was never re-established.

Bīr Shāh and his assassination.

39. On his death the crown devolved upon his son Bīr Shāh, a valiant and able prince, who ruled successfully. He gave his daughter in marriage to Durgpāl,[1] the son of

[1] This name is unknown to Deogarh history.

the king of Deogarh; but subsequently learning that Durgpāl had spoken insultingly to the princess, he vowed to Mahākāli that if victory were given him he would offer Durgpāl's head to her shrine; then mustering his forces he marched against the prince of Deogarh. In the battle which ensued the Deogarh army was assisted by a Muhammadan contingent, and the Chānda troops were driven back. Bīr Shāh was on the point of being captured, when unsheathing the sacred sword of his house, he rushed at Durgpāl, and with the cry, 'Victory to Mahākāli,' severed his head from his shoulders. The Deogarh army thereupon broke and fled, and Bīr Shāh taking the head returned to Chānda, where he offered it in fulfilment of his vow. His wife Hirai pulled down the old temple of Mahākāli and erected a new one on its site, and on the spire looking towards Nāgpur she fixed a stone bust of the slain Durgpāl, which gazes northwards to this day. Among Bīr Shāh's body-guards was a Rājput named Hīraman, who was supposed to possess a magic sword of wood, regarding which the king often questioned him, but questioned in vain. It so happened that when the ceremonies connected with Bīr Shāh's marriage to a second wife were in progress, and the day had arrived for the procession to the bride's house for which all the pomp and circumstances of the kingdom were marshalled in glittering line before the palace, awaiting their lord, and the king in regal dress was descending the palace steps, the thought came across his mind that unless he knew the truth regarding Hīraman some ill-fortune might ensue. Pausing where he stood while shouts and music rent the air he turned to Hīraman and peremptorily ordered him to produce the sword. Pressed before the crowd, the Rājput grew furious, and drawing his heavy brand struck the king down dead in sight of court and guards and people and then as rapidly despatched himself. Thus perished Bīr Shāh in the flower of his age. Over his remains rose the fairest of the temple tombs, which mark the resting places of his line; and no bridegroom of his house has since passed in procession to his future wife. This is said to have happened in 1672 A.D. Bīr Shāh having died without male heirs, his widow Hirai adopted the infant son of Govind Shāh, a member of the royal family who had settled at Chandankherā, and named him Rām Shāh, acting as regent during his minority.

The pious Rām Shāh.

40. Rām Shāh from his childhood was singularly humble, obedient and pious, and as he advanced in years the people came to regard him as an incarnation of the deity. On mounting the throne he proved a wise and excellent ruler, and so great was the awe created by his supposed divine attributes that crime, it is said, almost wholly ceased during his reign. Wise as he was, however, he did not escape family dishonour, for his daughter became enamoured of Bāgba, a Gond prince who dwelt south of the Wardhā, and many guilty visits resulted. One evening, so the story runs, Bāgba reached the Wardhā and found it in flood, but riding along the bank he came to where the stream narrowing rushes through sandstone cliffs on either side, and here he leaped his horse across. The intrigue was soon discovered, and Rām Shāh in wrath sent to seize Bāgba who resisted the messengers. The King then marched against him; and Bāgba with no hope of victory, but determined to die with honour, collected his followers, and accompanied by his brothers Agbā and Rāgba advanced to meet the sovereign. The opposing forces joined battle at Ghūgus, and the insurgents were totally routed. Agbā fell on the field; Rāgba was killed in the pursuit near Turodā, and Bāgba escaping home led his wife and children into a cavern hard by, where he put them to the sword and then slew himself. The king's troops traced him to the cave, which they filled with wood and straw, and firing the pile reduced the bodies to ashes. The Ramāla tank and the Rām Bāg (the latter near the present Chānda court-house) were made under Rām Shāh's orders; while the Govindpur

suburb and the Nagīna Bāg in which the Chānda mission orphanage now stands were constructed by his father Govind Shāh.

The Marāthā attempts to gain possession of Chānda.

41. In 1718 A.D. we find the Rājā of Sātāra attempting to obtain from the Delhi Emperor the cession of Chānda, and about the same year the former sent Kanhoji Bhonsla to invade Gondwāna. Kanhoji met with no military successes in the Chānda kingdom, and latterly betook himself to plundering, chiefly west of the Wardhā. He appears subsequently to have been recalled, but the summons having been disregarded, Raghujī Bhonsla was ordered to enforce his return, and about 1730 A.D., Raghujī captured him near Mundur in the Sirpur pargana (now of Berār), and forwarded him to Sātāra. Raghujī then proceeded to the city of Chānda, where he was courteously received by the king, and tradition states that the Marāthā soldier was so awed by Rām Shāh's calm mien and bearing, that in place of seeking a pretext for a quarrel he did him homage as a god. Rām Shāh was gathered to his fathers in 1735 A.D., and when Major Lucie Smith wrote he still lingered in the memory of the people as an aged saint-like man unruffled by the cares of earth, and inspiring a love not unmixed with solemn dread.

The last Gond king.

42. Well would it have been for the fame of his house had the fast failing thread of the Gond dynasty been severed at his death, for his son Nīlkanth Shāh, who succeeded to the throne, was an evil and cruel prince. He put to death his father's trusted Dīwān, Mahadāji Vaidya, and dismissed with contumely all the high officers of the former reign. The people he ground to the dust, and he interfered in the political disputes of Deogarh, but retribution overtook him swiftly, for in 1749 A.D. the Marāthās were at his gates, and the city fell, not by the award of battle, but by the treachery of an estranged court. Raghujī therefore dictated a treaty of partition, by which two-thirds of the revenue were alienated to the Marā-

thās ; but the remnant of power then spared soon vanished for in 1751 A.D. Raghujī took entire possession of the kingdom and made Nīlkanth Shāh a prisoner, the latter dying in confinement. Thus ended the dynasty of the Gond kings of Chānda. Originally petty chiefs of a savage tribe, they spread their sway over a wide dominion, reclaiming and peopling the wild forests in which they dwelt, and, save a nominal allegiance to the Delhi throne, preserving their soil for several centuries inviolate from foreign rule. When at length they fell, they left, if we forget the few last years, a well-governed and contented kingdom, adorned with admirable works of engineering skill, prosperous to a point no after-time has reached. The device of the Gond kings was a Singh or Griffin destroying an elephant, and probably had reference to their family name of Singh. This crest is carved upon wall and gateway and tower wherever Bhīm Ballāl Singh's line held sway, and is to be seen far beyond the boundaries of the present Chānda District.

The Bhonsla rule.

43. From the Marāthā conquest Chānda became a province of the Bhonsla family, and it will be sufficient to record only those events which directly affected this dynasty. In 1755 A.D. Raghujī died, leaving four sons, Jānoji, Sābaji, Mūdhoji and Bimbāji. Jānoji, the eldest, succeeded but the succession was disputed by Mūdhoji who was supported by the court of Poona ; and several encounters took place between the brothers. Mūdhoji having been worsted the matter was referred to the Peshwa, who confirmed Jānoji in the government of Nāgpur with the titles of Senā Sāhib ; while Mūdhoji was granted Chānda and Chhattīsgarh with the appellation of Senā Dhurandhar. Mūdhoji was wasteful and rapacious, and did much to ruin the country under his rule. In 1758 A.D. he left Chānda in the hands of his creditors and proceeded to Hindustān with Raghunāth Rao, the uncle of the Peshwa. On his return a good understanding sprang up between Jānoji and himself, consequent upon a project of the former's

to adopt as his successor Mūdhoji's eldest son; and in the hostilities which ensued between the Peshwa and Jānoji he assisted his brother. In 1769 A.D. Mādho Rao (the Peshwa) and Rukun-ud-daulah laid siege to Chānda, but were forced to retire, and peace was shortly afterwards declared. About 1772 A.D. Jānoji proceeded to Poona, and obtained the sanction of the Peshwa (Mādho Rao) to the adoption of Raghujī, Mūdhoji's eldest son. Mādho Rao died in November of that year, and was succeeded in the Peshwāship by Nārāyan Rao; while Jānoji expired in May following when on his march back to Nāgpur. Raghujī being a minor, Mūdhoji and Sābaji each claimed the regency; but Daryā Bai, Jānoji's widow, setting aside the pretensions of both, assumed the Government, and appointed Sābaji her General and Dīwān. Mūdhoji having always maintained relations with Raghunāth Rao found himself viewed with dislike by the Poona court, and he quickly saw that his only chance of success lay in his sword. He thereupon attacked Sābaji near Akolā in Berār, but was defeated with great loss. The Peshwa's agent then induced the brothers to agree to a truce, during which interval Daryā Bai deserted Sābaji for Mūdhoji. The latter again took the field, supported by the Pathān Governor of Ellichpur, while Sābaji was assisted by the Nizām. At this crisis the Peshwā Nārāyan Rao was murdered, and fresh complications arose, Mūdhoji espousing the cause of Raghunāth Rao and Sābaji that of the Poona ministerial party.

Local and family feuds.

44. In the meanwhile Chānda was not undisturbed. Ballāl Shāh, son of Nīlkanth Shāh, escaped from confinement in the Ballālpur fort, and collected a considerable force of Gonds with the intention of seizing Chānda and Mānikgarh. The insurgents, however, were routed at Gunpur in the Ghātkul pargana by Mahipat Rao, the sūbahdār of Chānda; and Ballāl Shāh, after receiving a gun-shot wound, was captured and sent in to Nāgpur. About this time a party of the Poona

Bemrose, Collo., Derby.

NANA SAHIB BHONSLA'S TEMPLE, CHANDA.

ministerial forces penetrated to Chormarhi, near Bhāndak, and made prisoners of the ladies of Mūdhoji's family; but Venkat Rao, zamīndār of Ahīri, and his brother Mohan Shāh, who were at the time military governors of the Chānda city, with a third brother Vishwās Rao, then in charge of the Mānikgarh fortress, attacked the Poona troops and rescued the ladies. Mūdhoji shared the reverses of Raghunāth Rao, and in January 1775 A.D. was vanquished and surrounded by his brother's troops at Pānchgaon near Nāgpur. Sābaji, flushed with success, drove his elephant up to that on which Mūdhoji was seated, exultingly calling him upon to surrender, when a pistol shot from Mūdhoji laid him dead in the very moment of victory. Mūdhoji thus suddenly undisputed regent of Berār had still many dangers to face, and he was glad to purchase a peace with the Nizām by the surrender of four forts among which were Chānda and Mānikgarh; but the surrender, never actually carried out, was shortly afterwards revoked.

Mūdhoji died in 1788 A.D. and his son Raghujī II, till then but titular Rājā, assumed the Government. He obtained from the court of Poona for his younger brother Venkoji the title of Senā Dhurandhar, and allotted to him Chānda and Chhattīsgarh. In 1789 A.D. he released Ballāl Shāh and granted him a yearly pension of 600 rupees. Venkoji commonly called Nāna Sāhib resided at Chānda, and was of a quiet and religious disposition. He rebuilt the Ballālpur fort and the Chānda citadel, both of which had fallen to ruin, and he erected a palace, a fragment of which forms the present Kotwāli. Several temples also owe their construction to him, the handsomest being the new building over the shrine of Achaleshwar, and the Murlīdhar temple within the palace precincts.

The decay of the Bhonslas.

45. In September 1797 A.D. the Erai rose to an extraordinary height, flooding the entire city of Chānda and submerging numerous dwellings. In 1803 A.D. Raghujī

II, by the treaty of Deogaon, lost Cuttack and the provinces west of the Wardhā, Mānikgarh and Sirpur; the ancient seat of the Ballāl Shāh dynasty thus passing away from Chānda. About this time the Pindāris first made their appearance in the District, and gradually overran the country, few villages escaping pillage, and many being rendered wholly desolate. Their visits roused the plundering classes into action, and the injury inflicted directly and indirectly was incalculable. In 1811 A.D. Venkoji died at Benāres, and his son Mūdhoji, known as Appa Sāhib, appears to have been born and brought up at Chānda, but no act of his prior to his becoming the head of the Nāgpur State has left his mark on the District.

Appa Sāhib.

46. In 1816 A.D. Raghujī II died, leaving but one son, Parsoji, who was imbecile in mind and body. After some opposition Appa Sāhib was declared regent, and sedulously courted the British alliance. In January 1817 A.D. he proceeded to Chānda, and during his absence from Nāgpur Parsoji died, murdered as it was subsequently learnt by Appa Sāhib's secret orders. The latter as nearest heir now became Rājā of Nāgpur. Avowedly a warm friend of the British, he privately intrigued against them in all directions until November following, when he threw off the mask and declared hostilities. The battles of Sītabaldī and Nāgpur followed in which he was signally defeated and was forced personally to surrender, and to agree to terms which rendered him wholly dependent on the British. In January 1818 A.D. he was permitted to resume the Government, and immediately recommenced his intrigues. He invited the Peshwa Bāji Rao to move on Nāgpur stirring up the Gonds to oppose the British, and ordered the Killadār of Chānda to recruit intending to escape to that city. But the Resident, Mr. Jenkins, was watching his plans, and on the 15th March caused him to be seized and brought a prisoner to the Residency. In the meanwhile his adherents were hastily making efforts to garrison Chānda.

Bhujang Rao, zamīndār of Ahīri, and his brother Kondu Bāpu, zamīndār of Arpalli, threw themselves with their followers into the place, and every able-bodied citizen of the lower classes was pressed into the ranks. On the 2nd April the van of Bāji Rao's army reached Warhā, ten miles west of Chānda, on the left bank of the Wardhā, but was there checked by Lieutenant-Colonel Hopeton Scott, who had been despatched from Nāgpur to prevent Bāji Rao getting into Chānda. Colonel Adams, with a second division, shortly afterwards arrived in the vicinity, and on the 17th April the combined forces attacked and routed Bāji Rao at Pāndarkaura west of the Wardhā.

Siege of Chānda by the British.

47. The British troops then laid siege to Chānda, one brigade taking ground at Kusara on the right bank of the Erai, north-west of the city, while the second was massed south-east of it, at the junction of the Jharpat and Erai, where batteries were posted on an eminence called the Māna hill. The garrison were now called upon to surrender, but their only reply was to kill the messenger; and the citizens are said to have been so confident of success that marriages went on amongst them as if no hostile force were near. The British guns thereupon opened fire, and a breach was soon made in the line of curtain between the Pathānpura gate and the Hanumān wicket. On the morning of the 2nd May the storming parties moved to the assault, and were met in the breach by the regular garrison, who are said to have fallen to a man in its defence, while the Killadār Gangā Singh was also slain, rewarding with his dying breath one Ali Khān, who claimed to have shot an English officer. The struggle, however, was of short duration, and the British were quickly masters of the place, which was given up to sack; but in the general plunder which ensued, the Killadār slain protected his home far better than his living arm could have defended it, for the English in admiration of his conduct at the assault caused his house to be scrupulously

respected [1]; and his family, it may be added, are now pensioners of the British Government. Appa Sāhib's repeated treachery having proved him unworthy of trust, the British Government decreed his deposition, and placed Raghujī, grandson of Raghujī II, at the head of the Nāgpur State.

Administration of the country under the British Resident.

48. As the new Rājā was only some nine years old, a regency was appointed under his grand-mother Bakā Bai and the administration of the country was conducted by the Resident, acting in the name of the Rājā, and assisted by British officers in charge of each District and department. The mean rapacious spirit which characterised the Bhonslas in all dealings with their subjects had caused infinite harm to the Chānda District, and from 1803 A.D. constant disturbances and lawlessness had added their evil fruits; indeed it is on record that the population was in 1802 A.D. double that in 1822 A.D., and that the houses in the city of Chānda had decreased during that period in nearly the same proportion. The able men, who from 1818 A.D. to 1830 A.D. now administered the District in succession, did much, each in his time, to restore the former prosperity of the country. The Gond chiefs who had rebelled were brought to submission, plundering was stopped, and order established, the heavy assessments on the land were reduced, deserted villages re-peopled, and ruined irrigation works repaired. Education was encouraged and during this period Subāji Bāpu, a Telugu Brāhman of Chānda, gained an Indian reputation by his published works in Marāthī, Telugu and Sanskrit, the scientific value of which particularly of his treatise on the Copernican system, was warmly acknowledged by the Government of India and the Asiatic Society of Bengal.

---

[1] After its capture Chānda was practically destroyed; besides the city walls, only the Ballāl Kilā (now the Jail) and the Killadār's house (now the Kotwāli) being left standing. When rebuilt the town was laid out on a different plan and the main thoroughfare the 'Victoria Road' now runs from north to south.

Raghujī III.

49. But in June 1830 A.D. the management of the country was made over to the Rājā Raghujī III, and progress stayed. Short-sighted grasping measures took the place of a broad and generous policy; men without interest found their lands taxed to almost their full return, while those with influential friends paid less than their just due; many of the old holders were ejected, and the best villages bestowed on relatives and favourites of the Rājā, or on official underlings. Thus sprang up a body of absentee landlords leasing the richest estates in the District, but knowing naught about them and having hardly an interest in common with the country or its people; anxious only to obtain the largest possible income, and utterly careless of the well-being of their tenantry; all in striking contrast to the policy pursued by the Gond kings. Plundering revived in spite of military parties posted thickly over the District, and as late as 1862 A.D. a Government treasure escort was attacked and robbed by Gonds on the Mūl road, not sixteen miles from Chānda.

Lapse to British Government.

50. In 1853 A.D. Raghujī died heirless, and the Nāgpur Province was then incorporated in the British Empire, the administration being conducted by a commission under the supreme Government. The first Deputy Commissioner of Chānda was Mr. R. S. Ellis of the Madras Civil Service (afterwards created a C.B.) who assumed charge of the District on the 18th December 1854 A.D. The swell of the great wave of rebellion which swept over India in 1857-58 A.D. was felt in Chānda, and the wild nature of the country, the predatory habits of the Gonds, and the proximity of the Hyderābād territory, combined to render the management of the District during this period a task of peculiar anxiety; but Captain W. H. Crichton (the then Deputy Commissioner) prevented any outbreak until March 1858 A.D., when Bāpu Rao, a petty chief of Mollampalli in the Ahīri zamīndāri, commenced plundering in the Rājgarh pargana,

and was shortly afterwards joined by Venkat Rao, zamīndār of Arpalli and Ghot. These two leaders then openly declared rebellion, and, collecting a mixed force of Rohillas and Gonds, withstood the troops sent against them. On the night of the 29th April a party of the insurgents attacked Messrs. Gartland, Hall and Peter, telegraph employés, who were encamped near Chunchgondi on the Prānhita, and killed the two first. Mr. Peter escaped into the Ahīri keep, and as soon as possible joined Captain Crichton, who was in the vicinity directing operations. Subsequently when it was desired to communicate with Lachmī Bai, the zamīndārin of Ahīri, Mr. Peter disguised himself as a native and safely delivered to her Captain Crichton's letter. The rebels made a stand at several points, but never with success, and at length by the exertions of Lachmī Bai Bāpu Rao was captured, and was immediately sent in to Chānda, where he suffered death on the 21st October 1858 A.D. Venkat Rao escaped to Bastar and in April 1860 A.D. he was arrested by the Rājā of that dependency, and on being handed over to the British authorities was sentenced to transportation for life, with forfeiture of all property. For the services performed during 1857-58 A.D. Lachmī Bai was granted sixty-seven villages of the Arpalli and Ghot zamīndāri. On the 2nd March 1861 the Nāgpur Province and the Saugor and Nerbudda territories were formed into the Government of the Central Provinces and Chānda then became a portion of the Nāgpur Division. Since that date the District has fully shared in the material and intellectual progress which followed the inauguration of the new Government.

The Rampā rebellion.

51. Only once has the peace of the District been disturbed and that by a local incident known as the Rampā rebellion. In 1879-80 some new forest laws caused considerable dissatisfaction among the forest tribes in the hills that bound the Godāvari valley. The oppressive and injudicious action of the

Tahsīldār of Bhadrāchalam and the forest ranger fanned the smouldering discontent, and a flame of insurrection ran along the hills. The forest tribes and villagers gathered in bands amounting occasionally to several thousands, looted villages, killed one or two policemen, and captured a steamer of the Godāvari river service. A military field force was sent from Madras to quell the insurrection and the company of troops stationed at Sironchā was called out. Sardār Ratan Singh, District Superintendent of Police, Chānda, distinguished himself by his prompt and able conduct of the police operations, and by his intrepidity and skill in one skirmish with a considerable number of the rebels won high praise from Viscount Guillamore, Special Assistant to the Agent of the Godāvari District, who was with him in the action. Sardār Ratan Singh in his own report states that if police action in the first instance had been promptly taken there would have been no need for military intervention. There were several subsequent disturbances during the next two years, but by 1882 the people had returned to their usual avocations, and since then the District has enjoyed the peace that 'has no history.'

ARCHÆOLOGY.

Scythian remains.

52. The District contains many antiquarian remains belonging to different ages. Scythian, Buddhist, Hindu and Gond have alike left characteristic traces of their occupation, which, in spite of their great interest, have never been systematically studied, so that materials for a scholarly and accurate account of Chānda antiquities are not at present available. Formerly, it is recorded, there existed in Chānda many cromlechs and kistvaens, which are declared to mark a Scythian invasion. The Rev. Mr. Hislop wrote that in each of fifteen villages in the vicinity of Mūl two cromlechs were to be found and in Chāmursi a group of twenty. Many of these cromlechs, if they ever existed, have entirely disappeared, and only one

authentic instance has been traced. Captain Glasfurd, Deputy Commissioner of what formerly was the Upper Godāvari District, sent some relics dug out of kistvaens in the Albāka tāluk of Sironchā tahsīl concerning which Mr. Hislop wrote: 'With reference to these remains I may state that the vestiges 'of an ancient Scythian raid in this part of India are very 'numerous. They are found chiefly as barrows, surrounded 'with a circle of stones, which when complete are styled 'kistvaens, and, when open on one side, cromlechs. The 'cromlechs are now found empty. The kistvaens, if they 'have not been disturbed, contain stone coffins, urns, etc. 'The tumuli are also rich in antiquities.' The objects described by Mr. Hislop as cromlechs or dolmens are found at Keljhar, Mūl, etc., and are fairly numerous all over the lower Waingangā valley, where the Kurumwārs, a shepherd caste, range, and there is some reason for supposing that they really are Kurumwār temples or shrines. The latter closely resemble cromlechs but the open side is always to the east. The shrines occur in pairs, one for the male god Mallana, and one for the goddess Mallani. Mr. Hislop's statement that the cromlechs are empty, that they occur in pairs in fifteen villages, and that they have one side open, strongly supports the hypothesis that he mistook these shrines for cromlechs. That they are shrines at present is certain, for the present writer has witnessed the worship of Kurumwārs at these shrines and seen them put little clay images of sheep under the stone to win protection for their flocks from the deities. The closed tombs or kistvaens and the relics dug up from tumuli are however sufficient to establish the occurrence of a Scythian raid, but the vestiges of it are not so numerous in this as in neighbouring Districts.

Buddhist remains.

53. The cave temples at Wijāsan (*Vidyā-asan*, abode of learning) near Bhāndak are described in the note on that village in the Appendix. They form the principal Buddhist antiquities in the District, and are to be clearly distinguished from the

Bemrose, Collo., Derby

TEMPLE OF DASAVATAR, MARKANDI.

Hindu cave temples, probably of still more ancient date, which are found at Bhāndak, Ballālpur, Ghūgus and Jharāpāpra.

Hemādpanthī temples.

54. The local legend of the birth of Hemādpanth, the temple builder, is the same as that told of Lakshmanīya Rājā of Gaur:—'When 'his mother's confinement drew near, the time was declared 'to be inauspicious, so she ordered her attendants to hang her 'up by the feet, till the auspicious hour arrived. She was 'then taken down and gave birth to Hemādpanth, but died 'herself immediately afterwards.' Hemād became learned in every science but more especially in medicine. When Vibhīshana, the brother of Rāwan, the prince of the Rākshasas, was sick Hemādpanth cured him and the grateful patient told him to ask a boon. Hemādpanth asked for the aid of the Rākshasas to build temples wherever he might require them. The boon was granted, but on condition that the Rākshasas were not to work for more than one night at a time. Hemādpanth accordingly built all the temples at Mārkanda, Bhāndak, Neri, etc., in one night. This story of the origin of Hemādpanthī temples is common throughout this District and Berār. Hemādpanth has been identified with Hemādri the Shrīkaranādhipa or superintendent of records of the Yādava kings of Deogiri, Mahādeva and Rāmchandra. He was a renowned Sanskrit scholar. But Hemādri's date is 1260 - 71 A.D. and archæologists date the Mārkanda temples about the 10th or 11th century A.D. Temples of the Hemādpanthī style are found in about 30 villages in the District, some of them being of remarkable beauty, and displaying wonderful stone carvings. Modern temples and shrines are still built in imitation of these, but the carvings are no longer of the same beauty and finish. Striking examples of ancient Hemādpanthī temples are found at Bhāndak, Neri, Bhatāla and Waigaon, but by far the most beautiful and extensive are the ruined temples of Mārkanda.

Gond architecture.

55. The buildings that mark the period of Gond ascendancy are mainly tombs and forts. Temples were not within the sphere of their philosophy. The tombs of the Gond kings in Chānda show quite an original form of architectural conception, different from either Hindu or Muhammadan memorials of a similar character, which almost rises to a distinct type. The town walls of Chānda and the still more distinctive masonry of Tīpagarh fort witness to a considerable knowledge of the art of fortification. The walls of Tīpagarh are remarkable for the huge size of the blocks of stone built into them. Large forts in a fair state of preservation are also to be found at Ballālpur and Wairāgarh, while those at Devalvāda, Bhāndak, Bhatāla, Neri and Segaon, though now fallen into ruin, must once have been works of considerable strength and size. The ruined palace built by Dhundia Rām Shāh on the tank *band* at Junonā with its large extent of stone steps down to the water, and the ruins of a similar palace within the circuit of the walls at Tīpagarh on the edge of the lake, are memorials of a style of building that has entirely disappeared from the District, which is the more to be regretted as these 'water palaces' must have been delightfully cool and pleasant.

Inscriptions.

56. The inscriptions in the District are not so numerous as the extent of the archæological remains would lead one to expect, and a large proportion of them are so defaced as to render them difficult if not impossible to decipher. The oldest inscription in the District is on a slab at Deotek. The characters are like those of the Asoka edicts 269—232 B.C., while on the same slab is an inscription in Gupta character. Probably next in age are those in the Bhadranāg (Bhāndak) and Mārkanda temples. None of them have been deciphered and all are fragmentary. In the Buddhist caves at Bhāndak are illegible inscriptions which from the lettering appear to belong to the 6th or 7th century A.D. An inscription of

the 9th century giving the names of three or four Buddhist kings of the Pānduvansi line has been referred to in the History chapter. Nāgri inscriptions later than the 10th century are fairly plentiful but none are of much importance; one on the Mārkanda temple 'Magardhwaj Jogi 700' has been the cause of considerable comment, but its meaning has at last been satisfactorily solved by Mr. Hīra Lāl.

Two copper-plates of the Vākātaka kings have been found in the possession of Gonds now living in Seonī and Chhindwāra. The ancestors of the families now in possession of them are said to have lived in Chānda, and brought away these plates with them, but no information can be obtained as to the locality whence they were removed.

CHAPTER III.

POPULATION.

STATISTICS OF POPULATION.

Changes of area, and statistics of population.

57. Both the external boundaries of the District and the internal distribution of its tahsīls have undergone extensive changes since the formation of the Central Provinces. In 1860-61 ten villages were added to Chānda from the Nāgpur District. On the completion of the 30 years' settlement in 1869 the District comprised about 9700 square miles, and consisted of three tahsīls, Mūl with an area of 5098 square miles, Bramhapurī 3321 square miles, and Warorā 1281 square miles. In 1874, the area of the District received a substantial addition by the transfer from the Upper Godāvari District (which was simultaneously abolished) of the tāluks of Sironchā, Nūgur, Albāka and Cherlā with an area of 1053 square miles, which were formed into a new tahsīl with its headquarters at Sironchā. From this date until 1895 the area of the four tahsīls of the District was as follows: Mūl 5058 square miles, Bramhapurī 3324, Sironchā 1085, and Warorā 1282, or a total of 10,749 square miles. In 1895, the headquarters of the Mūl tahsīl were shifted to Chānda and the tahsīl was thenceforward known as the Chānda tahsīl; no alteration of area, however, took place at this time. At the beginning of 1905 a new tahsīl with an area of 3708 square miles was formed with its headquarters at Garhchirolī, 1181 square miles being taken from the Chānda tahsīl, and 2527 square miles from Bramhapurī. At the same time an area of 2603 square miles, almost the whole of which consisted of the Ahīri zamīndāri, was transferred from Chānda to Sironchā, and another 100 square miles was transferred from Chānda to Bramhapurī. In October, 1907, four of the northern zamīndāris, comprising an area

of 838 square miles with a population of 47,428 persons were transferred from the Garhchirolī tahsīl to the Drug District and at the same time an area of 13 square miles was transferred from Sironchā to Garhchirolī. Besides these changes which have actually taken place, it has long been contemplated to transfer the lower tāluks of the Sironchā tahsīl to the Madras Presidency, and the transfer has been shown in the B. Volume as actually having taken place in 1905 but as a matter of fact the Lower Tāluks still remain (1908) attached to the District.[1] As the result of all these changes the District has, as at present constituted, an area of 9911 square miles divided among five tahsīls. Its population, which at the census of 1901 amounted to 601,533 souls, is now, allowing for territorial changes and neglecting this subsequent increase due to the excess of births over deaths, 554,105. The area and population of each tahsīl, as adapted from the figures of the last census, now stand as shown below :—

Tahsīl.	Area in square miles.	Population.	Population per square mile.
Chānda	1174	121,040	103
Warorā	1282	134,547	105
Bramhapurī	897	115,049	128
Sironchā	3675	75,154	20
Garhchirolī	2883	108,315	38
District Total ...	9911	554,105	56

Of this total, 273,607 were males and 280,498 females, or roughly, 40 females to every 39 males. The returns of vital statistics since 1901 indicate that the population has already

[1] The Lower Tāluks have since been transferred to Madras from is July 1909.

once more expanded to over 600,000. Since 1902, the birth rate has been exceedingly high ranging from 44 to 52 per mille, while the death rate, except in 1906 when it reached 34·6, has averaged only about 24 per mille. In proportion to its area, Chānda is the most sparsely inhabited District in the Provinces, a fact which is attributable to the huge areas of zamīndāri lands inhabited by a mere handful of aborigines. The incidence of population by tahsīls shows this clearly enough. Chānda, Warorā and Bramhapurī, which contain no zamīndāris, all have an average incidence of over 100 persons to the square mile, whereas Sironchā, which contains the Ahīri zamīndāri with its huge area of 2600 square miles almost entirely abandoned to jungle, and Garhchirolī, in which there are 15 zamīndāris covering an area of 1413 square miles, only boast 20 and 38 persons to the square mile respectively. The total *khālsa* area of the District is 5900 square miles with an ascertained population of 495,454 persons or 84 to the square mile, whereas the zamīndāri tracts with a total area of 4013 square miles have a population of only 58,651, or between 14 and 15 to the square mile. Even within the *khālsa* itself the distribution of the population is very uneven. Thus in Sironchā almost the whole of the population is confined to a narrow strip along the bank of the Godāvari: that strip supports nearly 700 persons to the square mile of occupied land, whereas inland the country is pure jungle and almost entirely uninhabited The population is most dense in the rice tracts, a fact which is reflected in the figures for the Bramhapurī tahsīl. In pure rice tracts the population often comes to over 600 souls per occupied square mile and is never below 550. The reason is not far to seek : rice gives a far heavier outturn than any other crop, and so we find holdings smaller and the pressure of population greater. The Bramhapurī Station-house area had at the last census a population of 194 to the square mile, while the adjoining Talodhī Station-house area had 192, whereas the Warorā Station-house area, representing the richest open field tract of the District, averaged only 157 to the square mile.

Towns and villages.

58. The District contains, according to the census figures and allowing for the territory transferred to Drug, two towns and 3134 villages, of which latter 935 are uninhabited, while 154 are ryotwāri and 39 forest villages. The urban population is confined to the towns of Chānda, 17,803, and Warorā, 10,626, and forms only 5 per cent. of the total population. Twenty-two villages boast a population of over 2000 persons:—Mūl (2847), Saoli Khās (2548), Talodhī (2494), Dābha (2320), and Chaudampallī (2227) in the Chānda tahsīl; Chimūr, (4088), Nerī (3362), Bhāndak (3188) and Bhīsi (2586) in Warorā; Bramhapurī (4328), Nawargaon Buzurg (4100), Nāgbhīr (2940), Sindewāhi Mokāsa (2932), Talodhī Rāj (2727), Pīpalgaon Maktā (2288) and Arher Nawargaon (2231), in the Bramhapurī tahsīl; Armorī (4802), Chāmursi (2449) and Garhchirolī (2077) in the Garhchirolī tahsīl; and Asaralli (3128), Ankīsa (3029) and Sironchā (2813) in the Sironchā tahsīl. Forty-seven other villages have between 1000 and 2000 inhabitants, while the very large number of 960 inhabited villages contain populations of less than 100 each.

Variation of population.

59. A census of the District has been taken on five occasions, in 1866, 1872, 1881, 1891 and 1901. There have, however, as has been explained at length in the preceding section, been considerable changes in the area of the District which vitiate comparisons between the earlier and the later returns. Making allowance for these changes, the population of the present area of the District as ascertained on the last three occasions of taking the census is shown below:—

1881	602,936
1891	639,483
1901	554,105

The total population thus increased by 6·1 per cent. during the decade 1881—1891, and decreased by 14·2 during the decade 1891—1901. During the first decade the increase was almost entirely due to the natural expansion of the population, not to immigration; it was most marked in the northern zamīndāris, but was there doubtless in large measure due to more accurate returns. The *khālsa* tract which showed the greatest increase was Warorā, where the increase was 6·1 or exactly equal to the average for the whole District. The appalling decrease in the population which took place during the next decade was of course in the main attributable to the bad years and famine immediately preceding the last census. Some of the loss was due to emigration, but much of it must be assigned to the heavy mortality of the decade. From 1895 to 1897 the number of deaths exceeded that of births by over 10,000, and although an abnormal birth rate in 1899 temporarily made good the wastage, the famine of 1900 resulted in a death rate of 96·62 per mille and the deaths of that year exceeded the births by nearly 37,000. It is very doubtful, too, if the mortality during the scarcity of 1897 was not a good deal heavier than was indicated by the official returns. The only part of the District which has steadily increased in population during the twenty years from 1881 to 1901 is the Sironchā tahsīl, where the increase during the first decade amounted to 4·8 per cent. and during the second to 22 per cent. According to Mr. Hemingway, the reason given for this locally is the immunity from dacoits under British rule, but, as he observes, this hardly seems an adequate explanation, and the true reason appears to be that this part, owing to the fertilising action of the river, never suffers an entire failure of the crops, a circumstance which has not only favoured the multiplication of the present population but has also encouraged a rapid influx of tenants from the Hyderābād side of the river. Since the last census, matters have, thanks to rather more favourable seasons, considerably improved, and, as has been remarked in a foregoing paragraph, the vital statistics indicate that the population has once more expanded to at least 600,000.

Effect of recent bad years on the population.

60. The effect of the cycle of bad years upon the population is summarised by Mr. Hemingway thus: 'The decrease over the rest of the 'District (*i.e.*, excluding Sironchā) var'ies very largely from group to group. A succession of poor 'rice years has encouraged the small tenants of rice tracts 'to seek their fortunes elsewhere in the open tracts where a 'greater variety of cropping is possible, and the probability of 'all crops failing utterly is very small. The Warorā tahsīl, 'for instance, has larger areas of open-field crops: the total 'drop in that tahsīl was 6 per cent. only, the best of the open 'field groups showing a good increase: in the *khālsa* portion 'of Chānda tahsīl the drop was 12 per cent., in the corres'ponding portion of Bramhapurī tahsīl it was 19 per cent. If 'the open tract at the extreme north of Bramhapurī tahsīl 'is excepted, the tract is purely rice-growing; and there are 'a large number of small villages interspersed between the 'large stable villages, where the area secured by irrigation is 'comparatively small and tenants had a succession of really 'unpropitious years for their rice. In the Chānda tahsīl 'the Ghātkul group returned a large increase in the popula'tion; this is an open-field tract, somewhat remote, and for 'that reason not fully occupied until poor rice years brought 'its soil into high favour. The increase here is mainly due 'to immigration from the poorer rice tracts ....To what 'extent the decrease in the population is a permanent loss or 'merely a temporary exodus in search of work must be 'largely a matter of conjecture. In certain tracts it has 'always been customary for the village labourers to repair to 'Berār after the rice harvest is over, in order to find employ'ment on cotton-picking; and the census is taken at the 'exact time when most of the labourers who make a practice of 'going to Berār have already gone. It may be said with 'some certainty that the drop in the figures of open tracts 'adjoining Berār was caused entirely by this temporary 'exodus, since there is now no marked want of labour for

'agricultural work in these open tracts. But it is equally 'certain that the loss in some of the rice groups is more 'permanent; to prove this, there are large areas of second 'rate rice land unoccupied, which in normal years were 'occupied by the village labourers and small tenants; and 'also a rough census was taken at attestation of a few vil-'lages which seemed to be very short of labour for the reaping 'of their rice: this rough census, though its figures are of 'little use in that they concern a very small area, showed 'that a very large proportion of the regular labourers of cer-'tain villages had been absent for three years from their 'villages, and it might safely be assumed that they would 'not return as permanent inhabitants until the rice crops 'were giving sufficient outturn to induce them to return. 'This want of labour was very marked two years ago (*i.e.*, '1903-04) when there was a bumper rice crop, but not 'enough labour to cut it in time: also the survey parties in 'railway employ could get no labour; and at the present 'moment the railway construction, and tank construction as 'well, is proceeding very slowly indeed, because there is not 'sufficient labour in the District. It may safely be said that 'the population of the poorer rice tracts will continue to be 'very short indeed, until a succession of good rice years has 'been enjoyed.'

Migration.

61. The statistics compiled at the census of 1901 do not, of course, reveal the ebb and flow of migration between different parts of the District, which Mr. Hemingway's remarks quoted above show to have been considerable. As regards the course of migration between this and other Districts of the Province and other parts of India, the figures of that census showed that 90 per cent. of the population was indigenous to the District, while of the balance about 6 per cent. came from other parts of the Province and 4 per cent. from the rest of India. The chief fields of emigration are Berār and Hyderābād. Twenty-eight thousand persons

born in Chānda were enumerated in Berār, while out of nearly 17,000 natives of the Province enumerated in Hyderābād the great majority probably belonged to Chānda. The Berār figures were, of course, much swelled by immigrants who had moved over merely for the harvesting season. Twelve thousand natives of this District were found in Wardhā and nearly 9000 in Nāgpur at the time of the census, while the corresponding figures for Bhandāra were 6000 and for the Feudatory States 5000. Some 60,000 persons hailing from other parts were enumerated in this District. The largest number of immigrants came from Hyderābād which claimed over 14,000: natives of Raipur numbered 10,000, of Bhandāra 7000, of Berār over 6000, while there were some 4000 immigrants apiece from Nāgpur and Wardhā and 8000 from the Feudatory States. On the whole, making allowance for the season at which the census was taken, the interchange of population with the outside is a very even one, the only marked streams of emigration being towards Hyderābād, and Berār, and of immigration from Hyderābād, mainly into Sironchā, and from Raipur and the Nāndgaon State into the northern zamīndāris since transferred to the Drug District.

Language.

62. Three distinct languages—Marāthī, Telugu and Gondī—meet in the Chānda District; and around and between each has accumulated a weltering mass of dialects which almost defies enumeration. Roughly it may be said that Marāthī is the language of the *khālsa* exclusive of the Sironchā tahsīl, Telugu of Sironchā, and Gondī of the zamīndāris. Marāthī is now far more widely spoken than either of the other two languages, and is the tongue of nearly two-thirds of the population. It does not appear that it always possessed this predominance, as Sir R. Jenkins wrote in 1826 that Marāthī and Telugu were spoken in nearly equal proportion, and this statement of course refers to the District exclusive of Sironchā which is now the principal seat of Telugu. Hindī and Urdū are comparatively little employed:

out of some 42,000 shown as speaking these languages at the last census, 30,000 were speakers of Chhattīsgarhī belonging to the zamīndāris since transferred to Drug.

Marāthī.

63. Marāthī was found at the last census to be the language of 382,641 persons, or 64 per cent. of the total population of the District. This language is the standard language of the whole of the Warorā and Bramhapurī tahsīls and of the northern half of the Chānda tahsīl. It is also found in all other parts of the District holding the field with competitors of varying strength. Roughly it may be said to be the predominating language of the whole of the *khālsa* except the Sironchā tahsīl. It is also the language of the courts. The variety spoken is that known as Nāgpurī Marāthī, which is identical with that of Berār, and is the typical Marāthī of the Province. The local dialect is sometimes called *Jhāri*, *i.e.*, jungle language, *Jhāri* meaning forest-country. Various dialects are distinguished which are really nothing more than jargons of the standard type. The most important of these is Kunbau, the dialect of the Kunbīs, stated in the Linguistic Survey to be used by over 110,000 speakers. Others are Gowāri (500), Kumhāri (1000), Koshti (3123), Mahāri (10,000), Kosri (630) and Netakāni (180). The figures in brackets indicate the numbers of persons using each dialect, but the classification of these appears to be somewhat rough and ready, and in some cases the classes overlap one another. Most of them are, as the names indicate, caste dialects, and these are all rejected by Dr. Grierson as essentially identical with the ordinary Marāthī of the locality. Netakānī is confined to a small body of persons in the Sironchā tahsīl, where Telugu is the principal language. It is based on the common Marāthī, but largely modified by Telugu, and must be looked upon as a broken form of speech.

Gondī.

64. Gondī belongs to the Dravidian family of languages, and forms a link between Telugu on the one hand and Tamil and Kanarese on

the other, on the whole approximating more closely to these latter languages. The language as spoken in Chānda, however, forms an exception to this generalisation in that Telugu influence is strong, increasing in power the further one goes south. At the census of 1881 Gondī was ascertained to be the native tongue of 132, 348 residents of the District: in 1891 the figure was 132,598 and in 1901, 98,428. Speakers of Gondī are to be found in almost every town and village in the District, but the true home of the language is in the tract east of the Waingangā. The Gonds speak Gondī among themselves, but talk Telugu, Marāthī or Hindī with strangers. The language has no literature and in fact no written character; there are however several popular folk songs, of which some were collected and transcribed by the Rev. Stephen Hislop. Three variations of the language, which are usually classified as sub-dialects, are found in the District, but Dr. Grierson does not consider that they differ sufficiently from the main language to be so classified and holds that the various denominations are only local names for the border dialects where Gondī merges into Telugu. The Māria dialect differs very slightly from ordinary Gondī: it is not confined to any particular locality, and is spoken, according to the census of 1901, by 9655 persons only. Koi is the dialect of 8144 persons: it is an advanced form of the language with more points of analogy with Telugu than is the case in other Districts. The Kois or Gonds of the hills, especially in Sironchā, are known as Gattu or Gotte Kois, and a dialect has been distinguished under the name of Gattu which, according to the last census returns, is spoken by 5483 persons. Dr. Grierson considers that both Koi and Gattu represent the same dialect, which can be characterised as a link between the forms of Gondī spoken in the north-east of Chānda and the adjoining Districts in the Bastar State on one side, and the Gondī dialects of Hyderābād and the Madras Presidency on the other. The chief local peculiarities of the tongue as a whole are the substitution of 'i' for standard Gondī 'r' when an initial letter, the possession of separate forms of the dative and accusative (this points to Aryan influence), and certain variations in the personal terminations of verbs. An interesting point about the Gondī language is that with one or two exceptions all its numerals above seven are borrowed from Aryan languages. The Gond is undoubtedly taking freely to the use of other languages than his own, and Dr. Grierson remarks that it is probably only a question of time when Gondī shall have ceased to exist as an independent form of speech.

Telugu.

65. Telugu is spoken by 71,811 persons, the majority of whom are residents of the Sironchā tahsīl, but it is also used freely in the south of the Chānda tahsīl and follows the course of the Waingangā as far north as Chāmursi and Garhchirolī. Telugu in many respects occupies an independent position among the Dravidian languages, and is the only descendant of the Andhra dialect of old Dravidian. It is supposed to be a most mellifluous language, the Italian of the east, but according to the Census Report of 1901 the euphonious nature of Telugu is not appreciated by the people of Nāgpur, among whom it is said to sound like stones rattled in a tin. It has a voluminous literature, mostly poetical, which is written in a dialect widely differing from the colloquial form of the language. The bulk of the Telugu speaking population of this District use the standard form of the language, but its purity and the quality of pronunciation markedly improve from north to south; when spoken in the direction of Mūl and Chāmursi it is to a great extent mixed with Marāthī. The wide divergencies from place to place may be illustrated by the translation of a simple phrase, 'Come again.' About Mūl and Chānda, this would be rendered '*Ayinaka rā*', in Sironchā '*Taruwāla rā*', in the pure Telugu of the south '*Malli rāndi*' or '*Thuthaku rāndi.*' Several minor dialects have been distinguished, such as Sālewāri, the dialect of the weaver, Komtau, the language of the Komtīs or shopkeepers, Kāpewāri, which is ascribed to a certain class of agriculturists, Golarī, spoken by

the nomadic Golars or Golkars, a dialect called Manthāni, and so forth, but Dr. Grierson does not think that the departures from standard Telugu which these forms exhibit are striking enough to warrant their separate classification. Mr. Russell in his Census Report lumps all these dialects together under the alternative titles of Golarī, Holiā or Komtau, and states that they are one dialect spoken by a number of castes whose native Telugu has undergone some modification by being brought into contact with Marāthī.

Halbī.

66. Halbī is spoken by 3258 inhabitants of the zamīndāris. Linguistic evidence indicates that the Halbās are an aboriginal tribe who have adopted Hinduism and an Aryan language. Their dialect is a curious mixture of Uriyā, Chhattīsgarhī, and Marāthī.

Occupation.

67. Out of the total District population of 601,533 as ascertained at the last census 412,212 were found to be actually employed in earning a livelihood. These were broadly divided into eight classes and the number of persons employed in each class and the percentage borne by that number to the number of actual workers in the District are shown below :—

Nature of employment.	No. of workers.	Percentage of total workers.
Government	4,421	1·1
Pasture and agriculture ...	299,567	72·7
Personal services	6,403	1·5
Preparation and supply of material substances	82,773	20·1
Commerce, transport and storage ...	3,344	·8
Professions	1,914	·5
Unskilled labour, not agriculture ...	7,859	1·9
Means of subsistence independent of occupation (mainly mendicants) ...	5,931	1·4
Total ...	412,212	100·00

Out of every 10,000 actual workers, 3723 are landowners or landholders, 2518 are field labourers and 657 are farm-servants. The proportion of herdsmen is 241, of cattle and small stock breeders and dealers 41 and of cow and buffalo keepers and *ghi*-sellers 27. In the preparation and supply of material substances, fishermen, fish curers and dealers number 319 in each 10,000 actual workers, persons employed on the provision of vegetable food 189, providers of drink, condiments and stimulants 98, of light, fuel and forage 79, oil pressers and oil sellers 77, cotton-spinners, sizers and yarn dealers 272, cotton weavers 420, workers in metals and precious stones 146, basket, mat and broom makers 101, workers in leather 79, potters 42, carpenters 47, tailors 44, and persons employed on building 25. Persons employed in administration number 107 per 10,000, this figure including village servants and persons in the employ of local and municipal bodies. In the same ratio, barbers number 42, washermen 63, professional men 46, money-lenders and bankers 33, unskilled labourers other than agricultural 190, and mendicants 137. This leaves a balance of 237 in each 10,000 workers who are employed in various occupations, whose followers do not in any instance total 1000 in the whole District.

Attitude of the people towards the census.

68. The people have by now learnt to look on the census merely as one of the many harmless eccentricities of the Sarkār, but it was not always so in earlier days, and it may be worth while to reproduce some of the stories originating in this District which are chronicled in the Report of the Census held in 1881. The counting operation was of course held to bring ill-luck, which was generally expected among the women of the lower classes to take the form of illness or death among their children. In Sironchā a story was current that the Sarkār had made a grand find of gold, and that it was intended to select one young man and one young woman from each household and march them

off to the diggings. In the Ahīri zamīndāri the number-boards supplied to each house were carefully stowed away underground in rice stores and similar places of concealment, because a story had been circulated to the effect that it was a settled plan on the part of the Police to have these boards stolen, and then to get every householders fined Rs. 25, who failed to produce his number-board on the night of the census. But the most ingenuous rumour was that which went round in Chānda itself. Here some waggish person spread a report that on the night of the census a brass measure would be applied to the breasts of the women, and that those too liberally endowed by nature were to be deprived of this superabundance by a surgical operation. A little timely ridicule, however, quickly scotched this canard.

Health.

69. Although the climate of Chānda is one of excessive heat, the fact that there are no great extremes of cold at any time of the year conduces to the general health, which is well up to the provincial average. In point of fact the District ranks eighth in the provincial scale of health. But to all but natives of them the jungle tracts are unhealthy all the year round owing to the prevalence of malarial fever in them, and the comparative immunity of their inhabitants is probably only due to their becoming 'salted' by survival from attacks during infancy, or possibly in some degree to heredity. The chief diseases are malarial fevers and bowel complaints. Fever as a rule accounts for fully half the mortality of the year. Only once in the fifteen years 1892—1906 did the deaths from fever fall below 10 per mille of the total population: in six years, they ranged from 10 to 15 per mille, in five from 15 to 20 per mille, and in three over 20 per mille, but one of these was the famine year, 1900, when circumstances favoured excessive mortality and the death rate from fever alone was over 37 per cent. Cholera seldom gets a fair grip on the District: for four years during the

period 1902—1906 Chānda was wholly immune from this disease : in seven other years the mortality fell below one per mille. From 1895 to 1897 there were three successive epidemics which in all accounted for nearly 8000 lives, and in the fatal year 1900 the mortality was over 8000 or 15·5 per mille. Plague broke out in this District for the first time in January 1903, five years after its first appearance in the neighbouring District of Wardhā, and seven years after the initial outbreak in Bombay. The mortality, however, has been small, the highest figure reached being 201 in 1904. Evacuation has been readily resorted to by the people, and the only other preventive measure found necessary has been the destruction of rats which was commenced in 1906, and thoroughly organised in the following year. Inoculation has not as yet been introduced into this District. Of other diseases, dysentery and diarrhœa are observed to be most common in tracts where juāri is the staple food. So far as is indicated by the hospital returns tubercular diseases are not prevalent, but Captain Fleming is of opinion that phthisical conditions of the lungs which would in the absence of microscopical examination be deemed tubercular are quite as common as, if not more so than, in England : he attributes this to the almost constant presence of fine dust in the air and to the results of neglected or imperfectly treated pneumonia. Apart from the lungs, tubercular diseases of the joints, glands, etc., do not seem to be so common as in England. Among nervous diseases, hemicrania or half-headache is very common, though it is somewhat difficult to understand why it should be so. Diseases of the eye are very prevalent, as elsewhere in the plains of India, and the usual forms of inflammation generally lumped together under the term ophthalmia, especially cataract, are common, but granular conjunctivitis or trachorna is seldom seen. Captain Fleming thinks that glaucoma is far more common than in England, and this is as might be expected from the fact that errors of refraction much more frequently take the hypermetropic than the allyopic form. The number of persons who have hypermetropia but have never suffered on account of it must be enormous. Night-blindness is common and is usually associated with errors of refraction. Diseases of the heart valves are rare, as also is abscess of the liver. There is a remarkable absence of cases of stone: only five cases came to Captain Fleming's notice in four years. Cancer of all sorts is found but does not appear to be common. Lathyrism is unknown. There is a disease called 'Gondī boil' the nature of which is somewhat obscure, but it is not improbably secondary syphilis or yaws. Cases of Madura foot are very rare, and guinea-worm is confined to imported cases.

RELIGION.

Statistics of religion.

70. The census returns for 1901 show that Hindus constitute approximately 76½ per cent. of the population, Animists about 21 per cent. and Muhammadans 2 per cent. Only 735 are shown as Jains, and 266 are Christians of whom 62 are Europeans and Eurasians and the remainder native Christians. The great mass of the people belong to some form of Hinduism. Notwithstanding that Chānda was once one of the great Buddhist centres, and Bhāndak has been identified as one of the cities visited by the Chinese pilgrim Hiuen Tsiang (629–45 A.D.) this ancient faith has utterly disappeared from the District. The caves and sculptured Buddhas at Bhāndak are almost the only memorials of its existence. It appears to have been superseded by Siva worship about the 10th and 11th centuries A.D., and to this day the majority of the people are Sivites, but nevertheless Buddhist influences may be traced in the more advanced theories of local religious thought.

Hinduism.

71. Hinduism is a comprehensive term and comprises religious opinions that range from the most transcendental theories of Hindu philosophy to the debased nature cults of primitive peoples,

and startling contrasts of advanced speculation side by side with savage magic are specially characteristic of Chānda Hinduism. A number of the more learned have studied the Shrīmad Bhagavad Gīta but only a very few know anything of the 'Systems,' and the majority prefer to leave the higher walks of the path that leads to *mukti* to a future birth. The learned Shāstris teach that all who would attain to *mukti* (freedom) must be enlightened and practise *yog*. For such there are four states of happiness as reward—(1) *Salokatā*, abiding in the heaven of the god whom one has worshipped; (2) *Samīpatā* (nearness), to be ever in the presence round about his throne; (3) *Sarūpatā* (likeness), to bear the likeness to the god served; (4) *Sāyujyatā*, absorption into the essence of Brahma. From each of the first three states, the soul, after enjoying the reward of its virtue, will return to the earth and be reborn, but *sāyujyatā* is perfect salvation, freedom from rebirth, from it there is no return. But this teaching is esoteric. Much nearer the hearts of even the educated is the worship of the gods according to the forms hallowed by immemorial custom. In every Brāhman household there is a *panchāyatan* of gods, whose emblems, placed in due order in a shrine, are worshipped daily. They are bathed and some of the water so used is applied to the forehead of the worshipper and a little of it is drunk. Food and flowers are offered them. The shrine is a square or oblong platform in the centre of which is placed Mahādeo, and round him are grouped four lesser gods whose emblems are placed one at each corner of the platform. These emblems are as follows:—Mahādeo in the centre is represented by a *lingam*, or by a white oval stone with a groove in it, brought from the Nerbudda river. Behind him at the back corners of the platform are Vishnu and Sūrya, Vishnu represented by the *shāligrām*, a black stone brought from the Gandaki, a tributary of the Ganges, and Sūrya by the *sphatik*, a clear transparent stone. In the front of the platform are Devi, represented by a brass image, and Ganpati whose emblem is a red stone. These stones are brought and sold by wandering Brāhmans. Besides the *panchāyatan* each household reveres a family god who may, or may not, be included in the *panchāyatan*. Rāma and Krishna are often so worshipped.

Lingam worship.

72. The *panchāyatan* of gods supplies a clue to the maze of polytheism in the District. The majority of the Hindus seem to worship one supreme god who is called Mahādeo, and identified with Ṣiva. The cult of the multitude of minor gods appears to have relation only to the wants of this present life, and corresponds to the "douleia" or secondary veneration paid to saints and angels in other lands. It could scarcely be said that they arrive at monotheism, but amongst the educated the worship of the supreme god stands out more distinctly and that of the lesser gods fades in importance, while amongst the ignorant the worship of the lesser gods is more prominent and the idea of Mahādeo becomes more dim and vague. Though 98 per cent. of Hindus at last census did not return any sect whatever, the majority of the people, as already stated, belong to the Sivite sect. More people may be seen here wearing the silver casket containing the *lingam* or phallic sign of Siva than in any other District of the Province. A child is invested with it seven days after his birth, and never parts with it, for it is buried with his body. Practically in every temple the *lingam* of Siva is worshipped. Siva may be regarded as the representative of the Vedic Rudra (Megasthenes (300 B.C.) identifies him with Dionysos), but in this District he is revered as the supreme god. The coarser elements in his worship represent a compromise between Vedic religion and the Dravidian rites of which local Hinduism is compounded.

Village gods.

73. In nearly every Hindu village will be found besides the temple of Siva, usually fashioned after the Hemādpanthī style, a shrine of Marai, another of Māroti, then probably outside the village

an earthfast stone smeared with red paint (*sendur*) representing Bhīmsen, and especially in the eastern and southern tracts, the highly ornamented earthenware horse who is Balkīdeva. Many other gods there are, the numerous incarnations of Vishnu, Nāg the holy snake; in fact the majority of the gods of the Hindu pantheon are commemorated in an occasional shrine within the District, but these represent the gods most widely venerated. By far the most important of these minor deities is Marai or Devī. She is sometimes identified with Kāli and protects against small-pox, cholera, ophthalmia, *madhurā*, *gowār*, cattle-disease and other ills, but if her worship is neglected, will bring these troubles on the people. She seems to have combined in her single person the virtues and vices of the seven Devīs of the Telugu country. The Seven, to whom according to one legend the Sāt-Bahini (seven sisters) hill near Nāgbhīr is sacred, are as follows :—(1) Pochammā, the goddess of small-pox, (2) Marammā, of cholera, (3) Muttiyalammā (pearl goddess) protects against *madhurā*, a form of typhoid, one of the symptoms of which is a garland of pimples on the breast like a necklace, (4) Duggalammā, the goddess of cough, (5) Bangārammā, of gold, (6) Mahishammā, of buffaloes, and (7) Illammā, the protectress. In propitiating the goddess to induce her to avert or to cure disease, an offering which typifies the symptoms of the illness, such as a necklace of pearls for *madhurā*, painted eyes for ophthalmia, etc., are usually presented. Marai is worshipped before all marriages. Miniatures of the wedding garments are left at her shrine, and brides fill the *oti*, or skirt of her garment, with rice that she may grant them fertility. On the day of the full moon in Ashādh (July) each family propitiates her to secure protection for themselves from all calamities and immunity for their cattle from the diseases to which they are liable in the rains. A joint *pūja* is engaged in by the whole village to avert cholera, or to bring rain. In a dry year work is stopped on Sunday, Tuesday, and Thursday and each family pours a *gharā* of water over her image to induce her to send the wished-for showers. Goats, sheep and fowls are sacrificed to her, the blood of the victims is sprinkled on the fields, and rice soaked in it is sown, in order that the crop may be abundant and free from blight. Wooden images of herself in *nīm* or mahuā and sometimes teak-wood are offered to the goddess and crowd her platforms. Curds or *nīm* leaves are indispensable in her worship as they are cooling substances in the native pharmacopœia and diseases sent by Marai are generally hot. Rice, *kunkū*, turmeric, water and cloth, which must always be sewn, are also commonly offered. Marai has numerous shrines all over the District, but the most distinguished is the Mahākāli temple at the east gate of Chānda where formerly human sacrifices were offered, and the Mahākāli *yātra* is still held in her honour.

Māroti or Hanumān, the warden of the village boundaries, is represented by the carved figure of a monkey with a very long tail, and usually armed with a very serviceable club. His shrine is a prominent feature of every village save amongst the Gonds, as witness the Hindu proverb, 'where there is no Māroti the place is *masān*' (a graveyard). In former times Māroti was enshrined in the four quarters of the village. In Bhatāla the ruins of which show that it was once a large city, there are still four Makardhwaja shrines. Makardhwaja was the son of Māroti begotten of a crocodile, who swallowed the phlegm that Māroti spat out on the water. His image is exactly like that of Māroti. The shrine of Māroti is usually found now under a banyan tree in the middle of the village, facing south or east. In the month of Shrāwan (August) a subscription is raised and the villagers join in a feast at Māroti's shrine and beseech him to ward off danger from their cattle. The name Hanumān connects the god with 'the son of the wind' whose adventures are told in the Rāmāyana.

Bhīmsen is an agricultural god. His emblem is some stone of a peculiar shape on the outskirts of the village.

It is smeared with *sendur* and offerings of fruit and incense are made to it. In a year of drought a goat is sacrificed to him, and his image is immersed in water to induce him to send rain. He is worshipped in Ashādh (July) at the beginning of agricultural operations and again when the grain is threshed in the autumn.

Balkīdeva or the 'Bullockman's' god is a familiar sight in the southern and eastern parts of the District. His image is a highly ornamented horse of baked clay set on a platform at some little distance from the village. His business is to ward off tigers from the village herds. In the night the tiger comes and mounts the horse who promptly rides off with him. Graziers worship Balkīdeva that their cattle may be free from the attacks of wild animals in the jungle. It is worthy of note that in the worship of these lesser gods the Bhūmak officiates. He is usually a Pardhān or a Gond as representing the people of the soil, but sometimes he is a Gowāri or a Dhīmar. The Bhūmak is a village servant and receives contributions of grain from the tenants. The flesh of animals offered to Marai is usually given to the Dhobi but he receives no other public contributions.

Saints.

74. The numerous tombs at which offerings and devotions are made bear witness to the prevalence of 'the worship of the sainted dead' in the city and District. If the 'legends of the saints' of Chānda are to be credited they may claim reverence for their possession of miraculous powers but scarcely for any pre-eminent innocency of life. Of the prominent Hindu saints whose tombs are in Chānda, Govind Swāmi is worshipped for seven days in the *saptāh* in Ashādh when Gurus are commemorated. He died about 150 years ago. He granted a boon to a barber that he should excel as a physician, and the descendants of the barber are still reputed to be skilled in medicine. On one occasion the saint drank water from the *lotā* of a low-caste woman. When his disciples objected he turned the pot of water into a perennial

Bemrose, Collo., Derby.

OLD TEMPLE OF CHANDIKA. BHANDAK.

spring to show that his sanctity had taken no hurt. He is reputed to grant the desires of his devotees. A cupful of *prasād* (offering of food) prepared at the tomb of Dāsoba, an Udāsi mendicant, will suffice to feed hundreds of people. Hayagrīva, whose tomb is near the girls' school, will cast out devils. In the District Someshwar Maharāj of Sindewāhi is most famed. He was Jangam by caste and died about 25 years ago. It is related of him that he restored a Mahār to life in the village of Bhiwāpur, and cured a concubine of leprosy in Umrer. He commanded this woman to carry home a dead dog. She obeyed and on reaching her house found the body converted into solid gold. A temple of Siva has been raised over his grave at Sindewāhi and on Sunday, the bazar day, hundreds of offerings are made at the shrine in the name of Someshwar. Dharmarao has *maths* connected with his name at Warhā and Arher Pīpalgaon where childless husbands and wives go through a twenty days' penance to remove their reproach.

Musalmān saints.

75. A tomb near the dâk bungalow at Chānda is raised to the memory of Bhabart-ullah Shāh. This saint had no teeth but could crush large bones in his mouth. He was loved by a Telin in the city and no severity of bolt and bar could prevent the saint from gaining access to her. His tomb is always tended and many devotees resort to it during the Muharram. A few miles to the west of Chānda are the tombs of Ināyat Shāh Mian and his tiger. The saint used to ride to Chānda on the tiger. One night a stranger visited the shrine and Ināyat Shāh Mian set him upon his seat. The tiger came and licked the stranger's feet, but seeing another man present, leaped on him and slew him. When he discovered that he had slain the saint, he dashed his head against the stones and killed himself. Near the Mahākāli temple is the tomb of Juman Shāh Mian, who stopped human sacrifices at the shrine of the goddess by offering himself as a substitute for the intended victim. When the goddess came to slay him,

he attacked her and drove her off. This legend is also told of an Ahīr. A few miles to the east of Chānda, in the jungle, is the abode of Pāpa Mian the hermit. He has renounced the world and has a great local reputation for holiness. He was formerly the Deputy Commissioner's chaprāsi, but will doubtless be a saint in time.

Festivals and fasts.

76. One of the best aids to getting a comprehensive grasp of the prominent observances of Hindu religion is a review of the fasts and festivals that recur throughout the year, and a short survey of the year is here given, with a brief note on the ceremonies performed on the more important dates. The calendar of the District is regulated according to the Saka year. Each month contains roughly 30 days, and is divided into the *Shuklapaksha* and *Krishnapaksha* or 'light' and 'dark' fortnights of fifteen days each. The *Shuklapaksha* is the period from new to full moon; *Krishnapaksha* the 15 days of the waning moon. This gives only 360 days for the Hindu year and the difference is adjusted by an intercalary month in certain years. It chanced this year, 1908, Saka (1830) that the 1st of Chaitra fell on the 2nd of April so that the Hindu and English months practically coincide.

Chaitra, April.

'Gudhi pādwa' or New Year's day, the 1st of Chaitra, is a festival observed by all save the untouchable castes. Most people erect a bamboo, on which a *lotā* has been tied with a new cloth, in the courtyard of their houses. The *lotā* represents the *kalash* (water vessel) which is an auspicious sign. On this day mango, tamarind, and other fruits are first eaten. Rām Navamī or Rāmajayanti, the birthday of Rāma, the hero of Rāmāyana, falls on the ninth day of the month. It is a festival kept by the higher castes only. A silk doll is made to represent Rāma and all the ceremonials connected with childbirth are gone through. Some Brāhmans keep the day as a fast.

'Akshaya Tritiyā or Tīj' falls on the third of the month.

Vaishākh, May.

On this festival every household must give food to a person of their own caste in memory of their deceased ancestors. All cultivators go to their fields and ceremonially plough a little to indicate that the work of the year has commenced. The day being a specially auspicious one, many weddings are arranged to take place then. On the last day of the month is 'Mothi Bhawai.' In country villages seven stones are set on *nīm* leaves and *nīm*-leaf shades are put over them. In front of these stones low-caste boys dance, and the bystanders throw water on them. The ceremony is said to induce the Devī to send good rains.

'Ashādhi Ekādashi.' In each month of the Hindu year

Ashādh, July.

there are two 'Ekādashis' or eleventh days, one in the bright, the other in the dark fortnight. By orthodox Hindus each of these days is observed as a fast, but only two are observed by all, the Ashādhi Ekādashi at the beginning of the rains and the Kārtiki Ekādashi after the rains have ceased. The festival of Marai in this month has already been described.

In this month many festivals fall, the more important

Shrāwan, August.

being 'Nāg Panchamī' on the 5th, when snakes are propitiated. Bowls of milk are placed near their holes, and pictures of snakes are painted on the walls. About this time snakes are driven from their retreats by the rising water and the festival is supposed to induce them not to harm those into whose premises they may come. The evening of Nāg Panchamī is devoted to wrestling contests. Rakshābandhan falls about the 14th of the month when twice-born castes change the sacred thread, and *rākhīs*, little charms of silk or cotton thread, are tied on the wrist as a protection against evil spirits. They are also put on furniture and trade implements. In most places they are tied on by a Brāhman, who receives a small gratuity for his services, but in Chānda they are tied by Kalāwantins (prostitutes). On the 8th day of the dark fortnight comes 'Krishna Ashtamī or Krishnajayanti,' the birthday of Krishna. This festival is similar to Rāma Navamī, only it is kept by night instead of by day, and a clay doll is used in the ceremony instead of a silk one. 'Polā,' the cattle festival, falls on the last day of the month. The ordinary ceremonial does not differ from that observed elsewhere. The cattle procession to the shrine of Māroti takes place in the afternoon, the cattle are stampeded back to the village and the mālguzār gives a small gratuity to the tenants. On the following day children mimic the ceremony with toy bullocks. The explanatory legend to account for the festival is that the bullocks complained to Mahādeo that men were oppressing them beyond endurance. Mahādeo appointed a day to enquire into the matter. Men got to know of this and that day treated the bullocks so well that when Mahādeo came he found their complaint utterly groundless. The bullocks were outwitted but they still claim their day. On the evening of Polā day the houses are thoroughly searched for mosquitoes, bugs, flies, etc., and at the dawn the Badge ceremony is performed. The head of the house, or a servant representing him, dressed in the meanest rags, goes forth carrying a pot in which bugs, mosquitoes, etc., with a little rice, fruit, spices, a small bit of iron, two cowries and a little fire have been put. As he goes he calls *Māsha murkute gheun jā, re Mārbot* (Take away all flies and bugs, Oh! Mārbot) and *Rai roggheun jā, re Badgia* (Take away all disease and calamity, Oh! Badgia); when he reaches a place where three roads meet he casts down the pot, breaks it with his stick and returns home without looking behind him. He enters the house quietly, taking no notice of any one until some one pours water on him. He is then given oil to anoint himself, sandalwood paste, and some sweetmeats, after which he may again speak to the household.

The third of the month is 'Kājaltīj,' a fast for women. If any woman eats rice or sweets on this day she will be a rat or an ant in

Bhādrapada, September.

her next birth. The following day is 'Ganesh Chaturthi' or 'Ganeshjayanti,' the birthday of Ganesh, the elephant-headed god. On this day no one looks at the moon lest a calamity should befall him. Should one see the moon accidentally, the remedy is to hurl stones at the houses of his neighbours till some justly incensed householder comes forth and abuses him. The calamity will then fall on the irate neighbour.

Ashvin, October.

The tenth day of the month is Dasahra or Vijaya Dashamī, the day on which Rāma conquered Rāwan. It is also the anniversary of the victory of Devī Kāli over the Buffalo Rākshasa and in some places a buffalo is slain in memory of it. It is a day of many pleasant ceremonies. People go out to the village boundaries as if ceremonially to reopen communications with neighbouring villages which have been interrupted during the rains, and everyone desires to see the blue jay (*nīlkanth*) a fortunate omen. People visit their friends and present each other with *shami* leaves in lieu of gold pieces calling them *sonā*. Trade implements are worshipped and a pumpkin (said to symbolise a human sacrifice) is cut up and offered. Twenty days after Dasahra comes 'Diwāli or Lakshmī pūjan' on the last day of the month. On this day Rāma was crowned king of Ajodhyā on his return from Lankā (Ceylon) and Lakshmī, the goddess of fortune, passes over the land and distributes her gifts of wealth. All illuminate their houses and shops in order that they may not be overlooked. The lights are often tastefully and beautifully arranged and the festival is one of the prettiest of the whole year. The day is also the birthday of Buddha. In country villages a peculiar ceremony is performed. A Govardhan or heap of cowdung cakes is built in which an egg is placed. Cattle or buffaloes are worshipped and driven over the heap. Should the egg remain unbroken it betokens immunity from all calamities for the year. Formerly Diwāli was the last day of the financial year for traders, and new accounts were opened then.

Kārtik, November.

Two days after Diwāli is 'Yama Bij' or 'Bhau Bij' when Yama, the god of death, was entertained by his sister at the river Yamuna (Jumna) in the United Provinces. On this day brothers visit their sisters and are entertained by them, and in the evening the sisters return the visit, perform the ceremony of *artī* and receive a gift. Ten days later is the festival of 'Tulsī vivāha,' the marriage of the Tulsī (Holy Basil plant) to Vishnu. From this day the season of weddings commences. The whole of Kārtik is considered a specially sacred month for women and during it they perform many ceremonies.

Mārgashīrsh, December.

On the 6th of this month Champā Shasti is celebrated in honour of Khandobā, chiefly by Marāthās, by whom he is regarded as an incarnation of Siva. Khandobā and his *vāhana* (vehicle), the dog, are worshipped; and alms and food are given to Wāghyas and Murlīs, who are devotees of Khandobā. *Bājra* cakes and brinjals are first partaken of on this day.

Poush, January.

About the middle of the month falls 'Til-Sankrānt,' the festival of the winter solstice. On this day all rise early and bathe, and *til* cakes and sweets are eaten. On the following day bullock-cart races are held in many villages. On the last day of Poush is 'Māhi' when the low castes worship their deceased ancestors. They offer fowls, cocoanuts and *mūng* cakes fried in oil. All offerings must be cut with a knife since they symbolise flesh. If the last day of Poush falls on Sunday, and the *nakshatra* be *Shrāwan* and the *yog Vyatipāt* it is the festival of 'Ardhodaya.' This astronomical conjunction happens once in forty-five years, the last occasion having been February 2nd, 1908. It is a most auspicious day and many pilgrims resorted to Mārkanda to bathe. On that day if one give a rupee in alms he will receive a crore in the next birth.

Māgh, February.

On the 5th of the month is 'Vasant Panchamī' on which day Kāmadeva, the god of love, is worshipped. Many weddings and sacred thread ceremonies are reserved for this date. It is one of the three great *muhūrtas* or times of auspicious commencement in the year. The other two are Gudhī pādwa and Dasahra. 'Shivarātri' falls on the 14th of the month when Mahādeo is worshipped and his devotees fast for 24 hours.

Phālgun, March.

The Holī festival falls about the middle of Phālgun, when Madan, the Hindu god of lust, is worshipped mainly by lower-caste people. Two fires, the fuel for which should be stolen, are kindled outside the village for Madan and Madanī. A cocoanut is hung from the pole in the middle of the fire, and when it falls the people secure the burnt core and eat it and smear themselves with the ashes of the fire. They also throw a red fluid over each other and grossly obscene songs in praise of love are sung. The explanatory legend is that Kāmadeva, the beautiful god of love, endeavouring to influence Siva with a passion for Pārvati, discharged an arrow at him. But Siva, enraged at his insolence, reduced him to ashes with a beam of fire darted from his central eye. Afterwards the god relenting caused him to be born again, as the son of Krishna with Māya (illusion). The fires are said to symbolise the death of love and the rejoicings, its rebirth. Another explanation is that the object of the festival is to avert the troubles that may be brought on the community by the Rākshasi Dhundhā or Holikā, which 'lady devil,' the Jyotirnibandha assures us, is satisfied with the unclean language of the hymns and leaves the revellers free from love troubles throughout the year.

Cultivator's calendar.

77. Amongst cultivators the months are named from some prominent feature, such as the occurrence of a festival, the ripening of a crop, or a special ceremony. Thus Chaitra is called *Tīj*; Vaishākh, *Nāch Bhāwai*; and Jyeshtha, *Chīkhal Bhāwai*, from the mud that is expected after the monsoon breaks. Ashādh is called *Jeoti* from the festival of Marai, but the name itself is derived from the fact that *jāmuns* ripen

then. Shrāwan is called *Polā* and Bhādrapada, *Akharpok*, a vulgar corruption of Pitripaksha, the dark fortnight of the month when *shrāddha* is performed to the manes of dead ancestors. Ashvin becomes *Diwāli* and Kārtik *Kodāwas* from the ripening of the kodon crop. It is also sometimes called *Pahili* as under the old system the agricultural year commenced from Diwāli. Mārgashīrsh is called *Somwār*, all the Mondays in that month being very sacred among Kunbīs, who call in Brāhmans to cook their food on these days. It is also called *Sart* or *Dūsari* (second). Poush becomes *Māhi*; Māgh, *Shivarāt*; and Phālgun, *Māndawas*, from the cultivators building *mandwās* and going out to live in their fields in that month.

Agricultural cults and gods.

78. Some peculiar agricultural festivals remain to be noted. 'Sājoni' is the cultivators' observance of Tīj. The carpenter is called in and ceremonially welcomed, *kunkū* and rice being applied to his forehead. He prepares a *wakhar* which is taken to the field next day by gaily caparisoned bullocks. The earth, the bullocks and the plough are worshipped and a little ceremonial ploughing is done. A feast is cooked in the field and eaten. On that day no one should give grain to his neighbour lest his own granaries should be empty all the year. In Jyeshth, Bijorā, the festival of the seed-god, is performed in the wilder tracts. It is a joint *pūja* to which the whole village subscribes. The god is enshrined outside the village. Seed sprinkled with the blood of the victims sacrificed is distributed to the tenants by the Bhūmak, and the handful of seed thus received must be that first sown in every field. The 'Dudhāra' (Milk-god) ceremony is performed on any Saturday or Sunday in Ashādh before commencing rice transplantation. The god is enshrined on the bank of a tank and goats and fowls sacrificed to him. Miniature winnowing fans and grain baskets with grain, fruit, etc., are presented and milk is poured over the god to induce him to grant good rains and a fertile year. The

flesh of the animals sacrificed is distributed among the tenants; the Bhūmak gets the heads. 'Palkāpoli' is celebrated on any Saturday or Sunday in Bhādrapad. Devī is worshipped in her form of Mahishammā (buffalo-mother). The usual offerings are made and grain dipped in the victim's blood is cast into the fields with the invocation that they may be free from weeds. The ceremony is performed at each tank from which cultivators obtain water for their fields. 'Sanjori' is the harvest festival to propitiate the Sanjorā god before commencing threshing operations. The blood of the victim is sprinkled on the winnowing fans, baskets and the sheaf of *dhān* which each cultivator brings with him to the place of worship. The sheaves thus sanctified are replaced on the stacks and threshing commences. During threshing a handful of grain is laid aside each day and taken home separately. It is called *deodhān* and food prepared from it is eaten by members of the family alone. It may not be shared with others. At the beginning of the harvest each cultivator offers a chicken to his crop and sets it free. It is caught by the Bhūmak for his own use. Should blight attack the crop it is believed that it may be averted by sending a woman in her courses round the field so that her garments touch the crop.

Musalmāns and Jains.

79. The Musalmāns number about 11,000 of whom nearly a fourth live in the two towns of Warorā and Chānda, but a considerable number of Warorā Muhammadans have moved on to Ballālpur with the opening of the new coal mines. They own 173 villages, but this number includes over one hundred villages belonging to the zamīndār of Gewardhā, who is a Musalmān. They have five *masjids* in Chānda and an Urdū school. Representatives of both the Shiah and Sunnī sects are to be found, and some are orthodox and strict, but the majority of Muhammadans in the District are ignorant and have assimilated various Hindu ideas. In rural villages they subscribe to the joint *pūjas* and some will worship even the Hindu gods. Hindus are equally tolerant and

accommodating. In many villages the 'Ashtāne-kā-tāzia' is built by public subscription from Hindus and Muhammadans alike and is given precedence in the Muharram procession. There is a sect even, which openly permits intercourse between Hindus and Muhammadans, though only for a time. It is said to have been founded by a Musalmān *fakīr* and a Mehrā from Hindustān from whose conjoined names it is called the 'Shādāwal or the Dāwalmalak' sect. Mahārs, Telis and even Kunbīs join in the ceremonies and reverence Bābā Sheikh Farid, a well-known Muhammadan saint. Every third or fourth year the priest of the sect, who is always a Musalmān, ties a *nāda*, or thread to the wrist of the saint's devotees. Those of Hindu race are then freed from all caste obligations until Farid appears to them in a dream and reveals to them the name of a shepherd from whom they must purchase a goat. The shepherd is also warned in a vision. When the devotees visit the shepherd the fated goat comes forth from the herd of its own accord, and the price fixed in the dream is paid. The goat is ceremonially killed and cooked by the Musalmān priest and its flesh partaken of by all. From the tying of the *nāda* till the closing meal, the devotees wander about shouting '*Dum Dum*' and eating whatever is offered them, regardless of caste. But after the last meal they return home and are readmitted to caste by going through a purification ceremony and giving a feast to their caste fellows.

Jains number 735, most of whom are merchants and traders, and they have a handsome Jain temple adjoining the Gol bazar in the city.

Christians.

80. Christians numbered 266 in 1901 of whom 48 were Europeans, 14 Eurasians, and 204 native Christians. During the preceding decade native Christians had increased by 81 and during the present decade they have more than doubled their numbers. The Episcopal Church of Scotland supports a Mission in the District which is staffed by two European clergymen and a number of native assistants. The Mission has four

schools in the town and District, and two orphanages, one of which the Claude Hamilton orphanage for girls, in the Nagīna Bāg, is in the charge of two European lady workers of the Mission. The Church of St. Andrew in the town belongs to the Mission, and the senior missionary is in charge of the Church of St. Jude in the civil station. Chānda is in the Diocese of Nāgpur and the Mission in under the Episcopal charge of the Bishop of the Diocese. In Sironchā there is a flourishing branch of the American Methodist Mission with an orphanage in charge of an American lady and a native pastor. The northern part of Chānda District is in the Roman Diocese of Nāgpur, the southern in that of Vizagapatam. There is a small Roman chapel at Warorā which is occasionally visited by a priest from Nāgpur.

CASTE.

Introductory note.

81. One view of caste would regard it as a social system which has been developed and elaborated from the custom called 'taboo,' an institution found among all primitive peoples. A caste might, therefore, be roughly described as a social group which observes the same taboos. But many other factors have tended to isolate social groups. In Chānda, hereditary occupation appears to be the least stable feature of caste life, and a considerable number of castes are at present rising in the social scale through changing the hereditary profession. Marriage regulations, especially the rule that a man may marry only within the caste, form the most stable characteristics of the system, and if they change at all, they change but slowly. Among the lower castes, in castes that are rising in the social scale, the tendency is to restrict marriage within the limits of the subcaste so rising. Among higher castes a very slight tendency to relax the rule has been observed, and subcastes, of equally good social standing that were formerly endogamous, occasionally intermarry. So many different races meet in Chānda that the

number of castes is double or treble that found in an ordinary District and the problem of unravelling them, if of greater interest, is more difficult.

Marāthā and Hindustāni castes occupy the north and west of the District, Telugu castes the south, and aboriginal tribes the east and centre and wherever jungle tracts are found. According to the table of social precedence adopted by the Ethnological Survey, the Hindu population of the District is distributed as follows:—

Group I. Twice-born castes that wear the sacred thread, such as Brāhmans, Rājputs, Baniās, etc., number 8832 and own 684 villages.

Group II. (*a* Higher cultivating castes from whom a Brāhman will take water, like Kunbīs, Ahīrs, etc., number about 150,000 and own 614 villages.

(*b*) Higher artisans of similar standing, Komtī, Sonār, Barhai, etc., number 16,000 and own 58 villages.

(*c*) Serving castes like Nais, Dhīmars, etc., number 41,243 and own seven villages.

Group III. Castes from whom a Brāhman does not take water, comprising (1) the lower cultivating castes like Māna and Kāpewār, etc., (2) artisans, traders, and miscellaneous castes like Kalār, Lohār and Dhangar, etc., number 105,972 and own 100 villages.

Group IV. The aboriginal tribes numbering 150,000 and owning 1912 villages are far in excess of any single Hindu caste and comprise over one-fourth of the total population of the District.

Group V. Impure castes, whose touch is pollution according to Hindu social law, number 91,000 and own seven villages. They are made up of Mahārs, Chamārs, Dhobis and the group includes all the lower stratum of Hindu society.

From this distribution it will be seen that in the District he Indo-Aryan element in the population is small, though its influence is out of all proportion to its numbers as practically the whole trade and wealth of the District is in its hands. In the numbers given in the above groups only castes which exceed 3000 have been included. The mixture of races has produced a large number of castes peculiar to the District, some of which cannot be dealt with because their numbers are small, but the study of their origin and customs presents some interesting ethnological problems.

82. Among the many tribes and races, which inhabit Chānda District, the most interesting both ethnologically and historically are the Gonds. The History chapter tells how for some centuries they were the dominant race in this District and far beyond its bounds. The representative of the ancient royal line, Dinkar Shāh, who is now a political pensioner in the city where his forefathers held sway for many generations, and the Gond *zamīndārs*, who are the landlords of most of the tracts east of the Waingangā, as representatives of the old Gond nobility, still uphold, in somewhat straitened circumstances, the crumbling prestige of the race.

Aboriginal tribes.

83. The Gonds still number 135,000, forming 22 per cent of the population and own more than 1900 villages in the District. They divide themselves into four endogamous tribes Rāj-Gonds, Māria or Mādia, Dhurve and Khatulwār Gonds. There are also other minor sub-tribes who would not class themselves with either of the above tribes but they are few in number and unimportant. The most notable of these are the Koyās and the Gaitās. These sub-tribes all speak dialects of the Gondī language which differ considerably, but the difference is mainly due to the fact that the limited vocabulary of the Gondī tongue is supplemented by words from the language of their nearest Hindu neighbours. In the south of the District the language thus drawn upon is Telugu, in the west and north Marāthī, and on the eastern

Gond.

and northern border, Hindī. It thus happens that a Dhurve Gond from the Raipur border would have some difficulty in understanding the language of a Māria from Ahīri. The Dhurve and Khatulwār Gonds are found in the northern zamīndāris along the Drug border. They are small sub-tribes numbering less than 5000 each. The Dhurve Gonds, or at least a portion of them, often call themselves Naik Gonds and their dialect Naikī. They hold themselves to be descendants of the soldiers of the Gond king's army and still prefer service as police or peons to agricultural work. Many of them were in the zamīndāri police before that force was reorganised under the Government; a considerable number of Naik Gonds have thus migrated to the southern parts of the District.

The Khatulwār Gonds have adopted many Hindu customs. They wear the sacred thread of the twice-born castes, use the title Thākur, and, as Major Lucie Smith says, 'try hard to believe that they have Rājput blood in their veins.' The Koyā dialect of Gondī is nearly pure Telugu. The name Koyā may be connected with the name by which the Gonds still call themselves 'Koitur' (men). The Gaitā Gonds are remarkable because they are almost alone in retaining the old Gondī custom, once universal, of building their village in two long barracks lying east and west facing each other about eighty feet apart. In these barracks the married people dwell, while the bachelors of the tribe are relegated to a barrack at one end of the village. In some cases the unmarried girls have a barrack at the opposite end of the village, but usually they live in the house of the Gaitāl or headman. The two main septs of Gonds in this District are the Rāj-Gonds and the Mārias. These divide the vast bulk of the Gond population of the District between them.

Māria Gond.

84. The Mārias inhabit the wilder tracts of the zamīndāris and are in their unsophisticated state a very attractive people. The villages are usually built deep in the jungle near some wide shallow stream, which offers facilities for the *gātā* cultivation,

elsewhere described, and the surrounding jungles supplement the fruits of their agricultural efforts. Few villages lack the customary grove of *tāri* trees, the juice of which, fermented or unfermented, is ever acceptable to the Gond. The Mārias are a lithe, active looking, well-built set of men. Their good looks are often marred by the ravages of small-pox and skin-diseases and a mild form of leprosy called 'Gondi rog' is fairly frequently seen. Their principal charm to Europeans is the open, hearty manner, and the cheerful smile of good fellowship markedly different from the schooled politeness of the Hindu, which distinguishes them. Their dress is scanty, consisting of a compromise between a *langotī* and a *dhotī*, a strip of cloth wound tightly round the waist in rope-like folds and passed between the legs with the spare end hanging down in front below the knees. Often this garment diminishes to the scantiest rag. They adorn their necks with handsome strings of beads and their arms occasionally with metal and glass bangles. Their ears are pulled out of shape by the weight of numerous brass rings with which they are usually garnished and occasionally they wear *pagrīs*. A curved knife with a brass mounted handle is stuck into the waist cloth and, from the shoulder dangles the ever handy axe without which a Gond seldom moves. Māria women wear a *lugadā* of strong cloth usually white with a coloured strip in the border. They wear no *cholī*, no Gond woman ever does, and their necks, like their husbands' are garnished with beads. They frequently tattoo their faces and limbs in ntricate patterns.

Gond dances.

85. All Gonds, but especially Mārias, are fond of dancing. It is the great amusement of the people. Night after night in the eastern tracts in the cool moonlit nights of the hot weather, the sojourner in camp is lulled to sleep by the rythmic lilt of a Gondī chorus as the villagers dance round a fire in some open space near the hamlet. The favourite dance is a peculiar rippling step forwards with the foot dragged, not very graceful when done

by a single individual, but looking quite different when done in unison by a great circle of dancers singing a 're-la' 're-la' chorus to which the step keeps time. In some villages where the headman is an enthusiast for the pastime, a trained band performs weird and wonderful step dances to the sound of the drum. At a big dance the trained band occupies the inner ring round the fire, while the common folk, men and maids, in separate rings move round in great circles in opposite ways. All are dressed for the occasion in their best bearing in their hands weird ornaments of wicker work, with garlands of flowers on their necks, and, in their hair, feather ornaments humorously or coquettishly placed. Seen in the red glow of a huge log fire, glinting on the shining beads and barbaric ornaments of the dancers, with the throb of the drums, and the beat of many feet moving in unison to the wild music of the voices in chorus, a Māria dance is a spectacle not easily forgotten, but lingers as a characteristic scene when other details have faded from the memory. Men and women ordinarily dance in separate circles, but in the dances where the young men choose their brides they dance in couples. A few *gharās* of country liquor are always at hand to slake the thirst of the performers.

Rāj-Gonds.

86. The Rāj-Gonds are to be found on both sides of the Waingangā, but few of them are found in the wilder tracts where the Mārias dwell. They are more sophisticated than the Māria and from intercourse with Hindus have adopted a larger number of Hindu customs. Major Lucie Smith suggests that they acquired the name of Rāj-Gond as being the sub-tribe connected with the royal house or perhaps because they first rose to power when Chānda passed under Gond rule. They are as a rule shorter and perhaps darker than the Māria but resemble him in features. They are tough wiry fellows and like the Māria 'wise in all manner of venary.' They are mostly tenants and farm labourers, but prefer if possible to do jungle work and many of them are to be found in Government forest villages. They

are addicted to drink as a race though not actually drunkards, but every marriage, death, birth, feast, or religious festival, is an occasion for consuming *dāru* in considerable quantities.

Gond institutions and internal social structure.

87. Certain institutions are common to all the septs of the Gonds. Their ceremonies at births, marriages, and deaths do not greatly vary and the remarks which follow on these subjects may be presumed to apply with slight local modifications to all Gonds in the District.

All tribes of Gonds are divided into exogamous groups which still bear dim traces of a half-forgotten totemism. For instance the Rāj-Gonds are divided into four groups each with a totem sacred to it. As given by Major Lucie Smith these are—

Group.[1]	*Totem.*
(1) Four-god Gonds ...	Tortoise and crocodile.
(2) Five ,, ...	Iguana.
(3) Six ,, ...	Tiger.
(4) Seven ,, ...	Porcupine.

The only group which retains any trace of these totems at the present day is the six-god group which still venerates the tiger and the Gond *singh* or *simha* (tiger) is used as the crest of the royal house.

These groups are again subdivided into 'Houses' or families distinguished by their family name or *pādi*. Among the Rāj-Gonds there are 28 such houses or families, amongst the Mārias 24, and amongst the Dhurve Gonds 17. The others have not been ascertained. The *pādi* of the Gond kings is Atrām.

The exogamous unit is the group. No Gond may marry within his own group but must mate with a woman belonging to a group with a different number of gods from his own. Commonly therefore in a village one finds the Gonds divided into two groups, say, seven-god Gonds and five-god Gonds. The children belong to the father's group. Mārias do not intermarry with Rāj-Gonds now, though the records of the Ahīri family show that they once did so.

[1] A group of three-god Mārias has lately been verified in Lahir.

Religion.

88. The Gond religion is described as animism. But the attitude of mind, which animism here connotes, is a tendency to attribute personality to every object animate or inanimate which influences the Gond at any time. It is the theory by which he explains the phenomena of the world around him and is rather a crude form of primitive science than a primitive religion. A current Hindu sarcastic tale against the Gond in these parts illustrates this attitude of mind. A Gond was sent to a neighbouring village with a basket of mangoes and a letter. On the way he carefully buried the letter, and ate two mangoes. Thoughtfully covering the basket and removing all traces of his delinquency he unearthed the letter, and proceeded on his way. On arrival he was intensely chagrined to find that the letter, in spite of his precautions, still gave him away. This story, which is probably true enough, shows that when the Gond personifies a thing he does not necessarily deify it or worship it. He only imagines it has a personality similar or even inferior to his own. His gods are quite different to his personification of natural objects. The chief god is called Pharsā Pen, who is worshipped under the form of a nail, and sometimes a piece of iron chain. These nails are prepared only by Māria Gonds and are kept for sale enclosed in bamboo tubes. Such a nail might cost from five to seven rupees. Formerly Pharsā Pen was worshipped by human sacrifices but they now besmear a spear head with human blood and wash it over the emblem of their god.

Human sacrifice.

89. About 50 years ago the *Hindkuris* or 'catchers of the victim' used to come out and capture some friendless stranger to be sacrificed at the Dasahra time. The last authentic instance of human sacrifice in the District occurred about ten years ago at Jāmgiri in the Garhchirolī tahsīl, where a Gond sacrificed a woman and sprinkled her blood in his field. This enthusiast fled the District and was never captured.

Formerly the worship of Pharsā Pen enshrined a reference to the peculiar groups of the Gond septs. Along with the long nail or spear head which is the emblem of Pharsā Pen the Gond would place a number of arrow heads equal in number to the number of gods in his group, less one, that is, a six-god Gond would put beside the large spear head five arrow heads to make up the number six and similarly for the other groups. These were put in a bag or pot and hung from the roof-tree or from a branch of a tree overhanging the door of the hut. The sacrificial blood was sprinkled over all the emblems when worshipped, but over the large one first.

Lesser gods and beliefs.

90. Besides Pharsā Pen the Gonds worship a considerable number of lesser gods some of whom like Marai, the goddess of plagues, diseases and death, and Bhīmsen, the Hindu demi-god, they have borrowed from their neighbours; others are local, like Tāroba, who dwells in the beautiful lake of that name, and Wāghoba whose image is so often seen on the outskirts of a village marking the place where a man has been slain by a tiger. One Gond belief is that the soul of the slain will inhabit the image of the tiger thus set up, and being inimical to his slayer will attack tigers at every opportunity and thus act as a village guardian. Once a year a great pilgrimage of Gonds and low-caste Hindus is made to Sāt-Bahini, the great flat-topped hill near Nāgbhīr, concerning which there are confused legends. The Gond believes in the immortality of the soul but his faith is a very vague one. Amongst some transmigration is dimly held and a curious ceremony is performed which tends to define their belief. A Gond like most of the inhabitants of Hindustān must not die on a bed but stretched on Mother-Earth. On the place where the man's head rested at the moment of death a small heap of grain is made and covered with a basket on which a lighted lamp is placed and kept burning all night. In the dawn the lamp is extinguished, the basket lifted, and the wise discern on the heap of grain the foot-print of the animal which the soul of the departed will inhabit in the next life.

Marriage.

91. The position of women amongst Gonds is practically that of equality with the other sex, and though the Hindu custom of child marriage is now creeping in, normally a Gond woman is free to be wooed by the man of her choice and few of them are married under sixteen.

(1) Normal or 'Marmi' ceremony.

The young couple generally agree first, but the negotiations are carried on by the elders. When a betrothal has been arranged the bridegroom's party come and plant a spear in the courtyard of the bride's house which none may pull up. If the bride's party consent, water is poured over the spear by the father of the girl and the ceremony may then proceed. Should he fail to do this the bridegroom's party consider themselves insulted and the father of the bride is heavily fined. A platform of cowdung cakes is built on which a blanket is spread ; on this the couple take their stand and exchange vows, the bridegroom puts an iron ring on the finger of the bride and the ceremony is complete. The pair then leave the wedding party and betake themselves to a temporary hut previously prepared in the forest

(2) By service.

When a man is unable to pay the bride-price, demanded by the parent, it is sometimes arranged that he serves for his bride. A parent may demand five, eight, or ten years' service. If during the first three years the bride is not known to have lost her chastity, the full marriage ceremony then takes place, but if the contrary prove the case, the marriage is by the *pāt* ceremony.

(3) Pāt.

In *pāt* or widow-marriage, the pair stand under the eaves of the bridegroom's house with an upright spear between them. A mixture of turmeric and oil is applied to the bridegooom's forehead and to the iron spear head. The bridegroom then ties a string of beads round the woman's neck, and the pair walk into the house man and wife.

In marriage by capture the bridegroom collects a party of friends and carries off the bride from her village. When they arrive at the bridegroom's house a pot of water is poured over their heads and they become man and wife, but are supposed to live apart until the full marriage ceremony can be performed.

(4) By capture.

Marriage by capture has fallen into disuse as it was apt to lead to complications with the Penal Code. But irrespective of the Indian Penal Code it was not free from difficulty. Major Lucie Smith records a case where a fascinating Gond maid of sixteen was carried off from her village and married to suitor No. 1. Next night a disappointed rival's party appeared, carried her off and married her to suitor No. 2. Then her own village party arrived and took her home. Considerable confusion now arose as to whose wife she was, which the young woman solved by declaring for No. 1. There remained the delicate question as to whether she was to be married with the *marmi*, the full wedding ceremony, or *pāt*, second marriage rites. 'It 'was finally decided by the elders that only *pāt* rites could be 'granted, which was certainly hard on the young woman.'

Birth ceremonies.

92. On the ninth day after the birth of a child a feast is given and the naming ceremony takes place. It may be named after the month or the season as Wanjā from *wanji* rice, one born in the rice harvest, or Irpā, from *irpū* the mahuā flower. Should a difficulty occur about the name, a little rice is tied in a cloth and swung in front of the child while a list of names is shouted out. At whatever name the child clutches the cloth that name is chosen. After the birth of the first son the names of the parents are merged in the name of the son. Thus if the son be called Rekā, the father is known as Rekaltapā, the mother as Rekaltālni.

Funeral rites.

93. Persons who die of cholera or small-pox, and young children are buried, but others are usually burnt. The body is borne by the mourners to the burning place and laid on the pile which is

fired and the skull of the deceased broken with a stake which is specially placed for the purpose. The mourners then leave the pile and wash in a stream. An ox is sometimes killed, but more often a goat or fowl and the flesh eaten by the mourners. The animal must be slain by a single blow from a heavy wooden axe. After the feast the mourners return home and refrain for three days from their usual occupations. A small cromlech is built on the spot where the body was burned and usually a pot with a few small coins is placed within it. Amongst the Mārias in the case of a man a stone or a carved post about five feet high is usually put up to mark the spot. Sometimes one comes across a forest glade strewn with these memorials, the only sign of some deserted village the very name of which has perished.

Witchcraft.

94. The intense hatred of the Gond for witchcraft in, which he is a firm believer, is mainly due to the fact that he conceives of it as the unlawful propitiation of supernatural powers, who are enemies of the village and of the racial gods to induce them to bring evil on members of the tribe. When a person is suspected of witchcraft—the victim is usually a woman—she is taken to the nearest stream or pool, in which three men stand. The woman is immersed in the pool while the first man throws an arrow to the second, who gathers it and throws it to the third, who throws it to the bank. If the woman remains under water while this is being done she is innocent, if she comes up she is a witch. Her head is shaved, her front teeth knocked out, and she is banished from the village.

A curious ceremony was performed at the funeral of the zamīndār of Khutgaon whose widow suspected that he had been done to death by witchcraft. Three Mārias who knew the ancient rites were sent for. They laid the body on a bier which was borne by the usual bearers. In front of the body one of the Mārias, repeating the necessary spells, crushed a chicken to death. The life then entered into the corpse which impelled the bearers to visit the usual places frequented by the deceased and finally hurried them towards the neighbouring village where he had breathed his last. This last movement the bearers endeavoured to resist but could not, and finally some 50 persons were required to force the bier towards the burning-*ghāt.* Here three *yen* leaves were placed, one named witchcraft, the other, ghost or spirits, the third, natural death. The bearers were impelled forward and stopped at the leaf named 'natural death.' The positions of the leaves were changed repeatedly without the knowledge of the bearers but invariably they stopped at the leaf named natural death. Had they stopped at the leaf named witchcraft the spirit of the departed would then have impelled the bearers to search out the delinquent from the assembled villagers, and the usual punishment would have followed. It will be many decades yet, ere these malignant superstitions die out, but the grosser forms of them can no longer be practised.

Sub-tribes: Pardhān.

95. There are a number of small forest sub-tribes or castes, who appear to have been subjugated by the Gonds. They are inferior to them in social rank and used to perform the usual village service exacted from subject races though now many of them, by taking to agriculture, have greatly raised their status. In features and general physique they bear a strong resemblance to the Gond type. The chief sub-tribes are as follows. The Pardhāns were formerly the musicians and bards attached to Gond families of distinction. In many Gond villages the Bhūmak is a Pardhān, he also performs priestly functions like blessing the cattle and fields. Now, as a caste, their occupation is spinning and weaving. In former days they were able to recite the genealogies of the Gond chiefs and sing ballads in praise of their valour. Some still follow the ancestral profession of village musicians and a few can relate in rather a halting fashion legendary tales of ancient days. Locally they are classed with Dhers, as a caste whose touch is pollution.

Māna.

96. **The Māna** caste numbers about 27,000 or 4 per cent. of the population and owns 14 villages. There is a legend that previous to the rise of the Gond kingdom they were the dominant race in the District and ruled from the fortresses of Mānikgarh and Surjāgarh. Thākur Deo on the summit of Surjāgarh is still their tutelary deity. They seem however to have lost this tradition among themselves and only remember that they once were soldiers, and the sword is one of their objects of worship. The true origin of the caste has not been discovered but they are supposed to be an offshoot of the Gonds who have greatly raised their status by becoming cultivators and adopting the whole of the Hindu pantheon. They are skilful farmers and rank just inferior to the Kunbī, but will take cooked food only from the hand of a Brāhman. They have the reputation as a caste of being very miserly, and though possessed of plenty, live only on the poorest and coarsest food. They both burn and bury their dead, but the corpse must be laid on the pyre or in the grave with its feet to the north.

Gowāri.

97. The grazier castes of the District number 17,000 or about 3 per cent. of the population; half of these are Gowāris, the remainder being allied castes of Gaolīs, Golkars and Ahīrs. The Gowāris are believed to be of Gond extraction although a considerable number of them, calling themselves Gai-Gowāris, have risen in the social scale and designate their less ambitious brethren Gond-Gowāris. They have a legend that their first ancestor was a foundling and set to tend cattle, which became the hereditary occupation of his descendants. They revere the green pigeon because its call is similar to the low whistle they use to call their herds, and have legends telling how by its call it rescued their cattle from thieves who were carrying them off. The Gowāris observe a marriage ceremonial very similar to that of the Gonds, and like them are divided into exogamous septs, but besides this,

they recognise certain other septs as Dūdh-bhais 'milk brothers' with whom also marriage is forbidden. This is supposed to be a relic of polyandry, the Dūdh-bhais being probably the offspring of the same mother by different fathers. The Gowāris are distinguished by a caste mark which is a vertical line tattooed on the forehead for males and a vertical line standing on a horizontal one for females. Without this caste mark a Gowāri's legitimacy is doubted and he is not admitted to caste privileges. The Golkars are cow-keepers of Telugu origin, and mostly tend herds of milk buffaloes. They number about 2500 and divide themselves into subcastes called Yerā, black, and Nāna, white, Golkars. The Ahīrs come from Hindustān, and the Gaolīs are immigrants from the Marāthā country; all these castes breed and sell cattle and deal in milk and *ghī*.

Kohlī.

98. The Kohlī caste numbers about 7000 or 1 per cent. of the population and own 115 villages. Relatively to their numbers they are one of the most important castes in the District. They are noted for their skill in tank building and irrigation, and take great pride in their work. The local status of a Kohlī is measured by the size of his tank and the length of his embankment. They cultivate rice and sugarcane and are the chief *gur* manufacturers of the District. Their trade suffered somewhat from the rise of the sugar-making industry in Northern India, but the impetus that is now being given to sugar cultivation by the Agriculture and Irrigation Departments of these Provinces is setting the Kohlī on his feet again. The origin of the caste is obscure. Tradition says they were brought by a Gond king from Benāres, on his return from a visit to the sacred city. Sherring, following Major Lucie Smith, holds that they are Hinduised aborigines and the latter points to their physical resemblance to the Gonds as proof. The Kohlīs themselves say they came from Bhandāra and the Bhandāra Kohlīs say they emigrated from Lānji in Bālāghāt. Mr. Marten suggests that they might be connected

with the Ponwārs of that District as they have similar characteristics. This rather points to a Northern origin, as does the similarity of their name to the Kohirīs, a gardening caste of Hindustān, but neither in their speech nor in their family names can any trace of Hindustāni origin be detected. They affect a slight peculiarity in dress, the men wearing a *bandī* over their *kurtā* and instead of a turban a small white handkerchief knotted round the head. Those who do wear turbans tie them in the Gāndli fashion. Their caste discipline is very efficient. All quarrels are settled by the caste *panchāyat* and Courts of Law are seldom resorted to. Like other castes engaged in spade cultivation the Kohlīs marry several wives, the first wife taking precedence of the others. A good harvest or the acquisition of a new field is a valid reason for marrying an additional wife as she is more efficient than an extra servant. The ordinary bride-price is Rs. 30, but for second and subsequent wives large sums have to be paid especially if they are beautiful. A widow of full age commands double the ordinary price. Conjugal offences are frequent and leniently dealt with. Divorce is seldom resorted to as it entails heavy penalties on both parties. The erring spouse is taken back by her husband and a trifling fine is imposed by the caste. Marriage ceremonies are rather peculiar. The status of the caste permits them to employ a Brāhman, but for the sake of economy all the marriages in a village are celebrated on the same day once a year. The officiating Brāhman ascends to the roof of a house and beats a brass vessel to attract the attention of the different parties and repeats the marriage *mantras* as the sun goes down. Simultaneously the various couples garland each other. The bridegroom ties the *mangalsūtram* (a necklace of black beads) round the neck of the bride and the ceremony is complete. Subsidiary ceremonies also take place. The bride's brother ties a thread round the marriage crowns and receives Rs. 2 for untying it, and one unexplained ceremonial is the presentation of wooden models of a shoemaker's knife and a *khurpā* or scraper. A widow is married to a sword which represents her second husband, who never attends the ceremony in person. Kohlīs eat flesh butabstain from liquor and take cooked food from the hand of a Brāhman. They take water from a Gond. They are dirty in their persons and belongings, but enjoy a fairly high social status, being classed in Group II-A, as cultivators from whom a Brāhman will take water.

Other aborigines.

99. The remaining forest tribes are—Kawars, Halbīs, Thotīs, Jharias, Araks, Pārdhis and others. They are mostly of the servant class or small tenants. The Halbīs appear to have been formerly soldiers but are now a cultivating caste of good status, though there are only a few in the District. The Thotīs are a small tribe of bamboo workers who formerly were wandering musicians. The Pārdhis are a tribe of wandering hunters and trappers. They are a black diminutive race who live in tiny tents. Their traps and snares are very ingenious, and are often manufactured from the sinews of bird's wings, but brass wire is displacing these. Major Lucie Smith says of the aboriginal races 'that they are in 'intellectual capacity no whit below the Hindus, while in sim-'plicity and manliness of character they are much superior.' The former statement is open to doubt, but most officers who have known the forest tribes will enthusiastically endorse the latter. The progress of education and cultivation among them is much slower than among the Hindus. But very considerable improvements are being made, and it is hoped the day is not far distant when the aboriginal races will be again, as they have been in the past, an important element of political strength in the District.

Hindu castes.
Brāhman.

100. The Brāhman caste numbers about 5000 or nearly 1 per cent. of the population. The majority belong to the Deshasth subdivision. In physical features they approximate more closely

to the Scytho-Dravidian type than to the pure Indo-Aryan races of Upper India and probably there is a good deal of mixed blood in the race. Though not numerically strong they own 571 villages, ranking next the Gonds as proprietors. They rose to prominence during the Bhonsla rule, so much so that that period is still referred to as the 'Brāhman rāj'. They are still by far the most influential caste in the District and the spread of education, since they have been the first to take advantage of it, has tended temporarily to increase their influence. As a race they possess marked intellectual ability and have courteous manners, but during the period of their ascendancy they earned a bad reputation which still clings to them. They are stigmatised as subtle and unscrupulous intriguers, grasping landlords, and hard creditors, as harsh to their inferiors as they are supple to their superiors. In the day of their power their rule impoverished the District, and drove large numbers of peaceful tenants, who were unable to meet their exactions, to join the wandering bands of Pindāris who ravaged the land. The mud-walled forts in every considerable village still bear witness to the misrule of the 'Brāhman rāj'.

At the present day the caste contains many individuals who are valued members of the upper class, distinguished for their intelligence, foresight, and skill in affairs. They are found in many walks of life, but chiefly as mālguzārs, money-lenders, grain dealers, priests, clerks, and large numbers are Government officers, an occupation for which, by their talents, they are well fitted. The Telugu Brāhmans have the reputation of being very learned in Sanskrit literature. The Brāhman caste still sets the standard of Hindu orthodoxy, but with the spread of English education old prejudices begin to disappear. Though the orthodox party is still strong, the number of those who have recourse to hospital remedies, drink soda water, and have less regard to the strictness of rules about food and ceremonial pollution, increases. But marriage regulations have always been more stable than the rules about food and drink and a more important sign of the loosening of ancient bonds is the relaxation of the rules concerning marriage within the subdivisions. There have been instances of marriage between the Deshasth and Nārbada subcastes, and occasionally girls are married whose age exceeds that prescribed by the rules of the Shāstras. Widow-marriage is not unknown but the parties are always outcasted.

Rājputs and Baniās.

101. These castes together number about 3000. They claim to be twice-born and wear the sacred thread, but doubt is expressed of the purity of the extraction of some of their number. The Rājputs or Thākurs are usually cultivators and own 47 villages. The Baniās are enterprising traders and money-lenders, especially the Mārwāris. They own 24 villages. Both these castes, though few in number, are respected and Mārwāris particularly are most useful as the larger portion of the trade of the District is in their hands.

Kunbī.

102. Amongst the agricultural castes of the District the Kunbīs predominate so greatly in number that the name 'Kunbī' in colloquial use means 'cultivator', and men of other castes, engaged in agriculture, will describe themselves as 'Kunbīs.' They number 95,000 or 16 per cent. of the population and 300 villages have Kunbī mālguzārs. The subcastes which are endogamous are Tirole, Khaire, Dhanoje, Khedulā, Jhāria and Wāndhekār. The Tirole Kunbīs are settlers from Berār, and have the reputation of being the most intelligent of the Kunbī subcastes, but are harder landlords and more intriguing than others. They eat with Dhanojes but do not intermarry with them, yet their own marriage laws are rather lax. The children of a concubine, though the mother be of another caste, are admitted to meals with the caste. Such children are called Kharse and are not allowed to marry within the caste. The Dhanoje subcaste is the wealthiest of the Kunbī class. They cultivate the lands on the east bank of the Wardhā as far south as

Tohogaon. They grow any crop suitable to the soil but chiefly juāri and oilseeds, and are noted for the excellence of their cattle. The women of the caste wear the badges of three different castes. At marriage and in child-birth they wear green bangles, a Muhammadan badge, and cocoanut bangles like the Dhangar women, while their tattoo marks are similar to those of the Marāthās. The explanatory tale is that the first ancestor of the subcaste was the son of a Musalmān by a Marāthā woman who was brought up by a Dhangar in a sheep pen, and for this reason the women must bear the symbols of these castes. The probability is that they are an offshoot of the Dhangars who have taken to cultivation and risen in the world. The Khaire-Kunbīs, whose ancestors probably manufactured *khair* or catechu, occupy the northern parts of the Waingangā valley and grow rice and juāri. They build excellent tanks and are skilful cultivators. The Khedulā, whose name is probably derived from *kheda* a village, are found mainly on the east bank of the Waingangā between Wairāgarh and Bramhapurī. The Baones are immigrants from Bhandāra, and the Jhārias are probably aborigines. Their wild appearance justifies the suspicion. A branch of the Kunbī caste, that has migrated to the Telugu country, is called Are, but they still retain these subcastes and their distinctive names. In social status the Kunbīs rank next to the twice-born castes and employ Brāhmans to perform their religious ceremonies. Widow-marriage is permitted. They believe that the souls of their deceased ancestors are embodied in crows, and are careful to invite them to all marriages. In the month of Ashvin an oblation of food is offered to them, and if the crows do not eat it the Kunbī is much disturbed and changes the food till they do. The respect in which the caste is held is shown by the proverb *Kunbī matta, Deva datta*, 'The opinion of the Kunbī is god-given.' He is held to be a simple-minded, just straightforward man, whose dealings are free from guile. They are charitable when they see good cause, but do not give very readily. They are the backbone of the Hindu agricultural castes in the District.

Marār.

103. The Marār and Māli castes together number about 30,000, constituting 5 per cent. of the population. They own 25 villages but are not very successful as mālguzārs. They generally irrigate a little patch of garden from an uncased well dug in the bed of a stream. They provide the vegetables and spices so largely consumed by all castes to give variety to the rather unappetising diet of pulse and rice. The great majority, about 27,000, belong to the Kosri, or Kosaria subdivision, a name which recalls Kosala, the ancient kingdom of which Chānda once formed a large part. The remaining subdivisions are mainly distinguished by the plants they chiefly cultivate. These are—the Phūlmālis, or flower growers, Jirya who cultivate *lahsan*, Vāngya, *bhāng*, and Hardyā and Ghāse, turmeric. These last subdivisions are immigrants from Berār. Phūlmālis socially rank highest and turmeric-growers lowest of the subcastes. Turmeric-growing is esteemed a low and vulgar calling. The Pahād subcaste is almost a separate caste. They refuse to serve any masters, and if poor, rather than do so, will sit at the door of a Marār whose superiority they acknowledge. The Marār feels bound to supply them with food, and for this he may exact a certain amount of work. The women of the caste are reputed pretty, coquettish, and expert in intrigue, as witness the proverb 'For a love messenger choose a Mālin.' The caste is industrious and of good status.

Teli.

104. The Teli caste numbers 31,000 or 5 per cent. of the population and owns 48 villages. The hereditary occupation of the caste is oil-pressing, but a large majority have abandoned it and become cultivators. They are subdivided into Ekbailā, Dobailā, Erandia, Sao-Teli, and Gāndli. Ekbailā Telis use only one bullock in their oil mill, while Dobailās use two. Sao-Telis are mainly cultivators and grow sugarcane and rice.

Sao, meaning 'banker,' is a title of respect. The Gāndlis are landowners, traders, and money-lenders and aspire to be classed as Baniās. Some of them have adopted the sacred thread of the *dvija* or twice-born. They appear to have raised their social status by change of occupation, and in their case this was perhaps rendered easier by the fact that they are Telugus by race and immigrants to the District. Erandia Telis are socially the lowest subcaste and they alone extract castor oil (*eranda*). Oil-pressing in any form, but especially castor oil, is regarded as a vulgar occupation and most Telis are anxious to rise in society by abandoning it. Telis are not greatly esteemed and it is considered inauspicious to meet one on first going out in the morning. All business undertaken that day will fail. They have made a peculiar and rather unpleasant addition to their marriage ceremonial. At the moment of throwing rice on the couple they burn chillies which sets the whole company sneezing. They are usually in easy circumstances being an industrious and enterprising caste. Small colonies of them have pushed out into the remoter jungles and their villages are found beyond Bhāmrāgarh and Lahirī.

Dhīmar.

105. The Dhīmar or fisherman caste is a large one numbering 31,000. Their subcastes are Bhanāre, Bendare and Machhinde. Also the Pālewārs or Bhois, though of Telugu race, and the Kewats, are locally classed as subcastes. The women of the subcastes are distinguished by the bangles they wear. Bhanāre women wear iron and Bendare women brass bangles on one arm only, Machhinde women having brass bangles on both arms, and if married one lac bangle. No Dhīmar may wear shoes, only open work sandals, and a caste penalty is exacted for any breach of this rule. The ancestral occupation is fishing, and they are the boatmen of the District, and in former times were the *pālki*-bearers also. They cultivate the *singhāra* nut in tanks, and grow water-melons, turmeric, hemp and tobacco on the slopes of river banks and alluvial islets. They also breed the tasar-silk worm which other castes will not

do. The men are usually of excellent physique, clean limbed, and muscular, and look the best set up fellows in the District. They share with Mahārs the *begār* duties of the villages.

106. The Mahārs or Dhers number nearly 75,000 or 12 per cent. of the population. They are a despised race, the helots of the District, whose touch is pollution. In most villages there is a Mahār quarter where they must live apart. There is little doubt that they are the descendants of an aboriginal race, reduced to complete subjection and made village drudges. They say that their original home is Poona, and their first forefather Māhā-Muni, a sage. The subdivisions of the caste are very numerous but none are of much importance save the Somsi who claim a higher rank, through some connection, which they trace, with the Rājput dynasty Somvansī. Their caste rules are complicated and strict but are laughed at by Hindus. A Mahār is outcasted and must pay a caste penalty, if a dog has a litter of puppies, or a cat has kittens, on his premises. The dog seems to be a sort of totem in the caste. They do not swear by his name nor injure one. If a man keeps a dog and names it after a Mahār, the Mahār is outcasted, and this is sometimes maliciously done. The majority of the caste are day labourers, some of the more enterprising are cultivators and seven villages have Mahār mālguzārs. A large number are weavers who provide a coarse strong cloth which finds a ready sale among labouring castes because of its durability. The kotwārs or village watchmen are mainly drawn from this caste. They are not unintelligent, and a good many of the cultivators and weavers have abandoned caste and joined the Kabīrpanth. Many Mahārs are anxious to have their children educated, and send their boys to school, though on account of caste prejudice they are not allowed to mingle with Hindu boys but must sit apart in the verandah or in a separate room. They are quite up to the average in ability.

Mahār.

Mālas are a Telugu caste who have the same status as Mahārs. They probably are pariahs in their own country but here they prefer the designation of Telangi Sadar Bhois. They formerly were zealous followers of the 'Right Hand' (*Dakshinachāri*). They may be distinguished by the loose method they have of tying their *dhotī* and the squarish shape in which they fold their *pagrīs*. They number about 7000 and their occupations are similar to those of Mahārs.

Kāpewār.

107 Kāpewārs, 5000, are a Telugu caste of cultivators like Kunbīs. They are also excellent stone masons, and Major Lucie Smith conjectures that they may have been employed in building the Chānda walls and took to cultivation afterwards. They have some peculiar marriage customs. On the 4th night of the ceremony the bridegroom, bearing portions of a plough, followed by the bride, carrying cooked food in a cloth, walks to the edge of the *mandwā*, and drills five furrows with an ox goad, in which he sows mixed cotton seed and juāri. The cooked food is then eaten by the pair who share it with all present, and the seed is watered by the company washing their hands over it. All girls must be married before they are ten years old or the parents are outcasted. If, however, the girl is taken to some sacred shrine across the Godāvari and then married, the penalty is avoided.

Komtī.

108. Komtīs, 5000, are a Telugu caste corresponding to the Baniās. They claim to be Vaishyas and wear the sacred thread, but their caste customs and marriage regulations, especially the rule compelling a boy to marry his paternal uncle's daughter, indicate a Dravidian origin, so the claim is doubtful. They do not permit widow-marriage, but occasionally their widows contract unions with men of other castes. Women are very scarce in the caste and the bride-price is high. The usual rate is said to be Rs. 100 for every year of the girl's age, so that a girl of ten, the ordinary marriage age, would cost Rs. 1000. They are usually married very young. The caste is wealthy and industrious and has considerable influence in the District, but owing to the timid and conservative character of

their business methods they are allowing trade to fall into the hands of more enterprising Baniās and Cutchis.

Dhangar and Kurumwār.

109. Dhangars (Marāthā), 3000, and Kurumwārs (Canarese), 3000, are shepherds. The Kurumwārs feed their flocks in the Waingangā valley. They mingle but little with the local people, and do not even learn the language but speak their own tongue. They worship the Hindu gods, but their special gods are Mallanā Deva and Mallanī Devī, who are the guardians of their herds. The shrines of these gods are generally placed under a banyan tree, and in form are very like Scythian cromlechs for which they are sometimes mistaken, but a Kurumwār shrine is always open to the east The caste do not use their hands in taking food but eat from a leaf plate, and drink from a tank or stream like animals. Both Dhangars and Kurumwārs manufacture *kambals* or woollen blankets which are in great request amongst labourers and field workers.

Velamā.

110. The Velamās are the cultivator caste of Telugus to which the superior proprietor of Sironchā belongs. They have a fairly high social status, and one subdivision secludes its women. They appear to have been originally a cultivating caste, some of whom took to military service and others became dyers. The former are now of high rank, zamīndārs and landlords, while their less ambitious brethren are dyers and weavers. The Velamās of Chānda are said to have separated from the Kammā caste, originally one with them, on the question of *pardā* which the Velamās wished to retain, the Kammās to discard. The caste numbers only 198 in the District but is rich and prosperous.

Other castes.

111. The artizan castes of Chānda have a reputation for considerable skill in their various trades. Their customs do not differ markedly from those of similar castes elsewhere and do not call for special notice. Sonārs (Marāthā) and Panchāl (Telugu),

9000, are goldsmiths. They are skilful but do not vary much from conventional patterns in making jewellery. The Pañchāls may sometimes work in iron as well as in the precious metals. Koshtīs (Marāthā) and Salewārs (Telugu), 10,000, are weavers. They prepare silk-bordered *sāris* and finer fabrics. Their work is more artistic but they are unable to compete with the mills, and are usually wretchedly poor. Kalārs, 10,000, are liquor sellers and distillers, but owing to the introduction of improved Excise regulations many have taken to cultivation. Lohārs, 9000, blacksmiths; Naīs, 5000, barbers; Banjārās, 6000, cattle dealers and traders; and Dhobis, 5000, washermen, do not differ from their brethren in other Districts. Washermen of Telugu race are called Warthi. Sutārs 4000, are carpenters and are famed for their skill in carving. Chamārs (Marāthā) and Mādgis (Telugu), 5000, are leather workers. They are a low caste whose touch is pollution. The Chamārs make pretty embroidered slippers, which have a considerable local reputation. Bestās are a caste of Telugu fishermen akin to Pālewārs. They too formerly were *pālki*-bearers. They are said to be eaters of rats and 'such small game' and are rather despised, but are nevertheless a sturdy and muscular race like the other fishing castes. Balijā (Telugu) is a caste of cultivators also called Naidu (Lord). In Chānda they have a fairly high social status because they neither eat flesh nor drink liquor, but their caste is said to do both in Madras. Gurao, Dāsari and Sātāni are castes of temple-servants and temple-keepers. Many Guraos officiate as village *pujāris*, Dāsaris are often religious beggars, and Sātānis are marked by the fact that they do not wear the sacred thread, and cut off the *shendī* or scalp-lock which nearly all Hindus wear.

Criminal tribes.

112. Chānda has no criminal tribes peculiar to the District, but most of those castes which are ordinarily classed as criminal in the Province are to be found here. Those most numerously represented are Banjārā, Waddewār, Māng, Kaikādi, and

Yerukalā. The Māngs move about with small tents and donkeys, and camp near villages ostensibly to engage in basket-making, purse-selling, etc., but really to pick up unconsidered trifles. They are called Uchhlās or lifters which is also the name of a subcaste. The Banjārās are reputed to be expert cattle thieves.

SOCIAL LIFE AND CUSTOMS.

Villages.

113. The villages in Chānda District are of two distinct types, the Gond village of the zamīndāris which has been described elsewhere, and the large village of the *khālsa* cultivator. The latter usually stands on a knoll, shaded by groves of mango or tamarind trees, and contains eighty to a hundred houses with a population of four to five hundred. In the Wardhā valley, at the end of the rains, its little cluster of brown thatched roofs is seen across wide undulating fields of juāri, cotton and til. In every field a little *mālā* (platform), roofed with a bamboo mat, rises above the greenness, from the interior of which a raucous *rakhwāla* (crop-watcher) hurls abuse and occasional stones at marauding birds. Along the village boundaries run strips of low scrub-jungle which serve as grazing grounds for the village cattle. In the Waingangā valley the juāri is replaced by green-gold stretches of rice, the fields are not so extensive and the strips of jungle heavier, almost suggesting a resemblance to a forest clearing. The village is built along a straggling ill-kept street, the haunt of disreputable 'pai' dogs, ragged fowls, and an occasional fat baby clothed in a bangle and a string round its waist. For the sake of shade and coolness the houses are built to face north or east, and so lie at all angles to the street, presenting an end or a back wall to it, as often as a front verandah. The Mahār quarter is usually a little apart.

[1] Grateful acknowledgment must be made to Mr. Hīra Lāl of the Ethnological Survey and to Major Lucie Smith many of whose val ble notes have been incorporated in the above account of caste.

114. The houses of the mālguzār and better-class tenants are built of unbaked bricks and mud plastered; sometimes the walls are whitewashed and the roof tiled. In the northern tahsīls many mālguzārs adopt the *sondi* style of building. It consists of a strong square room, having thick clay walls without windows, roofed over with planks which receive a thick clay coating on the top. Over this a light second storey is erected and verandahs enclose the sides. The doorway of the central room called the *sondi* projects from the wall and, being small and low, can be readily closed with brick slabs shaped to fit it. In case of fire all valuables are hastily thrown into this room as, when the doorway is closed, it is practically fire-proof. By the sides of the *sondi* are *kothrīs* or receptacles for grain, which open into the central room. Grain can be poured into them from the top and when full they are closed with earth. The house usually has a courtyard surrounded by a high mud wall, against the sides of which are *kothās* (cattle sheds), rooms for implements, and grain stocks. On either side of the gateway are rooms which serve as the mālguzār's *baithak* where informal village councils are held or as guest-rooms for such travellers as can claim his hospitality. The houses of the poorer tenants are mud-walled and occasionally of wattle and daub. They usually contain one large central room, and the roof of thatch or bamboo matting is extended to cover verandahs, which, when enclosed, form additional rooms used for cooking and sleeping. The front verandah is usually left open.

Houses.

115. Furniture is scanty consisting of a few *palangs* (cots) strung with rope made from *palās*-root fibre, hemp, or *sūm* grass. A clean corner of the verandah is occupied by the quern or hand-mill for grinding meal, and the *ukhal* for husking rice. Earthenware jars of various sizes are used to keep pulses, tamarind, chillies, and grain for immediate use. The roof is garnished with all sorts of farming tools, and from it hang

Furniture.

dandis or bamboo poles, suspended with string, from which is festooned the family bedding in the daytime. Along the mud walls are niches in which lamps and various oddments for household use are placed, and in one, arranged as a shrine, are the family gods.

Cooking, drinking, and water storing utensils in poor families are all earthenware. In well-to-do families they are brass or bell metal. But practically every one has at least one *lotā*, and one cooking-pot and cover of brass. By way of public buildings in a village there are the temple of Siva, half ruined, but in the shrine the lamp is still nightly lit and a few disconsolate rags wave from bamboo poles in front, as flags; the shrine of Māroti under a shady banyan tree where the village elders sit of an evening and discuss matters; a sanded open place for wrestling practice, and to these are occasionally added the Government school and perhaps a police outpost.

Village names.

116. Village names are a complicated study. They are mainly derived from Telugu, Marāthī and Gondī, but *ur* or *uru*, a Canarese termination meaning village, is quite common as Kothur 'new village.' Telugu terminations meaning village are *palli*, *gudiam*, or *gudam*, *petā*, and *puram*. These are generally found in Sironchā tahsīl but they have penetrated into the northern tracts also. Typical examples are—Etāpalli, hamlet of *sindi* trees; Mamidigudiam, mango-tree village; Muyyaboinpetā, village of wood cutting; and Kondāpuram, hill town. Glasfurdpetā commemorates a former popular Deputy Commissioner of Sironchā, and Chīchpalli is a mixture of Marāthī and Telugu, meaning village of tamarind trees, Chintāpalli being the pure Telugu equivalent. Marāthī terminations meaning village which are prevalent in the northern tahsīls are—*pur*, *gaon*, *peth*, *khedā* and *khedī*, while other favourite endings are *wāda*, palace; *garh*, fort; and *jharī* from *jhar*, a spring. Common instances are—Ballālpur, Ballāl's city, from the name of the founder Ballāl Shāh; Sonegaon, golden village; Ghorpeth, the horse ward; Rānkhedā, jungle

village; Rājgarh, royal fort; Gangewāda, the water palace; Ghorājharī, the horse spring. Other terminations are *tukum* [1] possibly derived from Gondī, meaning a small village settled out of a larger one, as Sattāratukum the suburb of Sattāra; *Buzurg* meaning large, and *Khurd* small, as Vehār Buzurg 'big Vehār' and Mehā Khurd 'little Mehā.' Common Gondī terminations are *tolā* equivalent to *tukum*, as in Mānpurtolā; *metā* a hill, as in Kukurmetā, dog hill; *nār* a village, as Raiknār, village of *chār* trees. The polyglot character of the District is shown by many different names equivalent in meaning as Dhānoli and Viyampalli both meaning rice village, Pulligudiam and Wāgholi, tiger village, Sātharā and Usegaon, sugarcane village. Names of founders and of gods are often preserved in village names as Shankarpur and Pochammapalli commemorating gods, and Bamhnī, Brāhman's village, Korambi, shepherd's village, etc., commemorating founders. Examples of miscellaneous names are—Mukkudigutta, noseless hill; Chorli, Chorāla and Chorgaon, thieves' village; Māldongrī, hill for depositing stolen property; Kothāri, granary; Lonī, butter; Kolsā, coal; and Ghantāchauki, the guard house with the bell. *Mendā* meaning *band* of a tank is a frequent termination in well irrigated tracts like Bramhapurī, as Aswalamendā, bear *band*, and Wāslāmendā, adze-shaped *band*.

Food.

117. Cultivators and labouring classes eat three meals a day. In the morning *ambil* (juāri or rice gruel) is drunk and some food left over from the previous evening is taken. The midday meal which is freshly cooked consists of *ghāla* a sort of porridge of wheat or juāri flour and vegetables. In the evening *khanyā* (thick porridge) and *bhākar* or *chapātis*, cakes of wheat or juāri meal, are eaten. A great variety of vegetables and tilli oil are used to form appetising curries and sauces. Amongst the lower castes a good deal of flesh and

[1] *Tukum* also implied a peculiar form of tenure. See History Chapter para. 34.

large quantities of fish are used, but are esteemed delicacies The evening meal is taken about 8 or 9 P.M.. and the cultivators usually bathe before partaking of it. Mālguzārs and better-class people eat rice, and usually take only two meals a day, one at midday after bathing, and the evening meal. Many people bathe a second time before the evening meal, but by some it is considered sufficient to wash the hands, particularly in the cold season. Rice is prepared in a great variety of ways, with *ghī*, milk, sugar, vegetable sauces, and *chatnīs*. It is the mark of a good housewife to know a large number of recipes for such sauces. No Hindu of good caste eats flesh, but some of the vegetable curries and *pulaos* they use are excellent. On festivals all classes prepare special dainties, which are generally some delicacy made from the crop or fruit which happens to ripen then. For example *pūranpurī*, a variety of gram cake made with sugar, is eaten at all festivals but specially at Polā, *modak*, balls of wheat *chapātis* rolled round a kernel of cocoanut are sacred to Ganesh Chaturthī, and til must be partaken of at Til-Sankrānt. Tobacco is used by all classes, and nearly all the lower castes and forest tribes drink country liquor, some to excess.

118. The ordinary dress of a man consists of a *dhotī*, *kurtā*, and *phetā* or *pagrī*. The *dhotī* is a strip of cloth 4½ to 5 yards long, arranged round the loins and passed between the legs, the *kurtā* is the upper garment shaped somewhat like a short shirt. A good many of the poorer people do not wear it but substitute a strip of cloth worn round the shoulders. Better-class people ordinarily wear a *bandī* or waistcoat over the *kurtā*. The *phetā* is a long strip of cloth wound round the head to form a turban; it is often of *kosā* silk. The small Marāthā turban worn by native gentlemen is a very smart and costly head-dress. For full dress the *bārakasī* and *uparnā* are donned. The *bārakasī* is an elaborate double-breasted coat tied with twelve strings arranged in pairs; three pairs fasten the inner flap and three the outer. The

Clothing and ornaments.

uparnā is a strip of fine cloth worn plaid fashion over the shoulder. Coats that button and small round embroidered caps are now very generally worn by young men. Heelless native slippers with turned-up toes are often seen, but English pattern shoes and boots are also quite common. Brāhmans wear a special garment of silk, linen, or woollen cloth at meals, and women also wear special clothes when preparing food. In the southern part of the District all classes take great care to avoid pollution and people even of the lower castes sit apart and turning their backs on their companions cast a blanket over their heads when eating. A gold ring inserted in the upper lobe of the ear is a favourite ornament among men; sometimes it is jewelled and has a fancy chain attached to it. Other ornaments are gold and silver finger rings and wristlets and many castes, especially cultivators, wear silver waist belts of beautiful workmanship.

A woman's dress consists of the *lugadā* and *cholī*. The *lugadā* is a strip of cloth about nine yards long, put on so as to form a sort of petticoat, with the *padar* or free end covering the breast and head and falling like a veil over the right shoulder. Kohlī and Dhīmar women have the *padar* on the left shoulder. The *cholī* is a very small short sleeved bodice, covering the breast but leaving the waist bare. Women belonging to the forest tribes may not wear it. Bright colours are greatly favoured, red, blue, green and yellow being commonly worn and the borders and *padars* are often beautifully embroidered. White, as the colour of widowhood, may not be worn unless the *lugadā* has a coloured border. The *sāri* is a very elaborate and expensive *lugadā* of silk often beautifully woven and delicately embroidered. Women wear a great variety of ornaments many of which are heirlooms. Nose-rings, studs for the nostrils, ear-rings, finger rings, toe rings of a great variety of conventional patterns are commonly worn. Silver and white metal anklets and bangles of gold, silver, white metal, lac, or glass are practically universal and many castes have special rules about the kind of bangles that must be worn. The *garsolī* or the *mangalsūtram*, a necklace of black beads with a gold pendant attached, is put round the neck of the bride at marriage and practically takes the place of the wedding ring amongst Europeans.

A widow must wear no ornament of any sort and hes *lugadā* should be white without a border, but this rule is often disregarded. High-caste ladies adorn their hair witn pretty gold ornaments, but Kunbīs and some other cultivating castes forbid this to their women. Marāthā ladies do their hair in a 'bun' at the back of the head, but Telugus arrange theirs with a coquettish tilt to the left side. Telugu women also have ornaments in both nostrils, while Marāthās adorn only one. Women of the lower castes and of most forest tribes frequently tattoo their faces and bodies in very elaborate patterns and even men are not always guiltless of this vanity.

Village life.

119. Village life seems to an outsider extraordinarily monotonous. The country folk know little of the world beyond the little circle of local bazars where their avocations take them, and they dread leaving home. Before taking a journey omens are watched, the astrologer consulted, and an auspicious day is anxiously selected. The cultivator rises at an exceedingly early hour and turns out the cattle to feed. From dawn to midday he ploughs or does other field work. He rests for about three hours in the heat of the day and from three o'clock takes up some light task, returning home at sunset. After supper he goes straight to bed, but in seasons when work is light he may go to the *chabūtra* of Māroti's temple to gossip and get bazar news. Here *bhajans* are sung, old stories retold and anonymous complaints concocted against the patwāri, the head-constable, or other unpopular officer. Sometimes an educated man will read the Purāns or a vernacular newspaper, and as education spreads the reading public grows larger. The visit of a troop of acrobats or of Lawande (dancing boys) is the occasion of a great *tamāsha*. Occasionally an enterprising school-master may start a dramatic club, and both

the plays and the acting are often surprisingly good. But even this little bustle of social life has not reached the Gond, and dance and song, and oft-told legend still make his evenings as happy as his day is free from worldly care.

Children's games here as elsewhere have times and seasons. *Tipal-dāndu* (tip-cat) and *dhandhār*, a sort of single stick play with farcical interludes, are favourites all the year round, except during the rains. From the beginning of the rains till Polā stilt-walking holds the field, but the *ghode* or stilts are discarded on the evening of the Badge ceremony. *Phugadī* is a romping dancing game played at Dasahra. *Lon-patā*, a complicated 'touch' game played in squares, begins at the end of the rains, and in Phālgun, *ghān-mākad*, a sort of see-saw, has its turn. A log is placed on an upright pivot, two boys seat themselves on the ends and set it whirling with a push of their feet, when sufficient velocity is attained they lift their feet and whirl. This log is usually burnt in the Holi fire. Marbles, called *goli*, is a favourite game in the hot weather. In many old temples stones are found showing deep cuts caused by village boys rubbing their marbles to make them round. In Chānda city hockey and cricket are beginning to be popular.

Marriage.

120. Amongst Hindu castes in this District child marriage is practically universal. If a girl attains puberty without being married her family are outcasted, but some castes may avoid the penalty by getting the wedding celebrated across the Godāvari. Bride-price is generally levied and in some castes it is very high. Wedding festivities usually last from three to five days and sums out of all proportion to the means of the parties are usually expended on them, parents cheerfully burdening themselves with enormous debts that their children may be married with due display. The ceremony usually takes place at the bride's home, but in some Telugu castes and among the forest tribes it is at the house of the bridegroom. A *mandwā* (marriage booth) is erected in front of the house and in it a raised platform is built on which most of the cere-

monial takes place. An axe is put on the top of the *mandwā* to the handle of which a *kankan* or wrist-band is tied as a protective charm and many household implements are similarly adorned. A marriage is usually performed with a vast amount of ritual that varies in different castes, but the essential part of the ceremony appears to be as follows :—

The bride and bridegroom stand under the *mandwā* with a curtain between them ; the *joshī*, or presiding priest, ascends the roof of the house so that he may see the sun touch the horizon. As the sun sets he recites the marriage *mantras*, the curtain is removed, the rice is thrown, the couple join hands, walk five times round the platform and the fire thereon, and are man and wife. In Chānda many peculiar rites, derived from primitive marriage customs, still survive. They differ in different castes and a few of the more striking ceremonies are briefly given here.

Kurumwārs, a shepherd caste who weave blankets, seat the couple first on the loom and then in a basket and throw coloured rice over them. Telugu Brāhmans also seat the pair in a bamboo basket and the explanation usually given is a mixture of sympathetic magic and a bad pun. The association with *vansh*, a bamboo basket, is supposed to ensure their having a numerous *vansh* (offspring). Among all Telugu castes great importance is attached to the tying of the *mangalsūtram* (wedding necklace), and among Komtīs the beads are strung by a Kalawantin (prostitute). A prostitute can never be a widow, hence a necklace prepared by her is supposed to confer *akhanda saubhāgya* or unbroken married life. Amongst Telugus, also, the bridegroom, at one stage of the ceremony, seizes a pot full of cakes and sweetmeats, and flees to another house pursued by all the children of the party who shriek 'the dog is stealing off.' When the children come back the father of the bride goes and beseeches the bridegroom to return which he refuses to do until a present has been given him. Amongst Telugu Brāhmans of the Vaishnava sect a wearisome performance called *raibhār*, which is supposed to preserve the *izzat* of the bride, is gone through. When the *barāt* (wedding procession) arrives at the bride's village it stops some distance away. The bride's party comes out to meet it and sits down about a field or so away and each party awaits the advance of the other. Embassies pass between the parties beseeching each other to advance, which they do about a yard or so at intervals, whiling away the time meanwhile with songs and watching the dancing of *nāch* girls. This goes on for hours, neither party wishing to show any eagerness, until every one is heartily sick of the whole thing and they adjourn to the bride's house for the ceremony.

Among Kānnava Brāhmans and Sonārs the bridegroom's father touches the *kachhotā* (part of the dress) of the bride's mother and gives her a *sāri* and a gift in money and she then serves him with food. The ceremony appears to symbolise the primitive custom of wife-lending to a guest. The *nanhorā* ceremony in which all the women of the party bathe naked under the *mandwā* is still performed among Kohlīs, and among some subcastes of Sonārs and Kunbīs the foot of the bride dipped in *kunkū* (red powder) is stamped on the bridegroom's back. Badwaiks, a subcaste of Mānas, give the couple an arrow and make them shoot at a clay idol. These instances, which could be greatly amplified, may serve to show how interesting a field the District presents for ethnological study. Remarriage of widows is permitted practically by all castes in the District save the twice-born. The ceremony is always by *pāt* or second marriage rites and the woman, even though remarried, is not considered an auspicious person to be present at any important ceremony. The marriage customs of the Gonds have been dealt with under aboriginal tribes.

Birth ceremonies.

121. Although a girl is married as a child she does not join her husband save for occasional visits of ceremony, till she has attained puberty. Among low castes when a girl shows the first

signs of maturity, her bangles are changed and new clothes are given her, but among high castes the *ritu shānti* ceremony is performed. It consists of the recitation of Vedic *mantras* and burning incense to *agni* (fire). The girl is given new yellow or green garments and is treated with great consideration for four days. On the fifth night her husband is sent for and the *garbhādhān* ceremony takes place after which she lives with her husband. During pregnancy special food is given to the mother and various rites to protect her and her child from evil influences, or to ensure the birth of a male child, are scrupulously complied with. When the time of delivery approaches the mother returns to her parent's house. At the time of the birth, two heaps of burning *dhān* husks between which a *tendū* log lies, bar the gateway to hostile spirits, and a shoe is kept in the room where the mother lies for the same purpose; among Gāndlis it is put under her pillow. Midwives are usually of the Gond, Nai, Māng, or Mahār castes as a woman at child birth is unclean. On the 5th, 6th and 7th nights after the birth Satwai is worshipped, as the goddess then comes to write the child's fate on its forehead. Satwai's writing is seen in the sutures of the skull. On these nights the child must be carefully watched, as if the goddess comes and finds all asleep, she will smite the child with *satwai* (a disease). On the 12th day the child is named and after that the mother goes to the well and having fetched a pot of water may henceforth mingle with the household again.

A *joshi* is usually called in to cast the child's horoscope. Should the child have been born in an inauspicious hour the *go-prasava-shānti* (birth from a cow) ceremony is performed. The child is placed between two winnowing fans and a cow is brought in and made to lick the child. This averts all calamity and the cow must be given to the *joshi*. In casting the horoscope the *joshi* classifies the temperament of the child according to its planets, as *devagan*, divine, *manushyagan*, human, or *rākshasgan*, demon-natured. These horoscopes are carefully studied at the time of arranging the child's wedding so as to secure a partner of suitable temperament. A *devagan* can marry any one, a *manushyagan* only into his own class or the one above, a *rakshasgan* may not marry a *manushyagan.* For three months after the birth of the child, the mother when she goes out must carry with her the *vīda* or the knife with which the umbilical cord is cut and wear a blanket or piece of black cloth lest evil befall her or the child. Amongst Khedulā and Baone Kunbīs a necklace of cowries is put on the child and until it is taken off the mother does not associate with her husband. For two months after the birth of her infant, the mother, when she meets the mother of another child, must stop though they be on the worst terms, and enquire kindly after the other's child, otherwise the child of the woman who shows offence will get diarrhœa. To avert this, however, she may carry a soiled rag of her own infant with her.

Death ceremonies.

122. When a man or a widow dies, they are placed on the bier in a white shroud, but for a married woman a red shroud is used. Amongst Hindus and aboriginal tribes the dead are disposed of both by cremation and burial, but Musalmāns and Hindus of the Lingāyat sect always bury. Whether it is to be burned or buried the Hindus lay the body on its face with feet to the north, but Lingāyats bury it in a sitting posture and carry it to the grave not on a bier but in a *jholī* (wallet). Amongst lower castes a fowl, goat, or cow is sacrificed to the manes of the dead. It must be crushed to death or slain with the blow of a club. No knife may be used in the sacrifice. Higher castes perform *shrāddha.* The period of mourning varies from two to ten days in different castes, but Telis mourn only till the ensuing Monday, no matter on what day the man dies. If he died on Sunday he would be mourned one day, on Tuesday six days, on Monday for that day only. The corpse must be handled by men of the same caste. A man without friends is buried by Māngs

Kunbīs, Telis, Dhīmars, Marārs, and Khātis have a strange rite called *utārna* or recalling the souls of the dead. A *bhagat*, a man who has communion with the dead, usually of the Dhīmar or Kunbī caste, is called. Before him the son of the deceased sits, holding in his hands a bowl of milk. Drums are beaten and prayers and invocations are sung till the soul of the dead man called descends upon the head of the *bhagat* and drives him to and fro in the house. His movements are closely followed by the son with the bowl of milk. At the shout 'He has come' they look in the bowl and find something like a grain of rice in the milk. This is taken out, touched with vermilion put inside a ball of flour, and placed among the family gods. It is worshipped annually at the Holi festival. After this the souls of other ancestors may be called and an extraordinary scene follows. The *bhagat* no longer himself but possessed by the soul of the dead inspects the store-houses and cattle sheds and surveys the present state of the family. He visits the women of the house and renews his relations with them. They weep and he weeps and they greet each other as if after long parting. This weird scene continues till the soul of the ancestor invoked departs from the *bhagat* and he becomes himself again. The special rites of the aborigines have been already described.

Pilgrimages.

123. Chānda has many sacred places to which pilgrimages are made. Tāroba Lake and Sāt-Bahinī are resorted to, once a year, by considerable numbers of Gonds and forest castes, and the Mānas still journey to be purified to the shrine of Thākur Deo on the summit of Surjāgarh, but in addition to these, four *yātras* or religious fairs are held annually to which Hindus come from long distances.

(1) Mārkanda *yātra* is a purely religious gathering. The people assemble to worship in the beautiful ruined temples there and to seek purification from sin in the cleansing water of the Waingangā. The fair begins from Shivrātri, the last day of Poush (January), and lasts fifteen days. The popularity

of the gathering is waning as only some 4000 people assemble during the fortnight.

(2) The other fairs are partly religious and partly commercial. The Mahākāli *yātra* at Chānda lasts a month commencing from the full moon in Chaitra (April). The devotees worship at the temple of Mahākāli and at the *tīrth* (purification) of Achaleshwar by the east gate. All shops in the town are shut and the traders of the bazar move out to the large open space in front of the temple where a little city of booths springs up. In 1908 a local exhibition was held and prizes and medals were distributed. Some 75,000 people attended in the course of the month.

(3) The Bālaji *yātra* is held at Chimūr near the Bālajī temple there. It occurs in February and lasts for 15 days. About 15,000 people assemble.

(4). The Bhadra-Nāg *yātra* at Bhāndak lasts one month from the 5th of Phālgun (March) to the 5th of Chaitra. It draws some 25,000 people, mainly from Berār. The temple is by far the most ancient in the District. In the early centuries of the Christian era, when under Hindu dominion, it was called the temple of Bhadra Nāth (Lord Bhadra), a name of Siva. A period of Buddhist domination supervened during which the cave temples of Bhāndak were built. When the Buddhist power was dispossessed probably by the rise of the Nāgvansi kings of Bastar, the old temple was renovated and became Bhadra-Nāg 'The Blessed Snake' which name it still bears.

These *yātras* are most characteristically national, redolent of the India that does not change with changing creeds or dynasties. In the semi-commercial *yātras*, the religious element is slight. It occupies only a short portion of the daily leisure of the visitors for three or five days. The *yātra* is practically a huge temporary bazar and agricultural show. The large open spaces near the temples are filled with the booths of traders, gay with wares and implements from distant marts, exposed for sale. Every one is in holiday attire and happy. It is a scene from the historic past of India

Bemrose, Collo., Derby.

IMAGE OF KALI. CHANDIKA TEMPLE, BHANDAK.

reconstructed. If Prince Siddhārtha and Channa once more 'passed beyond the gates' as in ancient song into the modern *yātra* at Bhāndak, they still might recognise as familiar

'The painted streets alive with hum of noon,
'The traders crosslegged 'mid their spice and grain,
'The buyers with their money in the cloth,
'The war of words to cheapen this or that,
'The shout to clear the road, the huge stone[1] wheels,
'The strong slow oxen and their rustling loads,
'The broad-necked *hamāls* sweating in the sun,
'The housewives bearing water from the well
'With balanced chatties, and athwart their hips
'The black-eyed babes, the fly-swarmed sweetmeat shops,
'.........the millstones grinding meal, the dogs
'Prowling for orts'[2]............

The prince would find the fanes, that his own life and doctrine had founded, all empty and deserted now, but if he passed to the half-ruined temple of Bhadra Nāth, with its squalid decorations clinging to the carven stone, he still would hear the dreamy monotone of the Sanskrit *mantras*, murmured before the image of the god, by a white-robed, low-toned Brāhman in the scented gloom. He still would see some woman with eager empty longing in her eyes pass up to the temple gates

'Stealing with cakes and garlands to the god,
'To pray her husband's safe return from trade
'Or beg a boy next birth.'[3]...........

The whisper of her feet upon the sand, the feet that seek and do not find, the tinkle of her silver anklets, mingling with the mystic murmur of the Shlokas in an unknown tongue, his own silent fanes, would tell the prince that the

---

[1] The poem describes an Indian street scene about 500 B.C. In this passage with the alteration of one word the description fits equally well a street scene at a modern *yātra*—but the prince would not see 'stone' wheels now. The change from stone to wooden cart wheels represents very fairly the measure of material advancement and civilisation that, apart from modern Western influences, 2500 years of history have introduced into the life of the peasantry of Chānda.

[2] Quoted from Arnold's 'Light of Asia.' | [3] *Ibid.*

ancient gods, whom, for a space, his teaching had banished, had returned again, and India had not changed.

LEADING FAMILIES.[1]

The Gond Rājā.

124. The present family of the Gond Rājās of Chānda are descended in the direct line from Rām Shāh, a member of the royal family, who on the death of the king Bīr Shāh without male heirs about the end of the 17th century was adopted by the deceased king's widow and in course of time succeeded to the throne. The sovereignty of the house came to an end with his son Nīlkanth Shāh, who was ousted from the throne by Raghujī Bhonsla in 1751. The family is now in much reduced circumstances, although they are in receipt of a political pension of Rs. 500 per mensem from Government, and also receive customary dues from the Gonds, whom they once ruled. Each Gond family pays them an annual tribute of R. 1 and a contribution of R. 1-4 is made on the occasion of a marriage between Gonds. The family is at present indebted to an approximate amount of Rs. 4000. The present head of the family is Rājā Dinkar Shāh, who has been recognised by Government as successor to Rām Shāh who died in 1905. The device of the Gond kings was a species of heraldic griffin, which appears to be a winged lion or tiger. It may still frequently be seen carved over the gates of buildings over which the dynasty once held sway. The family tree since Nīlkanth Shāh, the last of the ruling kings, is given below :—

NILKANTHSHAH (deposed 1751).

- Ballālshāh.
  - Rāmshāh.
    - Yādoshāh.
      - Rāmshāh.
      - Govindshāh.
        - Dinkarshāh.
      - Kesharshāh.
  - Govindshāh.
    - Kesharshāh.
    - Deoshāh Bāpu.
    - Ballālshāh.
- Krishnashāh.
  - Nīlkanthshāh.
    - Krishnashāh.
      - Nīlkanthshāh.
        - Akbarshāh.
        - Ballālshāh.
        - Bhagwānshāh.

[1] For Zamīndārs see Appendix under Zamīndāris.

The Gond Kings' Crest.

125. In the tahsīls of Chānda and Warorā the leading families are those bearing the titles of Deshmukh and Deshpānde, names which, originally signifying a certain official position, have come in course of time to be transmuted simply into surnames. The Deshmukh was originally, as it were, the head patel of a circle of villages and had both to apportion and collect the land revenue assessed upon that circle, while the Deshpānde was the head patwāri or kānungo and kept the accounts. The titles are of ancient origin and, though not invented by the Gonds, certainly existed under the Gond government and prior to the supremacy of the Marāthās. The seat of the Deshpānde family of the Chānda tahsīl is at Mūl, which was formerly the headquarters of a large pargana. The original grantee was one Purushottam Pant, who was granted *muāfis* and *maktās* in several villages by the Gond Rājās for loyal service; these *muāfis* were confirmed by Sir Richard Temple to the heirs of the original grantee and to their successors, subject to the conditions of loyalty and good behaviour. At present the family holds *muāfis* in 24 villages with an aggregate area of 858 acres. The head of the family used also formerly to receive a small annual pension from Government, but this was discontinued on the death of Atmārām Deshpānde in 1895. There are at present six adult male representatives of the family, all possessing fair educational qualifications, and but very slightly indebted. The Deshpānde family of Warorā can trace their descent for three centuries, the original grantee of the title being one Dewāji Pant who is said to have colonised the Warorā tahsīl which had till then been mere jungle. Under the rule of the Bhonslas, the family used triennially to draw up assessment papers for the Warorā pargana, about 70 villages in all, receiving in return a commission of 5 per cent per annum on the land revenue of each village so assessed, and also enjoying certain lands in perpetual *muāfi* right. They at present hold the *mokāsa* of one complete village

Marāthā Brāhmans.

Dahegaon and *muāfi* fields in 52 other villages of an aggregate area of nearly 1400 acres. The family property is at present divided among three shareholders, Deo Rao, who owns half, and Venkatesh and Nīlkanth Rao, who each own a quarter of the estate. The first named is a well-to-do man, and the two others are in moderately easy circumstances; they have all acquired landed property in various villages in addition to their ancestral estate. They are all men of influence in Warorā and its neighbourhood. All three have shares in Warorā, Deo Rao being lambardār, all are members of the Warorā Municipal Committee, while Deo Rao and Nīlkanth Rao are also Honorary Magistrates. They are literate in Marāthī, but have not any special educational attainments. The Deshmukh family of Tādur own *muāfis* in five villages in the Chānda tahsīl. They are non-residents, their abode being at Tādur in Hyderābād territory.

Gujarātis.

126. In Bramhapurī the two leading families are descendants of traders who are said to have immigrated thither from Gujarāt some two or three centuries ago, and who seem to have built up an estate out of their gains. Both families are said to belong to the caste of Jambu-Gujarātis, and it is explained that the prefix Jambu denotes that their original home was in a village of the name of Jambusar. One of the families, that of the Janis, was first brought into prominence in the time of the Bhonslas by the wealth and capability of Janārdan Vishnuji Jani. One branch of the family is now much reduced in circumstances and the present chief representatives, four in number, although in moderately affluent circumstances, are possessed of little energy or public spirit, and have not been admitted to the privileges of exemption from the Arms Act and of seats in Darbār enjoyed by their fathers. The other family is commonly known as Bhai, although its true name is Joshi. Its present head is Jairām, who is a *darbāri* and who is fairly well off.

Other Brāhmans.

127. The family of the late Rai Bahādur Chandi Prasād originally came from the District of Unao in the United Provinces. His father, accompanied by two brothers, came first of all to Nāgpur and then to Chānda where one of the brothers married the daughter of Sādhurām, a man of some position and property. He had no children by her and brought up his two nephews Chandi Prasād and his brother. The latter died in 1876 and Chandi Prasād succeeded to the whole or the property, which was considerable, at the age of forty. Though of no education, Chandi Prasād was a man of great intelligence and influence in the District. He spent large sums in charity and was a considerate landlord. He received the title of Rai Bahādur in 1902, was an Honorary Magistrate of the second class and President of the Chānda Municipality. He died in 1906 and left, as heir, his grand-nephew Girijā Shankar, a boy of some 10 years of age. The original surname of the Shāstri family of Chānda appears to have been Kanchanpalliwār. The first member of the family of whom anything is known was one Pandit Venkatrām, who came to Chānda from Manthan in the Nizām's dominions about the year 1771. He was a man of great learning in the Shāstras and the Bhonsla Rājā used to address him as Shāstrijī, and thus this name has been adopted as surname by the family and the original surname has been dropped. The reputation for learning possessed by the Pandit seems to have been maintained by his descendants who were all learned in the Shāstras and Vedas. Their learning appears to have stood them in good stead, and owing to it they have acquired considerable landed property both in the Chānda District, in Berār and in the Nizām's dominions. The present representatives of the family are Haribhau, who is a clerk in the District and Raoji who was, until lately, camp clerk to the Lieutenant-Governor of Bengal, and has now been appointed a Tahsīldār in the Central Provinces. The first member of the family of the Dābha mālguzār of whom anything is known

was one Jagannāth, the great-great-grandfather of the present mālguzār. The family came originally from a village named Kotakunda in the Nizām's dominions and from this takes its surname of Kotakundawār. Jagannāth held a position similar to that of a modern tahsīldār at Sirpur in Hyderābād State, and two of his grandsons also held such positions. Of these Rāmchandra, the father of the present mālguzār, was Kamaishdār of the Ghātkul pargana containing about two hundred villages. His refusal to go to Wairāgarh led to his resignation of service and subsequent to this he acquired the twelve villages which form the estate of the family. The present mālguzār is an old man who possesses considerable influence in the pargana.[1] His son Bhagwant Rao is a useful member of the District Council and Local Board.

Velamās. The Sironchā proprietor.

128. The leading families of the Sironchā tahsīl have a history of some interest. Before the cession of Sironchā to the British, the tahsīl formed part of a tract known as Alamgir Sarkār, which had been held, it is said, for some 400 years by the ancestors of the present superior proprietors on a quit-rent payable to the Nizām of Hyderābād. The holders of the fief had the status of zamīndārs, and were known by the title of Sirdeshmukh. Owing to internal quarrels and irregular payment the Alamgir Sarkār was resumed under direct management by the Nizām, but when the country was settled by the British, the former feudatories were, in recognition of their special position, given the status of superior proprietors. The present representatives of the family are Venkat Srīniwās Rao, the superior proprietor of the Sironchā and Cherlā tāluks, Venkat Rām Rao and Musammat Pullaka, who hold the Albāka and Nūgur tāluks respectively. It is said that prior to British rule, the arrangement among the Sirdeshmukhs was to cast lots every twelve years to settle the distribution of the tāluks between themselves, and that the distribution of tāluks among the proprietors by the British

[1] He died in February 1909.

simply confirmed the arrangements which happened to subsist at that particular time. The superior proprietors are of the Velamā caste; they are not well off and are fairly heavily indebted. At the settlement of 1866, the tāluks of Nūgur, Albāka and Cherlā were being farmed out to lessees known as *dhorwās* and these were given the status of inferior proprietors. In Albāka and Cherlā the status has become extinct owing to the death of the lessees without heirs, but the inferior proprietorship of the Nūgur tāluk still exists, and is at present held by Rāghava Rāju Yernam Rāju, a Kshattriya by caste, and a resident of the Godāvari District in the Madras Presidency. The only other prominent landholder in the tahsīl is Ahirimuttu Mudliār, who possesses seven waste land and one clearance lease villages. His grandfather was a zamīndār in the Nizām's dominions and had the title of Deshmukh there. He is a Vellalān by caste, is well educated being acquainted with English, is a *darbāri* and, not long ago, was the recipient of a *sanad* from the Chief Commissioner in recognition of assistance rendered by him to his tenants. He is slightly indebted.

Musalmāns.

129. The family of the mālguzār of Porlā was founded about 125 years ago by the grandfather of the present mālguzār, one Mīr Baxis Ali, who was a *risāldār* in the army of the Nāgpur Rājās. In recognition of a victory which Mīr Baxis Ali gained over the Nawāb of Bānda, the Rājā granted him some forest area which he brought under cultivation. The personal title of zamīndār is said to have been granted to him later by the Bhonsla Rājā, in recognition of his services in preventing a rising of the neighbouring zamīndārs. He was succeeded by his son Mīr Mardān Ali, who married a daughter of the Gond Rājā who was an illegitimate son of the Bhonsla Rājā. The present mālguzār, Mīr Yākub Ali, is in possession of 25 villages including one in the Bhandāra District of which 6 are *maktā*, 17 mālguzāri and 1 *thekedāri*.

CHAPTER IV.

AGRICULTURE.

SOILS.

Topographical distribution of soils.

130. The soil of the District falls into clearly defined longitudinal bands, and each of these bands displays cropping of a wholly different kind from that of its immediate neighbour. On the extreme west, on the left banks of the Wardhā and the Godāvari, there is found a deep and rich black loam overlying trap and itself probably largely composed of disintegrated trap. The impervious nature of the underlying trap makes the soil extremely retentive of moisture, and it is found to be peculiarly suited to the growth of open field crops such as cotton, juāri and staples of the *rabi* type. Further east occurs a belt of shallower brown or yellow loam overlying sandstone. This soil drains rapidly and would be of little value without irrigation, but when watered is ideal for rice and cane. As the country is interspersed with numerous hills affording excellent sites for tanks, we find this tract studded with villages devoted to the cultivation of rice, and for the most part possessing excellent tanks. Further eastward again, on either bank of the Waingangā, the black loam reappears and is accompanied by a prevalence of open field spring crops, with occasional rice villages intervening wherever a good site can be found for a tank. Eastward of the Waingangā valley the soil becomes poor and hills are abundant, the consequence being that rice is the staple crop of the zamīndāris which occupy this tract.

Different kinds of soil.

131. The various kinds of soil distinguished at settlement are nine in number. Their local designation varies according to the language prevailing in different tracts, but to secure

uniformity the Marāthī names have been applied in the official classification throughout the District. The best soil is known as *kāli*: it is confined to the riverain tracts and is only found to any considerable extent in the valley of the Wardhā. It is trap soil of great depth and fertility, without a speck of grit. In the hot weather it is chequered by deep and wide fissures, but with the advent of the rains it is rapidly transformed into a quagmire. It is so retentive of moisture and so heavy that it is impossible to plough it up until the rains are over, at any rate with the cattle at the command of the average tenant. Accordingly it is almost useless for *kharīf* crops. Next in order ranks *kanhār*, which is also characteristic of the river valleys, though it is also occasionally found in the beds of tanks and *borīs*. Little inferior to *kāli* in depth, retentive power and fertility, it differs from that soil in containing a minute admixture of grit in the form either of limestone or of small round pebbles. Though slightly more friable than *kāli*, it is nevertheless too heavy for *kharīf* crops, except in years of abnormally short rainfall: in the north of the District, however, it is often embanked and grows a light broadcast crop of rice in the rains, followed by more valuable spring crops.

Bersi kanhār only differs from the true *kanhār* in containing a larger proportion of grit and small stones: it is more sandy and drains more rapidly. It is the most common soil in the Wardhā valley proper, and in the best portions of the Waingangā valley. When the rainfall is heavy, it has a tendency to become water-logged, but otherwise it is an excellent soil for all crops: cotton and wheat thrive well upon it, and when found in irrigated rice positions it is generally double cropped. *Bersi kanhār* begins the transition from black soils to yellow, and is the only black soil found on comparatively large areas outside the riverain groups. *Morand*, the most common agricultural soil of the District, is a light coloured loam containing more sand than is found in *bersi* and larger particles of stone. It grows both *kharīf* and *rabi*, crops well, may be freely irrigated and yet will also give a good outturn without irrigation, and is easily ploughed and cropped. In the open fields, the principal crops on this soil are til and juāri, but when embanked for both rice and *rabi*, the favourite second crop is gram, which unlike the more valuable *rabi* crops does not require to be manured. *Khardī* is a very poor soil, of light colour and full of stones, but when embanked sometimes improves itself into *morand.* In the open it grows only til and juāri and the outturn is low. Even so, it requires plenty of manure or frequent resting. *Wardī* is the principal rice soil of the heavy rice tracts. It is a light coloured soil, being purely sand with just sufficient clay to keep it from crumbling in the dry season. If unirrigated it would be a very poor soil indeed, but, the irrigation in this District being extensive, *wardī* is a most popular soil: it never gets water-logged, and with full irrigation and some manure it gives a very full crop of rice and fair crop of cane. When dry it is almost as hard as stone, and cannot, as a rule, be ploughed before the rains have well set in. *Retāri* and *bardī* are soils which are quite useless without irrigation; the first is almost pure sand and the second is nothing but pebbles. Neither soil is often brought under the plough. The ninth and last class of soil is known as *pāndhri*, which is really an artificial soil. It is the grey soil that is found on and around a village site obtaining its colour and its fertility from the ashes and refuse that accumulate upon it from the neighbouring houses. It grows maize, tobacco and similar crops well, without irrigation.

In the Sironchā tahsīl an alluvial soil known as *kachhār* occurs freely along the banks of the Godāvari, and has been recognised as a distinct class for purposes of assessment. This soil is also known and recognised in other parts of the District that border on a large river, but the capriciousness of the floods that control the deposit has prevented *kachhār* land from being ranked as a distinct soil class except along the Godāvari, where floods are of annual occurrence and reach certain limits with great regularity almost every year.

Position classes.

132. The value of a field being dependent on its position and the lie of the ground as well as on the actual soil, position classes were given at settlement to the soils which grow wheat, rice and garden crops. For *mutafarikāt* or miscellaneous crop land no separate position classes were deemed necessary. For wheat land there are three favoured positions: *bandhān*, land with a high embankment, *bandhia*, land with a low embankment, and *lawan*, low-lying land receiving drainage but not embanked: one neutral position, *sādhāran*, that of an ordinary flat field, neither receiving moisture from elsewhere nor transmitting its own, and two disadvantageous positions, *wahūri*, land cut up by small nullahs, which is drained somewhat rapidly, and *pathār*, land lying at the top of a slope and apt to be scoured away in years of heavy rain.

The rice positions fall into two classes, irrigated and unirrigated. The unirrigated positions are three in number, *viz*, *tekrā*, *sawān* and *jhilān*, corresponding respectively to the *pathār*, *sādhāran* and *lawan* positions of the wheat land with the exception that the rice land is always embanked. The irrigated positions are *warsalang* and *murkhand*. Properly speaking, *warsalang* land is land irrigated from a side channel which does not tap the deepest water in the tank, while *murkhand* is that irrigated from the centre channel. But in actual practice the distinction is one between first and second class irrigation. If a tank is too small to hold water all the year round, the land below it is classed as *warsalang*, while land which is fully secured against drought is classed as *murkhand*. Garden land also falls into two main classes, dry and irrigated. Dry land which can grow garden crops without manure is always very high class soil: it is found in the riverain groups and generally receives some silt from the river, when it is called *bāri marhān warpāni*. If near the village site it is called *bāri abādi warpāni*. If the garden is irrigated *walit* is substituted for *warpāni* in either class. For cane land the *walit* positions are again subdivided into *pātasthal* and *motasthal* according as it is irrigated by direct flow from a high level tank or from a well. There remain two position classes which are common to all kinds of land—*khāri*, which is applied to lands receiving the fertilising drainage of a village, and '*rān*' which denotes fields liable to damage from wild animals: owing to the extensive forests found in this District, the area of cultivation in this latter position is very large.

Of the total cultivated area of the District at the time of the recent settlement *kāli* covered 1 per cent; *kanhār*, 9; *bersī kanhār*, 32; *morand*, 40; *khardī*, 5; and *wardī*, 13; other soils being of no importance. The average soils of the District are thus not very rich: the Garhchirolī and Chānda tahsīls are particularly deficient in deep soils, and Sironchā, excluding the Ahīri zamīndāri, with 27 per cent. *kanhār*, 2 *kachhār*, 31 *bersī* and 26 *morand* is by far the most naturally fertile tract. Twenty-three per cent. of the whole cultivated area was classed at settlement as growing wheat, 23 per cent. as rice land, 3 per cent. as garden cropped, and 51 per cent. as devoted to miscellaneous crops. There was however great variation in these figures from tahsīl to tahsīl: wheat land varied from 40 per cent. in Warorā to 3 per cent. in Sironchā, rice land from 48 per cent. in Bramhapurī to 9 per cent. in Warorā, garden land from 6 per cent. in Bramhapurī and Sironchā to 1 per cent. in Warorā and miscellaneous crop land from 74 per cent. in Sironchā to 6 per cent. in Bramhapurī. In Sironchā practically the whole of the cultivated area, excepting soil inferior to *morand*, would grow wheat. That crop is however not in favour with tenants, for it is little used in the tract itself or the markets to which grain is exported: juāri is the staple food of the tract, and the local juāri, sown directly after the floods have subsided, gives an outturn of from 1500 to 2000 lbs. per acre in the richer soils.

STATISTICS OF CULTIVATION.

Proportion of area occupied.

133. Prior to the transfer in October 1907 of four zamīndāris to the Drug District the total area of the District as ascertained by professional survey was 10,749 square miles. Three thousand one hundred and eighty-eight square miles of this area consisted of unsurveyed areas of zamīndāris and waste lands for which no returns exist. The balance for which returns exist was, according to professional survey, 7561 square miles, but the corresponding area as given in the village papers amounted to 7781 square miles, or 220 square miles in excess of the area as ascertained by professional survey. Out of the area of 838 square miles transferred to Drug, all except 354 square miles consisted of unsurveyed lands. The District as now constituted thus comprises, according to the professional survey, 9911 square miles, for 2704 square miles of which no returns exist: the balance for which returns exist should be, according to the professional survey, 7207 square miles, but is actually according to the village papers 7427 square miles. This area of 7427 square miles is composed as follows: 3019 square miles or 30·5 per cent. of the total area of the District is under Government forest, 410 square miles or 4·1 per cent. is classed as not available for cultivation, 2588 square miles or 26·1 per cent. as culturable waste other than fallow, 217 square miles or 2·2 per cent. as current fallow, and 1193 square miles or 12 per cent. as the net cropped area. The most closely cropped tahsīl is Warorā in which 55 per cent. of the total and 73·4 per cent. of the total village area is occupied for cultivation. In Sironchā on the other hand only 31 per cent. of the total village area is occupied, while in the zamīndāris the percentage is as low as 15, and only about 4 per cent. of the total zamīndāri area is under occupation.

Statistics of crops.

134. Excluding the figures for the Sironchā tahsīl and including those of the zamīndāris recently transferred to Drug the total

rise in the area under crops since the first settlement has been from 644,000 to 853,000 acres or by 34·6 per cent. The groups in which the advance between the first settlement and attestation at the recent settlement was most marked were Sironchā (176 per cent.), Nūgur (93 per cent.), Ghātkul (88 per cent.), Nāgri (51 per cent.), Chimūr (27 per cent.), Kurul (23 per cent.), Bramhapurī (20 per cent), Arher Nawargaon (20 per cent.), Rājgarh (17 per cent.), and Ensa Segaon (16 per cent.). In the Wairāgarh group during the same period the cropped area declined by 29 per cent., in Gunjewāhi by 20 per cent., and in Garhchirolī and Kothāri by 19 per cent. The present total cropped area of the District as it now stands since the transfer of the zamīndāris to Drug is 763,000 acres. But in order to set forth the progress made in cropping of recent years it is necessary to include the area recently transferred to Drug, as it is not now possible to disentangle the statistics for the transferred area without a wholly disproportionate amount of labour. The most striking feature in the statistics of recent years is the great fluctuations in the areas under *kharīf* and *rabi* crops respectively: this is illustrative of the fact that in large areas of the District the choice of crop is dictated by the nature of the particular monsoon or its immediate predecessors. The following table shows the great fluctuations in the *kharīf* and *rabi* areas of recent years :—

Year.	Total area under *kharīf* crops.	Total area under *rabi* crops.
1891-92 ...	306,000	366,000
1892-93 ...	381,000	310,000
1893-94 ..	296,000	378,000
1894-95 ...	456,000	233,000
1895-96 ...	517,000	187,000
1896-1900 (average)	485,000	315,000
1900-1906 (average)	451,000	390,000

During the last six years the proportion between the two crops has been fairly constant, the *kharīf* area having regularly been from one-fifth to about one-fourteenth greater than the *rabi* area.

Turning to particular crops, rice invariably occupied the largest area, until the advent of bad seasons ousted it in favour of juāri. At the original settlement, it occupied 235,000 acres as compared with 199,000 acres under juāri. From 1891 to 1896 the average area under rice was about 206,000 acres while that under juāri was 137,000 acres. From 1896 to 1899 there was a marked advance in the area under rice, the average rising to 304,000 acres; the juāri area at the same time expanded slightly to 151,000 acres. In 1899-1900 the rice area sank to 189,000 acres and in 1900-1901 it reached low water mark at 144,000 acres. The juāri area meanwhile expanded and from 1899 to 1903 averaged nearly 240,000 acres. Thereafter, however, with the gradual recovery of the rice tracts it dropped off very notably, and from 1903 to 1907 only averaged 136,000 acres. Meanwhile the rice area has steadily expanded, the average area under that crop amounting to over 220,000 acres. Of other crops, cotton after undergoing an eclipse for the thirty years following the cessation of the American Civil War began to expand in the early nineties, and by the beginning of this century had almost reached the figures obtaining during the war. During the last six years the average area under this crop has amounted to 44,000 acres, and these figures, now that the railway has been carried through to Ballālpur, may be expected to increase very substantially in the near future. Linseed has always been a popular crop, and except during the famine years has usually covered an area of from 50,000 to 80,000 acres: in 1906-07, the record area of 105,000 acres was under this crop. The area under wheat is usually slightly in excess of that under linseed, and has remained fairly steady except during and immediately after the famines: 70,000 acres were sown with it in 1906-07. The area under til has fluctuated very greatly from year to year: for instance, in 1894-95 it was only 9000 acres, while two years later it rose to 63,000; in the years 1899-1900 and 1900-1901 it covered 90,000 and 87,000 acres respectively while from 1903 to 1906 the average area under til amounted to little over 12,000 acres: in 1906-07, however, it recovered to nearly 46,000 acres. The area under kodon-kutkī has remained fairly steady at between about 40,000 and 50,000 acres since 1896. *Lākhori or lākh* has also fluctuated comparatively little except for a temporary drop succeeding the last famine: in 1906-07 it covered nearly 36,000 acres. Gram usually covers 15,000 to 20,000 acres. Sugarcane, the only other crop which requires mention, has fallen off greatly since the first settlement, when it covered 8000 acres: in the quinquennium 1891—1896 it averaged 3350 acres: in the ensuing quinquennium, the average area dropped to 2000 acres, and from 1901 to 1906 to 1000 acres. Since 1903, however, it has shown a slight tendency to recover, and the next quinquennium should show improved figures.

Fallow.

135. Excluding the abnormal years 1899-1900 and 1900-1901 the area under old fallow has varied since 1891 between 160,000 and 247,000 acres: since the last famine it has never fallen below 200,000 acres. During the same period the area under new fallow has varied from 82,000 to 204,000 acres. It is not possible to draw any strict deductions as to the normal amount of fallow from these figures. To quote Mr. Hemingway: 'The alternation of cropping, which makes it almost 'impossible to give the normal areas under each crop, 'frustrates completely any accurate, or even approximate 'estimate of the fallow areas in holdings in normal years; it 'is impossible to say what is a really normal year in groups 'that have all classes of land. To prove this, it is necessary 'to give but few figures: I will quote those of one Warorā 'group only, namely, Chandankherā:—

Year	Wheat.	Rice.	Juāri.	Cotton.	Occupied.	Old fallow.
1866 ...	1973	3060	6410	5025	23,848	3351
1898 ...	1401	3934	2395	1215	26,496	7829
1901 ...	597	1069	6445	2136	27,613	5284

'In this group, the area under til rose from 2454 acres in 1898 'to 3959 acres in 1901. Considering the large amount of old 'fallow in holdings that have been broken up since 1898 and 'the extension of the occupied area, it would appear that this 'group has made actually great progress; but it has lost all or 'rather a great proportion of its valuable crops: it has been 'able to make a rapid recovery by the variety of its cropping; 'but it cannot be said what is the correct amount of old fallow 'for holdings to contain in normal times. The above is a 'typical case, illustrating the variations over the whole of 'Warorā tahsīl, half of Chānda, and a third of Bramhapurī. 'It is manifestly impossible to define normal conditions in a 'District with so much cultivation of this type.'

Double-cropping.

136. Considering the large area of irrigated land in this District, double-cropping is comparatively little practised. Only twice since 1891 has the area double cropped exceeded 50,000 acres while in five years during the same period it has fallen below 30,000 acres. The only areas in which it is regularly practised to any considerable extent are the north of Bramhapurī in the *gātā* cultivation tract, and in the Sironchā tahsīl where rice is grown as a second crop. In the rice tracts, where there are ample opportunities for double-cropping, tenants seem to care for nothing except their rice crops.

CROPS.

Harvests and chief crops.

137. As elsewhere in these Provinces there are two main harvests for field crops, the *kharīf* or autumn crop, which is gathered in at the beginning of the cold weather,

and the *rabi* or spring crop which comes to the sickle in January and February. The chief autumn crops are rice (*Oryza sativa*), juāri (*Sorghum vulgare*), cotton (*Gossypium indicum* and *Gossypium neglectum*), kodon-kutkī (*Paspalum scrobiculatum*) (in the zamīndāris) and maize (*Zea Mays*) (in Sironchā); the chief spring crops are wheat (*Triticum sativum*), gram (*Cicer arietinum*), linseed (*Linum usitatissimum*), the lesser pulses, and, in Sironchā, juāri.

The cultivation of the zamīndāris is of an extremely primitive type, and it will be convenient to describe it separately. The opening portion of the chapter will therefore treat simply of the *khālsa* area of the District.

Cultivation of the khālsa. Conditions determining cropping. (i) Fundamental: soil.

138. It may be laid down as an axiom that the character of the crops in any particular area is determined fundamentally by the natural conditions of that area and more particularly by its soil and proximately by a variety of more or less transitory and changeable influences. It has already been seen, when treating of soils, that the soils of the District fall into distinct belts. Along the banks of the Wardhā, in the west of the Warorā and Chānda tahsīls, lies a broad strip of deep black loam, very retentive of moisture, and excellently adapted for the growth of wheat, juāri and other open-field crops. A similar strip of soil, though somewhat inferior in character, occurs along the banks of the Waingangā, and upon it open-field crops are also found. Nearly all the Bramhapurī tahsīl together with the Ghot pargana of Garhchirolī is occupied by sandy soil which, under the excellent irrigation provided by past generations, is admirably adapted for rice and sugarcane, but unsuitable for most other crops. Hence we find these crops so predominating that there is a current saying that 'a *bāri* of sugarcane and a stalk of rice are all that Bramhapurī produces.'[1] Besides these two distinct types of soil, there are large tracts, especially in the east of Warorā, but also to a

[1] *Unsāchī wādī, dhānachī kādī.*

considerable extent in Chāndā, Garhchirolī and Bramhapurī, in which the soil partakes more or less of the character of either type, and where the cropping follows suit. These tracts may be termed intermediate to distinguish them from the open-field and rice tracts. In the foregoing remarks no mention has been made of Sironchā. This tahsīl consists, with the exception of the jungly inland Sirkondā group, where rice is the staple, of purely open-field tracts. But these open-field tracts are not composed of the black soil characteristic of the other open-field tracts of the District. The soil though deep, at any rate in the Upper Tāluks, is lighter in colour than the true black cotton soil. The tract is one of exceptional fertility, chiefly owing to the alluvial deposits which are received each year from the Godāvari river. The influence of the river differentiates the cultivation of Sironchā from that of the rest of the District. Maize and juāri are the two main crops, and the juāri is of a very different type from that found elsewhere. In speaking of the open-field tracts of the District, it will therefore be understood that those of Sironchā are excepted.

(ii) Proximate.

This fundamental factor of soil absolutely determines the cropping of the true rice tracts, since the conditions practically admit of no crop other than rice and sugarcane. But in the open-field and intermediate tracts large latitude in the choice of crops is allowed by nature, and a number of less permanent influences come into play, which are the immediate arbiters of the crop to be sown in any particular year or series of years. The chief influences to be distinguished are the condition of foreign markets, the state of local communications with the outside world, and the character of the monsoon and also of its immediate predecessors.

(a) State of foreign markets and communications.

Since expenses of transport have to be set off against the prices obtainable in foreign markets, the first two of these considerations may be touched upon together. Cotton and oil-seeds are among the most important crops raised in the non-rice area of this District, and these are grown almost entirely for export. Of these two crops cotton gives the more signal illustration of the operation of the influence named. At the settlement of 1869, an area of some 57,000 acres was estimated to be under cotton; prices had gone up sky high as a consequence of the American War, and even Chānda, remote though it was, was tempted into a liberal extension of its cotton cultivation. Prices came down as America recovered from the effects of the war, and Chānda was forced to abandon an unequal competition with better developed tracts. Until 1900, the cotton area of the District rarely approached 20,000 acres, and was often much lower. Prices have however again gone up, and the area under cotton is now nearly as large as it was in the sixties, having averaged over 52,000 acres in the last decade. But the state of communications has hitherto practically limited the area of production to a radius of 40 or 50 miles from Warorā station, since it does not pay to cart cotton over a longer lead. Thus soils naturally adapted for the growth of cotton, such as those of the Kothāri and Ghātkul groups in the Chānda tahsīl, have so far not been utilised for its production. It is safe, however, to prophesy that, if prices continue high, the extension of the railway southwards will have the immediate effect of inducing tenants in those groups to turn their attention to this crop.

(*b*) Variations in the monsoon.

The effect of the variations of the monsoon in these tracts is thus described by Mr. Hemingway: 'In the open tracts, as 'contrasted with the rice tracts, the 'cropping varies greatly between *kharīf* or monsoon crops 'and *rabi* or winter crops. This is due entirely to the varia- 'tions in the monsoon; the soil in these open tracts rapidly 'becomes water-logged if the rainfall is heavy in August 'and September, and the *kharīf* crops in this soil suffer 'heavily from excessive moisture in these months; if, how-

'ever, the rainfall is both heavy and prolonged well into 'October, the soil is the easier to plough and sow for 'winter crops. If therefore in any series of years the rainfall 'continues heavy, the tenants, after experiencing poor har-'vests in the first two years through excessive moisture, com-'pletely change their cropping, and sow *rabi* crops instead of '*kharīf*. Similarly when a series of years are giving short 'rainfall, the ground is generally too hard for the *rabi* crops, 'and tenants make the best use they can of it before the 'rains cease; that is, they grow *kharīf* varieties of juāri and 'cotton in land which in more normal years is reserved for 'wheat and *rabi* pulses.' In the intermediate groups the same considerations come into play as regards the open crops, but here the choice is not limited to the alternative between autumn or spring open-field crops; the tenant has also an option between committing the major part of his fortunes to rice or to *rabi*. On this point, Mr. Hemingway may again be quoted: 'Where the holdings do allow of 'this alternation between rice and *rabi* the loss of the rice 'has now been followed by an extension of the *rabi* area, 'unless tenants have relied too long on their one crop. And 'there are distinct indications in certain groups, which have 'only poorly irrigated rice land and *rabi* land of compara-'tively good soils, that the present rice area is remaining low 'because tenants have adopted a policy to suit the seasons at 'present prevailing, and are purposely leaving their rice land 'fallow while their *rabi* land is more fully cropped. This 'applies to intermediate groups only, and is most noticeable 'in those groups of the Warorā tahsīl and Rājgarh of 'Chānda; in these tracts it cannot be said that tenants are 'poor, short of cattle, or not in a position to find rice seed; 'unless their rice land is well irrigated they are simply 'waiting for years of better rainfall before fully cropping 'their land. And when they do fully crop their rice land 'once more there is the possibility that their *rabi* land may in 'turn be neglected, unless the experience of the last decade 'has taught them how to crop both classes of land 'whenever they have the opportunity; in past years they 'have not made the most of such opportunity; they have 'waited until actually compelled before changing their 'methods.'

In Sironchā, the proximate influences described above scarcely operate at all save in a negative sense in that in the Upper Tāluk the entire lack of communications has resulted in an utter stagnation of trade, and there is consequently no reaction of the foreign markets upon local agriculture. There is no particular fluctuation in the crops according to the character of the monsoon as the tract is one which can grow good crops even when the rainfall is short. The river is another Nile, and its regular action produces a similar regularity in the cropping upon its banks.

No monsoon ideal for the whole District.

139 The foregoing description will have made it clear that the cultivation of the District is such that no monsoon, however distributed, if uniform over all the District, can be welcome to all parts alike. Heavy and fairly continuous rains in the early monsoon are excellent for the rice tracts, but result in the water-logging of the black soil tracts, or render weeding operations impossible. On the other hand that quantity and distribution of rain which is ideal for the open-field tracts is certainly too meagre and probably ill-distributed for the rice tracts. Man to a great extent has levelled up the inequalities of nature by providing irrigation in the rice tracts, and every year sees a larger area secured against drought. When the irrigation policy of Goverenment is fully developed (a consummation which must be placed in a somewhat remote future), the rice tracts—and these are the more precarious—will no longer have to dread a year of short rainfall, while the open-field tracts, although their autumn harvest cannot be artificially secured against excessive rainfall, are already automatically compensated for a loss of it by their capability of growing spring crops instead.

140. Having thus broadly considered the distribution of crops in the *khālsa*, we may next turn to the actual methods of cultivation commonly followed. Commencing with the open-field tracts, it will be convenient first to give a sketch of the farmer's calendar, and, having thus obtained as it were a bird's-eye view of the operations common to most open-field crops, to proceed shortly to particularise the more important species sown, offering such remarks as may appear necessary upon each.

Methods of cultivation.
(1) The open-field tract.

141. The first active measure of the cultivator's year is usually the manuring of his lands. This generally takes place in the hot weather; the manure is simply carted to the fields and dumped down *in situ* in large heaps. No attempt is made to prevent its losing its virtue by evaporation. The cultivator then waits for a shower of rain to soften the ground and render it amenable to ploughing. A hot weather shower sufficiently heavy to secure this result acts as the *reveillé* to all good cultivators, and in almost every field the paring plough may be seen converting the unkempt and gaping wastes of the hot weather into an orderly tilth. The object of this hot weather ploughing is to expose as much soil to the air as possible and to kill weeds; it also serves to distribute the manure and mix it with the soil. It is repeated according to the opportunities and diligence of the farmer; most tenants go over their fields at least twice before the arrival of the rain, and as often after. The seed of the autumn crops is then sown. Henceforward the most important function to be performed is the weeding of the young crop. For this a break in the monsoon is absolutely necessary, for if heavy rain persists in falling weeding with the scarifier is impossible and weeding by hand very tedious. Most autumn crops receive at least two weedings, one while the crop is only a few inches above the ground, and the other a few weeks later. By the time the second weeding is over, it is time to think of preparing the land for

The farmer's calendar.

the spring crop, an operation which is carried out in much the same manner and with the same implements as are employed for the autumn crop. Meanwhile that crop is fast ripening for the sickle, and it has become necessary to guard it against the depredations of bird and beast. The *improbus anser strymoniaeque grues* of Virgil have in this country worthy compeers in the *corvus impudicus*, the parrot, the *mainā*, and hosts of other feathered depredators, each of whom comes with his claim for a 'daimen icker in a thrave,' small requests individually, but collectively, if conceded, tantamount to a free gift of the whole crop. The birds cease awhile from their pilferings with the approach of night, but are replaced by more doughty if not more destructive foes, pig and deer. These are particularly harmful to the spring crops. 'A pig,' to quote Mr. Hemingway, 'will root up a field of unguarded 'wheat in a single night, and then will lie up for the day in 'the adjoining juāri field, after reaping a goodly quantity of 'the juāri to form a soft couch. Deer, on the other hand, are 'comparatively mild offenders; they will do an untold amount 'of damage if allowed to stay peacefully in the field; but 'they are easily kept out by a very small amount of noise. These animals are warded off from the fields partly by fencing and in forest villages also by night watching. Watching in the daytime is unintermittently necessary to check the ravages of birds. The operation is a familiar one, but the following description of it by Major Lucie Smith appears worthy of reproduction:—'As the crop progresses, the '*machān*, or raised platfrom, is run up in the centre of each 'field. In the more open country it is made just high enough 'to give the watchers a clear view over the field, but as the 'jungle is approached and entered, the *machān* rises higher 'and higher until it stands some twenty feet above the 'ground. From this as the centre radiate to the outer bound-'aries of the field cords hung with rags and wooden clappers, 'so that a pull in the *machān* creates a rattle and a flutter of 'cloth to the furthest corner, and whitewashed earthen pots 'and skulls of cattle perched on poles, with other scarecrows, 'are liberally dotted about. In the day, the watchers pull 'the cords, sling stones, and shout volleys of abuse at their 'feathered foes; while those temporarily relieved from the '*machān* while away their leisure below by an occasional 'cock-fight with some brother watcher from a neighbouring 'field. As evening draws on large fires are lighted, and the 'hardest part of the work commences, for now begin to steal 'out of the forest herds of deer and droves of pig, and if the '*machān* men be not quick of ear and loud of voice, the morn-'ing's light may show the crop trampled down and half 'devoured.' After the sowing of the *rabi* crop, the *kharīf* harvest is close at hand, and by the time all the operations in connection with that, cutting and gathering, drying, threshing and winnowing are over, the spring harvest (which has all the while required careful watching and a certain amount of weeding though a good deal less than is requisite for the autumn crop) is almost due and has to be treated likewise. Add to this the business of disposing of his crop, and it will be seen that there is but little intermission in the farmer's labours. Only in the hot weather, and not throughout that, can he, if he be conscientious, take a holiday and call his time his own.

Cultivation of juāri.

142. Incomparably the most widely sown open-field crop is *Sorghum vulgare* commonly known as juāri. Omitting from consideration the Sironchā variety, which will be described separately when dealing with the crops of that tahsīl, there are two general classes, *kharīf* juāri and *rabi* or *ringni* juāri. *Kharīf* juāri is the more widely sown and of it there are numerous varieties differing from each other in colour, shape, hardness of grain and outturn. Of the spring crop, *ringni* is practically the only variety.

There is nothing remarkable about the cultivation of the crop. *Kharīf* juāri should be sown in July and in any case not later than the middle of August; about four *pailīs* of seed are sown to the acre and in sowing either the *sartā* or *tifan* is employed. The crop flourishes best with light and intermittent rainfall at the beginning of the monsoon, followed by good showers in October. It should be given two weedings, but as a matter of fact often only gets one. It is cut towards the end of December or early in January. The standard outturn for the District has been fixed at 600 lbs. per acre, but Mr. Hemingway would, as the result of recent crop experiments, have this raised to 650 lbs. The crop does almost as well on inferior soils such as *khardī* and *wardī* as it does on such good soils as *kanhār* or *bersī*. Rice and *kharīf* juāri require such opposite conditions that they are seldom both found to cover large areas in the same tract simultaneously. In tracts capable of growing both, rice would ordinarily be grown in a series of wet years, while juāri would tend to oust it when a cycle of dry seasons supervened.

Ringnī juāri.

143. *Ringnī* juāri, however, is a common spring crop in rice tracts. Its cultivation differs little from that of the *kharīf* variety except in the matter of times and seasons. It is sown in October, by which time both man and beast are likely to be flagging in consequence of their previous labours, so it probably gets less adequate ploughing. Of weeding it requires comparatively little, as weeds flourish less riotously towards the close of the rains. It is cut in January and gives an average yield of some 500 lbs. per acre, or rather less than that of the *kharīf* crop; the grain is rather hard, and often coarse. The chief advantage of the crop is its great capacity for withstanding drought. Both species of juāri are very liable to smut, which turns the grains to a fine black powder. The cultivator of the Georgics knew the remedy for this disease,[1] but the Chānda cultivator is only now beginning slowly to learn the virtues of pickling through the emissaries of the Agricultural Department.

---

[1]Semina vidi equidem multos medicare serentes,
et nitro prius et nigra perfundere amurca.

(*Virgil. Georgics I, 193-194.*)

144. Next in importance, if not in actual area, among the open-field crops comes cotton, the chief export crop of the Warorā tahsīl.

Cotton cultivation.

The full account of the methods of cultivation adopted for this crop which is given in the Wardhā Gazetteer applies in essentials to the practice of this District, and may be referred to for more detailed information than the scope of this chapter admits. Both the *banī* and the *jari* varieties are found, and the latter here figures as a spring crop. *Banī*, which is a rains crop, will not flourish except upon the true black cotton soil of the riverain tracts, and is not found east of Bhāndak. In this District it is usually interspersed with a few lines of tūr. Free ploughing and heavy manuring are essential to both kinds of cotton, and *banī* cotton requires very careful weeding. Sowing is conducted by means of the *sartā* or by the two-coultered *mogāda*; the choice of drill depends on the saturation of the soil; the *sartā* is used in conjunction with the deep plough when the surface is dry and deep sowing advisable; the *mogāda* when the ground is moist. To prevent the cohesion of the seeds by their lint, they are previously treated by immersion in a compound of water and cow-dung. Six *paserīs* or nine seers of seed are sown to the acre. *Banī* is sown in June and begins to flower in September, just about the time the *jari* sowing commences. By November it is ready for the first picking, and altogether it gives five or six pickings, of which the second, third and fourth are the most important. *Jari* comes into blossom about February, and the first picking takes place during the following month. There are usually four pickings, but a fifth is occasionally necessary. It is a less prolific crop than *banī* and its lint is not of such good quality. Owing to the difficulty of conducting experiments on this crop, it is not easy to estimate the average outturn with accuracy, but *banī* is usually credited with yielding some 300 lbs. to the acre, and *jari* with about four-fifths of that amount. Cotton is a good drought-resisting crop, and this quality has helped to bring it in favour of late years. As remarked earlier in this chapter, the extension of the railway will inevitably lead to an expansion in the area under cotton.

Wheat, til and other open-field crops.

145. Wheat requires more labour than most crops. The land has to be dressed with the *wakhar* every fortnight from June till October, and free manuring is advisable. In Warorā, tenants grow wheat on that portion of a field which lies about the site of the previous year's *mandwā*, and so secure the fertilising effect of the manure of the cattle which have been picketted there during the open season. In Bramhapurī, wheat is generally grown in embanked land. A good black soil is essential for a good crop. The seed is sown late in October or early in November, and the crop cut in February or March. The standard outturn is 580 lbs. Linseed is a troublesome and precarious crop, but popular, since, if successful, it is a very paying investment. Like wheat, it is usually sown after juāri or cotton, but, unlike wheat, it is very exhausting to the soil, and it is said that no good crop, except perhaps cotton, can be obtained for two or three years from land where it has been sown. Two hundred and fifty pounds is a normal outturn. Til is sown chiefly as a spring crop; the seed is so small that it is mixed with powdered cow-dung previous to sowing to prevent an excessive quantity passing through the coulter at one time. Only one and a half or two pounds of seed are required to the acre, and the outturn is about 200 lbs. for the *kharīf* and 300 lbs. for the *rabi* crop. When dry the seeds run out of the pods by the mere force of gravitation when the plant is held head downwards, so all the labour of threshing is obviated. Gram, lākh and peas are generally sown after rice in black soil. Gram requires no weeding, but before the plants flower, they are pruned to stimulate their growth. One advantage of gram is that birds do not eat it, but it has of course to be guarded against cattle and wild animals. The standard outturn is 550 lbs. Tūr in the Wardhā valley is

generally found as a mixed crop in connection with cotton or juāri. The customary proportion is one line of tūr to every seven or eight of cotton, and two contiguous lines to every ten or twelve of juāri. Elsewhere it is found as an unmixed crop. When sown alone, the lines are three feet or so apart in order to allow the bushy plant to expand freely. It is sown early and cut late, and only requires one *wakharing* and one ploughing. Four hundred pounds is an average outturn. *Lākhori*, a small variety of lākh, is generally sown as a double crop in rice *dolīs.* It is simply scattered in the still, wet ground shortly before the heavy rice is cut; it requires no weeding or watching. It is said not to possess the paralysing properties of the kindred lākh. Mūng and urad are sown as mixed crops. The castor plant, or *eranda*, is preferably grown in black soil, sometimes by the simple method of throwing it into cracks of the soil if the latter is too stiff for the plough. Castor needs no watching, as animals are aware of its medicinal effects, and avoid it.

(2) The rice tracts. Cultivation of rice.

146. Rice (*Oryza sativa*) occupies in normal years a far larger area than any other crop, although in some recent seasons when the rainfall has been short or uncertain, it has been outstripped by juāri. It is of two distinct species, known respectively as light (*halkā*) and heavy (*bhāri*), the former being an early and the latter a late crop. The varieties of rice are very numerous, and Major Lucie-Smith distinguishes no fewer than fifty, which he divides into three classes. Light rice requires little water and ripens quickly, but on the other hand the rainy season is not over when it is harvested, and so the ripe crop runs a risk of injury from the final showers. If transplanted, it requires to be watered up to the middle of September only, while, when sown broadcast, it does well without any irrigation in a normal year. Heavy rice on the other hand, while it needs more water and takes longer to mature, ripens when the weather is settled and gives a larger outturn than light rice; tenants therefore prefer to sow

heavy rice if they can do so, but it can only be grown in land which has really first class irrigation. It is not necessarily of better quality than light rice; indeed, according to Mr. Hemingway, epicures prefer many of the lighter varieties.

Methods of rice cultivation.

147. In the *khālsa* portion of the District there are three distinct methods of rice cultivation, *viz.*, *rohnā*, by transplantation, *autia*, by sowing broadcast, and *mulkā* or *kaorak*, by previous germination. In all three systems alike, embanked land only is employed.

(i) By transplantation.

The method by transplantation is always employed when irrigation is available, and frequently also when it is not. The ground to be cultivated is ploughed up with the *nāgar* three or four times as soon as the first showers fall, and a small plot is selected for a nursery, and, after being very heavily manured, is sown broadcast and scarified by means of the *wakhar*. The area of the plot is usually about one-twentieth of an acre; such a plot is sufficient to supply young plants to about half an acre of land. Transplantation in a normal year begins shortly after the middle of July and lasts till Polā, and heavy rain is absolutely necessary for its success. The embanked fields, or *dolīs*, which are to receive the young plants are worked up into a thick pasty mud by repeated ploughing or by trampling with young bullocks and the seedlings, which have by now attained a height of about a foot, are removed from the nursery and dabbed into the ground with sticks in small bunches at intervals of four or five inches. This operation is usually carried out by women, who sit in a line and take the plants as they are thrown into the field. The young plants are sometimes dragged from the nursery plot to the fields in which they are to be transplanted on wooden sledges called *khirlīs*. Little weeding is necessary. Seed beds are hardly ever weeded at all, while for the *dholīs* one weeding by hand at the end of August is all that is required after transplantation, since the preparation of the land for that process has already destroyed the free growth of weeds that springs up in the early part of the rains. After transplantation, light showers only are needed for a time, as very heavy rainfall is apt to induce rot, but the fields should be filled with water at least once more before harvesting. It is calculated that about ten *kuros* of seed are required for each acre, and the normal yield would be five *khandīs* or tenfold.

(ii) Broadcast.

For the sowing of rice broadcast there are two alternative methods. In the first, which may be called the dry method, the seed is sown before the rains, while in the second the preliminary showers are awaited, and the land is given one ploughing before sowing commences. In either case, the *modus operandi* is very simple; the seed is scattered by hand, and a harrow is drawn over the field to cover it up. Four or five *kuros* of seed are sown to the acre, and should normally give a yield of about 1½ *khandīs*. Weeds are kept down by hand, and there are always two, if not three, weedings, otherwise this method is much less expensive than that of transplantation, as less ploughing is required and the very heavy item of wages for transplantation is avoided. In the zamīndāris practically all rice is broadcast, but the only part of the *khālsa* in which broadcast rice is regularly sown to a large extent is the northern part of the Bramhapurī tahsīl where the system known as '*gātā*' cultivation (which will presently be described), generally obtains.

(iii) By previous germination.

When rice is planted by the method of *kaorak* or *mulkā* the land is prepared by three or four ploughings with the *nāgar* as for transplantation, but the sowing and subsequent operations follow the broadcast method. The feature of this system is that the seeds are made to germinate previously to sowing by soaking them in water for twelve hours and then letting them stand for another twenty-four.

Rice nurseries are always heavily manured and the fields in which the crop comes to maturity are also manured as often as the tenant's means permit. With this object even small tenants keep a few cows in addition to their plough cattle.

Light rice is ready for cutting about the end of September, but heavy rice is not cut till the end of November or in December. The hot-weather rice of Sironchā is cut as said above in April or May.

The standard outturn of rice in this District has been placed at 1500 lbs., and experiments conducted during the recent settlement operations indicated that this standard is approximately correct. With the aid of manure, rice can be, and is, grown year after year in the same field without deterioration of the soil. 'Many fields,' wrote Major Lucie Smith, 'are believed to have been continuously cultivated for 'the last 150 years or more, yet they are in no way inferior 'to land reclaimed from the jungle about 15 years ago.'

In many of the true rice tracts, tenants appear to care for nothing but their rice land, and, when enjoying a series of good seasons, systematically neglect their *wāwar* or open-field land. The cultivators of the Bramhapurī tahsīl however form an exception to this rule, and Mr. Hemingway says of them: 'Even in the heaviest of the rice tracts the open-field crops are 'highly esteemed where the soil is of moderate fertility, and 'tenants in average years grow a good class of crop in their '*wāwar* land. Thus in place of the perpetual juāri in the 'second rate soils, the tenants will be found sowing gram, 'linseed, peas or other fairly useful crops as a mixture with 'the juāri; this is a very common feature in both the Garbori 'and Wairāgarh parganas, wherever the soil is at all 'suitable. On the other hand, such fields are held in little 'respect over the greater part of the Chānda and Warorā tahsīls, and no pains are taken to secure any rotation of crops.'

'Gātā' cultivation of Bramhapurī.

148. Mention has been made above of a third system of agriculture, known as the *gātā*[1] system, which pervades a great part of Bramhapurī, and is of considerable import-

[1] *Gātā* means a field or plot.

ance. Mr. Hemingway's description of it runs thus: 'In the 'riverain groups of the Bramhapurī tahsīl the cultivated 'lands contain heavy *kanhār* or *bersī kanhār* soil; a very 'large proportion of this is embanked, and in normal years 'grows both *kharīf* and *rabi* crops. The *kharīf* crop is 'invariably light rice, generally sown broadcast; this is reaped 'in October, and the fields are again ploughed and cropped 'with gram, linseed and *rabi* pulses; occasionally wheat is 'the second crop. This system is quite distinct from the 'ordinary double-cropping, when pulses are sown as a catch-'crop after rice; here, the light rice is a "catch" crop, and 'the second harvest is the more important; but the profits 'from the cultivation are high, because the outturn of the rice 'is heavy, and the expenses of transplantation are saved.'

Cultivation of the Sironchā tahsīl.

149. There are several features which distinguish the cultivation of Sironchā sharply from the other types prevailing in the District. Rice is, indeed, one of the staples, and it is sown broadcast much after the fashion of the other parts; the *mulkā* system also is known, but the methods of inducing previous germination differ slightly from the procedure prevailing elsewhere. The seeds are wrapped in teak leaves and laid on straw. Pressure is then applied in order to generate heat, and the mass is sprinkled with water every evening for four or five days until germination takes place. But there is a great lack of irrigation; tanks, once not infrequent, have generally been allowed to fall into disrepair; there are no *borīs* and practically no embankments except in Māria villages. What irrigation there is is mostly dependent on perennial springs, and the land protected by these is fully occupied. Sironchā is furthermore unique in possessing two rice harvests. Besides the usual rain crop, there is a hot-weather crop, which is sown after the rain crop has been garnered. This crop requires extremely heavy manuring and constant irrigation, but does not give much of an outturn. Were the tract less

isolated, it probably would not pay to grow the crop, but under existing conditions it is in high demand locally. Its local name is *jimsarā* or *grīshma kāl.* Maize or *makai*, elsewhere a comparatively insignificant crop, is one of the *kharīf* staples of the tahsīl. It is carefully manured, and is a crop which never fails. The chief spring crop is juāri. A fair amount of this is the ordinary *ringnī* juāri, but this crop pales into obscurity beside the magnificent juāri which takes its name from the tahsīl. Of this Sironchā juāri there are nine varieties, the *bhuttas* varying considerably in colour and shape, some being red and others black, but all alike are prolific in the extreme. The crop is sown in September after the floods have subsided, mūng or cotton being mixed with it, and is cut in February or March. Mr. Hemingway thinks that it is probably *kharīf* juāri acclimatised to a later sowing. The outturn ranges from 2000 lbs. per acre on the best soils to 700 lbs. on the worst, and Mr. Hemingway estimates that a standard of 1500 lbs. would not be outside the mark. Other *rabi* crops are wheat, gram, linseed and cotton, but the cotton is an inferior *jari* grown for purely local consumption. In the Lower Tāluks til and hemp are quite considerable crops. Garden crops bulk more largely than in other parts of the District, and tobacco is a popular and extremely lucrative crop, high rents being obtainable for suitable land. But the absence of trade and the lavishness of nature have resulted in an apathy on the part of the cultivator, particularly in the Upper Tāluk, such as is not found elsewhere. There is no deep ploughing; almost all crops are sown broadcast; little attention is paid to double-cropping or to the introduction of new varieties of crops; weeding is systematically neglected; manuring is confined to *bāris* and double-cropped rice land; the value of rotation is not recognised; improvements are unknown, and trouble is not even taken to keep existing tanks in repair. Everything is left to soil and climate, but climate and soil are such that the cultivator, so far from suffering for his negligence, regularly reaps crops that the more diligent toilers of less favoured tracts might well envy.

Cultivation of the zamīndāris.

150. To the bulk of the population of the zamīndāris, cultivation is merely a secondary means of winning a livelihood, and agricultural produce simply serves to supplement the food supply forthcoming from the jungle. The call of the jungle is for ever in the ears of the Māria, he is for ever, so to speak, agog to 'pull out on the long trail,' and his hereditary instinct for migration appears to have lost little, if any, of its primeval power. So, although in the neighbourhood of the *khālsa*, we do find a certain amount of fairly stable cultivation, the typical cropping of these tracts is slovenly and shifting and bears the impress of the woodman rather than that of the farmer. Rice and the lesser millets practically monopolise attention, and although the transplantation method is found, the broadcast system predominates. When the tenant owns or can hire bullocks, or for the matter of that cows, for the Māria yokes cows and bullocks alike to the plough, he will carry out broadcast cultivation on the same lines as the cultivator of the *khālsa*, though a good deal more casually. But the typical cultivation of the zamīndāris is the *khamori* system, well known elsewhere in these Provinces under the name of *dahiā*. For this, a level or slightly sloping plot of ground is selected and, towards the close of the hot weather, cleared of its jungle. When it has been covered with wood to a depth of a few inches, the mass of timber is set alight and allowed to burn down. Rice is simply thrown broadcast among the ashes, and nature is left to do the rest. No ploughing is required, so from the cultivator's point of view the process is the acme of economy. Only light rice is sown after this fashion, and the outturn is very great, a normal crop yielding as much as eighty-fold. When *mandiā* is the crop sown the term *sampod* is used in place of *khamori*. Usually the plot is abandoned after one crop has been taken off it, but

occasionally a second crop of kutkī is produced in the ensuing year, and in this event the term *hiwar* is applied. After one year or at most two the plot is abandoned, and the brushwood upon it allowed to recuperate. It either reverts permanently to its pristine state of jungle, or remains undisturbed for a period of at least ten years until the new growth is sufficiently luxuriant to tempt somebody to repeat the process. The system is a very wasteful one, and a good deal has been done to restrict it in estates under the management of the Court of Wards, but it is suited to the simple appliances of the aborigines, and within limits, and provided that care be taken to conserve valuable timber, it is the best that could be devised for these stretches of wilderness, which are simply in the pioneer state of civilisation. The rent paid for *khamori* cultivation is reckoned by the 'axe,' *i.e.*, that area of land which a single axe can clear, a variable measure usually connoting rather more than an acre. The payment is not truly to be reckoned a rent, as it is simply a forest due for the timber cut; whether there is a *thekādār* farming the rents of the village or not, *khamori* payments like other forest dues always go to the zamīndār. The rate for an axe of land is eight annas.

Gātā cultivation.

151. Another method of cultivation peculiar to the zamīndāris is that known by the name of *gātā*.[1] The essential condition of this is a small valley with gently sloping sides and watered by a stream. Substantial timber dams are built across the stream at intervals during the hot weather, and are continued on either wing by embankments of earth until they almost but not quite merge into the rising sides of the valley. A series of perhaps twenty such *gātās* may be constructed one below the other. When the rains come, a large shallow basin of water is dammed up above each *gātā*, superfluous water being passed on to those below it by the escape passages left at the end of either wing or else cascading over the top

[1] This differs in method from the cultivation described in para. 148 though the name is the same.

of the dam. Rice is planted in the shallow water thus held up, the irrigated area thus being above, not below, the dam. Many of these *gātās* are ambitious works of great size and requiring no mean engineering skill, and it might have been thought that their construction would conduce to stable cultivation. But, so far from this being the case, Mr. Lancaster, in his report on the southern zamīndāris attested by him, mentions having seen villages containing large dams, 30 feet high and 600 feet long, which have been allowed to go to ruin, the cultivators having abandoned the village in a body owing to some fancied ill-luck pervading the site.

In spite of these savage methods of cultivation, it must not be supposed that the crop obtained is of poor quality. On the contrary according to Mr. Lancaster the rice grown by the Māria is of the very finest description and far superior to any kind usually to be met with in the *khālsa*.

The only crop of importance besides rice in these tracts is kodon, kutkī or *harak*, which appeals to the jungle population by the simplicity of its cultivation. It does quite well on the most stony soil and asks for but a minimum of attention. It only requires one *wakharing*, it does not need manure, very little seed is required and can be sown broadcast, while the outturn is very large in proportion to the seed sown. The hill Mārias on the Bastar border also grow considerable quantities of a small millet called *kosri* which is said to be very nourishing.

Garden crops.

152. Of garden crops the chief are sugarcane, tobacco, *pān*, chillies, turmeric, brinjals and ordinary vegetables.

(i) Pān.

Pān cultivation is carried on principally at Bhāndak and Chichordi by communities of Barais and is chiefly interesting for the high degree of co-operation and organisation which it exhibits. The *pān* has not the reputation of that which is grown at Rāmtek, and is less favourably situated for disposal, and the Barais are far from being in a prosperous condition.

(ii) Tobacco.

In the Sironchā tahsīl, where garden crops play a very prominent part in agricultural economy, tobacco is a very important crop. It is always irrigated, and in the Upper Tāluk is generally grown by Marārs in land situated on the edge of a *nullah* and irrigated from a *kachchā* or unlined well. Sometimes a big tobacco garden is cultivated by a large community jointly. In the Lower Tāluks, a good many expert tobacco-growers have immigrated from Madras. These water the tobacco by hand and after one or two waterings pick off the head of the plant, thus inducing it to spread and ripen early. Very high rents are paid for these tobacco gardens.

(iii) Sugarcane.

The only other type of garden cultivation which requires detailed description is sugarcane. Cane cultivation is found in Warorā and the Rājgarh pargana of Chānda, but the chief seat of production is the Garbori pargana of Bramhapurī. Lean years and the competition of *gur* from the United Provinces and Bengal have combined to reduce the cultivation of sugarcane to a somewhat languishing state, and the crop is now hardly important enough to justify a detailed description of the processes employed, interesting though they are. The first necessity is a stable source of irrigation, and this may be either a well or a tank. In the first case the cane garden is termed '*motasthal*' from the leathern *mot* employed to draw up the water and in the second it is known as '*pātasthal*' to signify that it is irrigated by a channel or *pāt* coming from a tank. *Pātasthal* gardens are comparatively rare in other Districts. One marked peculiarity of the cultivation is the method of allotting land for it. 'In cane-growing villages of this District,' writes Mr. Hemingway, 'it has been the 'custom from time immemorial for tenants to hand over their 'holdings in rotation to the mālguzār for cane. The cane 'when irrigated from a tank is almost invariably grown by a 'community of which the mālguzār is not of necessity a 'member; if a certain number of tenants in the village 'express a desire to grow cane, and the tank contains enough 'water to supply the demand, the mālguzār may sublet a 'plot of his *sīr* to them for the purpose, or he may call upon 'a tenant to surrender his holding for cane; the mālguzār has 'full control over the land thus taken up; he is supposed to 'give the tenant land of equal value in exchange, or if that 'cannot be arranged he remits the rent for the time that 'the land is out of the tenant's possession. The mālguzār 'then apportions the land to the men who want to grow 'cane, and he or the owner of the tank, if the tank does not 'belong to the mālguzār, takes water-dues from the cane-'growers according to the area which each member of the 'community has under cane in his garden.' There are many minor variations of this system into which it is not necessary to enter here. Two classes of cane are grown, the better being a thick purple variety known as *kālā* which gives only one cutting and occupies the ground only one year. *Kathai* is a smaller and inferior cane; it is harder and contains little juice, but it has the advantage of giving three cuttings in successive years, though the second and third cuttings are comparatively poor. Cane growing is an extremely expensive form of cultivation; it requires heavy manuring, preferably by the costly method of picketting sheep and goats on the area to be planted; very substantial fences have to be erected as pig and jackals find the cane very toothsome; constant irrigation is required, and, finally, the cane occupies the ground for a whole year before it is ready for cutting, so that the capital invested takes much longer to give a return than is the case with most crops. The triple cutting which the *kathai* variety yields makes considerably for economy in these expenses, and has therefore rendered it more popular than the superior variety. When the crop has been cut, the juice is expressed by mills, which are generally of the wooden-roller type though iron-roller mills are becoming increasingly popular especially in the Chānda tahsīl, and it is then boiled down in country pans. Cane is planted in February and takes a year to arrive at maturity. Cane cultivation is being assiduously pushed by the Irrigation and Agriculture Departments and the area thus cultivated has greatly expanded in the last two years. Local experiments made in the Ahīri estate show that though the risk may perhaps be greater than with ordinary crops, sugarcane is very profitable.

Agricultural implements.

153. For ploughing the two principal implements employed are, as elsewhere, the *nāgar* and the *wakhar*, the former of which is a heavy tearing or cutting plough which is used for breaking up new land, while the latter is much lighter and acts as a paring plough. Both these implements are also used for weeding, the *wakhar* frequently, the *nāgar* only occasionally, when the soil is light and the space between the rows of plants narrow. For the smoothing of sugarcane land, a *mohī* or heavy wooden clod crusher, drawn by from two to four pairs of bullocks, is used. For sowing with the drill, a long bamboo funnel is usually attached to the back of the plough. The *tifan*, or three-coultered drill, is only common on the borders of Wardhā and Nāgpur, a light one being employed for *kharīf* sowing and a heavy one for *rabi*. Weeding is commonly carried out by means of the *daurā*, which is a miniature *wakhar*; the *eli* is also used for weeding certain crops; it resembles the *daurā*, but, instead of having one broad share, it has two short shares about six inches apart in the same plane. For clearing rice land previous to transplantation, a wooden harrow called a *phan* is employed; this is the same instrument as is elsewhere known by the name of *dantāri*. Reaping is carried out by means of an ordinary sickle, called *irā* or *darāti*. Threshing is done by hand, and by the scriptural method of treading out the grain with oxen and for winnowing the cultivator is dependent on the aid of the wind; he stands on a platform or a stool and lets the grain fall slowly out of a basket, so that as it falls the wind may blow the chaff and dust away.

154. On the subject of weeds it is sufficient to reproduce the observations of Mr. Hemingway's Settlement Report: 'Noxious 'weeds are little found in the pure rice tracts; they do not 'flourish in the sandy soil of those groups, and are easily 'eradicated when they appear. Similarly in the open tracts 'they are seldom found in the very heaviest soils, unless 'years of abnormally short rainfall have encouraged their 'growth; when the soil is easily water-logged during the 'rains, or regularly flooded by the river, as in Sironchā 'tahsīl, their appearance is rare. But in the open tracts 'where the soil varies from good to moderate, *kāns* with 'light rainfall becomes a scourge which is particularly disheartening to the tenantry. It can be kept down by deep 'ploughing, but few tenants have large enough cattle, or the 'inclination to eradicate it by these means. They generally 'leave it to die down and the process takes as long as ten 'years. In the Waingangā valley a variety is found known 'locally as *padyāl*; this is an extremely troublesome 'variety; deep ploughing has but little effect upon it, and a 'long fallow period appears absolutely necessary. This 'variety is generally found in villages that border small 'feeder nullahs, and is not suppressed by inundation. During 'the last few years this species has put out of cultivation a 'very large area of land in the Murjhā group.

Weeds.

'Though weeds of any vitality are seldom found in the 'rice land there is a plant which appears in that land when 'under cane crops which is extremely noxious. This is 'locally termed *tarup*, and it is apparently the same weed 'as is found in other Districts where cane is largely grown 'under the name of *agia*. When this plant has once 'made its appearance it spreads rapidly, and the whole of 'the cane in its neighbourhood dries up at once. It is never 'found in gardens in which cane is grown at long intervals 'and its appearance denotes that the cane-cropping has been 'too incessant, and the land requires resting from that crop.

'It is seldom found in the lightest soils; and since those soils 'are used by preference for cane, when available, the damage 'done by it in any particular year is seldom extensive.'

Manure.

155. Cultivators fully recognise the value of manure, and it is freely employed in the rice tracts both for rice and sugarcane. The only forms of manure, however, which are at all common are cattle droppings and house-sweepings; these are kept till required in an open pit. Many tenants keep several cattle in addition to their plough-bullocks simply for the sake of obtaining their manure; in rice tracts even the smallest cultivators have two or three such cattle, while a well-to-do man may keep as many as a score or two. The most heavily manured crops are rice and sugarcane, particularly the latter, for which the expensive process of picketting goats and sheep on the field at night is ordinarily employed. The charge for picketting a flock is Rs. 4 for twelve days. Where firewood is readily available, all the cattle-droppings are carefully conserved, and wood alone is used for fuel. In the zamīndāris, wood ashes are used to make up any deficiency of animal manure. In the open tracts, cotton and wheat are often manured, and juāri occasionally; but except in the Warorā tahsīl, comparatively little use is made of manure in these tracts. For this Mr. Hemingway assigns two reasons: 'Firstly, the tenant has generally a small plot 'of rice land also, to which he devotes the whole of his 'supply; secondly, on account of the distance from the 'railway, the price of open-field land is very low, and the 'tenant has generally in his occupation a far greater area of 'this land than he actually needs for cultivation and resting 'fallows. Instead of regularly manuring a plot of moderate 'fertility and cropping it yearly, the tenant cultivates only 'a small portion of his holding in years when the rice crop 'promises well, and frequently changes the position of his 'crops in order to plough land yearly that has had long, 'almost too long, rests.'

Bemrose, Collo., Derby.

WATER BASTION, RAMALA TANK. CHANDA.

IRRIGATION.

156. In the extent of its irrigated area, Chānda ranks second only to the Bhandāra District. According to the agricultural return for 1906-07, the total area under irrigation in the District amounts to 123,823 acres, of which 118,400 acres are irrigated from tanks. This area is equal to more than one-fifth of the total area under irrigation in the Central Provinces and Berār. Prior to the famine of 1900, the area irrigated usually amounted to 150,000 or 160,000 acres, but that famine threw a vast quantity of land under insufficiently stable irrigation out of cultivation. Since 1902, however, when the irrigated area stood at under 110,000 acres there has been a fairly steady recovery to the present figures.

Area irrigated.

157. The chief sources of irrigation are the large lakes usually known as tanks, and the pond known as *borīs*. The number of these latter fluctuate considerably from year to year, but at a rough estimate it may be said that there are 1500 large tanks and as a rule some 4000 *borīs*. The best tanks in the District are found at the base of the hills in the Garborī pargana, and in the adjoining tracts of the Chānda and Warorā tahsīls: Ghot, Rājgarh and Amgaon have also several very fine tanks. In Garborī almost every village has a large high level tank capable of irrigating up to 300 acres, and this pargana is so studded with these reservoirs that is has earned the title of the 'Lake District' of Chānda. It is calculated by Mr. Hemingway that in the heavy rice tracts over 80 per cent. of the rice land is well irrigated, and over 50 per cent. is secure against the ordinary deficiencies of rainfall, but it has to be remembered that this calculation was framed at a time when the poorest rice lands had been abandoned to waste, and consequently the percentages are rather more favourable than they would have been in more normal years. Looking purely to statistics of irrigation, Gunjewāhi is the pargana best protected, Mūl, Keljhar, Talodhī, Garborī, Ghot

Tank irrigation.

and Wairāgarh follow in the order named. If Sironchā be excepted, the District really possesses but few tank sites within village areas of which full use has not been made. For this the present generation of cultivators owes a debt of gratitude to its ancestors, and also to the wise provision of the Gond kings who, under the system of *tukum* grants, allowed each builder of a tank to hold the land irrigated by that tank rent free for a term of years. The Sironchā tahsīl once contained a fair number of good tanks, but most of these have now fallen into disrepair; when this happens, the land beneath the tank is simply abandoned. The tenants do not attempt to keep the tanks in good order, while the attitude of the Velamā proprietors is analogous to that of Seithenyu ap Seithyu Saidi towards the embankment of Gwaelod: 'It 'was half rotten when I was born, and that is a conclusive 'reason why it should be three parts rotten when I die.'

Construction of tanks.

158. Tanks are formed by closing the outlets of small valleys watered by a stream, or by throwing a dam across sloping land intersected by rivulets: the dam should be short, and not exposed to any violent rush of water, and the position should allow of an ample escape channel being dug, in firm rocky soil, with a course which will take off the flood waters without injury to the dam or to the cultivation. Finally, good land for wet cultivation must lie below the tank at such a level as to permit of the tank water freely flowing over it. In order to effect irrigation, the water of the tank is passed through the embankment (*band*) by means of a sluice or *turum*, having a simple but effective arrangement of vertical ducts arranged in a series of descending steps and leading as their lower ends into a horizontal channel which is pierced through the embankment. The highest vertical duct is nearest the inner face of the embankment and can only be used when the tank is full: as the level of the tank becomes lowered the other ducts come into play in descending order. Less ambitious tanks are simply provided with a wooden

tunnel, generally the hollowed trunk of a mahuā tree, but this is a source of weakness which frequently leads to breaches in the embankment. The smaller tanks which go by the name of *boris* are not provided with sluices: their dams are cut through to let the water run off as required, and the breach so made is repaired before the break of the ensuing monsoon. In the rains, the embankment needs constant care and is watched day and night. 'When floods are out 'and the level rising fast, the watchers beat the alarm drum 'and the whole village thereupon hurries to the tank, some 'to keep the escape channel clear, others to repair on the 'instant aught that gives sign of yielding in the dam. Thus 'hours go by in battling with the waters, and at last the 'crisis is over, and the workers return glad and wet and 'weary to their homes.'[1] Many of these tanks are extremely picturesque, and there are few more grateful sights to the official touring in the heavy rice country than the broad clear blue sheet of water which awaits him at the end of the morning march, reflecting perhaps the contour of surrounding hills and rocks and verdurous forests, and at any rate affording, in the duck riding on its bosom and the snipe haunting its margin, both a pleasant recreation and a welcome addition to camp fare.

Kohlis.

159. The most expert tank builders found in this District are the Kohlīs, a caste apparently of Dravidian origin, and perhaps akin to the Māria Gonds. The Kohlī is not found (except, to borrow a forester's phrase, as an 'escape') outside the Chānda and Bhandāra Districts, and indeed in this District is seldom found outside the heavy rice tract of Garborī. For this reason as well as for his own intrinsic merits, no apology is required for the reproduction of the following sketch of him from Mr. Hemingway's Preliminary Assessment Report on the Bramhapurī tahsīl: 'As a builder of tanks he is without 'equal in this District, if not in these Provinces: he

[1] Major Lucie Smith's Settlement Report, para. 224.

'constructed very nearly all the large tanks in Garborī, and 'besides taking advantage of the obviously good sites he has 'succeeded in irrigating many very unpromising stretches of 'land from sources that must at the outset have been far 'from being so obvious. The one fault that can be found 'with his large tanks is the want of a good waste weir; if he 'makes any allowance at all for surplus water, he can never 'gauge the force of that water in years of prolonged and 'heavy rainfall; in such years the weak end of the embank-'ment where the waste weir should have been is frequently 'washed away, and a large sum of money has to be 'spent in repairs. But necessary repairs are always done. 'I have not discovered a single case of a Kohlī mālguzār 'failing to keep his tank in effective working order; in 'this respect he forms a very pleasant contrast to the 'Brāhmạn mālguzār of other tahsīls, who will never spend 'a penny on his tank himself, and will certainly not let his 'tenants do so when re-settlement operations are pending. 'It is somewhat curious that only a small proportion of the 'men who made these big tanks in Garborī were rewarded 'with privileged tenure; in other tracts such tanks are almost 'invariably *tukums*. It can only be inferred that the Kohlī 'had little influence at the Gond and Marāthā courts.' After extolling the Kohlī as a first class cultivator of rice and cane, a kind and just though not weakly indulgent landlord, and a co-sharer, who dwells in unity with his brethren, Mr. Hemingway concludes: 'Some of these Kohlīs have 'developed a wonderfully minute knowledge of their villages; 'one or two of them will walk across their village and tell 'you from memory the *khasrā* number of every plot that 'they pass: such men belong to the younger generation and 'are perhaps thought less truthful than their elders; all, 'young and old, might give lessons in courtesy to many of 'the classes that rank above them socially and have better 'education. With all the above virtues it is hard to find a 'better mālguzār than the Kohlī, at least in this District.'

Besides the proficiency in the construction of the actual tank, the Kohlīs exhibit a wonderful skill in arranging distributive channels and taking out levels: some of the very largest tanks are over a mile away from the land that they irrigate—the Rajolī tank is even more distant—and the water channels are brought at different levels along the surrounding slopes to irrigate every available square yard of land.

Well irrigation.

160. The area irrigated from wells only amounted to 1823 acres in 1906-07. The crops irrigated are garden crops, chief among which is the *motasthal* sugarcane crop. The leather *mot* worked by bullocks, the pole-lift and the hand-lift are the chief means employed for raising water from wells. Sironchā is more particularly the home of this type of irrigation, and it has already been mentioned how Marār immigrants into the Upper Tāluk frequently sink *kachchā* wells for irrigation purposes on the edge of a nullah. In the big tobacco gardens of this tract, an unusual method of working the *mot* is employed. Instead of starting from the level of the well mouth and pacing down an incline hollowed out of the surrounding ground, the bullocks work from a high wooden platform down to the ground level, and thus the water can be distributed to all parts of the sloping field. Wooden troughs are employed to carry the water to the field and much time and care must be spent in elaborating these arrangements.

Other sources of irrigation.

161. The remaining area of 3600 acres is classified as irrigated from 'other sources.' Foremost among these is the system of *gātā* cultivation already described in dealing with the cultivation of the zamīndāris. But besides this, many of the hilly parts of the country are favoured with tiny perennial springs from which 'infinite streams continually do well,' and these are eagerly seized upon by the Māria and guided into small reservoirs for the purposes of his favourite *jhilān* cultivation. The Sironchā tahsīl, includ-

ing the Ahīri zamīndāri, and the vicinity of the Mūl hills are the chief localities in which these perennial springs occur.

State irrigation.

162. The active history of Government enterprise in irrigation commences, so far as the District is concerned, with the inquiries made in 1901-02 by the Irrigation Commission. The rough investigation of projects made in connection with this inquiry showed that if a rate of Rs. 2 per acre could be obtained for irrigation it would pay Government to construct schemes which would cost Rs. 60 or less per acre completely protected. When in May 1902 the irrigation circle was formed, Chānda was included in the Waingangā Independent Executive Charge having its headquarters at Nāgpur. Tanks at Tekrī and Saighatā were immediately taken in hand as small contract test-works for local labour, and drew well. The big Asolā-Mendhā scheme for which the original estimate was 4·81 lakhs was sanctioned by the Government of India and put in hand shortly afterwards. In September 1903, owing to the increasing burden of work, the South Waingangā Independent Subdivision was formed and put in charge of an Assistant Engineer with headquarters at Chānda, but the charge continued to grow in importance and in December 1905 it was constituted a Division under the name of the Mūl Irrigation Division.

Irrigation in the Division has so far been confined to tank work. The area of operations lies almost entirely to the west of the Waingangā, the Kunghāda tank being the only exception to this rule, and the majority of works undertaken lie in the Bramhapurī tahsīl. Progress on major works has been much impeded by scarcity of labour, particularly since the commencement of construction operations on the Gondia-Chānda Railway, and also by the difficulty of securing satisfactory contractors. The policy has accordingly been to concentrate attention on the Asolā-Mendhā project, and to go slowly with the other major schemes until the completion of the railway shall have released a more liberal supply of labour. The revised estimate for Asolā-Mendhā amounts to 10·38 lakhs, and up to the end of February 1908 work to the value of 3·16 lakhs had been done. It is calculated that, when completed, the tank will irrigate an area of 20,000 acres and command an area of 40,000 acres; the water spread area will be 7·3 square miles and will submerge seven villages, while the distributaries will extend the whole length of the *doab* between the Waingangā and Andhāri rivers. The only other major works on which any progress has so far been made are Ghorājhari and Khairī. Ghorājhari is anticipated to cost 8·33 lakhs, to irrigate 26,000 acres and command 39,700 acres: work to the amount of 1·15 lakhs has hitherto been done upon it. Khairī is a smaller work: its cost will be only 1·17 lakhs, it will irrigate 2000 and command 2550 acres: up to the end of February 1908 Rs. 15,700 had been spent on it. Other major projects which are under preparation or revision are Naleshwar, Katwān, Bhainskhandī, Kāsarla, Bunder, Metāpār and Mohāli Mokāsa. The estimates for Naleshwar and Katwān are 5·62 lakhs and 1·24 lakhs respectively; the former will completely protect 7500 acres and the latter 830 acres.

Minor tank works have been undertaken either at the entire cost of Government or else on what is known as the grant-in-aid system. Under this system, which was devised by the Hon'ble Mr. Craddock, when Commissioner of the Nāgpur Division, half the cost of a tank in a mālguzāri village is borne by Government, and half by the mālguzār, or by the mālguzār and tenants jointly, the share of the cost not borne by Government being advanced as a loan recoverable in small instalments. Six tanks have so far been completed on this system, *viz.*, Mangrūr (Rs. 8500), Saighatā (Rs. 2000), Mehā (Rs. 1700), Chichlī (Rs. 1400), Chārgaon (Rs. 1000) and Saolī (Rs. 800); the figures in brackets indicate the total cost of each tank in round numbers. Of minor works undertaken wholly by the State the following have been completed: Paunā (Rs. 5800), Mahābāra

(Rs. 8600), Ghorpeth (Rs. 5400), Junonā (Rs. 14,600), Janāla (Rs. 5500), Tekrī (Rs. 3250), and Kunghāda (Rs. 4700). The last named has been a particularly successful tank: water-dues amounting to Rs. 1453 were recovered for the year 1904-05 from 830 acres irrigated by it, and in 1905-06, no less than 960 acres of rice representing a full assessable revenue of Rs. 1808 were irrigated. Minor works are under construction at Chindī (Rs. 30,000), Kachapār (Rs. 9500), Maregaon (Rs. 14,000), Paunpār (Rs. 33,600), Rudrapur (Rs. 16,000), and Itolī (Rs. 7000). The numbers in brackets indicate the estimate of total cost. All these with the exception of Chindī were practically complete at the end of the irrigation year 1906-07. The total area which all these works, both grant-in-aid and State, both those completed and those under construction, are expected to irrigate amounts to 7518 acres. By the end of that year the total expenditure of the State on the construction of minor irrigation works in this District since the inception of the irrigation programme amounted to Rs. 1,17,650, which was distributed thus: contributions to grant-in-aid tanks Rs. 5100, expenditure on State minor works in ryotwāri villages Rs. 59,843, on State minor works in mālguzārī villages Rs. 50,280, and on repairs to tanks and tars Rs. 2427. Thirty projects for minor works were under preparation during 1906-07.

So far irrigation has only been effected from minor works. The area irrigated from State minor works amounted to 374 acres in 1904-05, to 1120 acres in 1905-06, and to 1698 acres in 1906-07. Rs. 1976 were assessed as water-dues in 1905-06 and the whole amount was recovered in that or the following year. In 1906-07 Rs. 2949 were assessed as water-dues, but only Rs. 70 of the current demand was collected. Water was in many cases granted free. The cultivators were found to have immediately fully realised the advantages of irrigation, but a new and more cautious policy had been adopted to regulate assessment. To quote the Chief Commissioner's Resolution on the point: 'Further 'experience has been gained in the regulation of rates and the 'choice of the system under which they shall be levied. It 'is found that more rapid progress is secured at the beginning 'by a low and gradually increasing crop rate. The cultivator understands and accepts it more readily, and gets to 'learn the full value of irrigation sooner, because he applies 'it fully to his crops. In the case of payment by waterings, 'he is apt to hesitate at each watering, hoping that nature 'will give him rain, and he therefore often loses in yield. He 'will eventually realise that by this short-sighted action he 'has to pay the same rate to save the remains of a poor crop 'as would have secured him a bumper harvest if invested at 'the right time, but the lesson takes some time learning. 'With a low initial crop rate, the returns to Government per 'acre to begin with are smaller, but irrigation spreads more 'rapidly and with it the knowledge of its value. It is most 'essential, however, that the ryot should know from the outset that low rates are temporary and also the rate which he 'will eventually be required to pay. As the rate increases, 'he may find that he prefers to pay by waterings, or he may 'prefer a fair crop rate; and this matter can be left for future 'decision.' At present the rates at which crops are assessed in this District are Rs. 7 per acre for sugarcane, Rs. 2 for garden crops, and from R 1 to R. 1-12 for field crops. The amount of irrigation done from grant-in-aid tanks has fallen from 1,720 acres in 1904-05 to 570 and 308 acres in the two subsequent years.

CATTLE.

Cattle-breeding.

163. The breed of cattle found in the District is small and poor. Breeding for sale in neighbouring Districts is carried on extensively in all jungly parts where there is plenty of grazing, but there is no selection and immature bulls are allowed to run free with the herds. Castration is effected very late, and in the usual cruel and primitive manner by pounding with a stone: Gonds and Māngs perform the operation for one or two

annas or for a free meal. Attempts have been made to encourage more systematic selection and early castration, but so far with little result. In 1902, an annual grant of Rs. 300 was sanctioned by Government to be disbursed in prizes to cattle-breeders at the Mahākāli fair which is held annually at Chānda, but the experiment was a failure and the grant was subsequently withdrawn.

Plough bullocks.

164. The plough cattle of the District are broadly classified into two groups—(i) the Māhurpattī group, which come from Māhur, Jungaon and Khamonā in the Nizām's dominions and are sold in large numbers at the annual cattle fair at Wūn in Berār; (2) the Telangpattī group, hailing from Ahīri, Dābha, Sironchā and the Ghātkul pargana. The former are good-sized and strongly built animals, suitable for work in the open fields of the juāri growing country, and the great majority of them are to be found in the Warorā tahsīl; a pair of good plough bullocks of this breed will cost Rs. 100 to Rs. 200, and a good cow from Rs. 40 to Rs. 50. Telangpattī bullocks are of much smaller build, and are reserved for rice cultivation, in which the limited size of the fields necessitates the employment of small animals. The best cattle of this species come from the Ghātkul pargana. The cost of a pair of good bullocks ranges from Rs. 60 to Rs. 125, while a cow costs from Rs. 10 to Rs. 30. The cattle of the rice country are usually white, while those of the open country are reddish or speckled red and white: a red animal is locally called *lākha*: if the animal has a red body with a white stripe on its forehead, it is styled *lākha bhondā*: a bull speckled black and white all over is termed *dhamnā*. An ordinary pair of plough bullocks should last 10 or 12 years in the open-field country, but in the rice tracts the usual duration of life is only about five years, for the work is hard and tells heavily on the animals.

Feed

165. 'Plough cattle,' writes Mr. Hemingway 'are as a 'rule well fed and tended; in the rice 'tracts there is excellent grazing, and

'cattle are well fed the whole year round; in the open tracts 'also with one exception, there seems no lack of good fodder; 'all the period that the cattle are working they are fed with '*bhusā* and the husks from the threshing-floor. During the 'hot weather, the cattle are kept out in the fields at the '*mandwās* that tenants construct on their holdings, and where 'they themselves live during the hot weather. The *karbī* of 'juāri is an invaluable cattle food in these tracts; and the sur-'plus that tenants do not require for their own cattle finds a 'ready sale in the local bazar. The one exception above 'referred to is the open tract at the bend of the Waingangā 'north of Bramhapurī, here the cropping is very close indeed; 'there is practically no waste land in the village, and cattle 'appear to be muzzled when loose until the month of April, 'when there is little for them to find in the fields. In this 'tract, tenants are content with the very thinnest and oldest 'cattle that they can procure; they seem perfectly happy if 'they get a full season's work out of their pair, before the 'latter expire, and new cattle of equally little value take their 'place.' Besides *karbī*, cattle are fed on *popat* or beans, *tākh* and cotton seed, the allowance being 1 to 2½ seers daily. Cultivating bullocks are only dieted in this fashion when actually engaged in cultivation, but trotting bullocks are fed all the year round.

In Warorā and Bramhapurī well-to-do mālguzārs and tenants give salt to their cattle five times a year; the amount given is one or one and a half chittacks at a time to plough cattle, and half a chittack to other cattle. The same custom is followed in the Havelī pargana of the Chānda tahsīl, but in the rest of that tahsīl, and in the west of the Garhchirolī tahsīl, salt is given to plough cattle only, and even to those only half a chittack is administered three times a year. In the Sironchā tahsīl, well-to-do cultivators give their cattle one or two tolās of salt twice a month during the cold weather and rains: poorer tenants do this only once a month. In the zamīndāris the practice of giving salt to cattle is unknown.

Cows.

166. Many tenants keep a large stock of cows for the sake of milk and *ghī*; and also for manure. Cows are also kept for breeding purposes, especially in parts where grazing is easily obtainable: in the eastern half of the District, almost every village has large herds of spare cattle which are disposed of to outside dealers at the local bazars. One bull is able to serve 30 or 40 cows. In the zamīndāri and wild tracts adjoining them the Gonds frequently plough with cows, disposing of all their bullocks for profit: Sao Teli residents of the zamīndāris are also in the habit of ploughing with cows.

Buffaloes.

167. In the Waingangā valley and the zamīndāris, milch buffaloes are very extensively kept for the sake of *ghī*, and in the villages that adjoin Chānda and other large towns also, the income from this source is so considerable that tenants habitually keep large fallow areas in their holdings purely to secure grazing. In the more remote tracts buffaloes are freely used in cultivation; they are used in rice cultivation to drag the *khirlī* or sledge and the *phan* or harrow. A male buffalo costs Rs. 15 or Rs. 16, and a she-buffalo Rs. 30 to Rs. 50: many of them come from Wardhā. Male buffaloes are not much in request. In Sironchā, a particularly fine breed of buffaloes is produced which is exported to Nellore in Madras.

Horses, etc.

168. Horses and ponies are very few in number and poor in quality: mālguzārs and other persons of note prefer to travel in *rengīs* drawn by bullocks.

Goats, sheep, etc.

169. Large flocks of goats and sheep abound. Sheep are principally kept by Dhangars and Kuramwārs for the sake of their wool, which is worked up into blankets, while goats are designed chiefly for food, and are sold into Umrer and Nāgpur for this purpose. Both goats and sheep are valued secondarily for the sake of their manure, and many tenants keep goats both for manure and food. The price of a

goat is Rs. 4 or Rs. 5 and of a sheep Rs. 2. Sheep are always kept outside, as they sicken if under cover: they also sicken and die off at once if there is heavy rain. In Sironchā, there is a special breed of sheep known as *dhor mundī* or the Godāvari sheep. This is a large, long limbed weedy looking animal, which grows to a height of three feet at the shoulder, and is covered with white or reddish brown hair. Its flesh is coarse, and is not much eaten by Hindus, who see a resemblance between the animal and the cow. The ewes, however, are of value and give half a seer to a seer of milk a day: the milk is used for making *dahī* and *ghī*. These animals are kept by Golkars, and cost Rs. 10 each. Fighting rams are bred in Chānda, but are only kept by a few people because, if they are well fed, they become fierce and attack children. They are set to fight and the one who turns or runs away is considered to have been beaten. They sometimes break one another's horns or foreheads, but they do not kill each other.

Cattle markets.

170. The most important cattle markets of the District are held at Warorā, Madherī, Chimūr Jāmbulghāta, Bhāndak, Nawargaon, Gāngalwādi, Chānda, Rājgarh, Dābha, Kunghāda-Talodhī, and Nāndgaon. Cattle come on from the big Wūn fair to the annual Mahākāli fair at Chānda. In the Sironchā tahsīl a few cattle come to the weekly bazar at Asaralli.

Numbers of stock.

171. The total number of agricultural stock during 1906-07 is returned as shown below:—

Bulls and bullocks	204,712
Cows	261,936
Male buffaloes	22,654
She-buffaloes	77,692
Young stock	172,534
Sheep	43,111
Goats	96,220
Horses and ponies	988
Mule	1
Donkeys	169.

The number of actual plough cattle is 192,266. In spite of heavy losses from recent outbreaks of rinderpest and foot and mouth disease, there has been a marked recovery in the number of plough cattle since the famine of 1900, when the total number fell to below 158,000. In some groups the loss during the famine was so great that rents, which would otherwise have been freely enhanced, had to be left practically untouched.

Cattle diseases.

172. The local names of the ordinary cattle diseases that occur in the District are *sad* and *tadak phānsi* for anthrax, *pai khuri* and *tondi khuri* for foot-and-mouth disease, *māta* for rinderpest and *dūkria* or *ghatsarap* for hæmorrhagic septicæmia. *Sad* is the name for gloss-anthrax ; the veins of the tongue are distended with black blood and the tongue becomes much swollen especially at the base. This disease appears in the hot weather and is probably caused by the animal drinking bad water. The local remedy is to brand the veins of the tongue and sometimes to cut the ears so as to let the blood flow from them. Linseed oil and turmeric are given internally. When there is congestive fever and the lungs are affected anthrax is called *tadak phānsi.* This is the most obscure of all its phases, and is said to be much more fatal. *Tondi* and *pai khuri* or foot-and-mouth disease is a contagious fever accompanied with vesicular eruptions in the mouth and on the feet. Sometimes the mouth only is affected, at other times the feet. The tongue is the principal part of the mouth affected, but the gums and roof of the mouth and the inside of the cheeks are also in some cases attacked. The eruption in the feet is found at the junction of the skin with the hoofs and between the hoofs. The local remedy is to wash the mouth of the animal with salt and water or with alum and water, while coriander leaves are given freely to eat. For eruptions on the feet tar is applied to the affected parts, or the animal is made to stand in hot ashes or sand. This disease is most virulent in the cold weather. *Māta* or rinderpest is said usually to be prevalent

in the hot weather, but accounts as to the time of its appearance vary so much that little reliance is to be placed on them. The most characteristic symptoms are a viscid discharge from the eyes, nostrils and the mouth, and ulceration of the gums and the other parts of the inside of the mouth and dysenteric fæces. All these symptoms are not invariably present but some of them will always be found. The duration of the disease is generally from 24 hours to 3 to 9 days, but sometimes extends to 12 to 16 days. Camphor and oil are given as internal remedies and rice gruel, heavily salted, is given the animal to drink, but some owners give no treatment at all, relying rather on religious observances and charms. The animal affected is taken once a day to Devī's temple and she is asked to give relief. *Dūkria* or *ghatsarap* known as hæmorrhagic septicæmia occurs principally during the rains, but it may appear at other seasons, the Christmas rains being frequently followed by an outbreak. The symptoms of this disease are high fever and the appearance of a circumscribed swelling, usually of the throat. The swelling rapidly increases and the animal breathes and swallows with great difficulty; a rattling noise, made in breathing, can be heard many yards away. If the animal lives longer than three days it will probably recover. The local remedy is to foment the swollen throat with a decoction of *nīm* leaves (*Melia indica*) or to treat the local swelling by scoring it in lines with a red hot iron. Linseed oil is given as an internal remedy. Rice gruel with a little salt is given for nourishment.

CHAPTER V.

LOANS, PRICES, WAGES, MANUFACTURES, TRADE AND COMMUNICATIONS.

LOANS.

Indebtedness.

173. The indebtedness of the people of this District is on the whole small. The reason of this is that the poverty of communications has hitherto deterred the exploitation of the District by foreign capital to any great extent. The value of land is generally speaking low, and investments in the more remote tracts are risky as recovery is a matter of some difficulty. The people have thus learnt to rely largely upon local and merely semi-professional money-lenders for their loans, men who do not as a rule care to involve their clients too deeply and who exact more punctual repayment than the regular *sāhukār*. Indebtedness is most heavy in open tracts such as the *havelī* of Chānda and the northern part of Bramhapurī; in the latter tract free credit is obtainable owing to the vicinity of Nāgpur, and many tenants have been induced by this circumstance to raise their standard of living unduly and to involve their holdings beyond hope of recovery.

Rate of interest: Various forms of borrowing.

174. Ordinarily, the lowest rate at which money is obtainable on the security of land is about 12 per cent. per annum: if jewels are pledged, interest is sometimes as low as 6 per cent or, if the loan be a very large one, perhaps only 9 per cent is charged, but the average rate of interest may be placed at from 12 to 24 per cent. For grain loans, there are two recognised rates known as *sawai* and *derhī*. According to the former rate, a quarter of the amount borrowed is taken as interest at the time of repayment, while according to the latter, half the original amount is so taken. Sometimes the

sawai rate is also used for cash loans, especially to cultivators, the loan being for a term of six months or a year.. Grain loans are advanced at the time of sowing and recovered at harvest, so the rate per annum is quantitatively a good deal higher than the nominal 25 or 50 per cent., but on the other hand it has to be remembered that grain is at a premium when advanced and at a discount when recovered. Wheat and juāri are advanced on *sawai* rates : oil-seeds and rice on *derhī*. These latter grains are more heavily charged for because in the case of rice the seed has to be kept distinct, while the amount of oil-seeds advanced is usually very small. It is said that sometimes even twice the quantity of seed-grain advanced is recovered. The only notable alteration in the rates of loans is that wheat, which used formerly to be charged at *derhī* rates, has within the last 15 or 20 years been reduced to *sawai*. In advancing small cash loans, the lender usually takes a bond from the borrower, but, in the case of approved clients, an entry in his account books is sometimes deemed sufficient, while very rarely the matter is settled simply by oral agreement. The procedure appears to be less rigid in respect of grain loans than in regard to cash transactions, doubtless owing to the fact that grain loans are repaid with far more regularity than cash. Large cash loans are of course always secured by a bond or deed which in the case of landed security will be registered. Grain is ordinarily borrowed for both harvests, except in Sironchā where borrowing is confined to seed for the spring crop of juāri. As a rule a tenant will go to his mālguzār for a loan in preference to a *sāhukār*, although the terms obtainable are probably the same in either case. Even in good years, most tenants make a custom of taking a small loan from their mālguzār or *sāhukār*, the idea being that, as regular clients, they will have the preference over casual customers in a bad season, and this right of precedence is more or less tacitly recognised by the lender. Grain loans are often taken for mere subsistence by the poorer classes, in which case they are known as *porgā*: the rates do not differ from those charged for loans of seed-grain. The system of borrowing known as *lawanī* is said to be common in Bramhapurī, where Cutchi money-lenders go on regular tours from village to village inducing people to take loans according to it, but it is not generally popular, and people appear to be beginning to look askance at it. It is also found in the rice tract of the Chānda tahsīl, and seems to owe its existence in both tahsīls to a succession of bad rice harvests. Under this system, the lender makes an advance of cash stipulating for its repayment in grain at a fixed rate at harvest. This fixed rate is always considerably lower than the market rate likely to prevail at the time, so the borrower is at great disadvantage, particularly if the harvest be short. But even in the remote parts of Garhchirolī, the rising prices of produce have opened the eyes of the people to the drawbacks of this system, and it is now resorted to only by the most helpless of the tenants. The ethics of repayment exhibit a curious duality. Mr. Hemingway remarks upon this point: 'With a very strange 'but very marked inconsistency, the tenant of this District 'yearly repays his grain debts with interest as soon as the 'crop is harvested, as a matter of course; but as a matter of 'honour he never repays his cash debts until he is positively 'forced to do so. He occasionally goes even further; he 'repays his grain debt to the *sāhukār* in preference to repay-'ing his Government taccavi. He knows that the Govern-'ment kist is a trifling sum; but it is a cash debt, with a 'lenient *sāhukār*, which should be paid under compulsion, 'for preference. Honour is then more than satisfied and the 'tenant has a most comforting grievance. A large tenant 'who has never borrowed grain in his life, and has married 'off his children from his own resources, will owe Rs. 5 to a '*sāhukār* all his life. As an experiment, I once induced a 'large tenant owning large herds of cattle and grain stocks 'worth about Rs. 500 to pay off the debt of Rs. 5 that he 'owed to the local *sāhukār*; he paid it, and borrowed Rs. 10

'in order to keep his name on the books as a matter of 'honour; he had never in his life had occasion to borrow 'money for an actual want of his own.'

Money-lender and tenant in the Sironchā tahsīl.

175. The Sironchā tahsīl, exceptional as it is in almost every way, presents a most remarkable condition of affairs in the relation between money-lenders and tenants. The natural conditions of the tract are such that, under any sane regulation of their affairs, the tenantry should be in circumstances of singular affluence. But a pernicious system of borrowing has reduced them to a state of absolute and abject dependence on their *sāhukārs*, who in this part are usually Komti shopkeepers from Madras. These men dole out everything the tenant requires in driblets as occasion arises. Each cultivator has a running account for food, seed, clothes and small sums of money: even rent money comes from this source. To recoup themselves, the Komtis take possession of the borrower's crop before it has been removed from the threshing-floor. The crop is then valued at a rate fixed by agreement amongst the Komtis, and credit is given to the cultivator at this rate. Needless to say, this '*sāhukār's* rate,' as it is called, is considerably below a just tariff, and it is but seldom that anything finds its way back into the pocket of the borrower. Not content with their '*sāhukār's* rate' the Komtis privily swell their gains by illicit recourse to a '*sāhukār's* measure,' a vessel with a generous capacity for all incomings. The hapless tenant, thus robbed and defrauded in every way, is not only content to acquiesce in this state of things, but actually looks on the *sāhukār* as his saviour from want. Something is being done to retrieve the situation by means of co-operative credit. Three rural societies, two financed by share capital and one by deposits, were commenced in 1906. Ten more rural societies are shortly to be started in affiliation to a Central Bank at Sironchā. But the conservatism of the people and the opposition of the *sāhukār* are formidable obstacles to rapid

reform, although final success, particularly with the impending opening up of communications, is beyond doubt. It should be remarked that the system described above, while practically universal in the Upper Tāluk, is in the less insulated Lower Tāluks practically confined to petty tenants.

Village sāhukārs.

176. The following account of the village *sāhukārs* of the District is reproduced from Mr. Hemingway's Settlement Report: 'The village *sāhukārs* of the District fall into two classes—'(i) the *sāhukār* class pure and simple with a hereditary 'profession of money-lending, (ii) cultivating classes who 'have supplemented their farming with a little *sāhukārī*. 'The first class need little description: they are the same 'all over India in their caste, manners and methods of busi-'ness. In this District the largest trading firms of this stamp 'belong to either Komtis, immigrants from Madras, or 'Gujarāti Brāhmans; firms of less repute are those of 'Marāthī Brāhmans, Hindustāni Brāhmans and a few 'Muhammadans. Of those castes the only firms who regu-'larly prefer a crooked to a straight transaction are the Guja-'rāti Brāhmans: others, though their dealings will not all 'bear the open light, are not professional sharpers: the Guja-'rāti Brāhman is. One well-known Gujarāti landowner has 'invented a *machla* system: in his villages when rents are 'collected, he takes the rent with one hand, gives it back 'with the other, and collects it plus 25 per cent. interest the 'following year. Since this is done with the greatest 'regularity from every tenant, his actual rent-roll is 25 per 'cent higher than the *jamābandī*. The tenants say they like 'it: it is slightly more difficult to recover as a cash debt than 'as a rent, but the risks are small to the mālguzār, and the 'yearly payments go down to the debt account: there is 'therefore an interest at 25 per cent. on the rent yearyl 'accumulating in the debt account. In the Bramhapurī 'tahsīl another firm of Gujarātis has obtained a bad reputation 'for sharp practice when dealing with tenants: the principal

'complaint against them is the production of forged resigna-'tions of land and leases reserving *sīr* rights. The tenant in 'this part of the District has now in self-defence generally 'adopted the plan of getting a petition-writer to draw up 'resignations and he sends them by registered post. Since 'this has become a general practice, any resignation written 'and produced by the Kāmdār, with the tenant's mark only, 'may, with few exceptions, be set down as fictitious. The 'Komti firms reside in Chānda city, but they are gradually 'extending their trade over the whole tahsīl. As plain money-'lenders their treatment of their clients is generally moder-'ate: but when they get possession of a village it takes only 'a very few years for them to get a mortgage on nearly every 'holding. Luckily, the true *sāhukār* classes in this District 'have not as yet obtained much land. In the north of 'Bramhapurī, both Būti and Chitnavīs of Nāgpur are rapidly 'increasing their clientèle. In the distant parts of their sphere 'of influence they lend little money to tenants, but confine 'themselves to the mālguzār classes, or small grain loans. 'When they begin to take mortgages, it is a sure indication 'that communications have improved the value of land: at 'present both these firms are taking up as much land as 'possible in the northern portion of the District. The second 'class of village *sāhukār*, the cultivator who supplements his 'farming with a little trade, is found in all parts of the Dis-'trict. The mālguzārs of this type are Kunbīs, Kohlis, Gānd-'lis and a few Gurdis. As village *sāhukārs* these men are with 'very few exceptions extremely lenient to their clients, and 'their villages do not deteriorate: they lend grain and only 'very small sums of money, and these loans are repaid with 'regularity. Luckily, the greater portion of the District is 'still financed by men of this type: and since the majority of 'these small firms have kept their place in recent years, 'there is every hope that they will further extend their 'transactions when communications are improved. The 'most oppressive indigenous *sāhukār* is the Mahār who has 'taken to lending money: his low caste seems to assist him 'in resisting all attempts to oust him, when once a plot has 'been leased for debt to him, and he has reaped the debt 'several times over from its produce.'

Principal money-lenders.

177. Chānda city contains some thirty money-lenders in a fairly big way of business. Paikannā Māmidwār is assessed to income-tax on an estimated income of Rs. 5000, Srīnivās Nārāyan Sharāf, Nānu Ganeshu Māmidwār, Sītārām Nārāyan Mungantiwār, Sambanā Somayā Tangadpulliwār, Sītārām Malayā Arkurwār, Vithoba Atmārām Kotpalliwār, Krishnayā Rājgopālu, Siddhakaran Agarchand and Bālkisan Hukumchand Mārwāris are assessed on supposed incomes ranging from Rs. 2500 to Rs. 3500, and four others have incomes of over Rs. 2000. But the money-lender who pays the biggest income-tax in the tahsīl is Saiyid Ismail Musalmān of Dābha, whose income is placed at Rs. 7000, and the interior of the tahsīl has some twenty-five money-lenders who are supposed to make over Rs. 1000 each a year. In the Warorā, Bramhapurī and Garhchirolī tahsīls, there is a good deal of business transacted with money-lenders from outside the District Foremost among these are Gopāl Rao Būti and Gangādhar Mādho Chitnavīs of Nāgpur, whose taking of mortgages has already been quoted as a sure harbinger of the rising value of land. Vināyak Jāgeshwar Būti of Nāgpur, Yādorao Brāhman of Bhandāra, and Rekchand Mahesri Baniā of Hinganghāt, have from half a lakh to a lakh and a half each out at interest in the Warorā tahsīl. Raotmal Mārwāri and Ganesh Harbāji Brāhman of Warorā, Someshwar Sakhārām Komti of Nerī, Krishna Patel Kunbī of Soit, and Rājeshwar Krishnāji Naik of Chimūr, are money-lenders domiciled within the tahsīl, whose incomes are reckoned at from Rs. 2500 to Rs. 5000 each. In the Bramhapurī tahsīl, the most prominent local money-lenders are Nārāyan Shrīdhar and Janārdan Dāmodar Naiks and Tejubhai Cutchi, with estimated incomes of

Rs. 3000, Rs. 5000 and Rs. 2000 respectively, and seven others pay income-taxes of Rs. 50 or more. Among the more prominent money-lenders of the Garhchirolī tahsīl may be mentioned Sadāsheo Bālkrishna Petkar, Nathu Kalār, Muhammad Bhai Cutchi, Girdhāri Bhau and Guljārmal Mārwāri, the last of whom is assessed on an income of Rs. 3000. Sironchā is the field of Komti money-lenders, but a few Kalārs have also lending transactions on a moderately large scale. The most prominent *sāhukārs* are Padisala Luxmia Komti, Tota Rājanna Komti, and Suiramballa Rājaramayā Brāhman.. One Totābālam Komti, who recently died, was also in a very large way of business, and distinguished himself by heavily involving the present zamīndār of Ahīri by none too scrupulous methods. He made a claim for nearly Rs. 60,000 in the Civil Courts against the Court of Wards, but finally accepted Rs. 40,000 as a compromise.

Between *sāhukārs* themselves, the ordinary rate for loans is R. 0-7-9 per mensem or Rs. 5-13-0 per annum.

Government loans.

178. The loans granted by Government to needy cultivators under the Land Improvement Loans Act and under the Agriculturist's Loans Act are of great benefit to those classes whose credit is not sufficient for them to borrow at reasonable rates from the ordinary *sāhukārs*. In a few remote parts, a little persuasion is needed to induce aboriginal tenants to take loans, but as a rule applicants are eager to take taccavi. The joint responsibility system, which is usually enforced at any rate for agricultural loans, is not, however, very popular, but is submitted to as a necessary condition for obtaining the money. Loans under the Agriculturists' Loans Act are expended on the purchase of seed-grain and bullocks. Land improvement loans are generally devoted to the construction or repair of tanks, *borīs* and wells, the construction and improvement of field embankments, or to breaking up new land. Of recent years a fair number of these loans have been taken under the grant-in-aid system. It is comparatively rare to find money taken

ostensibly for one of these purposes misapplied, but from time to time cases occur in which the borrower diverts the loan to such uses as paying off his debts or to a marriage ceremony.

Loan transactions were comparatively small prior to the famines: during the famines they were naturally very heavy and subsequently they have been generally on a larger scale than in pre-famine days. Altogether from 1874 to 1905 3·42 lakhs were advanced under the Land Improvement Loans Act: of this amount 2·47 lakhs were recovered, and Rs. 27,500 were remitted. Under the Agriculturists' Loans Act, the total amount advanced from 1885 to 1905 amounted to 5·20 lakhs, out of which 4·02 lakhs were recovered and Rs. 79,500 were remitted.

Material condition of the people.

179. Taking first the land-owning and land-holding classes, these were classified at settlement into five classes, according to the prescriptions of the Settlement Code, and the results are shown in the following table in the form of a percentage on the whole body:—

Class.	Percentage.	
	Mālguzār.	Tenants.
A. Prosperous	53·6	7·3
B. Substantial	18·1	25·1
C. In average circumstances...	20·7	49·3
D. Deeply indebted ...	7·6	17·7
E. Indigent	...	·6
Total ...	100·00	100·0

The boundaries between each class are necessarily elastic, but the classification is sufficiently accurate for practical purposes, and the broad conclusion that all save 7·6 per cent. of the mālguzāri body and all save 18·3 of the tenant body are comfortably off, or fairly so, may be accepted. The very low percentage of indigent tenants is, however, deceptive, and is merely due to the fact that the recent bad years have practically wiped out the E. class tenant by forcing him to migrate or to abandon his holding. Below the tenant class and constantly interchanging with its lower ranks comes the body of field labourers, a class which the depletion of population has raised of recent years to comparative affluence. Ordinary unskilled labourers are similarly in great demand, and are commanding wages such as would not have entered into their most sanguine dreams little more than ten years ago. Finally, the bulk of the remaining population is composed of artizans and 'base mechanicals' practising hereditary crafts. These have, as will be seen in the section on Manufactures, in many departments gone to the wall before outside competition, and, although numerous exceptions are to be made in favour both of particular occupations and of especially skilled individuals, this class is at present the most to be commiserated in regard to their material condition. They have, many of them, had to watch the dwindling of their earnings and to learn that hardest of all lessons, how to reduce their former standard of living.

The surroundings of the people, to western ideas bare, comfortless and even squalid, are pleasant enough for a race that neither knows nor desires anything better: indeed, when all is said, the average village homestead will bear comparison with the Scotch crofter's hut of little more than a century ago, the front doors of which were regularly flanked by a noble dung-heap. If the Indian cultivator's door were similarly adorned it would be a hopeful sign; at present he wastes and misuses manure horribly. In the interior of the District, two distinct standards of comfort may be observed, that of the aboriginal tribes and that of the Marāthā or Telugu; the difference extending to habitation, food, clothing and luxuries.

The Gond wants but little beyond what the jungle and the *bāri* around his house will provide: salt, liquor, some grain and tobacco, a minimum of clothing, iron for his axe and a few other simple tools, gaudy beads for himself and his wife: give him these, and the run of the jungle, and he will ask for nothing more. He loves, in fact, 'to live in the sun, seeking the food he eats, and pleased with what he gets.' Incidentally it may be remarked that this simplicity is by no means incompatible with good living. To say nothing of forest berries and 'roots of relish sweet,' it is to be feared that many a fat buck finds its way into the family pot, and, even without this surreptitious addition, fowls, mice, and "such small deer" lend variety to a *menu* which no scruples of caste circumscribe. The Māria Gond's house, too, in the remoter parts of the zamīndāris, is occasionally a very substantial erection: the walls are formed of barked logs laid horizontally and kept in position by upright posts: the interstices are daubed with mud, and a thatch of jungle grass covers all in. Withal, the whole costs the builder little beyond the labour of construction. The normal Gond dwelling is, however, built of strong wattle, supported by thick posts at the four corners, the inner surface of the walls *leeped* with clay. The roof is thatched and the whole surrounded by a strong wattle fence within which he has sometimes cattle sheds and shelter for goats, hens and other domestic animals. The ordinary transactions of life are carried out by barter, because money is scarce: this scarcity, however, does not by any means imply poverty.

Among Marāthās and Telugus the standard of living is higher, and the family budget contains more items. Houses cost more: an ordinary tenant will spend Rs. 50 to Rs. 100 or more on his house; a mālguzār Rs 150 to Rs. 300, or, if the house be of brick and tiled even up to Rs. 600 or Rs. 700. Poor men live in houses of wattle and daub thatched with grass or bamboo matting. Tiles and even corrugated iron are coming more generally into use, and are, as elsewhere, a sign of wealth and progress. On food, a Brāhman mālguzār would ordinarily spend from Rs. 20 to Rs. 50 a month for a normal family of two or three adults and as many children. A considerable item in a mālguzār's monthly bill is the entertaining of travellers and native officials on tour, such as police and revenue officers; a Kunbī mālguzār would in this way spend from Rs. 15 to Rs. 25, but a Brāhman mālguzār is required to dispense hospitality on a more liberal scale. Expenditure on clothing has increased considerably of late years, and a substantial mālguzār will spend up to Rs. 50 a year in providing raiment for his family. Even a coolie can nowadays launch out into a number of luxuries. A coolie family consisting of a husband regularly earning five annas a day, his wife earning 3 annas a day, and two children will probably spend his wages in some such fashion as follows: on food, roughly Rs. 8 a month at the rate of two *pailis* of juāri and half a *paili* of rice per diem; on spices and condiments inculding salt some R. 1-4 per mensem; on oil for culinary purposes 5 or 6 annas; on kerosene oil, about 8 annas, at the rate of a pice a day, and at least Rs. 3 or Rs. 4 a month on country liquor and tobacco. Clothes have to be bought once or twice a year at an expenditure of perhaps Rs. 20. With a little care this income is ample, but as a rule that care is not forthcoming, and in any case as a matter of principle the coolie is sure to be in debt to the extent of a few rupees. The personal ornaments of his wife would ordinarily be worth some Rs. 10 or Rs. 15. The great pitfalls in the way of the unthrifty are drink and the love of ostentation; the former is the curse of the aboriginals and lower castes, while the latter appeals to all classes alike all over India, taking, as is well known, its most acute form in the expenditure on marriages on which the income of one or two years is often squandered in a lump. There seems much in the view that attributes this lavish expenditure on vain show to the low standard of material comfort: the people really know very few other ways of spending their money. Hosts of dependants, love of litigation, subdivision of inheritances are contributory causes to unthrift: all of these are well known, none are peculiar to the District and they need not therefore be emphasised. It is of more interest to consider what effect western civilisation has had or is having on raising the standard of comfort. So far this influence has gone for little, outside the towns of Warorā and Chānda, and even in those towns it has done little more than add a thin veneer to the old mode of living. The use of kerosene oil and matches is universal, but the small chimneyless bazar-made lamp of tin or earthenware still practically holds the field: the triumph of foreign cloth and iron has simply been gained by supplanting the local products, and need not here be taken into consideration except in so far as to admit that the people are nowadays better and more cheaply clad than formerly. In the towns, some of the higher native officials have chairs, tables and lamps and a few other minor pieces of furniture after the European fashion, but the ordinary well-to-do native non-official has not followed this lead: indeed, such innovations are still regarded with some suspicion, and those who introduce them are apt to incur the invidious sobriquet of 'reformers' and find themselves in a fair way to achieve social ostracism. Some-time ago, a soda-water factory which guaranteed Brāhmanical soda-water was opened in Chānda but the concern became bankrupt. Despite this, the use of ordinary soda-water is becoming more and more prevalent. Two bakeries which purvey European bread have recently been opened in the town but are patronised solely by Musalmāns. Refined sugar is gradually superseding *gur*, and for the first time in 1905-06 outstripped the latter in the Chānda octroi returns.

A few Swadeshī enthusiasts have, during the last few years, been preaching a crusade against refined sugar, the story that it is cleansed with bullock's blood being widely spread; its sale has thus been considerably reduced but it is slowly recovering. On the whole the old order shows but little disposition to yield place to the new.

PRICES.

Agricultural produce. General course of prices.

180. Before the development of communications, the prices of agricultural produce were regulated almost solely by local conditions, and variations were characterised by great abruptness from year to year according to the conditions of the particular season. So long as the monsoon was regular and harvests favourable, prices ruled at what would now be deemed an absurdly low figure, but a failure of the crops immediately sent them sky-high. The only regulating influences which operated to tone down the violence of these fluctuations were the habit of hoarding sufficient grain to meet the consumption of two years, and the maintenance of public granaries. This period of insularity continued practically all over India till about the middle of the 19th century, and the Mutiny may be taken as the dividing line which separates it from the modern condition of affairs under which India is bound up in the commercial comity of nations, and the state of the cotton crop in Carolina reacts on the prices of cotton at Chānda. Thus prices prior to the Mutiny have, broadly speaking, but a topical value, and it need not be a matter for much regret that we have no reliable figure previous to 1832. Subsequently to the Mutiny, the chief influences which have permanently affected the course of prices in India as a whole are—(1) the transfer of the territories of the East India Company to the Crown, a step which immediately resulted in a great development of commercial and industrial activity accompanied by large imports of the precious metals, and (2) the opening of the Suez Canal in 1870, which led to the development of the grain trade with Europe. Turning to more local influences, for Chānda the crucial date is 1877 when the rail was opened as far as Warorā; and the present year 1908, when the Warorā line was extended to Ballālpur, thus bringing large tracts of hitherto insufficiently developed country within reasonable

distance of the railway, should also mark the beginning of a new era. More temporary influences have been—(1) periods of scarcity and famine, notably from 1861—1869, in 1897, and in 1900, at all of which periods the District itself suffered distress, and the great famine of 1877-78 in western and southern India, which caused a general rise in the price of food-grains all over India, and (2) the American War of Secession in 1861—1865, which created a strong demand for Indian cotton, and sent up the prices of agricultural produce in general.

Development of communications and greater command of money have had the inevitable result of inflating the prices of agricultural produce. In considering the course of prices of such produce in this District subsequent to the Mutiny the following periods are to be distinguished:—

(1) 1859—1861.—Normal period prior to development of communications.

(2) 1861—1869.—Period of high prices culminating in famine.

(3) 1871—1878.—Normal period : communications in course of development.

(4) 1878—1880.—Period of high prices caused by famine in other parts of India.

(5) 1881—1896.—Normal period: communication by rail now established as far as Warorā.

(6) 1897—1902.—Famine period.

(7) 1903 to date.—Period of gradual recovery, crops approximating to normal.

It is the normal periods that are of most permanent interest to the economic historian as displaying the steady upward trend of prices which accompanies development, and a fair idea of this upward tendency can be obtained by summarily comparing the rates of the three principal food crops raised in this District in various normal series of years. In the tabular statement below abnormal years are neglected. The prices entered are taken from the official returns and relate to petty retail transactions: they give a somewhat higher rate than the figures found in the books of *mahājans*, and they are by no means absolutely correct; but as a guide to the relative prices at various periods they may be accepted as fairly accurate :—

Year.	Rice.	Juāri.	Wheat.
	SEERS PER RUPEE.		
1859—1861	22·89	59·82	33·33
1871—1877	14·50	28·00	19·00
1881—1885	15·90	33·70	24·50
1886—1890	13·40	25·20	18·00
1891—1896	12·50	20·30	16·15
1903—1906	10·74	20·73	13·74

The prices given above relate to Chānda city only. Rates differ in the various tahsīls and within each tahsīl itself, but the variations are not so extraordinary as to call for particular remark. At the recent settlement it was calculated that the rise in the prices of agricultural produce since the settlement of 1868 amounted to over cent. per cent. in the Chānda tahsīl and the Upper Tāluk of Sironchā, to 70 per cent. in Warorā and the Lower Tāluks, and in Bramhapurī to 40 per cent. for rice, 70 per cent. for wheat and linseed, and to 50 per cent. for juāri. Percentages are however too rigid to be satisfactory in calculations of this type, and perhaps a better idea of the general rise of prices may be gained from the following quotation from Mr. Chhotelāl's Inception Report, dated 1896: 'It is well to add what the people 'relate regarding the rise of prices when they compare the 'current prices with those in pre-settlement days. They say 'that *dhān* was sold in pre-settlement days at Rs. 2-8 to Rs. 3 'per *khandī*, while it is now sold at Rs. 5 to Rs. 6 per '*khandī*; juāri was then sold at Rs. 4 per *khandī*, while it is 'now sold at Rs. 10 per *khandī*; til was sold at Rs. 7, Rs. 10 'or Rs. 12 per *khandī*, while it is now sold at Rs. 20 or 'Rs. 23; and linseed was then sold at Rs. 3 to Rs. 5 per '*khandī*, while it is now sold at Rs 20 per *khandī*. This 'shows that the people consider that prices have doubled since 'settlement.' And striking a rough average of all crops, it is safe to say that prices have again gone up by between one-third and one-half since Mr. Chhotelāl wrote the passage just quoted.

Prices of staple food-grains in Sironchā.

181. The course of prices in Sironchā calls for some brief remarks. At the first settlement in 1866 they stood at an abnormally high figure owing to the fact that the construction of the Godāvari Navigation Works had brought about a large influx of outside labour. But, taking the years immediately preceding this artificial inflation of prices and excluding those years in which prices were forced up, the average price of the staple crops from 1847 to 1861 was—rice 39, juāri 51, and til 29 seers to the rupee. A good deal of difficulty was experienced at the recent settlement in determining how far these prices had advanced. There was practically no open bazar, and the official returns of the Upper Tāluk were not to be trusted, as they related only to retail transactions on a very petty scale, while for the Lower Tāluks there were no official returns at all. The *mahājan's* books again are unreliable, for, to secure their own profits, they fix an artificial rate, at which they take grain at an unjustly low rate from the tenants in order to settle the running accounts which the latter keep with them. The rates prevailing in 1902 are given by Mr. Hemingway as follows:—

SEERS PER RUPEE.

	Rice.	Juāri.	Til.
Upper Tāluks.			
According to official returns ...	12	23	...
According to *mahājans'* books ...	22·5	45	...
Lower Tāluks.			
According to *mahājans'* books ...	18	42	15

The general rise of prices has, therefore, not been without marked effect even in the landlocked Upper Tāluk. The rise has indeed been even more marked there than in the more accessible Lower Tāluks, as the figures of the original settlement appear to give the prices at which food was bought up for the market at Rājahmundry. Considering the lack of communications, this sharp increase is somewhat difficult to explain, but the existence of the railway at Warangal appears to have influenced the course of prices.

Prices of staple food-grains in the rest of the District. Rice.

182. Excluding Sironchā, we may now consider the course of prices for each of the three staple food-grains of the rest of the District, rice, juāri and wheat. During the period from 1834 to the Mutiny, the price of rice at the headquarters of the District ranged between 25 and 30 seers to the rupee. From 1859 to 1861, which are generally regarded as normal years, the average price was 22·89 seers. Thence forward until 1869 a series of bad years and, in a lesser degree, the improvement of trade due to the American Civil War, caused a sharp upward rise, and the course of prices ran as follows: 1862, 15 seers; 1863, 12·5; 1864, and 1865, 9; 1866, 11·6; 1867, 7: 1868, 10·2; 1869, 5·9 [1]. Ensuing years witnessed a return to the normal which may be said to have lasted till 1896, with one break in 1878—1880 when prices went up owing to the Madras and Bombay famines From 1871—1878, the average rate was 21·3 seers: during the abnormal period 1878—1880 it rose to 10·7 seers. The remaining 15 years of the normal period may be divided into three quinquennia, during each of which a gradual but persistent rise in value may be remarked. For this, improved communications are accountable, but the inflation of prices in rice is less remarkable than in the case of other crops, chiefly because rice is mainly grown for local consumption but partly also because it was yielding uniformly

[1] Figures from 1834 to 1869 are for uncleaned rice and later ones for cleaned rice.

good outturns during these years. The average prices for each quinquennium were:—

1881—1885 ...	...	... 15·90 seers
1886—1890 ...	...	... 13·40 ,,
1891—1895 ...	...	... 13 ,,

The year 1896 with an average price of 12·2 seers was the last of the normal seasons and since then the average price has been 10·6 seers. In the famine of 1897, which was a period of heavy exports, prices averaged 8·9 seers, and went as high as 7·2 in August; in the 1900 famine, 8·7 seers was the average, and 7·3 the highest price reached. The course of prices since 1897 is shown below in the form of a chart:—

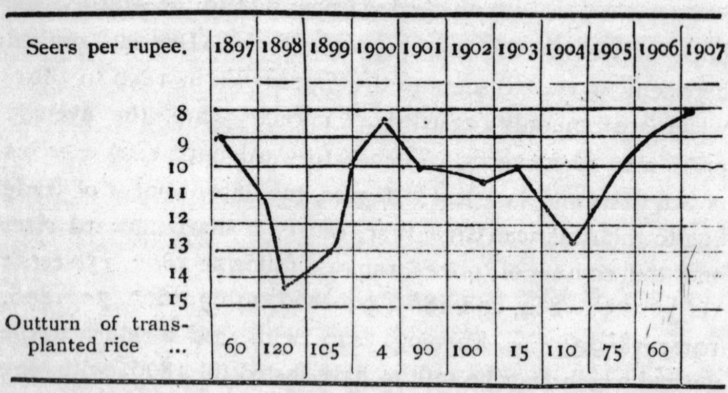

Juāri.

The price of juāri in 1832 is given by Major Lucie Smith as 34 seers to the rupee. From 1834 to 1859, the price varied between 40 and 60 seers to the rupee, and in 1860 the extremely low figure of 80 seers to the rupee was recorded. There was a sharp rise in 1861, when prices went up to 38 seers, and in the ensuing eight years of distress very high quotations were reached. In 1862 the rate was 20 seers, by 1864 it had risen to 13·7: it then declined to 20 seers in 1866, but again went up, this time to the high figure of 10·3 seers in 1869. Then followed the period of normal prices, in which the fluctuations of juāri display exactly the same characteristics as have already been noted in dealing with rice. Excluding the exceptional years 1878—1880, when the rate went up to 19 seers, the gradual rise of prices consequent on the opening of the railway in 1877, is shown by the periodical averages given below:—

Years.			Average price in seers per rupee.
1871—1877	...	...	28
1881—1885	...	...	29·5
1886—1890	...	...	24·5
1891—1895	...	...	20·5

In 1896 the rate stood at 17·5 seers. The next quinquennium 1897—1901 includes both famines, and the average price of juāri rose to 15·1, reaching its highest annual figure in 1900 when the average price was 9·7 seers. Three times, *viz.*, during the months of August 1897, and June and August 1900, the prevailing rate rose to 8·1 seers. In the following quinquennium 1902—06 there was a marked fall and the average price attained 20·6 was equivalent to that obtaining in the years immediately preceding the famines. The chart below shows the course of prices since 1896:—

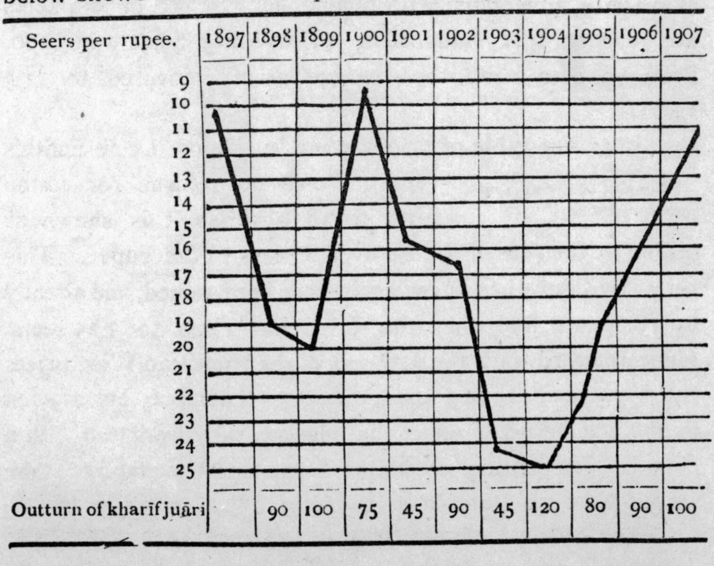

Wheat.

183. In 1832, according to the figures given by Major Lucie Smith, the average price of wheat at the headquarters of the District was 22·8 seers. From 1839 to 1860, the rate fluctuated between 32 and 41 seers, the latter figure being recorded in 1859, which may be looked upon as the last year of patriarchal cheapness in Chānda. From 1861 to 1869 the rise was rapid, the rates, according to the same authority, being 25 seers in 1861, 16 seers in 1862, 13·7 in 1863, 11·7 in 1864, 12·5 in 1865 and 1866, 7·7 in 1867, 11·8 in 1868, and 8·7 in 1869. During the ensuing normal period, the figures were as follows:—

Years.			Average rate in seers per rupee.
1871—1877	...	...	19
1881—1885	...	...	22·5
1886—1890	...	...	19
1891—1895	...	...	16

During the temporary pressure of prices in 1878—1880 wheat was forced up to 13 seers per rupee. In 1896 the retail price of wheat was 14 seers. In the ensuing quinquennium of scarcity, diversified with famine, an average of 9·9 seers was reached, the culminating price being 8 seers in 1900. From 1902 to 1906 the average price recovered to 12·5 seers.

Prices of other agricultural produce.

184. The table of prices given in Major Lucie Smith's report shows no returns for cotton prior to 1839, when it is shown as selling at the rate of a little over 8 seers to the rupee. This very low figure has never again been approached, and already by 1844 we find that the price has risen to 3·25 seers. Henceforward until the outbreak of the American War, prices ruled between about 3 and 4½ seers to the rupee, but as soon as the war began to affect the market they went up with a bound. According to Major Lucie Smith's figures they ranged between 1 and 2 seers from 1862 to 1869, but, in

view of the general drop in prices all over India after 1865, it appears probable that there is some mistake in his figures for the later years. From the cessation of the war until 1884, prices seem to have continued with very slight fluctuations at the rate of about 5 to 6 seers to the rupee, the only exceptional years being 1871 and 1872 when the rates rose to 1·5 and 2·5 seers respectively. In 1885, the price went up to 2 seers, and from that date till 1903 the rate never fell below 2½ seers: in 1907 it stood at 1½ seers. Linseed sold at 11 seers to the rupee in 1866: from 1867 to 1894 the rate varied from 8 to 15 seers: in 1895, it rose to 6·7 seers, but fell again to 10 in 1898. In 1901 and 1902 it stood at only 6 seers, but decreased in 1903 to 8 seers. In 1907 it stood at 7 seers. Til stood at 10 seers in 1866, varied from about 8 to 12½ seers between 1867 and 1887: it made a sharp advance in the following year, and between 1888 and 1894 fluctuated between about 6 and 7 seers. In 1907, the rate was 6 seers. Gram sold at an average rate of 13·7 seers from 1891 to 1895, of 12 seers from 1896 to 1900, and of 13·2 seers from 1901 to 1905. In 1907 the rate was 9 seers.

185. Salt. From 1862 to 1874 the trade in salt was hampered by the existence of the customs line, and the average cost was 13 lbs. per rupee. On the abolition of the line in the latter year, the price immediately fell to 17 lbs. In 1878, when the salt duty was lowered from Rs. 3 to Rs. 2-8 per maund, the price stood at 18 lbs. per rupee, at which figure it remained until 1882 when it fell to 20 lbs. In that year a further reduction of duty to Rs. 2 per maund was effected, and from 1883 till 1887 the cost of salt averaged 22 lbs. to the rupee. In 1888 the duty was again raised to Rs. 2-8 per maund, and thenceforward until the policy of reducing the duty was renewed in 1903, the average cost was 19 lbs. The recent reductions of duty, *viz.*, to Rs. 2 per maund in 1903, to R. 1-8 in 1905, and to R. 1 in 1907 have naturally resulted in a correspond-

ing decline in the cost of salt which is now sold at 36 lbs. (18 *pailīs*) to the rupee.

Prices of other common articles.

186. The following are the present retail prices in Chānda bazar of the common necessaries of life most in demand. Bricks for building houses cost from Rs. 3 to Rs. 6 per 1000; country tiles Rs. 2-8 to Rs. 4 per 1000; sand, 4 cartloads a rupee; bamboos, Rs. 2 to Rs. 7 per 100; small *tattās* for thatching 1'6" × 1' 2" Rs. 7 to Rs. 10 per 1000; large *tattās* 6' × 6' are sold at two to the rupee; small beams cost R. 1, large Rs. 6 each; rafters (*siwars*) if of teak cost R. 1 each, of other kinds of wood Rs. 15 per 1000. A bottle of country liquor holding 60 tolās or three-quarters of a seer, is sold at 10 annas or R. 1-4 according to strength. Country sugar is retailed at 2¾ seers to the rupee, other sugar at 4 seers, *gur* at 6 seers; potatoes 8 to 10 seers per rupee; brinjals 2 pice and onions 4 pice a seer; chillies 3 seers the rupee; cloves 14 annas a seer; cardamums 20 tolās to the rupee; cocoanut oil 12 annas, and linseed, til and castor oil 10 annas per seer; milk 8 seers to the rupee; *ghī* R. 1 to R. 1-4 per seer; cotton, seed (*sarkī*) 17, and oil-cake 13 seers per rupee; tamarind fruit, two maunds of 12 seers each per rupee. Firewood costs R. 1-8 to Rs. 2 per cartload; cow-dung cakes 4 annas per 100; *karbī* Rs. 6-4 per 100 bundles, grass Rs. 4 to Rs. 6 per 1000 *pūlas*. Cooking utensils are retailed at R. 1-12 per seer if of brass, at Rs. 2 to Rs. 2-12 per seer if of copper: if of the alloy of zinc and copper or brass called *bharat* the price is R. 1-2 per seer. Large iron buckets cost from R. 1 to R. 1-4, and small from 8 to 10 annas a piece. Common kerosene oil is sold at Rs. 2-8 per tin or 2 annas a bottle. Among leather articles, *mots* cost from Rs 10 to Rs. 20, hand buckets Rs. 3 to Rs. 5, ropes 75 feet long and 1½ inches in diameter Rs. 7 to Rs. 10 a piece; shoes, R. 1 to R. 1-8 a pair. Common cloth sells at 3 to 4 annas a yard; a pair of ordinary *dhotis* fetch Rs. 2 to Rs. 3-4 and the coarse cloth known as *khādi*

is sold at R. 1-4 per *thān* of 20 by 1½ cubits. Cotton and *newār* tape for cots is sold at from Rs. 4 to Rs. 6 for a piece 100 cubits long and 4 inches broad; ordinary sewing thread is sold at three pice a reel; a box containing 20 white *muttās* of No. 30 and weighing four seers is sold at Rs. 6. The prices of country carts are Rs. 40 to Rs. 100 for a *dhamnī*, Rs. 20 to Rs. 30 for a *rengī*, Rs 20 to Rs. 40 for a *khāchar*, Rs. 20 to Rs. 40 for a *bandī*, and Rs. 100 or Rs. 150 to Rs. 200 for a tongā.

WAGES.

Statistics of wages.

187. An able-bodied agricultural labourer earned Rs. 4-8 per month in 1893, Rs. 5-2 in 1895, Rs. 4-12 in 1897 and Rs. 5 in 1898. His wages were reduced to Rs. 3-12 in 1899, a rate which continued till 1901, as a result of the famine of 1900. They recovered to Rs. 4-11 in 1902 and 1903 and at the present time (1908) the wages of agricultural labour vary from 2 annas to 3 and 4 annas a day. In the towns of Warorā and Chānda coolies can earn 4 to 6 annas daily. These rates are for males only. Females get half the wages of males. A common blacksmith earned Rs. 9-8 per mensem in 1893. During the next four years his earnings varied between Rs. 10 and Rs. 10-8 and fell to Rs. 9-8 in 1898 as a result of famine in 1897. Since then they have improved and we find Rs. 11-4 recorded during the following three years. In 1902 they rose to Rs. 13-2 and in 1903 to Rs. 15 a month. Now (in 1908) he receives 8 annas a day in Sironchā, 12 annas in Chānda and up to a rupee in Warorā. A common mason is shown as having earned Rs. 10-6 a month in 1893, Rs. 13 in 1895, Rs. 12-8 in 1897, Rs. 10-5 in 1899 and Rs. 11-4 in 1900. The wages improved in 1902 and 1903 when he received Rs. 13-2 as his monthly income. In 1908 he got 10 annas a day rising to a rupee in Warorā. A common carpenter who is better paid than either the blacksmith or the mason earned Rs. 12 a month in 1893, Rs. 12-4 in 1869, Rs. 14 in 1898 and Rs. 12-9 in 1899. In 1900 he

received Rs. 13-2 and since then his wages have decidedly improved, having risen to Rs. 14 a month in 1901, Rs. 15 in 1902 and Rs. 18-12 in 1903. In 1908 he was getting from 12 annas a day to R. 1-4, the latter being the rate obtainable in Warorā.

Farm-servants.

188. In Chānda tahsīl the common term for an agricultural servant in regular employment is *awāri*, and in Warorā he is called *Sahā korvyā mānus* or the man getting 6 *kuros*. In Sironchā the Telugu word *palerū* is used. The dependants of an *awāri* or *Sahā koryvā mānus*, *i.e.* his wife or his small son, if they assist him in his duties, are called *râpte.* Farm-servants receive the bulk of their wages in grain, an arrangement which tells in their favour when, as of recent years, the prices of agricultural produce range high. There has, it is true, been a tendency in the rice tract to reduce the actual amount of grain paid to the farm-servant, but this reduction has not been effected in anything like inverse ratio to the increase in the price of grain. Thus, at the first settlement the servant of a rice cultivator received 740 seers of rice as his yearly wage besides grain perquisites amounting to 315 seers: now he only gets 600 seers and grain perquisites amounting to about 130 seers, but meanwhile prices have risen roughly cent. per cent. In the open-field tract the amount of grain remuneration has risen from 635 seers of juāri at the last settlement to 725 seers at present, and thus, having regard to the rise in the price of juāri, it is obvious that the farm-servant of this tract has considerably improved his position.

At present the fixed monthly wage of a farm-servant in regular employ in the rice tract is 5 *kuros* of *dhān* per mensem in most tracts, and 6 *kuros* in the Warorā tahsīl. In the open-field tract the monthly rate is 5 *kuros* and 2 *pailīs* of juāri. But in either case this remuneration is swelled by perquisites of various kinds. Thus in the open tract, the farm-servant gets a *pailī* of each kind of grain sown: when employed in watching the crops he may take three *pailīs* of juāri each day as remuneration, and besides this he will probably have a fighting-cock to bear him company which with its living will pick up a free living among the juāri pods[1] : he has the right of *sarwā* or gleaning the field, and in addition to this he gets about three *kuros* for cutting and bringing the crop to the threshing-floor. In this latter task his wife assists, and the dues he receives for it are known as *wātā-wadgā*, because the woman holds out her cloth so as to form a hollow (*wātā*) which is filled with ears of juāri while the man gets a *wadgā* or basketful of grain for his share of the work. Besides this the wife gets an allowance of three *kuros* for bringing food to the field: this is called *upsarā*, and she also grinds the master's grain and makes cow-dung cakes for him, taking half of the latter in reward for her labour. In the rice tract the servant gets four annas as a *pourboire* during the damp process of transplantation : he has the right of gleaning, while at reaping time he takes a handful out of each *bojhā* or head-load that he carries to the threshing-floor. If employed on *rakhwāli* or watching the crops, he can cut two *pailīs* of *dhān* per diem. In both the rice and open tracts alike, there are various other perquisites and privileges Thus each year the servant gets Rs. 2 to buy himself a blanket (locally called *wāz*) and R. 1 or R. 1-4 to buy a pair of shoes and free food is given at the cost of the master at the festivals of Polā and Nāgpanchamī. Another right, known as *māterā* is that of taking the sweepings of the threshing-floor after threshing is over and extracting the grain from them. Again, being as it were the natural priest of the god of the threshing-floor, the farm-servant gets an allowance of grain called *khātdeo* for offerings prior to threshing. Other privileges are free fire-wood to the extent of two cartloads and a rupee's worth of thatching grass. It is rather difficult to calculate what all these extras amount to in the aggregate, but they may roughly

[1] These cocks are worth as much as Rs. 5 : on bazar days in the cold weather they are set to fight each other with iron spurs tied on to their feet, and the owner of the winning ock takes the vanquished bird.

be estimated to average between half a *khandī* and one *khandī*, apart from the cash doles.

Casual agricultural labourers.

189. Casual agricultural labourers, employed at periods of exceptional pressure, usually get two *pailīs* a day, or, if required to watch a crop at night, three *pailīs*. For sowing and weeding women are as a rule employed, and are remunerated at the rate of one *pailī* a day for the former and three pice a day for the latter. For transplanting rice, a man is paid R. 1 for five days and a woman R. 1 for ten days. For reaping juāri men get 4 *pailīs* and women 2 *pailīs* a day, for wheat the rate is two *pailīs* of the grain for men and one *pailī* for women. Other grains are usually paid for in cash at 2 annas a day. The picking of cotton is paid for by a share of from $\frac{1}{16}$ h to $\frac{1}{20}$th of the amount picked.

Village grazier.

190. The regular village grazier is called the *dhorkī* and gets 1 anna per month for each head of cattle under his charge. The cattle are grazed at the owner's risk, and the grazier is exempted from making good any losses, an irresponsibility which is sometimes, though not often, abused. Two or three tenants often club together and hire a boy to look after their animals, while very well-to-do persons have a private grazier employed exclusively in their own service. Wealthy landlords hire a women as *shenakari* to collect and stack the cow-dung of their cattle. She either stacks it for fuel or pits it for manure, and she has also other duties such as *leeping* the floor and white-washing the walls.

Village servants.

191. Village servants in name and duties usually correspond to those found in other Districts of the Province, and their functions are for the most part so familiar that they require no detailed description. The Lohār or Khāti gets 2 or 3 *kuros* a year for attending to each tenant's ploughs, but the tendency is, as elsewhere, growing yearly stronger to remunerate him by the job. So also with the Barhai or village carpenter, who is

even more commonly paid by the job. The Mhāli or barber (called Mangali in Sironchā) and Wāthi or washerman (called Chakali in Sironchā) receive three to four *kuros* a year. On festive and ceremonious occasions they are generally given food and a small cash perquisite for drink in Sironchā. In some places the rate is one *kuro* of juāri for each adult male in the family and perquisites amounting to about a *kuro* with some food on festivals. They are however not engaged by all tenants but only by mālguzārs and big tenants, poor tenants paying 2 pice each time they require their services.

The Bhūmak also called Deohari and in Sironchā Permadu worships the village gods and keeps off evil influences from the village. He also supplies *pān patrāwali* or leaf-plates on festivals and at feasts, and cleans the cooking pots of Government officials visiting the village. For these services he receives one *kuro* or more according to circumstances from each tenant and perquisites amounting to about a *kuro*. He is sometimes given a piece of land rent free (rent Rs. 3 or Rs. 4).

The Joshi or village priest has no fixed *hak*. He fixes the date of *sājoni* when the mālguzār with his tenants starts ploughing. If he goes to the farm, every tenant gives him from 4 to 8 *pailīs*. He is generally paid by the job. His free for officiating at a marriage may be R. 1-4 and for reciting *kathā* R. 1. The Chamār known as Mādgi in Sironchā is not a regular village servant and is said to be remunerated by job work in Chānda and Garhchirolī tahsīls and by a fixed contribution in Warorā and Sironchā tahsīls. In Sironchā he receives one *kunchā* of juāri (14 seers) for each species of articles he supplies, *e.g.*, for a pair of shoes one *kunchā*, for leather thongs one *kunchā*, and so on. Besides he is customarily allowed to collect the remnants of the harvest floor. In Warorā he gets 4 *pailīs* to a *kuro* of juāri per plough for the repairs of shoes, etc. For an ornamental shoe for which this District is famous he generally gets from R. 1 to R. 1-12. The ornamental work is generally done in silk and takes the shape of flowers or pictorial fishes. An ordinary pair of shoes will fetch from 14 annas to R. 1-4.

MANUFACTURES.

The tasar silk industry.

192. The tasar silk industry has for some years attracted the attention of Government as a valuable and interesting cottage industry capable of considerable development. It divides itself naturally into three branches, the first being concerned with the rearing of the silk cocoons, the second with the spinning of yarn from the cocoons, and the third with the weaving of the yarn into the finished article. Chānda is more famous for its spinning industry than for the other two departments.

(i) Rearing of tasar silk worms.

The rearing of the tasar silk worm is conducted in the forests of the Bramhapurī, Garhchirolī and Sironchā tahsīls. This branch of the industry is entirely in the hands of Dhīmars, except in Sironchā, where, curiously enough, the Bhois or local Dhīmars absolutely refuse to have anything to do with the rearing of worms, and this task falls to the Gonds and a few Naiks. The operation is hedged about with countless superstitions and, while engaged upon it, the Dhīmar entirely cuts himself off from all intercourse with his family and lives a life apart. In this District, seed cocoons are invariably wild, and this is an advantage as the cocoons deteriorate under the influence of domestication. On the other hand, they are small and of poor quality even in their wild state, while the domesticated Chānda cocoon is the worst in the whole Province. This dependence on wild cocoons has another drawback. Each rearer is only able to collect a few cocoons, and he has therefore to breed two preliminary crops merely with a view of increasing his stock so that it is only when he has raised a third crop that he is able to sell to the spinner. The disadvantage of this is that the worms, which are heirs to countless dangers, are exposed to those dangers for a much longer period than is usual elsewhere, and, in addition to this, the third or *jadnī* crop on which the breeder solely relies comes at the beginning of the cold weather at a period when the worms are subject to a particularly great risk of disease. Frequently, especially in the last few years, crops have been entirely lost from this cause. The worms are always reared out of doors, generally on the *sāj* or *yen* tree (*Terminalia tomentosa*) which is roughly pollarded for the purpose. The risks to be faced come not only from birds, against which the worms can be more or less guarded, but also from the uncontrollable forces of wind and weather. Long drought, severe cold, storms or continuous wet weather are all in different ways fatal: heavy rain after protracted drought induces the much dreaded disease known as grasserie. Cocoons are sold to the Koshti spinners at rates varying from Rs. 2 to Rs. 5 per 1000; the latter rate, however, is only approached for superior cocoons or in bad years when the supply is short. An average crop for one breeder would be about 5000 cocoons. Tasar-worm rearers are not usually welcome guests to the Forest Officer, as their operations bring in no revenue to speak of and are destructive to the jungle. The policy of Government has therefore been in the direction of placing the rearers under the wing of the revenue officials, by setting aside areas of suitable B-class forest and handing over the management of these to the revenue authorities. Twenty acres of forest, worked in rotation for periods of four years, were laid down as a sufficient allowance for the support of one Dhīmar family. The main object in view in these proceedings was to increase the supply of cocoons, as it was held that the demand for tasar silk was ample, and that the great want was an increased outturn of cocoons: it is doubtful, however, if this view is well founded. The average area set aside for rearing the tasar worm in Government forest during the last three years is 1882 acres

(2) Tasar silk spinning.

The spinning industry is conducted by Koshtīs or Koskātis, who prepare the cocoons for reeling off by boiling them in an infusion of water and castor seeds or the ashes of the *agrā* plant. Probably there are about 200 families of tasar spinners in the whole District, and they are for the most part concentrated into Saolī, Chāmursi, Garhchirolī, Armori and Nāgbhīr. Nāgbhīr is the most famous centre of the industry, and before the famine there used to be 100 families of spinners in this place alone. The Nāgbhīr spinners make a very uniform and high class yarn in the preparation of which they reject the inferior surface fibre and frequently mix the native cocoons with superior cocoons imported from Bengal. One person can reel from 25 to 75 cocoons per diem, the average number being 50 or 60. According to the statistics collected by Mr. Mukerji, 10,000 cocoons yield from 30 to 37½ tolās of silk: the yarn is sold in bundles called *punjās* and 100 *punjās*, weighing from 40 to 55 tolās, sell at rates varying from Rs. 5 to Rs. 8, according to the quality and the demand. Thread is made of various strengths from 3—ply up to 12—ply. There is much room for improvement in the methods of reeling, which are of a very primitive kind: the spinning machine is, however, of a superior type to that used in adjoining Districts.

Imitation silk made in Germany of cellulose has of late years reduced prices and to some extent threatened the industry. But there is a good demand for Chānda yarn at Umrer, Paonī and Nāgpur, and the spinning industry is fairly flourishing.

(3) Tasar weaving.

In the weaving of tasar silk this District does not excel and weavers are but few in number. Four families at Armori and six at Chāmursi appear to exhaust the roll: these do their own spinning as well as weaving. The material produced is coarse in texture and is not for a moment to be compared with the products of Sambalpur : it has, however, good wearing qualities, and for this reason is more popular than the more delicate fabrics of that District. At Armori *sāris* are made with ornamental *ruiphuli* borders, but at Chāmursi plain *sāris* or at most *sāris* with a plain border were till lately all that could be produced. These were of a dirty white colour—the colour of widow's weeds, and no woman would wear them. In 1903, however, Government deputed a weaver from Sambalpur to show the weavers of Chāmursi how to dye thread and to weave the ornamental pattern which takes its name from the village of Barpāli. A few of the weavers succeeded in learning the desired lesson; but as they are unable to produce a *sāri* of this type for less than Rs. 30 or Rs. 35 and as they received no orders the experiment has not been an unqualified success. It is doubtful whether even from the artistic standpoint much is to be gained from the introduction of this pattern. The texture of the local fabric is so rough that the pattern, graceful on the more delicate fabric of Sambalpur, here loses much of its effect. *Pagrīs* or *phetās, sāris* and *dhotis*[1] are the principal articles turned out, and Mr. Mukerji mentions with approbation one very neat pattern of the latter which he saw at Armori; it was, however, very highly priced as compared with similar articles made in Bengal. Tasar silk as well as ordinary floss silk is looked on with favour by natives as particularly pure and suitable for ceremonial purposes: it is not polluted, like cotton, by the touch of an unholy thing. A piece of finished tasar 9 yards long by 24 inches broad fetches Rs. 4 at Chāmursi and Rs. 5 at Chānda, but superior pieces may run to Rs 6; these prices fluctuate with the supply of silk, in bad years as much as Rs. 8 or 9 being charged.

Formerly there was a fair export trade in tasar yarn and silk from about Dābha to the Nizām's dominions, but this has now altogether declined under the competition of German imitation silk. All branches of the tasar industry suffered heavily during the famines, but have since to some extent recovered.

---

[1] *Dhoti*, a flowing cloth bound round the waist and legs. It is generally bordered with purple or red, blue or green like the *toga prætexta*, and in Mysore the *dholī* is called *togataru*. —(Birdwood.)

Silk weaving other than tasar.

193. Apart from the tasar industry, the silk weaving of the District is of little importance. In Chānda itself there are some seven or eight houses at which families of a caste called Patwī weave cloths of pure silk, and at Dābha there are two more such houses. The silk used is imported from Bengal, and the articles produced are *pitāmbars* or loin-cloths for men and *cholis* or breast-cloths for women. These are nearly always of a red or a yellow colour, but Patwīs can also use green and rose tints of silk. Correctly speaking a *pitāmbar* should be yellow, since the word Pitāmbara, one of the most ancient epithets of Vishnu, means 'clothed in yellow garments.' A *pitāmbar* measuring 10 by 2¼ cubits costs some Rs. 9 or Rs. 10, and a *choli* R. 1 or R. 1-4. A *sāri* measuring 16 by 2¼ cubits costs from Rs. 18 to Rs. 25. Silk cloths are also sold by the piece called *khan* measuring 2¼ cubits by 1 cubit: these pieces are made up into *cholis* by women purchasers. The local silk fabrics are not in demand among the really well-to-do for important festive occasions such as marriages: for these, silk *sāris* from Poona and Jeolā costing anything up to Rs. 100 are in request.

Fabrics of mixed silk and cotton.

194. Much more common and more adapted to the popular purse are fabrics of mixed silk and cotton manufactured by the local Koshtīs. Cotton cloths with silk borders are woven in many villages, more particularly in the north of the District. Probably 250 or 300 families are engaged in weaving of this type in Chānda alone, and in both Armori and Chimūr there are said to be at least 100 families so employed. *Dhotis* are the articles most commonly produced in most villages, while in Chānda itself *sāris*, *pātals*, *phetās* and other cloths are also made. The *dhotis* generally have red borders with a pattern, and are also embroidered with gold or silver thread: in villages adjoining the Umrer tahsīl of the Nāgpur District, a few families of Koshtīs make silk-bordered *sāris* and *dhotis* of the well-known Umrer stamp. A *dhoti* of

mixed cotton and silk usually costs from Rs. 4 to Rs. 12: *sāris* for women, here called *pātrans*, range from Rs. 5 up to Rs. 30 or Rs. 40, but the usual price is from Rs. 5 to Rs. 8 for a white *sāri* ornamented with gold thread. A very neat pattern of mixed *sāri* for marriages, locally called *triguni*, is turned out in Chānda at popular prices, and a small girl-bride can cut a very presentable figure in one of these at a cost of Rs. 3-4. *Phetās* or turban-cloths measuring 16 by 1½ cubits and diversified with gold thread are sold at Rs. 4 or Rs. 4-8.

The silk used in these fabrics originally comes from Bengal: it is converted into white or yellow yarn at Nāgpur before being sent on to Chānda. The cotton thread employed is usually of a finer quality than can be produced in the local mills, and probably at least three-quarters of it comes either from England or from Sholāpur: the counts used range up to 60's, but 40's are the finest commonly in use. The gold and silver thread used for decorative purposes is of German origin.

Cotton fabrics.

195. The cotton fabrics of Chānda formerly possessed a wide reputation for excellence and durability: they used to be largely exported to western India, and Sir R. Jenkins mentions that prior to 1802 A.D. coarse cloths made at Chānda found their way as far afield as Arabia. White cotton *selās* for loin-cloths, white cotton *dorias* and *param*, a coarse white cotton fabric used for native saddle-cloths, horse clothing, etc., are the articles singled out by Sir R. Jenkins as the special products of Chānda; but none of these are said to be made now. The same authority also wrote that 'the chintzes of Chānda are much worn in Gondwāna and Berār by the women.' Much of this glory has now departed, although the *sāris* of Chānda still possess a more or less extended reputation, and a certain amount of local cotton cloth is exported to Amraoti and Akolā in Berār. The anticipations of Major Lucie Smith, who was confident that Chānda, thanks to its possession of coal and cotton in close juxtaposition, would ere

long command the markets of Central India with its piece-goods, have fallen very wide of the mark. So far from commanding other markets, the piece-goods of Chānda have to a large extent been elbowed out of their own: according to the estimates of local cloth merchants of the town, the annual cloth transactions of Chānda city amount to five lakhs: of this three lakhs represents the value of cloth imported from outside, while of the remaining two lakhs worth, which is produced locally, only one half is consumed locally, the other half being exported: this is of course avowedly only a very rough estimate. The mills of Hinganghāt and Nāgpur are easily able to flood the local market with cheap cloth: a common cotton *sāri* with a red and blue check made by Momins of Nāgpur and sold at Chānda for R. 1-10 easily undersells any similar article of local manufacture. In spite of these facts, there is still an extensive manufacture or coarse cotton cloths in nearly every village. Dhers of Mahārs are usually the weavers. They turn out coarse *dhotis* which sell at Rs. 2 to Rs. 3 the pair, and *sāris* at a similar price, and these garments are largely worn by the lower classes. The counts of thread employed are coarse, never higher than 20's and usually not above 12's or 16's, and this thread is now practically all obtained from local mills. After manufacture, the cloth is often dyed or printed in colours by local Chhīpas or Rangāris. Mahārs also prepare a coarse red cloth called *toshak* which is stuffed with raw cotton and sold in the form of a quilt for about R. 1-8. Probably there are at least 250 families of Dhers in Chānda alone who are engaged in the manufacture of cotton cloths, and a proportionate number would be found in most of the larger villages.

Dyeing.

196. The subordinate industry of dyeing merits a brief notice. In this department again Chānda once boasted a considerable fame which it has now lost, and possessed a flourishing export trade which has now ceased. Aniline dyes have, as

in most places, killed the old vegetable dyes which won the District its reputation. For a time the red dye obtained from the *al* or Indian mulberry tree (*Morinda citrifolia*) held its own, but even this branch of the industry is now completely extinct. In Mr. Russell's monograph on the Dyeing industry it is stated that one large dealer, who had formerly exported *al*-dyed cloths to the value of Rs. 4,000 a month, had within a few years practically lost all his trade, and did not export above Rs. 100 worth a month. This was in 1896: *al*-dyeing has now completely collapsed in this District, and cloths dyed by this process are now imported from Nāndurā in Berār where some peculiar property in the water is said to give a brilliance of colour surpassing that of the old local product. There are now perhaps eighty families of dyers in Chānda: some of these are Chhīpas, who get their name from their practice of printing or stamping the cloths which they dye with various ornamental patterns, generally black and white on a red ground: the rest are plain dyers, Rangāri or Rangrez.

Woollen manufactures.

197. In woollen fabrics, the only local manufacture is that of blankets. The castes employed in these are Dhangars and Kurumwārs, the latter being a caste of Kanarese origin not found elsewhere in this Province. Both castes unite the occupation of keeping sheep with that of weaving blankets. Dhangars make better blankets than Kurumwārs. The blankets produced are of a dirty grey colour approaching black, this being the natural colour of the wool out of which they are made: they are sold at prices ranging from a few annas up to Rs. 3 according to size: an ordinary sized blanket measuring 7½ feet by 3 feet fetches about R. 1-8. The industry is not a lucrative one.

Metal work. Brass and copper ware.

198. Chānda is the only District of these Provinces the metal work of which receives any notice from Birdwood in his 'Industrial Arts of India.' He says of it: 'Chānda

'was formerly distinguished for its workers in the precious 'and baser metals, but much of their fame has now been lost 'owing to the decreased demand for their wares under British 'rule. The District, however, still (1880) possesses good 'goldsmiths and silversmiths, whose work is marked by the 'strongest local character.' Brass work is still carried on to a considerable extent, the chief seats of the industry being Chānda, Neri and Bramhapurī: at the same time utensils of brass, copper and alloys are extensively imported from Poona, Nāsik, Mirzāpur, and Bhandāra. At Neri cast and wrought work is done with an alloy called *bharat* consisting of two parts copper to one part of zinc. A good deal of work is also done at various places in bell-metal, an alloy composed of four parts copper to one part tin or tinfoil. Bells of fair size and excellent tone are moulded from this amalgam, and plates or saucers in which anything acid in the way of food is to be kept are also made of it, since acids do not affect such ware in the manner that they do brass and copper. Copper articles of ordinary household use are made by three methods, simple hammering, heating and welding, and by preparing the article in two or more parts which are subsequently soldered together. But the domestic use of copper is not regarded with favour by orthodox Hindus, and copper utensils are consequently not in much request. Pots made of brass with a copper rim are called *Gangā Jamuni*, as they are supposed to symbolise the confluence of the dark water of the Jumna with the muddy stream of the Ganges: a small trade is done in brass and bell-metal ornaments, but these are only worn by the lower castes, and the ordinary Panchāl, deeming it beneath his dignity to produce them, has left this branch of manufacture to a caste known as Watāri. Ornaments for bullocks are freely produced; well-to-do mālguzārs and Seths delight to see their bullocks' horns tipped with a cone of brass, and their necks graced with a brass necklace in the shape of a linked chain in figure of eight pattern or with hollow globes of bell-metal which make a musical tinkle when a stone is placed inside them. Little is attempted in the way of ornamental work: enterprise in this direction is confined to inscribed and scroll work, which is, however, of fair merit. Two or three artisans of Bābupeth near Chānda have received certificates of merit for their productions in recent years. They produce a very pleasing design of *lotā*, in which a burnished copper centre is set between artistically inscribed upper and lower portion of brass. They can also turn out lamps of graceful shape and charming workmanship, but such things not being much in demand are only taken in hand when specially ordered. Compared with the celebrated brass work of other Provinces, the local industry of course ranks low, but within the limits of this Province, the artistic standard of Chānda ware ranks higher than that of any other District save Saugor.

Working in iron.

199. The smelting industry of this District was formerly one of considerable importance, ranking second only to that of Jubbulpore. As will be shown in describing the minerals of the District, iron is abundant and widely distributed: it is also easily extracted and broken up and therefore eminently adapted to the simple native methods of mining and smelting. Of late years, however, the industry has been rapidly on the decline owing to the pressure of foreign competition, and this downward tendency has been accelerated by the recent famines: heavy charges for fuel and the rise in wages caused by railway construction have also in large measure contributed to the general depression of the smelters. In 1900, there were 52 furnaces in the District; during the three following years the number fell to between 14 and 16: it recovered to 41 in 1904, but declined again to 14 in 1905 and to 9 in 1906, and smelting operations are confined to a few villages in the Wairāgarh range. The following are the statistics of production in alternate recent years:—

Year.			Tons of ore extracted.	Resulting quantity of iron.
1900	...	...	529	125
1902	...	...	202	40
1904	...	...	115	23
1906	...	...	89	18

These statistics are no doubt very rough, but they give a sufficient idea of the decline of the industry. When the railway now under construction to Gondia is open, it will doubtless, running as it will through the heart of the iron-producing country, lead to a still further decline, but probably the industry will not altogether die out, as the local iron is far superior to imported iron for certain restricted purposes where great malleability is essential. Smelting takes place in a conical furnace 5 or 6 feet in height: the fuel used is charcoal, three units of charcoal being fed into the furnace for each unit of ore. The operation takes about six hours, and the resulting mass of spongy crude iron weighs about 20 seers having a bulk of only one-fifth of the weight of iron ore used. In its crude state the iron is locally called *kīt* and is worth about R. 1-8 or Rs. 2 per maund. Before being brought to the market it is as a rule heated in a refining furnace and hammered so as to express the slag, a process which reduces its weight by about one half but much increases its value. The refined bloom or *chūl* is cut almost in two, in order apparently to show its quality, and is then sold to the Lohārs, who work it up into the usual household and agricultural implements. Various castes are engaged in smelting: in Bramhapurī the chief are Gonds, Gowāris, Dhīmars, Telis and Khaire Kunbīs: in Garhchirolī, Telis generally own its furnaces, while Dhīmars are employed by them as coolies, and in Sironchā the smelters are a tribe of Mannewārs. The manufacture of articles of iron is confined in this District to the simplest wrought work and requires no description.

Gold and silver ware.

200. Chānda city contains some forty families of gold and silver smiths, but there is really very little to say about the local industry, which only receives a few cursory notices in Mr. Nunn's monograph on the gold and silver ware of the Central Provinces. The people regard ornaments primarily in the light of a portable savings bank, and do not care to pay for artistic workmanship when the ultimate destination of their jewels may not improbably be the melting pot. The work of Telugu craftsmen does however make some pretensions to artistic merit, and in grace and lightness far surpasses that of the ordinary Sonār of the Central Provinces. Head ornaments, called *rākhris*, made with a base of gold and a top of silver and fitted up with lac in the centre, are popular among both Telugus and Marāthās. It would be impossible to enumerate the countless varieties of other ornaments. Most of the gold and silver smiths are compelled to eke out their living by also working in baser metals: not to be reduced to this necessity gives a certain social distinction: the Sonār's position as a pawn-broker also, as is well known, gives him an opportunity of making money in various ways which will not bear too close a scrutiny, and often brings him into contact with the police. Sonārs, Panchāls and Kamsaliwārs are the castes occupied in the gold and silver craft of this District: the last named are a Telugu caste who ape Brahmanical customs and are anxious to be called Vishwa Brāhmans. Some local ware was sent to the Delhi Exhibition.

Leather goods.

201. Chānda and Bramhapurī have, according to Birdwood, a great reputation in the Centra Provinces for the manufacture of nativel slippers. These are decorated with ornamental patterns in silk thread stitched on to the leather: some specimens were

sent to the Delhi Exhibition. Saoli and Chāmursi have also at best a local reputation for their slippers. The cost of a pair of slippers is from R. 1 to R. 1-8. Drums, bellows, *mots*, buckets, water bottles, *jots* for young bullocks and ropes are the other chief articles which are manufactured in leather. Sironchā and Mūl are the villages which produce the best *mots*: these are sold at from Rs. 10 to Rs. 20 in the Chānda bazar. Travellers for Cutchi firms go on regular tours in outlying villages and buy up hides, especially those of horses which no Chamār will touch. Chamārs and Mādgis are the only castes who work in leather in this District, and they have of late years felt the pressure of Cutchi competition in the demand for skins. In Sironchā, there survives one Chamār, the only one in the whole tahsīl, who learnt superior methods of working leather from the troops who were quartered there many years ago, but his field for exercising his attainments is very limited. Chānda city has also two or three superior craftsmen, one of whom boasts that his uncle used to be Chamār by royal letters patent to the Bhonsla Rājās of Nāgpur, and received a stipend of ten Nāgpuri rupees per mensem out of the royal purse. This man's embroidery work displays some skill, and slippers and *chārjāmas* made by him were sent to the Delhi Darbār.

Manufacture of *pohe*.

202. A special industry of a rather peculiar type, which is confined to the western portion of the District, principally in the zamīndāris and the adjoining tracts that contain plenty of forest, is the manufacture of *pohe*, a special preparation of rice. Mr. Hemingway gives the following account of this industry. The grain is prepared by tenants immediately the new grain is available; the unhusked rice is boiled directly after threshing, and is then pounded with the ordinary *mūsal*; in the pounding it becomes husked and flattened out; it is then roughly cleaned and is ready for consumption. It is prepared and exported in large quantities from the zamīndāris and the Wairāgarh pargana to both Nāgpur and Hinganghāt, and it is a most

marketable commodity: it may be eaten raw, or with sugar or salt according to taste and means : and it is a favourite food for tenants to carry about with them on long journeys, since it needs no further preparation. It is a bulky grain to export; but the *dhān* cannot be taken to the bazar and prepared there, since a large amount of fuel is needed for its preparation : and it can be made only when the grain is perfectly fresh. For these reasons it is prepared only in the tracts where fuel is cheapest, and only during the months of November and December.

Other manufactures.

203. A coarse kind of paper used once to be made at Chānda after a very primitive fashion by means of pulping old gunny bags. This industry is now extinct. Of more importance was the brick and tile factory which used to be kept up in connection with the Warorā Colliery. This was opened in 1891 and closed down in 1906 when the subsidence of the colliery rendered the further extraction of fire-clay impossible : during the interval it supplied large quantities of bricks and tiles to surrounding Districts and to the Public Works Department. The manufacture was extremely lucrative : not only was the original capital outlay of Rs. 57,000 redeemed within the first two years, but surplus profits amounting to over 1·71 lakhs were realised during the whole period of the working of the factory. In 1902, 276,000 bricks valued at Rs. 38,900 and 126,000 tiles valued at Rs. 13,600 were turned out. Stone carving is carried on at Bhatāla and Jāmbulghāta in the Warorā tahsīl, and also near Chānda itself, where a stone is obtained from a white argillaceous band which is very skilfully carved into minute forms of ornaments. But the black soapstone of Jāmbulghāta has the widest reputation in the District, and is extensively used for shaping into bowls and platters, pestles and mortars, etc.; just at present, however, the quarry is closed for lack of bidders. Pestles and mortars are also fashioned out of gneiss and granite at Jāmbulghāta.

The stone carving of Chānda is mentioned with approval by Birdwood. Glass bangles are made at Chānda, Bhāndak, Warorā, Bramhapurī and other places; sometimes, too, glass is worked up into globes to ornament the roofs of houses. The glass used in these manufactures is obtained from Kamptee and Nāgpur. Bracelets of cocoanut-shell are made by Panchāls and are largely worn by Kunbīs. The village of Pombhurnā is locally famous for the manufacture of lacquered articles of wood, generally in the form of sticks, boxes, plates or children's toys. These are manufactured out of some soft wood, *Wrightia tinctoria*, *Wrightia tomentosa* or *Holarrhena antidysenterica*, particularly the latter which is called in the vernacular *kūda;* the lacquer is applied simply by pressing a stick of lac against the article as it revolves on a lathe. Four houses of Panchāls are thus employed in Pombhurnā. Bangles of lac are also made in many places. The bamboo and grass matting work of the District is also distinctly good, and is widely practised. Along the banks of the Indrāvati and the Tālpir grows a rush called *tunga* which is woven by the Mārias, Gottes and Koīs into mats, very soft and cool and pleasant, which are much in demand as sleeping mattresses, and resemble a coarse China matting. Ahīri and Sironchā are the chief seats of manufacture and the mats of these places are freely retailed in the Chānda bazar at six annas each. Large bamboo tattis 20 cubits long by 9 inches broad called *gontāls* come to Chānda from Mūl and the adjacent bazars, and are sold at Rs. 2-4 a piece. Hemp ropes are made at Chānda. Carts and cart-wheels are extensively manufactured in many villages, particularly in the north of the District, where Chimūr and Neri supply most of the Wardhā District with cart-wheels.

Weights and measures.

204. The chief measures in use in this District are the *pailī* weighing 100 tolās or $2\frac{1}{2}$ English pounds, and the *kuro* composed of eight *pailīs*. In a few places, *e.g.*,

Rājgarh and Talodhi the *pailī* is somewhat larger and is equal to 105 tolās. *Kuros* are of two kinds: the *lambari kuro*, comprising 8 *pailīs* or 20 lbs., and the *bhatya kuro* comprising 6 *pailīs* or 15 lbs; the latter is the one employed in calculating the grain remuneration of farm-servants. One hundred and sixty *pailīs* make one *lambari khandī* while 120 *pailīs* make a *bhatya khandī*. The *pailī* itself is made up of 4 seers of 25 tolās each. These seers are known as *pailī chā ser*, and must not be confused with the ordinary seer of 80 tolās or 2 English lbs. The lowest unit of weight is the *ringa*: 4 *ringas* make one *pailī chā ser*. Standard weights have not as yet been introduced, but it is proposed to introduce them into the municipalities of Warorā and Chānda very shortly. These standard weights are the *chhatāk* of 5 tolās, the seer of 80 tolās, and the maund of 40 seers. The maund is of very varying composition, differing in weight with different commodities. Thus only 12 seers go to the maund of lac, gum or *harrā*, while the maund of *gur* is 11 seers in Warorā and 10 seers in Chānda: the unit here is the *mudda* or ball, a lump of *gur* about 1½ seers in weight: eight of these go to the maund. Similarly 12 seers go to the maund of *haldī*, chillies and cotton seed, and twenty such maunds constitute a *khandī*. The maund of uncleaned cotton weighs 24 seers. A maund of iron contains 14 seers, while a maund of brass or copper contains 14½ seers Locally grown *singhāras* and ground nuts are sold by the maund of 12 seers, while those that are imported are retailed by the maund of 10 seers. There are numerous other instances of such varieties in the significance of the term maund.

Sironchā has a table of weights and measures peculiar to itself. The most important weight here is the *tawā*, which is equal to 1¾ seers or 140 tolās. Eight *tawās* make 1 *kunchā* or *handī*: the latter term signifies an earthen pot, and the name of the measure has been derived from this. The table of weights and measures in Sironchā is given on the next page.

2	*arigiddās*	=	1 *pirsodū*
4	*pirsodūs*	=	1 *tawā*
8	*tawās*	=	1 *kunchā or handī*
8	*kunchās*	=	1 *giddā*
20	*giddās*	=	1 *putli* (2240 seers or 2 tons).

Markets.

205. The District contains 66 weekly markets of which 7 lie in the Chānda tahsīl, 21 in Warorā, 14 in Garhchirolī and 5 in the Sironchā tahsīl. This is equivalent to a market for every 154 square miles and 57 villages. Of these the principal cattle markets are those held at Chānda, Warorā, Jāmbulghāta, Madheri, Garhchirolī, Armori, Garbori, Nawargaon and Bramhapurī. At Madheri and Jāmbulghāta a considerable number of bullocks are sold. Those sold at Madheri are usually of the fine Berār breed, while at Jāmbulghāta are found heavy bullocks from Nāgpur for black soil and the small hardy breed from the eastern jungles of the District suitable for rice country. At Nawargaon about 500 cattle are brought every week for sale. But sales of cattle are registered at two places only, *viz.*, at Chānda and Warorā. Registration is compulsory at Warorā and optional at Chānda, and a fee is levied at the rate of three pies per rupee. The amount realised on this account in Chānda was Rs. 1106 in 1906-07 which would indicate sales of the value of Rs. 70,000. In Warorā during the same year the fee realised was Rs. 233 showing that the value of cattle sold was about Rs. 15,000. . Cattle are also sold at Pāthri and Rājgarh markets.

The most important markets for the ordinary produce in the open and semi-rice tracts are held at Chānda and Dābha in Chānda tahsīl, Warorā, Chimūr and Jāmbulghāta in Warorā tahsīl and at Bramhapurī in the Bramhapurī tahsīl. Dābha is important since it is the *entrepôt* of all export trade to Hyderābād. Jāmbulghāta is a large cloth bazar. The position Mūl occupies makes it an important feeder market to

Chānda and it is, as it were, the neck of the bottle through which all cart traffic between Chānda and a large part of the interior of the District must pass. Armori has naturally become the most important mart of the eastern half of the District and the weekly bazar held on Friday is a very considerable one, the traffic in cloth and cattle being particularly heavy. Formerly also this was the great *entrepôt* for the disposal of iron smelted in the east of the District, but of late years the output of this has much declined. A good deal of forest produce also is brought here. These two, Mūl and Armori, along with Nawargaon near Garbori are the best bazars in the heavy rice tracts. From Nawargaon the grain is taken across country by cart-tracks to Hinganghāt or Nāgpur: from Armori it goes to Bramhapurī and from Mūl, as said before, to Chānda. These three bazars are therefore simply feeder markets for the larger markets of this District and the Districts adjoining. At Nawargaon and Armori cloth is also largely sold; so also at Bhāndak. Chāmursi and Talodhi are also bazars of some importance. With the exception of the apology for a bazar at Asaralli there is absolutely no open market in the Sironchā tahsīl. The consequence is that there is practically no trade transaction worthy of the name. Each cultivator, rich or poor, has a running account for food, seed, clothes and small sums of money with one or other local *sāhukārs*. He borrows his rent from the same person and in payment hands over the whole of his agricultural produce. Very occasionally the *sāhukār* returns some of it to him over and above his needs for the year; such surplus is peddled out in the Asaralli bazar. During the last three years Sironchā trade has been slightly stimulated by the arrival of a Mārwāri from Chānda who is said to send juāri occasionally to Chānda, but it will be some years before he can create much competition. The itinerant petty traders in the District are known as Bhusares who may be either Telis, Marārs, Kalārs, Kunbīs or Dhers. They go round from village to village buying grain of all kinds and in any quantities from tenants which they subsequently sell in the bigger markets to wholesale dealers who are either Cutchis, Komtīs or Mārwāris. Cotton is collected from the growers of the Wardhā valley by petty traders or large dealers who are usually Mārwāris of the Wūn tāluk. It is ginned locally and sent by road to Hinganghāt mills. Til, linseed, juāri and wheat are also brought to market in small quantities, but the greater part is taken by dealers at harvest either in accordance with a specific agreement in repayment of an advance on the harvest or in satisfaction of some other debt.

Fairs.

206. Fairs are held at six places in the District, *viz.*, at Chānda, Chimūr, Mārkanda, Warhā, Nāgbhīr and Bhāndak. A large part of the wholesale business of the year was formerly transacted at these fairs, those at Chānda and Bhāndak being by far the most important. In 1866 these two fairs were attended by 229,010 persons, while the value of the sales effected amounted to Rs. 20,55,843 and gave the District a surplus in cash of Rs. 1,17,776. Fairs of commercial importance at present are the Mahākāli fair held at Chānda and the Chimūr fair. The Mahākāli fair held outside the Achaleshwar gate is supposed to be held on Chaitra Paurnimā (full moon day of Chaitra), but in practice lasts from 15th April to 15th May and the attendance from Chaitra Badi 10 to Chaitra Badi 15 is about 3000 persons daily, while the total attendance during the fair is estimated at 100,000 persons. Last year (1908) the attendance was 75,000. Cattle, tobacco and garlic are the principal articles sold. The total sales are estimated at 10 to 15 lakhs of rupees. About Rs. 80,000 worth of cattle are sold. The Chimūr fair takes place in February-March. The principal day is Māgh-Paurnimā (full moon day of Māgh). Two days before the Paurnimā the *rath* procession known as *ghodā* is taken round the village in honour of the god Bālajī. The usual merchandise is brought for sale, but *rengīs*, carts and cart-wheels are specially in evidence. Cattle are also brought for sale. The fair lasts

Bemrose, Collo., Derby.

ACHALESHWAR TEMPLE, CHANDA.

for 15 days and the average daily attendance is 1000 persons. The remaining four fairs are purely religious. The Mārkanda fair usually held in February (for fifteen days) attracts now 4,000 visitors, instead of 30,000 formerly, who come here to wash away their sins in the waters of the Waingangā. Mārkanda is a village with but a score of houses situated on the left bank of the Waingangā about 40 miles east of Chānda. The village derives its name and fame from a beautiful group of temples built in stone and finely situated on a high bluff overlooking the river, by far the largest and most elaborately sculptured temple being that of Mārkande Rishi. Bhāndak fair, one of the most important formerly, has now come to be a purely religious fair with a daily attendance of about 2000 persons from Nāgpur, Bhandāra, Wardhā, Nizām's dominions and Berār: some trade is also done. It is held in the month of March for about three weeks. The place is 18 miles north-west of Chānda and 12 miles from Warorā. The architectural remains in and around Bhāndak are of remote antiquity and great interest. Nāgbhīr and Warhā fairs are simply local fairs, the latter lasting for a day and the attendance is about a thousand people at each.

TRADE.

History of trade.

207. Under the rule of the Gonds Chānda was an important trade centre, and it is said that produce used to come to it from the country to the south to a distance of nearly 250 miles. But after the Marāthā conquest, the traffic dwindled away, as the town no longer lay on one of the main routes of traffic. Chānda does not receive any particular mention by Sir R. Jenkins as a seat of trade, although its manufactures are mentioned more than once. According to that authority, the internal commerce of the Nāgpur territories in his day was trifling. Nāgpur received from the outlying parts of the kingdom the common necessaries of life, together with cloths of different descriptions, partly for its own consumption and partly for exportation, and in return transmitted articles of

prime necessity imported from foreign countries, such as saltpetre, sulphur, metals, cocoanuts, spices and cloths both of city and foreign manufacture. Practically all foreign imports to the country south and west of Nāgpur passed through the hands of traders in that city, the only important exception being salt which was brought up from the East Coast by large caravans of Banjārās. With the restoration of tranquillity which followed the suppression of the Pindāris the trade route from Upper India was diverted westwards to Amraoti, and the transit trade of Nāgpur had by 1827 sunk into comparative insignificance. From this period until the opening of the railway from Bombay to Nāgpur in 1868, foreign goods came to Chānda chiefly by the Amraoti route, but the internal commerce in country produce with Nāgpur and Wardhā continued to be important, while there was also trade on a smaller scale with Chhattīsgarh, Bastar and Hyderābād. With the advent of the railway, goods from Bombay and Amraoti were as a rule sent on by rail to Wardhā, and thence brought by road *viā* Hinganghāt. In 1877 the railway was extended to Warorā, which thereupon assumed a paramount position as the main gate of the District which it held unchallenged for the next thirty years. Until 1861, trade had suffered from the existence of a transit duty which brought in a revenue to Government of more than half a lakh annually, but this was abolished early in the history of British rule. The chief obstacles to trade at the time of the first settlement were the Hyderābād transit duty, which was at that time being exacted on all goods crossing the frontier save grain imports with a rigour previously unknown, and the inland customs line established in 1865. This line traversed the District longitudinally from north to south in the west, and from south to north in the centre of the District, and created a series of bewildering jurisdictions, the annoyance being aggravated by the fact that the line lay along, not across, the main routes of traffic. The customs line which practically killed the trade in salt was abolished in 1874, but the Hyderābād transit duty still exists to discourage exports from that quarter. Major Lucie Smith wrote of the trade of his day as follows:—'A large part of the 'wholesale business of the year is transacted at fairs, which 'meet annually at Chānda, Bhāndak, Chimūr, Mārkanda and 'Warhā, the two first being by far the most important. Up 'to the end of 1866 the Hyderābād transit duty was worked so 'as not to interfere seriously with trade, and taking that year 'we find that the Chānda and Bhāndak fairs were attended by '229,010 persons, while the value of the sales amounted to 'Rs. 20,55,843, giving the District a surplus in cash of 'Rs. 1,17,776.'

Trade routes.

208. Poverty of communications has greatly retarded the development of the trade of the District. By far the greater bulk of its external trade goes to Warorā, and in many cases the lead to the rail is a very long one. Warorā forms the focus of the external trade of most of the Warorā and Chānda tahsīls, of the south of the Bramhapurī tahsīl, of the Garhchirolī tahsīl as far east as Dhanorā, and also of portions of the Yeotmāl District in Berār and the Edlābād District in the Nizām's dominions. The produce of the interior of this District is collected at Mūl, and so ultimately finds its way *viâ* Chānda to Warorā. Chānda also serves as a collecting and forwarding station for large tracts of country. The position of Warorā at the rail-head and the concentration of the export trade of the interior and the south of the District at Chānda, have naturally made the Chānda-Warorā road incomparably the most important trade route in the District and, till the opening of the Warorā-Ballālpur extension in the current year, it formed the main artery of the District. Next to it ranks the Mūl-Umrer road, which gives an outlet to a good deal of produce from the north of Bramhapurī and the north-east of Warorā towards the Nāgpur market, and is the only other made road connecting the District with the outer world. Of country roads, the most important are

those from Chimūr to Nāgpur and from Chimūr to Hinganghāt, from Bramhapurī to Paunī and Lakhāndur in the Bhandāra District, and from Dābha, south of Chānda, to the Nizām's dominions. In the remote east of the District, the outlet for produce is towards the rail at Nāndgaon, and exports consisting principally of rice and forest produce are put on the road leading to that station at Ambāgarh Chauki or Mohallā in the zamīndāris lately transferred to Drug. River-trade, except in Sironchā, is unimportant, although in the rains a certain amount of traffic comes down the Waingangā from Paunī to Armori. Sleepers and scantlings used also to be floated up the Wardhā from the Government saw mills at Alāpalli as far as Warorā, and on the Kanhān as far as Kamptee. In Sironchā, however, the Godāvari is the chief highway of trade. Enormous distances and bad *ghāts* cut off this tahsīl from the rest of the District, and there is very little trade in the direction of Chānda. As far as the Upper Tāluk is concerned, the river is of value only as an avenue of export: the small boats which used formerly to come up, can now no longer do so as the anicut was broken down some years ago, and the river traffic from this tāluk is now confined to the floating of timber down stream. The Hyderābād transit duties prevent free intercourse with the country lying across the river. The Lower Tāluks are more happily circumstanced; although equally cut off from traffic with Hyderābād on the west and landlocked to the north by a *ghāt* impassable to wheeled traffic, and further pent in by hills to the east and south, communication is possible both up and down stream during the rains and cold weather, and a big trade is carried on with Rājahmundry in Madras. To the north, however, bad barriers prevent traffic even by river with the rest of the District.

Trading centres.

209. Fair-weather tracks, too numerous to specify, link up all the most important villages in the District with each other, and, except in Sironchā, are very easily negotiable by carts in open

weather. The chief trading centres within the District are Mūl, Dābha and Chānda in the Chānda tahsīl; Warorā, Madheri, Chimūr, Jāmbulghāta and Bhāndak in Warorā; Bramhapurī, Talodhī and Nawargaon in Bramhapurī, and Garhchirolī, Armori and Chāmursi in Garhchirolī. Sironchā has no trading centre worthy of the name.

Exports.

210. The exports are purely agricultural produce, and food-grains are the chief commodity taken to Nāgpur from the northern portions of the District. Cotton and oil-seeds go from Warorā to Hinganghāt and Nāgpur by rail, and from Chimūr to those same outside markets by road A small trade in good cloth is carried on between Nāgbhīr and Umrer, and a little *kosā* is sent from the eastern side of the Waingangā both to Nāgpur and Chānda by either of the two main roads. Since the bulk of this trade is by road, none of it has been registered. This is to be regretted, for the trade with Nāgpur by road is very important. But the octroi receipts in Chānda and Warorā and the statistics of the rail-borne traffic from Warorā, are of considerable value in determining the development of trade in recent years. The net income of the Chānda municipality from octroi from 1890-91, and of the Warorā municipality from 1894-95 is available and is as follows:—

Chānda.		Income Rs.	
1890-91—1894-95	...	11,714	average for 5 years.
1895-96—1899-1900	...	16,324	„ „ „
1900-01—1904-05	...	20,785	„ „ „
1905-06 ...	...	22,183	for one year only.
1906-07 ...	...	24,820	„ „ „

Warorā.			Rs.
1894-95—1899-1900 (average)	...	...	8,467
1900-01—1904-05 (average)	...	...	12,809
1905-06 one year	...	...	18,410
1906-07 one year	...	...	14,058

Very little income is made by the Chānda municipality from cotton, the increase representing the improvement in the trade of food-grains; in the case of Warorā, the rapid increase in recent years is caused by the expansion of the area under cotton, which in Warorā is an article of trade, and also by the increased demand for juāri and *rabi* food-grains in a series of unpropitious years for the rice.

211. It is impossible to arrive at any definite estimate of the annual trade of the District, as there is no registration of the traffic by road. But as regards external trade, the statistics of the railway traffic at Warorā are an important guide, since nearly all the produce exported from the *khālsa* portion of the District, except the northern parts of Bramhapurī and the neighbourhood of Chimūr in the Warorā tahsīl, ultimately finds its exit by Warorā. At the same time it has to be remembered that the Warorā statistics include much of the traffic between adjoining tracts of Berār and Hyderābād with the outside world—a circumstance which notably affects the figures, especially those relating to cotton. Mr. Hemingway gives the total quantity of exports, with details about grain and cotton from 1894 to 1901. These figures show an average total export of 1,715,309 maunds, grain and cotton contributing 29,563 and 11,786 maunds respectively. While reviewing these figures Mr. Hemingway says:—'Much of 'the cotton comes from the adjoining district of Berār; but 'there has been a large extension of the cotton area within 'this District also, in the tracts that are in touch with the 'railway (the trade in this article was next to nothing from '1894 to 1898 when it varied between 44 maunds in 1894 'and 3692 maunds in 1896. In 1899 it reached 27,000 'maunds and in 1901, 45,000 maunds). The grain exports 'are of interest. Much of the rice from the northern portions 'of the District finds its way to the rail by roads through 'Nāgpur or Hinganghāt; but there is a good traffi in rice 'between Warorā and the more southern parts of the District

Rail-borne traffic.

'when there is a good foreign demand: prior to 1896 there 'was little demand for the Chānda rice, because all Districts 'in the Provinces had then been enjoying fair crops; but in '1896-97 other Districts felt famine severely and Chānda 'was called upon to supply grain very largely; consequently, 'the export rose enormously that year (exports recorded in '1896 being 59,000 maunds and in 1897 126,500 maunds). 'Probably there would have been a large rise in 1900-01 also 'if the stocks in the District had not almost failed that year; 'there was then no surplus to export. The total exports 'have not fluctuated so greatly as have the figures of grain 'and cotton, because there has always been a large trade in 'coal which has varied comparatively little.' The statistics for the last five years show a very marked expansion, both of imports and exports, especially in the years 1905 and 1906; the commencement of work on the Ballālpur extension largely accounts for the great increase in traffic during these last two years. The expansion is not confined to one or two classes of goods, but is, with the exception of coal exports, general. The following are the statistics for exports from Warorā:—

Articles.	1902.		1906.		Average for 5 years, 1902—06.	
	Maunds, in thousands.	Value, in lakhs.	Maunds, in thousands.	Value, in lakhs	Maunds, in thousands.	Value, in lakhs.
Coal ...	1746	4·36	340	·85	1177	2·94
Raw cotton ...	36	5·64	109	20·61	71	13·19
Grain and pulse ...	28	·66	84	2·72	44	1·22
Hides ...	2	·50	6	2·00	5	1·56
Castor oil ...	3	·38	2	·28	3	·33
Oil-seeds ...	269	14·97	509	20·35	401	15·90
Timber ...	14	·31	16	·35	14	·30
Other articles ...	109	4·88	38	2·43	63	3·51
Total ...	2207	31·70	1104	49·59	1778	38·95

The corresponding statistics of imports are as follows :—

Articles.	1902.		1906.		Average for 5 years, 1902-1906.	
	Maunds, in thousands.	Value, in lakhs.	Maunds, in thousands.	Value, in lakhs.	Maunds, in thousands.	Value, in lakhs.
Cotton manufactures ...	15	7·66	21	11·07	17	8·92
Grain and pulse ...	88	1·92	106	4·35	81	2·66
Gunny bags ...	5	·42	8	·96	7	·69
Metals ...	14	1·42	27	3·30	22	2·48
Kerosene oil ...	16	·71	26	1·22	20	·90
Provisions ...	14	1·57	17	2·00	14	1·55
Salt	87	3·26	92	2·42	98	3·10
Spices ...	11	1·24	12	1·93	9	1·33
Sugar ...	39	2·28	61	4·18	48	3·22
Tobacco ...	4	·35	6	·78	5	·48
Other articles ...	28	1·99	67	12·94	42	5·11
Total ...	321	22·82	443	45·15	363	30·44

Exports of agricultural produce.

212. The principal exports by rail are coal, oil-seeds cotton, pulses and hides. Of these the coal traffic simply represents Government enterprise, and need not be dwelt upon here. Owing to the shutting down of the Warorā Colliery and the infancy of the new colliery at Ballālpur, the exports under this head are at present at a low ebb. Under raw cotton there has been a rapid and uninterrupted advance throughout the quinquennium. In 1906, the exports of raw cotton amounted to 109,000 maunds valued at nearly 21 lakhs, or between three and four times the figures for 1902. But it must be remembered that much of the traffic in raw cotton comes from the adjoining parts of Berār and Hyderā-

bād. On the other hand a good deal of cotton is also collected from growers in the Wardhā valley by petty Teli or Mahār traders, or by the large Mārwāri dealers of the Wūn tāluk and elsewhere; this is ginned locally and sent by road to the Hinganghāt mills. The most important export crops raised in the District itself are oil-seeds. In 1905, the quantity exported of these was more than double the amount exported in 1902, and though there was a slight decline in 1906, still in that year over half a million maunds with a value of 20½ lakhs were sent out. The principal oil-seeds are linseed and til, the average exports of which during the quinquennium were, linseed 185,000 maunds, valued at 8·26 lakhs, and til, 128,000 maunds valued at 5·92 lakhs. A certain amount of castor, rape and mustard seed is also exported, while there is a growing trade in mahuā oil. All these oil-seeds go to Bombay. There is also a considerable traffic in rice, but as this almost all leaves the District by road, no figures are available. The unhusked rice known as *bagar* is largely exported by cart to Berār, Hyderābād, and Wardhā. A little wheat goes from the Bramhapurī tahsīl to Nāgpur. From the northern zamīndāris and the Wairāgarh pargana, and to a certain extent from the heavy rice tract, there is a fairly important traffic in the special preparation of rice known as *pohe*: this goes by road *viâ* Armori to Nāgpur and Hinganghāt.

Exports of forest produce.

213. The best timber in the District is unfortunately situated too far from the seat of demand to be of much value for purposes of export. Nearly all the largest timber is found in the south of the District, and the expense of carting it north is prohibitive. Timber is floated down the Godāvari to Dumagudiam, both from the Government forest and from the Ahīri zamīndāri, and this is absolutely the only means of disposing of timber in the log from these parts. But there is a fair demand for cut timber of small size in Warorā, where teak poles and scantlings are stocked for sale

in Berār and Wardhā. From the northern forest division there is a good deal of trade in bamboo with the open parts of Warorā, Wardhā and Berār and much of the produce collected at Warorā ultimately finds its way to Nāgpur. At one time, the bamboo forests near Chānda and Chimūr used to be extremely valuable, but all the bamboos in this tract seeded in 1900, and it will be some time before trade can recover. The abundant mahuā produce of the District also suffers from being distant from good markets; much of it is used locally; but there is a flourishing trade in it from the parts adjoining Chimūr to Wardhā and Hinganghāt. Imports of mahuā into Hyderābād are discouraged by a heavy import duty. In years of agricultural depression tenants extract a comparatively large amount of timber and take it to foreign markets for sale; but usually distance renders the profits insignificant, and they do not find it advisable to work their cattle during months when they would ordinarily be resting. Most of the produce of the forests which is exported is, therefore, taken out by outsiders. Other forest products are *chironjī*, lac, gum and myrobalans: some of the northern zamīndāris make a good income out of these latter. Sāmbhar horns are also exported to make knife-handles.

Exports of manufactured articles.

214. In manufactured articles the export trade is not of importance. A small trade in good cloth is carried on between Nāgbhīr and Umrer, and a little *kosā* is also exported to Nāgpur. Silk-bordered cloths are sent to Nāgpur, Berār and Hyderābād. Tiles and bricks used to be manufactured in the Government colliery at Warorā and sold for Rs. 10 a hundred. Oil is pressed in Chānda, and sent to places where there are mills employing machinery. Bamboo tatties are exported to Amraoti and Berār. Shoes, leather ropes (Bramhapurī), wooden cart-wheels (Chimūr), *rengīs* (Bramhapurī, Armori, and Chānda) are other articles of export.

215. Salt, sugar, thread, cotton piece-goods, spices, provisions, food-grains, and metals are the principal imports. The imports of salt have steadily expanded since the reduction of the duty from 87,000 maunds valued at Rs. 3¼ lakhs in 1902 to 109,000 maunds valued at Rs. 3·09 lakhs in 1905. The consumption per head of population averages 13 lbs. or exactly the same as the provincial average. Sugar imports have increased at a uniform rate of about half a lakh a year from 2·3 to 4·2 lakhs. About three-quarters of the sugar imported is *gur* from Bangalore and Northern India; the whole of the trade in it has sprung up within the last few years. Other kinds of sugar come from Mauritius and Northern India, chiefly from the former. The consumption of sugar averaged 13lbs. per head of the population during the quinquennium 1902 – 1906. Imports of cotton manufactures have risen from 15,000 maunds in 1902 to 21,000 maunds to 1906, and average 17,000 maunds for the quinquennium. The corresponding values are 7·66, 11·1 and 8·92 lakhs. The imports of piece-goods, both foreign and Indian, are on the increase, foreign piece-goods having risen from 4000 maunds to 7000 and Indian from 3000 to 4000 in the five years. Thread comes both from Bombay and from country mills. While the imports of foreign yarn remain stationary at about 3000 maunds, Indian yarn has advanced from 5000 to 7000 maunds. The imports of metals have almost doubled themselves within the last five years, and stood at 27,000 maunds in 1906. Gold and silver, brass and copper in sheets, iron, zinc and tin all come from Bombay. There is also a growing demand for kerosene oil, of which 26,000 maunds were imported in 1906. Among food-grains rice is the principal kind imported, accounting for 60,000 out of an average import of 80,000 maunds during the quinquennium. Out of the 14,000 maunds of provisions annually imported 6000 maunds consist of cocoanuts. Country blankets come from Hyderābād for export to other Districts, and *sāris* from Madras *viâ* Rājahmundry. Matches are imported from Bombay.

Imports.

Excess of exports over imports.

216. The excess of exports over imports (by rail) was Rs. 8·88 lakhs in 1902 which rose to Rs. 8·91 lakhs in 1904 and to Rs. 18·20 lakhs in 1905. The year 1906 records a sudden fall to Rs. 4·44 lakhs. The quinquennial average excess of exports over imports comes to Rs. 8·52 lakhs.

COMMUNICATIONS.

Early state of communications.

217. Prior to 1891, Chānda presented the remarkable spectacle of a British District nearly 11,000 square miles in extent but possessing only one metalled road, 29 miles in length and a section of railway measuring 17 miles, and both of these means of communication hugged the western border of the District so closely that they might appear to have wandered into it by accident, and for the vast bulk of the District might just as well have not existed. When it is considered that the railway was created solely to carry coal to other parts of the country, it is not unfair to call Chānda the Cinderella among the Districts in the matter of communications. A charge whose confines extended well over 100 miles from headquarters in one direction and quite 200 miles in a totally different direction, which was cut in two by a mighty river and seamed with innumerable water-courses, was to all intents and purposes devoid of all civilised means of communication until within twenty years ago. An important step was taken to remove this slur by the construction, in 1891, of the Chānda-Mūl-Umrer road, which opened up the Bramhapurī tahsīl, but it was not until the famine of 1900 that the task of developing the communications of Chānda was systematically taken in hand. Since then communications have been continuously, if not rapidly, developed: the existing railway has been extended till it now runs through 56 miles of the District, while another railway is being driven right through the heart of the rice country; a comprehensive system of roads linking together all the most

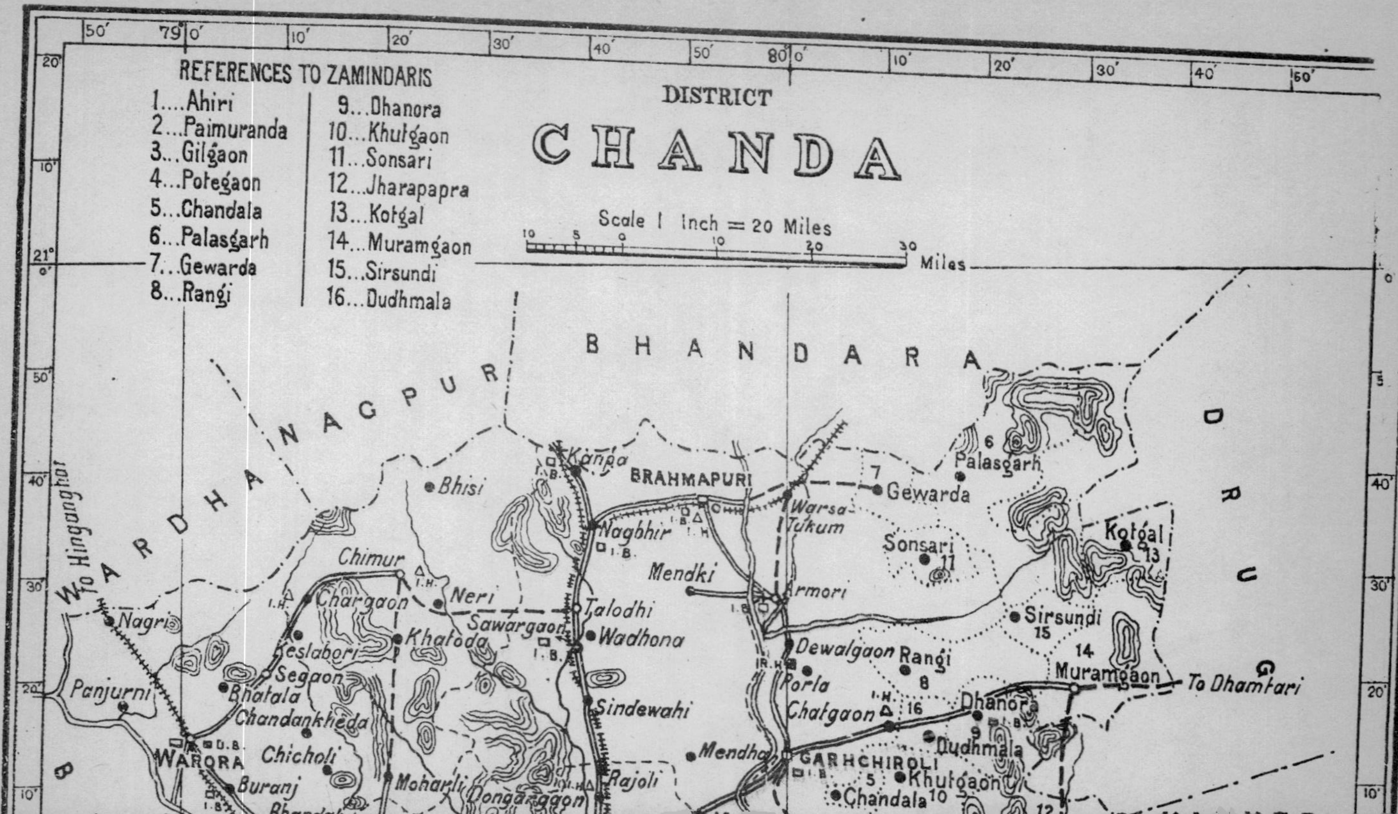
DISTRICT
CHANDA
Scale 1 Inch = 20 Miles
10 5 0 10 20 30 Miles
REFERENCES TO ZAMINDARIS
1....Ahiri
2...Paimuranda
3...Gilgaon
4...Potegaon
5...Chandala
6...Palasgarh
7...Gewarda
8...Rangi
9...Dhanora
10...Khutgaon
11...Sonsari
12...Jharapapra
13...Kotgal
14...Muramgaon
15...Sirsundi
16...Dudhmala
BHANDARA
NAGPUR
WARDHA
DRUG
To Hinganghat
To Dhamtari
BRAHMAPURI
WARORA
GARHCHIROLI
Kanpa
Bhisi
Chimur
Nagbhir
Mendki
Armori
Warsa Tukum
Gewarda
Palasgarh
Sonsari
Kotgal
Sirsundi
Muramgaon
Dewalgaon
Rangi
Porla
Chatgaon
Dhanora
Dudhmala
Khutgaon
Chandala
Mendha
Talodhi
Wadhona
Sawargaon
Neri
Chargaon
Khatoda
Keslabori
Segaon
Bhatala
Chandankheda
Chicholi
Buranj
Nagri
Panjurni
Sindewahi
Rajoli
Moharli
Dongargaon

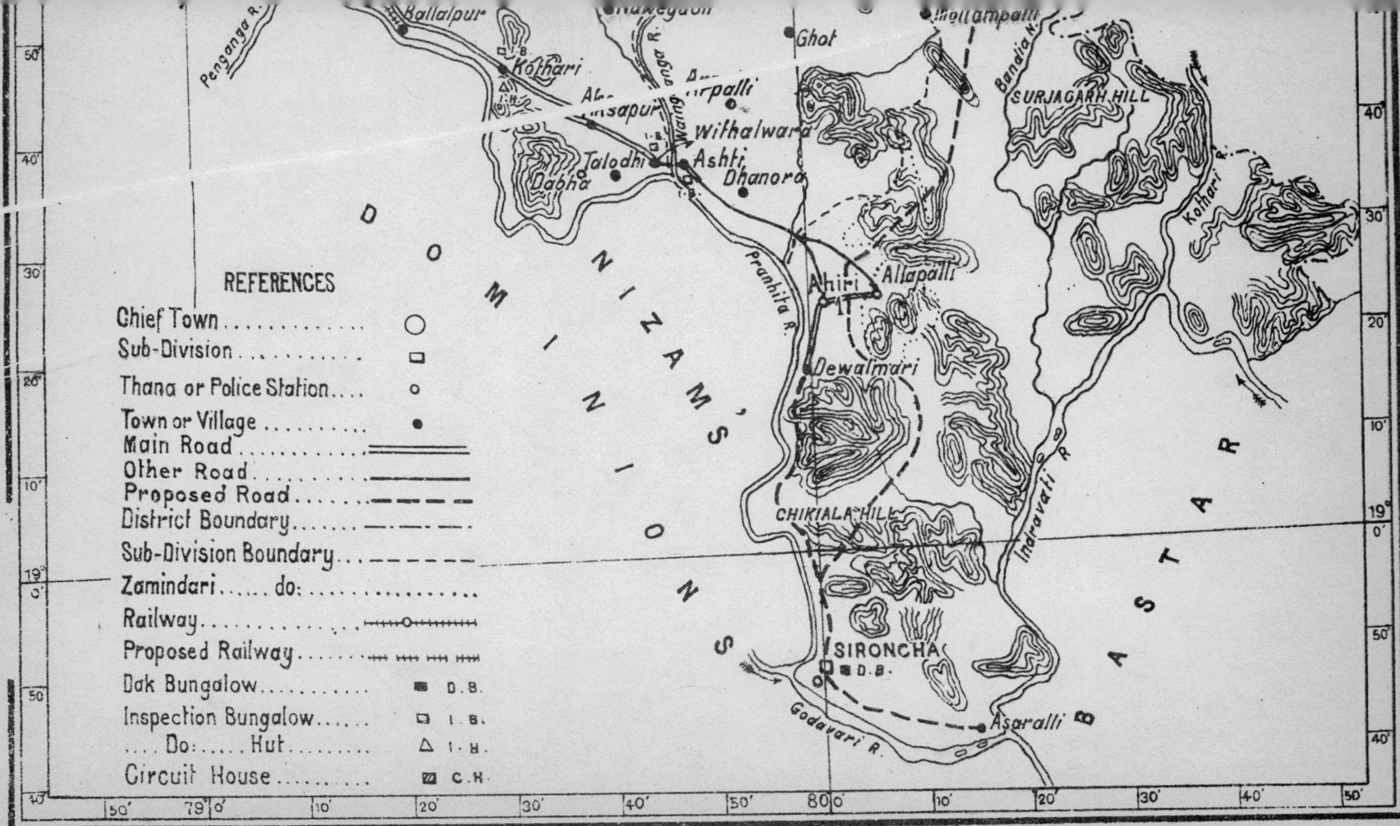

Specially prepared for the Superintendent Gazetteer C. P. from an original supplied by him.

important points in the District is also in process of construction. Unfortunately dearth of labour prevents these works being carried through with the rapidity which would have been possible in the days before the famine, and it will be some time before all these schemes are actually translated into the region of fact.

Railways.

218. Until the current year (1908) the railway communication of the Chānda District was confined to a section 17 miles in length on the Wardhā-Warorā branch of the Great Indian Peninsula Railway in the extreme north-west corner of the District. This line was opened in 1877 to afford an outlet to the coal of the Warorā State Colliery. It is built on the broad gauge, and, joining the main line at Wardhā, connects Warorā *viâ* that station with both Bombay and Calcutta. It was at first worked by the Great Indian Peninsula Railway Company, but during the twelve years from 1879 to 1891 it was under the direct control of Government, being known at this period as the State Coal Railway. In 1891, it was once more handed over to the Great Indian Peninsula Railway Company, by whom it has since been worked. There are two stations on its course within this District, Nāgri and Warorā, which has hitherto been the terminus of the line, and has naturally dominated the trade of the District, since practically the whole external traffic of the *khālsa* area has converged upon it. This commanding position, however, it is now about to lose. With the approaching exhaustion of the Warorā Colliery, it became necessary to seek for another source of supply, and when it had been finally decided to sink a shaft at Ballālpur, the extension of the railway to that place *viâ* Chānda was taken in hand. This extension commenced towards the end of 1904 and was completed at the beginning of 1908 at a total cost of 39 lakhs. Its length is 39 miles and it passes through four stations—Bhāndak, Tadāli, Chānda and Ballālshāh (Ballālpur). The principal obstacle in its course is the Erai river, which has been

negotiated by a bridge of eight spans of 100 feet each. It is in contemplation ultimately to link up this line with that from Bombay to Madras, and a line has been surveyed to Warangal passing through Ahīri and Sironchā. The new extension closely hugs the western border of the District, and its main importance, apart from its prime object of serving the Ballālpur Colliery, lies in the fact that it brings large tracts of country suitable to the growth of cotton within easy reach of the rail, and will render it feasible to grow that crop in quarters hitherto debarred from its cultivation by considerations of distance. Otherwise it will have but little effect on trade, save of course to stimulate it and make much of it debouch on points more southerly than hitherto, and vast areas of the District will be wholly unaffected by it. Chānda is distant 544 miles from Bombay and 823 miles from Calcutta by this line.

Of more interest perhaps to the District at large is the line on the 2′ 6″ gauge now under construction between Chānda and Gondia on the main line of the Bengal-Nāgpur Railway. This line will pass through the centre of the rice-producing tract of the Chānda and Bramhapurī tahsīls. At Nāgbhīr, 66 miles from Chānda, a branch is to be thrown out linking up Chānda with Nāgpur 67½ miles distant *viâ* Umrer, while the main line will proceed to Bramhapurī, crossing the Waingangā a little to the east of that town, and having its terminus at Gondia, 82 miles from Nāgbhīr.[1] The approximate cost of this railway will be 120 lakhs of rupees. The Waingangā bridge, is 2592 feet in length, and consists of 14 spans of 100 feet and 6 spans of 170 feet each: the foundations are all open, and rest on rock at a depth not exceeding 20 feet below low water level. The total cost of the bridge has been about 8 lakhs. As a means of facilitating the administration of the Bramhapurī and

[1] The Gondia-Nāgbhīr-Nāgpur line was opened on the 9th November 1908 by the Chief Commissioner Mr. R. H. Craddock.

Garhchirolī tahsīls, the importance of this line cannot be over-estimated, while its existence will solve the problem of getting grain into the interior of these tahsīls in times of famine and prevent a recurrence of the enormous difficulties of transport which were the most serious obstacle to famine administration in 1900. It will also bring the backward Garhchirolī zamīndāris within hail of civilisation, and encourage the influx of tenants into a quarter where population is sadly deficient. But it will carry away little agricultural produce save rice, since the bulk of the trade in this with the exception of rice will always be with Bombay and merchants will as a rule prefer to put their cotton and oil-seeds on the rival railway. It is as yet undecided whether the terminus at Chānda will form a joint station with that of the Great Indian Peninsula Railway.

Roads converging on Warorā.

219. As mentioned above until within the last twenty years the only metalled road in the whole District was that section of the old Southern Road which connects Warorā and Chānda, a distance of only 29 miles. Even this road was until 1901-02 only partially bridged and the mails were often considerably delayed by floods. Raised causeways or Irish bridges have now, however, been provided except at the crossing of the Erai, which is traversed by a temporary bridge and roadway during the open season, and by a ferry during the monsoon. This road has hitherto been incomparably the most important in the District, as Chānda gets all the trade from the *havelī* as well as traffic which the Mūl bazar collects and hands on from Rājgarh and the markets across the Waingangā, and passes it on in turn to the railway at Warorā: while, in the opposite direction, all the traffic between the south of the District and the outside world must necessarily filter through the same channel. The extension of the Great Indian Peninsula Railway to Ballālpur will, however, very greatly reduce the importance of this road as a trade route. A short but important trade route for the north-western area

of the District is the road between Warorā and Wūn, which is the great avenue of the cotton and grain trade with East Berār and the Edlābād District in the Nizām's dominions. This has been made a first-class road within the last few years. A second-class road, 33 miles in length, which was commenced as a famine work in 1899-1900 connects Chimūr with Warorā *viâ* Shegaon and carries a fair amount of traffic. It is shortly to be raised to the status of a first-class road. Northwards towards Wardhā runs a District Council road which is at present only a third-class road, but which is to be metalled. A second-class road has also been proposed which will connect Warorā with Moharlī *viâ* Chandankherā, and from Moharlī will run to Sindewāhi, thus bringing the heavy rice tract into much needed communication with Warorā.

Road in the Bramhapurī tahsīl.

220. Second only in importance to the Chānda-Warorā road is the road which links up Chānda with Nāgpur *viâ* Mūl and Umrer. This is metalled and partially bridged between Chānda and Mūl (27 miles), and for the ten miles north of Nāgbhīr, after which it passes out of the District, while for the 37½ miles between Mūl and Nāgbhīr it is laid with *muram*. The produce of the Rājgarh and Wairāgarh parganas and also that of the southern half of the Garborī pargana goes to Mūl and thence on to Chānda by the southern section of this road, while the northern part of the Garborī pargana and all the Bramhapurī pargana send their commodities along the northern half to Nāgpur. Bramhapurī is linked up with Nāgbhīr by a gravelled road 12 miles in length. It is proposed to raise both the sections from Mūl to Nāgbhīr and from Nāgbhīr to Bramhapurī to class I.

Central and eastern roads.

221. The central and eastern portions of the District are opened up, so far as they have as yet been opened up at all, by two roads which meet at Garhchirolī. The more

southerly of these two roads runs from west to east. To the west of Garhchirolī, it connects that place with Mūl (and so ultimately with Chānda) by a gravelled road 25 miles in length which was constructed in 1894. A little to the east of Garhchirolī it passes into the zamīndāris and affords a good *muram* coated thoroughfare as far as Dhanorā 21 miles away. The earthwork over a further distance of 15 miles as far as Muramgaon on the borders of the District was completed in the last famine, and the road is now being carried on to the railway at Dhamtarī in an easterly and to Nāndgaon in a northerly direction. It is intended to metal the length of 25 miles from Mūl to Garhchirolī and to improve the portion from Dhanorā to Muramgaon. The second of the two roads converging at Garhchirolī runs through Armori in a northerly direction to Bramhapurī, a distance of 33½ miles. At present it is merely gravelled, but it is intended to metal it. Westwards from Armori runs a second-class road to Mendkī, a length of 8 miles, which is to be linked up with the Mūl-Umrer road at Talodhī.

Southern roads.

222. South of Chānda, the District was prior to the famine of 1897 absolutely devoid of roads. A road to Sironchā *viâ* Alāpallī is, however, at present in course of construction. This road will be first-class as far as Alāpallī, and thence onward will be laid as a gravelled track. The first 22 miles as far as Kothāri have already been completed as a first-class road and construction is proceeding steadily over the whole of the remaining length. The road when completed will open up the lower Waingangā and Wardhā valleys, and tap the considerable grain traffic of the valley of the Prānhita, besides affording a connection between the timber depôt of Alāpallī and the railway. Another road is also in course of construction which runs from Alāpallī in a north-easterly direction to Muramgaon. When this is completed Alāpallī will be the apex of a great triangle of roads, the extremities of whose base will lie at Chānda and Muramgaon.

The District Council maintains third-class roads of some importance between Bramhapurī and Gewardhā, Garhchirolī and Chāmursi, and Chānda and Chimūr, besides that from Warorā to the Wardhā border and the second-class road from Armori to Mendkī which have already been mentioned. It also maintains 61 miles of village roads at an annual cost of Rs. 10 per mile.

There are altogether at the present time 101 miles of metalled and 286 miles of unmetalled roads in the whole District. The whole length of metalled roads and 197 miles of unmetalled roads are maintained by the Public Works Department at a cost of about Rs. 60,000 per annum, while the remaining 89 miles of unmetalled roads are kept up by the District Council at a cost of about Rs. 2500. The programme of future construction includes 23 new roads extending over 394 miles, the cost being estimated at 13 lakhs of rupees.

Methods of transport.

223. Although so far poorly provided with made roads, the District is fortunate in possessing for the most part of its area a hard red *muram* soil which furnishes most excellent village tracks for eight months out of the twelve. For the transport of goods, the carts most in use are the *bandī*, *gādā* and *khāchar*, all rough but strongly built two-wheeled contrivances with a capacity of about ten maunds; and drawn usually by bullocks but occasionally by buffaloes. Prices depend mainly on the type of wheel used. Wheels are of three patterns—'*wandio*' which is a primitive wheel of solid wood fashioned out of three boards and now only surviving in the zamīndāris and other jungly regions; *navi* and *pailī*, these two latter being spoked wheels distinguished from each other by the shape of the nave. A cart and a pair of bullocks can be hired for 12 annas or R. 1 per diem. For human transport, the *chhakrā*, the *rengī*, the *rerū* and the *dhamnī* are the types most familiar. The first two are of the familiar pattern, the *chhakrā* being a hoodless vehicle for fast light travelling meant for a driver and one passenger, the *rengī* having a *tattā* cover and

a capacity for three or four persons, or, on occasion and by the aid of almost incredibly compact bestowal of limbs, for five or six. The *rerū* is not unlike the *chhakrā*, but has a box-like seat upon which the driver and another sit straddle-wise: it is drawn by small country ponies. The *dhamnī* is a more ambitious vehicle built on the principle of the tongā, provided with springs and designed for travelling on metalled roads.

The Godāvari navigation works.

224. No account of the communications of the District would be complete without some reference to the Godāvari navigation scheme. The Godāvari, the Prānhita and the Wardhā rivers would all be practicable for navigation as far inland as the falls of the last named river were it not for the existence of three long stretches of rocky shoals usually known as the barriers. The First Barrier begins at a point about 132 miles above Coconada, and is situated without the limits of this District. Sixty-eight miles of free water lie between the head of this barrier and the foot of the Second or Enchampalli Barrier, which begins at the junction of the Indrāvati and Godāvari rivers and stretches down stream for 14 miles. Seventy-five miles of navigable stream then intervene until the foot of the Third or Dewalmāri Barrier (so called from the place of that name in the Ahīri zamīndāri), which again interposes a bar to navigation for a stretch of 35 miles. Another 101 miles of clear fairway are obtained above the head of this barrier, and then near Soit in the Warorā tahsīl a sheet of limestone stretches from bank to bank of the Wardhā and marks the point above which the river ceases to be practicable to navigation except for small boats. To overcome these obstacles by a series of anicuts and canals was the central idea of the Godāvari navigation scheme. This task successfully performed, it was considered that the whole length of the river would be rendered passable to vessels or flats with a draught of from 3 to 6 feet for six or seven months during the rains and early cold weather, and to

smaller vessels for eight or nine months. The idea even seems to have been mooted of negotiating the falls of the Wardhā, and thus making the river practicable as far as Hinganghāt. The scheme in its entirety was not confined to the main rivers, but embraced various affluents such as the Indrāvati, Pengangā, Waingangā, Sevari and Tāl. The first person to press the project on the attention of Government was Colonel Arthur Cotton, who drew attention to the subject in 1849, and in 1853 drew up a preliminary scheme of operations which was not, however, sanctioned. In 1855 Lieutenant Goddard made an expedition as far up stream as Chānda, and this was followed by another expedition which was, according to the instructions of Government, to be 'one chiefly of exploration and investigation' and was conducted by Lieutenant Haig. As a result of this expedition, it was reported to Government that at a cost of 30 lakhs 473 miles of the main stream could be rendered navigable for three-quarters of the year, and that at a proportionately increased cost altogether 873 miles of river, including affluents, could be similarly thrown open. Even then, however, Government hesitated to commit itself to any step involving the actual inception of work on the barriers, and investigations continued until, in 1863, a detailed report was submitted on the whole circumstances of the river and the country on its banks, which embodied proposals for building anicuts and canals with locks at each barrier, for the clearance of detached rocks in the fairway, for the construction of groins in shoaly parts, and for the laying down of towing-paths, the whole estimated expenditure being placed at a minimum of 75 lakhs of rupees. The Government accepted these proposals as far as they related to the First and Second Barrier, and work on the former commenced in 1865-66. Later on, the veto on the operations at the Third Barrier was withdrawn, but as a matter of fact no work worth mentioning was done on this barrier, although a road was constructed from Chānda to Dewalmāri in the anticipation that the river would be made

Bemrose, Collo., Derby.

OLD HINDU BRIDGE, BHANDAK.

navigable to that point.[1] In 1868-69, the work at the First Barrier was completed, but the Second Barrier, on which work was commenced in 1867, proved more difficult to negotiate, and matters never seem to have progressed satisfactorily in relation to it. Climate, want of labour, want of funds have all been assigned as the cause for this unsatisfactory state of things, but whatever the true reason, the fact remains that the work was abandoned under the orders of Government in 1871-72 after some progress had been made on the anicut, locks and guard walls. Since that date, nothing beyond ordinary repairs has been done on these works, and above the Second Barrier traffic on the river is practically confined to the floating of timber. Altogether 62·80 lakhs were sunk in the operations, and their practically total failure, as far as this District is concerned, is a somewhat melancholy page of history.

[1] All traces of this road have now disappeared.

CHAPTER VI.

FORESTS AND MINERALS.

FORESTS.

Situation and extent.

225. The Government forests of the District cover an area of 3354 square miles, of which all save 82,000 acres are situated in the *khālsa* taking up 56 per cent. of its entire area. The 82,000 acres referred to constitute the Alāpallī range, one of the few forests which Government has acquired by purchase; it comprises three blocks, two of which, Mirkalu and Bhimāram, with an area of 20,000 acres were purchased in 1873 from the zamīndār of Ahīri for one lakh, while the third amounting to 62,000 acres including the Elchil block was purchased in 1883 for Rs. 60,000 in order to consolidate the Government estate.

Forest Divisions.

226. Prior to the year 1904 all the Government forests of the District were included in one Forest Division, but with the expansion of work and revenue this charge was found to be too heavy a burden for a single pair of shoulders and it was consequently split up in that year into two divisions, both with their headquarters at Chānda. The North Chānda Division, as at present constituted, has a total area of 1731[1] square miles, composed of 1307 square miles of A class and 424 square miles of B-I forest; all Government forests lying within the Warorā, Bramhapurī and Chānda tahsīls and those in the north of the Garhchirolī tahsīl are included within its limits. The South Chānda Division, which takes in the forests of the rest of the *khālsa* and also includes the Alāpallī range, has an area of 1623 square miles with 1280 square miles of A-class, and 343 square miles of B-I class. By 'A-class' are denoted areas permanently reserved as forest, and by 'B-I class' areas declared to be available for cultivation.

---

[1]The Dābha range comprising 168 square miles of A class and 53 square miles of B-I class has subsequently (1-7-08) been transferred to the Southern Division.

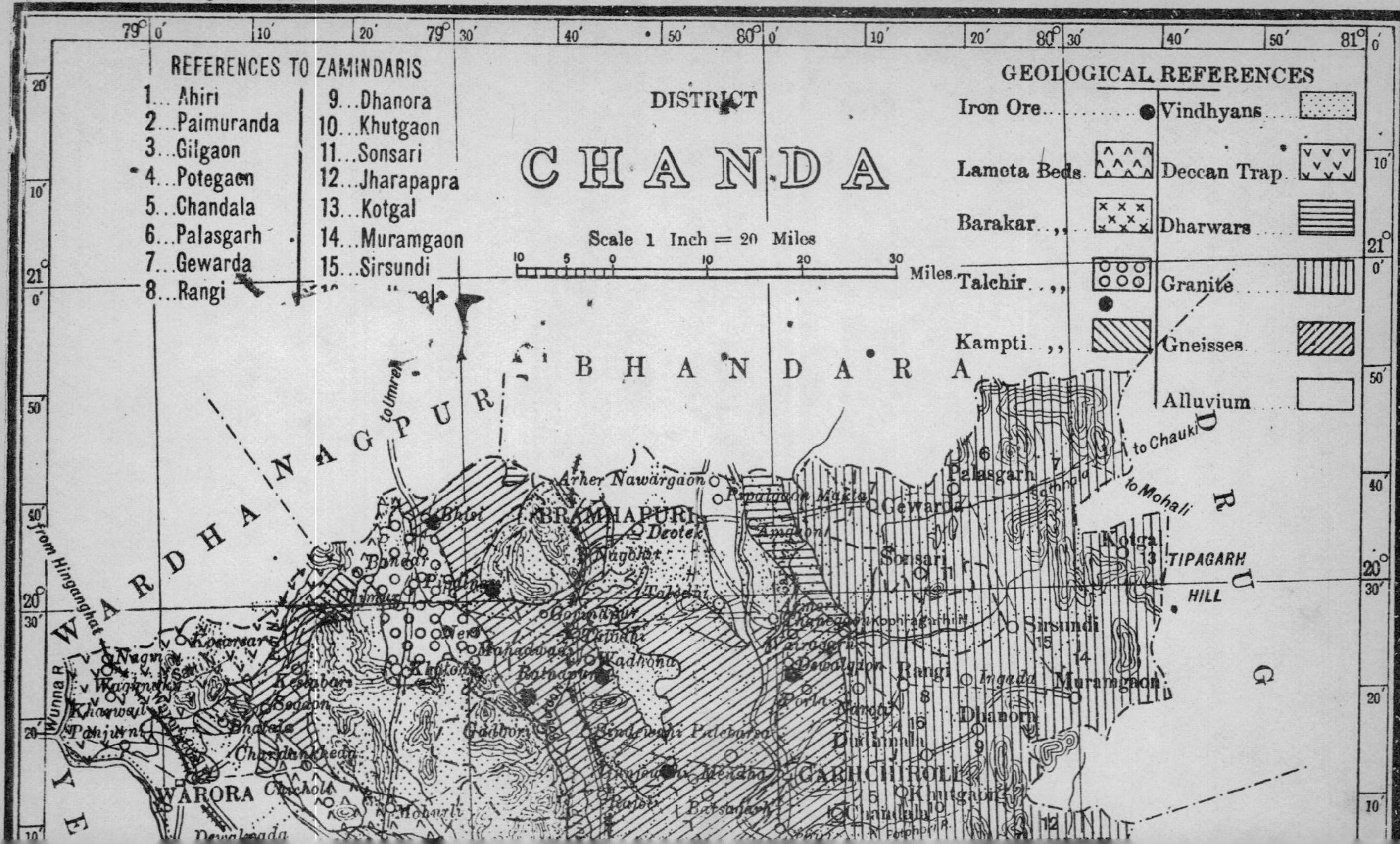
DISTRICT
CHANDA
Scale 1 Inch = 20 Miles
REFERENCES TO ZAMINDARIS
1...Ahiri
2...Paimuranda
3...Gilgaon
4...Potegaon
5...Chandala
6...Palasgarh
7...Gewarda
8...Rangi
9...Dhanora
10...Khutgaon
11...Sonsari
12...Jharapapra
13...Kotgal
14...Muramgaon
15...Sirsundi
GEOLOGICAL REFERENCES
Iron Ore
Lamota Beds
Barakar
Talchir
Kampti
Vindhyans
Deccan Trap
Dharwars
Granite
Gneisses
Alluvium
BHANDARA
NAGPUR
WARDHA
DRUG
TIPAGARH HILL
to Umrer
to Chauki
to Mohali
from Hinganghat
Wunna R.
Arher Nawargaon
BRAMHAPURI
Deotek
Palasgarh
Gewarda
Sonsari
Kotgal
Sirsundi
Rangi
Muramgaon
Dhanora
GARHCHIROLI
WARORA

Prepared specially for the Superintendent Gazetteer Revision. C. P. from an Original supplied by him.

Note.—The longitudes are referrible to the Greenwich meridian, taking that of Madras observatory as 80°-17′-21″ East. They require a correction of −2′-27″ to make them accord with the most recent value of the geodetic longitude of that observatory, viz., 80°-14′-54″.

Helio, S. I. O., Calcutta.

Reg. No. 2387 E. 08.—450.

227. For administrative purposes the forests of the northern division are divided into seven ranges, *viz.*, Moharlī, Havelī, Dābha, Warorā, Bramhapurī, Gunjewāhī and Wairāgarh, and each range is in charge of a Ranger or Deputy Ranger according to its importance. The present strength of the staff is 1 Forest Divisional Officer, 2 Rangers, 5 Deputy Rangers, 11 Foresters and 212 Forest Guards. The forests cover an area where the underlying rock is metamorphic sandstone, while laterite also occurs frequently; the resulting soil is a sandy loam, changing to brown clay, with alluvium deposits of considerable depth in ravines. Wherever sufficient moisture exists, these soils are capable of supporting fairly dense mixed forests, but the excessive heat and dryness of the climate retard the height growth, and active vegetation is restricted to the four months of the monsoon. Timber has been divided into four classes, according to the present market value of each species; the first two classes consist of hard wood suitable for building and furniture, the third of soft and non-durable woods and the fourth of bamboos. First-class woods comprise teak (*Tectona grandis*), *bijasāl* (*Pterocarpus marsupium*), and *shīsham* (*Dalbergia latifolia*), none of which are common in this division. Teak is sprinkled throughout the whole area, but the percentage is small; it is most abundant in the east of the Dābha range, where specimens 50 feet high and of a diameter of 4 feet 6 inches breast high from the ground occur, but the average girth does not exceed 3 feet. Drought has very seriously affected this species of recent years and thousands of stems have had to be cut out annually owing to stagheadedness. The finest *bijasāl* occurs in the Kanhārgaon block of the Dābha range where trees having a girth of 7 to 8 feet and a height of 50 feet may be seen. The average girth, however is seldom more than 3 or 4 feet and the tree is not common. The *shīsham*, familiar as the wood used for black-wood furniture, is also comparatively rare and undersized. Second

The North Chānda Division. Principal trees.

class timbers comprise many fine species, which are either insufficiently known or do not attain a considerable growth, and are therefore relegated to use as poles in the building of huts or devoted to the manufacture of agricultural implements. By far the most common is the *yen* or *sāj* (*Terminalia tomentosa*) which is almost as numerous as all the other species combined. It here seldom attains timber size and is principally used for pit-props in the local colliery and for hut building. The *dhaurā* (*Anogeissus latifolia*), *bhirā* (*Chloroxylon Swietenia*) or satin wood, the *garāri*, *temrū*, *kalam*, *haldi*, *kosam*, *anjan* and *babūl* are the other most common species of this class. Bamboos abound in the Moharlī and Havelī ranges and in parts of the Dābha range, and until 1902-03 formed a most valuable source of revenue. In that year, however, gregarious seeding took place, and bamboos died down almost completely over wide tracts. The old stock was replaced by a full crop of seedlings, but these are still undersized, and cutting has therefore been kept down with a strict hand. The resulting annual loss amounts to at least Rs. 15,000 or Rs 20,000 and must continue until the bamboos are again fit for regular working which will not be till three or four years hence. The principal edible fruit bearing trees are the mango, which occurs chiefly as an escape, the mahuā, which is very plentiful especially in the Gunjewāhi and Bramhapurī ranges, the *chār* (*Buchanania latifolia*), the fruit of which is called *chironjī*, the *khirnī*, and *aonlā*.

Minor products.

228. The chief minor products are lac, gums, mahuā and *chironjī*, wax and honey, and hides and horns. Lac is the product of an insect, *Coccus lacci*; trees are artificially infected with it by fastening on to them twigs encrusted with this insect which have been taken from already infected trees. The production of lac is greatest in years when there are heavy mists, and this has given rise to a popular superstition that the lac insects are born of the morning mist. The finest quality of lac is grown on the *kosam* (*Schleichera trijuga*) and attempts

have been made to cultivate it departmentally on this tree, but the late years of drought have so far baffled these experiments. Success is, however, inevitable with more favourable seasons, and a large increase of revenue will eventually be obtained from this source. Lac is collected departmentally in the Moharlī and Havelī ranges, but with this exception, all minor forest produce is disposed of on annual leases sold by auction. Forest produce is generally removed and revenue collected on licenses, but commutation for *nistār, paidāwār* and grazing on the village assessment system is also permitted.

Management of the forests.

229. Until about 1893, fellings appear to have been allowed to take place indiscriminately, but the removal of produce was subsequently localised to some extent, and eventually by 1899 the forests in each range had been brought under regular working-plans. Under these working-plans, each range is divided into a felling series or a number of working circles, and each felling series is again divided into twenty or thirty coupes; one coupe is opened annually, and after being worked is closed to grazing for ten years. The method of treatment prescribed is termed 'Improvement fellings,' but owing to the limited demand and the large proportion of inferior timber, this method fails to attain the object in view, and therefore the system actually applied partakes more of the nature of a thinning out of poles after reservation of the most promising stems.

Financial results.

230. The main sources of revenue since the constitution of the division have been in round figures, as shown below:—

Year.	Timber.	Fuel.	Grazing and grass.	Bamboos.	Minor forest produce.	Commutation.	Miscellaneous.	Total.
	Rs.	Rs.	Rs.	Rs.	Rs.	Rs.	Rs.	Rs.
1904-05	30,000	12,000	39,000	16,000	7000	17,000	3000	1,23,000
1905-06	44,000	7,000	58,000	15,000	10,000	17,000	2000	1,53,000
1906-07	38,000	12,000	58,000	11,000	7000	14,000	3000	1,44,000

The revenue and expenditure for the same period have been :—

Year.		Revenue.	Expenditure.	Surplus.
		Rs.	Rs.	Rs.
1904-05	...	1,23,000	78,000	45,000
1905-06	...	1,53,000	80,000	73,000
1906-07	...	1,44,000	83,000	61,000

The South Chānda Division.

231. The forests of the South Chānda Division form three compact blocks,[1] the most northerly being composed of the Ghot and Alāpallī ranges, the Sironchā range lying in the centre and the Cherlā range to the south. All these forests have a natural outlet to the south by means of rivers. The Prānhita forming the southern boundary of the Ghot range flows within eight miles of Alāpallī, and passes down the entire length of the Sironchā range to the west, while the Indrāvati similarly bounds this latter range to the east. The Cherlā range is a long strip of country along the left bank of the Godāvari which for the entire length of the range is open to navigation from the south for several months in the year. The mart to which these rivers give access is Rājahmundry in the Madras Presidency.

Nature of forests.

232. The forests of this division lie midway between the dry zone of Central India and the moister tropical forests of the Eastern Ghāts. Such southern species as *suria* (*Xylia dolabriformis*), the ironwood tree of Burma (this, however, occurs chiefly in the pole class only) and *polgu* or *polki* (*Givotia rottleriformis*), with shrubs such as *Webera corymbosa* and *Homonoia retusa* begin to make their appearance while *sāl* is not found at all either in

[1]The Dābha range was added on 1st July 1908, the Cherlā range was transferred to Madras on 1st July 1909 and the Ghot range was split up into the Ghot and Mārkhandā ranges on 1st April 1909.

this or in the northern division. The forests are mainly of the composition known as the Central Provinces types, *i.e.*, grass land sparsely or densely covered, according to the character of the soil, with poles of *sāj*, *lendia*, *dhaura*, *garāri*, *khair*, *rohan*, *aonli*, *tendū*, *mowai*, *salai*, *chār*, *mahuā*, *gongal*, the *semal* or red cotton tree and the *safed phetrā* (*Gardenia turgida*), with varying proportions of *bijasāl*, *haldū*, *shīsham kaini* (*Mitragyna parvifolia*) and teak. In Ghot along the Prānhita and for 10 or 12 miles up the Waingangā river there is an almost pure teak pole forest with a lower storey of thorny species, chiefly *zizyphus* and *khair*. A similar but better type is found in the B-I class areas in the south of Sironchā along the Godāvari. The rest of Sironchā contains a type of forest rarely met with elsewhere in the Province ; in this *anjan* (*Hardwickia binata*) is the characteristic tree, and is often found as a natural standard over a Central Provinces type, or on richer soils with teak, *bijasāl* and *sāj* of good height-growth ; in the extreme north-east it forms almost a pure forest.

Principal trees.

233. The most important species of timber is teak, which except in the south of the Ghot range is usually found mixed with other species. The Alāpallī, Elchil and Machhlīgattā blocks contain the finest teak in the Central Provinces, the largest specimens attaining a height of from 120 to 130 and a girth of 8 or 9, or even exceptionally 10 to 12 feet. The best crop is met with at the foot of the Bhimāram hills in the Alāpallī range, and its excellence is to a great extent due to continued immunity from fire and grazing, which has converted the open grass land type of forest, still to be seen across the boundary-line in the unprotected zamīndāri area, into a dense coppice of fine straight stems. Teak growth deteriorates as one goes further south, being inferior in Sironchā and still worse in Cherlā. The best stems have almost everywhere been cut out in former unregulated working, and much of what remains, of the older timber at any

rate, is unsound. The species delights in well-drained rich soils which, unfortunately for it, are also the most attractive to the cultivator. Teak is the only timber for which there is a real demand from the direction of Chānda. When sawn scantlings were carted to Warorā, the bulk of the stock was purchased by traders from Berār. The long lead has hitherto made it impossible to exploit less highly priced timbers in this direction. *Bijasāl* grows to a large size in Alāpallī and Sironchā and is found throughout the division; owing to the high price of teak, it is coming more and more into use as a building wood, but Government *bijasāl* has hitherto always been undersold by that brought from private forests. *Shīsham* attains a girth of 6 or 7 feet in Alāpallī, but the larger trees are generally hollow, and there is little demand for this wood. It occurs in less size in other ranges. The most common timber tree of these forests is the *sāj* or *yen* (*Terminalia tomentosa*) which is found everywhere and under favourable conditions attains a height of 100 to 120 feet and a girth of 8 or 9 feet; the other species which occur most frequently are those already enumerated in dealing with the northern division.

Bamboos and minor forest produce.

234. Except in the east of Sironchā and Cherlā, where the large thorny bamboo (*Bambusa arundinacea*) forms almost impenetrable forests along the banks of streams, the common bamboo of the Province (*Dendrocalamus strictus*) is the only one found. Since the seeding of bamboos in North Chānda the trade in this produce has slightly improved. The *kosam* is common along the banks of streams, and in this division also there should be a great future for the lac industry. *Harrā or hirdā* is not nearly so common as in the more northerly forests of the Provinces, and not more than Rs. 500 or Rs. 600 worth of myrobalans is collected annually. Tasar silk worms are reared in the north of Ghot and the south of Sironchā, but the present methods of rearing are said to be extremely destructive to the forests, and the

industry is not a popular one with forest officials. There is a small export of lac, wax and myrobalans chiefly to the south, where also hides of animals dying in Government forest fetch a better price than elsewhere. The gathering of mahuā and *tolī* is left to the villagers who make large profits by selling this produce to the lessees to whom it is annually auctioned.

The Alāpallī saw-mills.

235. Before the separation of the two divisions, a Sub-Divisional Officer used to be in charge of what is now the South Chānda Division, and had his headquarters at Alāpallī. Departmental working on an extensive scale has always been concentrated on Alāpallī, the forests of which have been exploited by Government since 1867. Before the range was purchased, a royalty of 3 annas on each cubic foot extracted used to be paid to the zamīndār. In 1871, saw-mills were started at Alāpallī chiefly with the object of supplying sleepers to the Bengal-Nāgpur Railway for the Bilāspur-Katnī line and to the Great Indian Peninsula Railway for the extension from Wardhā to Warorā. The feat of establishing and keeping up these saw-mills at a distance of over 100 miles from the nearest railway and in a notoriously unhealthy part of the country was one of enormous difficulty, but it was successfully accomplished. Sleepers and scantlings were floated up the Wardhā as far as Warorā and also up to Kamptee on the Kanhān. At one time, there were 17 elephants and nearly 5000 men employed either in the forest or in the floating and sale depots. The largest annual outturn was in 1879-80, when 7813 trees containing 358,490 cubic feet were converted. The timber was brought to the depot from the coupe in carts till December 1902 when a monorail tramway four miles in length was laid down. In November 1907 the saw-mills were closed to Government working, and three annual coupes, as prescribed by the working-plan which was drawn up in 1894—96, were for the first time sold to a contractor.

Working-plans and fire-protection.

236. The result of this concentration of attention upon Alāpallī has been that not until 1899 was a working-plan made for Ghot, while even now the large and valuable forests in the south have never been touched. The Alāpallī working-plan embraces a period of forty years and covers the southern two-thirds of the range. Altogether 80 compartments are demarcated, in 40 of which only works of improvement are prescribed. The forest is closed to grazing and to commutation, and is only exploited for large timber, the quantity of bamboos removed being insignificant. The Ghot plan covers a period of 15 years and divides the range into eleven blocks. The demands of the people are fully met from the B-I class areas, and except for small departmental operations in one or two compartments during the last few years no work has been done, but probably most of these blocks will be worked profitably in a few years' time when trade from the south has developed. The timber trade down stream is growing rapidly and almost anything that will float can be sold at good rates in the more southerly parts of the division. Already in Sironchā *sāj* is more remunerative per cubic foot than teak used to be in Alāpallī under the old departmental working. At present the policy is to work the more valuable forests under improvement fellings in order to remove unsound stock and make room for a better crop that will have had the benefit of fire-protection and conservation from its youth. Fire-protection was begun in Bhimāram in 1873, and there are now 571 square miles under protection. The intensity of protection varies in the different forests; in Alāpallī the cost of protection is over Rs. 20 per square mile, while in areas where no special fire establishment is maintained, it is only a few annas. The forest staff of the division at present consists of a Divisional Forest Officer, 3 Rangers, 1 Deputy Ranger, 7 Foresters and 65 Guards. The headquarters of the division continues to be at Chānda, though that city is about 40 miles from its nearest boundary.

237. The following statement shows the receipts under different heads for the last three years in even hundreds of rupees:—

Financial results.

Year.	Timber	Fuel.	Grazing and grass.	Bamboos.	Minor forest produce.
1904-05 ...	42,100	400	15,000	800	1100
1905-06 ...	76,000	200	30,000	1000	1200
1906-07 ...	76,500	200	28,100	1000	1300

and the statement below gives the statistics of revenue and expenditure for the same period:—

Year.	Revenue.	Expenditure.	Surplus.
1904-05 ...	68,500	66,700	1800
1905-06 ...	1,19,300	70,900	48,400
1906-07 ...	1,19,200	75,300	43,800

238. The zamīndāri area of the District is practically one unbroken forest. At settlement, the proportion of scrub jungle and forest to the total area of each zamīndāri ranged from 98 per cent. in Muramgaon and Jhārāpāpra to 54 per cent. in Rāngi; five other zamīndāris contained over 90 per cent. of forest, and six over 80 per cent., while Sonsari and Gewardhā are comparatively open with 65 and 66 per cent. of forest respectively.

Zamīndāri forests.

239. The most remarkable and the best developed forests are those of the Ahīri zamīndāri, which in 1906-07 covered 2527 out of the 2600 square miles of the estate. Four types may here be distinguished—(i) the bamboo type

Forests of the Ahīri zamīndāri.

which occurs mainly on the hills in association with teak, and in the plains along the banks of streams and nullahs and in depressions in conjunction with *bijasāl, yen, tendū* and *baherā* and also with a sprinkling of teak and *anjan* at the water's edge. *Kosam* is also found in this type in the valleys and along the bases of hills; (ii) the teak type which is found over about one-third of the whole forest area being especially conspicuous in the Mallampalli tāluk and along the banks of the Bandia river. Here teak of large dimensions is abundant, forming the predominant species and in places tending to become almost pure forest. Associated with it are found individual large trees such as *bijasāl, yen, tendū, shīsham dhaurā, kaim*, and scattered trees of less importance; (iii) the mixed forest type, which constitutes more than half the area of all the forests. This falls into two distinct subtypes—(*a*) that occurring in high lands where the forests are dense, and composed mainly of superior species, and (*b*) that on low, heavy, binding soils; here the forests are poor and more open, and are of the ordinary Central Provinces type with a great deal of grass; (iv) the *anjan* type, which occurs on sandy and gravelly soil, and is more or less restricted to an area about two miles broad lying to the south-west of the Alāpallī reserve, and extending from the borders of the Ahīri range to the foot of the Dewalmāri hills. In this tract, the *anjan*, which is of a remarkably gregarious habit, tends to form a pure forest. Individual large trees of the same species are also found in the dense mixed forest to the south of the Dewalmāri hills, and attain very large dimensions; some now standing have a girth of from 10 to 15 feet.

The crop is irregular, and every variety of density is to be found from open grassy plains to dense forest. This is attributable to the annual occurrence of severe fires, which had till recently been allowed to run over the forests unchecked. Prior to the assumption of management by the Court of Wards in 1902, immense damage had also been done by reckless felling; contractors were allowed to enter the best teak areas and cut out as many first class trees as they could obtain; of these they only removed the best and soundest logs. When the estate was taken under management, thousands of small and unsound logs thus rejected were found lying in the forests; of these many were collected and sold, a work not of months but of years, but the annual fires caused the destruction of vast numbers before they could be so salvaged. Shifting cultivation (*jwālapod*) had also been allowed to proceed unchecked and caused incalculable damage to large tracts of valuable jungle.

Since assumption, however, an end has been put to this maladministration, and the forests are now efficiently worked by a manager under the control of the Deputy Commissioner and in accordance with the provisions of the rules under section 124-A of the Land Revenue Act. Sylvicultural principles have been adopted so far as the undefined limits of the forest will permit. Fellings have been located, and not more than 500 trees are felled annually, the trees to be cut out being selected and marked under the direct supervision of the manager. At first, the indebtedness of the estate necessitated very economical working, and, although the demarcation of the more valuable teak areas had been recognised as essential as soon as the estate was taken over, it was not until 1905-06 that the necessary funds were forthcoming. The survey and demarcation of the Mallampalli tāluk was then taken in hand and pushed on rapidly. When this is completed, it is intended to frame a simple working-plan on somewhat general lines to render the working of the forests systematic and preclude the risk of over-cutting. The same year also saw the initiation of the first attempts at fire-protection in the forests of this zamīndāri. The experiment was entirely successful, the whole area of 863 acres treated being saved from fire. It is intended to put each compartment as it is felled under fire-protection, until the whole area now in course of demarcation is fully protected. Creeper cutting and the restriction of shifting cultivation are other important features of the reformed management of these forests. *Jwālapod* is now restricted to areas within village lands which are at least two miles distant from the forest boundary, and, although careful handling of the custom is necessary, it is hoped that it will in course of time give way to permanent cultivation.

Forest income of Ahīri.

240. The forest income since assumption of management is shown below:—

Head of revenue.	Realisations.				
	1901-02.	1902-03.	1903-04.	1904-05.	1905-06.
	Rs.	Rs.	Rs.	Rs.	Rs.
Sale of timber ...	18,500	22,250	25,000	36,700	27,800
Sale of teak *dongas* ...	...	...	...	3200	2000
Forest licenses... ...	150	250	650	1050	1400
Commutation fees ...	400	1550	1800	1750	550
Mahuā and *toli* ...	1900	2400	2350	2200	2350
Grazing	900	1800	2150	2250	4150
Minor forest produce ...	750	450	250	450	300
Total ...	22,500	28,700	31,800	47,700	38,450

The net revenue cannot be estimated, as the estate is worked as a whole in all its branches of administration. The fluctuations of forest income depend mainly on the rate obtainable for teak; for instance, this rate dropped from R. 1-7-9 per cubic foot in 1904-05 to R. 1-3-3 in 1905-06, the decrease being due partly to the closing of the anicut at Dumagudiam for repairs and partly to large auctions of timber by the Forest Department in North Kanara; the former of these circumstances deterred the Rājahmundry contractors from attending the sales, while the latter diverted the attendance of many bidders from Hyderābād, who would have otherwise appeared at Ahīri. One noticeable feature in the receipts is the income from the sale of teak *dongas.* These fetch from Rs. 2 to Rs. 2-8 per cubic foot, and are made of unsound timber, which could not otherwise be disposed of at so considerable a profit. A good many are purchased by the Public Works Department, but the demand is not large enough to make it a permanently important source of revenue.

Mālguzāri forests of the Ahiri estate.

241. The Ahīri estate also owns 77 mālguzāri villages in the Ghot and Amgaon parganas of the Garhchirolī tahsīl. These villages comprise an area of 55 square miles of which 38 are covered with jungle. In 62 of the villages the forests consist of a mixed species of poor growth, with abundant spaces of grass and an irregular scrub jungle on the border of cultivation. But in the other 15 villages, which lie within three or four miles of the Waingangā and of the Prānhita, is found an area of some 4000 acres composed of an irregular pure forest of teak poles which attain an average height of 40 feet and a maximum girth of 4 feet. Most of the trees are deformed through bad treatment in the past and will never yield timber of very large dimensions But in one village, Sidāpur Rit, which is situated in the middle of the Government forest, the fire-protection of the surrounding tracts has given scope for an abundant growth of young trees which is a striking visible testimonial to the advantages of fire-protection. The mixed forests are available to the people for *nistār*, and all that has been done since the assumption of the estate is to forbid the removal of the green wood except under a license; in the teak-producing area, all unregulated fellings have been discontinued, and a system of moderate thinning substituted which will improve the growth and convert these forests into a valuable source of income.

The forest establishment of the estate consisted in 1906-07, in addition to the Manager who is a trained forest official, of 1 Darogā, 1 Forester, 4 Moharirs and 8 Guards.

Other zamindāri forests.

242. There is little to be said of the forests of the other zamīndāris. From Major Lucie Smith's Settlement Report it would appear that in his day, though wastefully cut, they contained plenty of good timber and promised well. Since then, however, wasteful cutting has gone on without check, and for some time there has been little wood of value left in them. The reckless felling has been to a great extent dictated by the necessities of the zamīndārs, many of whom are heavily in debt. Much damage has also been done by forest fires which annually run over a large area; many of these are started deliberately to facilitate the collection of mahuā and also partly as a safeguard against tigers. Small teak is still obtainable in Murramgaon, Dhanorā, Kotgul and occasionally elsewhere, but in the main the estates are dependent on bamboos and other minor produce. The bamboos east of the Waingangā did not seed to the same extent as those nearer Chānda, and consequently there has been a fair demand for them of recent years. The only estates for which reliable statistics of income are available are Gewardhā and Rāngi, which are under the Court of Wards, and whose average annual income from forests during the years 1903–06 amounted to Rs. 4000 and Rs. 2100 respectively. These estates, however, benefit by comparatively scientific management; the independently managed estates have much smaller incomes. The forest receipts of Palāsgarh, undoubtedly the wealthiest among them from the forest point of view, were only placed at Rs. 1800 for purposes of assessment at the last settlement; and Khutgaon with an estimated income of Rs. 1500, Kotgul with Rs. 1250, and Muramgaon with Rs. 1200 are the only other estates whose income from this source is supposed to exceed Rs. 1000, while the average income for all 16 zamīndāris exclusive of Ahīri amounts, according to the same estimates, to only Rs. 873. Doubtless, with careful management, this income might expand considerably, but even those zamīndārs who make any attempt

to look after their forests are handicapped by the difficulty of adequately managing large areas with the small staffs which their means can command.

Mālguzāri forests.

243. The mālguzāri forests of the District cover a considerable area but do not call for detailed notice. At the original settlement, each village was allotted waste lands of an area twice as large as its total area of occupied land: much of this land was, and still is, covered with jungle of varying characters. The care with which the village forest is managed depends on the ability and energy of the mukaddam; as a rule, its comparatively small area enables him to look after it more closely than a zamīndār can look after his forest; but nothing like scientific management is attempted. In the north of the District the mālguzāri forests supply a good deal of grass, small timber and firewood to the markets of the Nāgpur and Wardhā Districts, and there is also a very brisk demand from the same quarter for mahuā produce. In more remote parts, such as Rājgarh, where there are good mahuā forests, the lack of demand renders this produce of little profit. As a rule, villages in this District have at least sufficient jungle area to satisfy their tenants' demand for *nistār*, and more often than not the forest is also sufficiently extensive to be worked with an eye to commercial profit, but the possibility of so doing naturally depends on the proximity of a suitable market which is somewhat of a rarity.

Roadside arboriculture.

244. Of a length of 297 miles on 8 roads in charge of the Public Works Department 12 miles are provided with established avenues and 102 miles pass through forest where they are not required. A length of 114 miles is thus provided for. Of the remainder 43 miles have partial or incomplete avenues and 140 miles are without them. The principal established avenues are 7½ miles on the Warorā-Chānda road and 4½ miles on the Mūl-Umrer road from Nāgbhīr to the border of the District towards Umrer. The greater lengths of incomplete

avenues lie on the Warorā-Chānda (11 miles), Warorā-Wūn (4½ miles) and the Chānda Station roads (3½ miles). The District Council has charge of five roads with a total length of 89 miles. Of these only 2½ miles have avenues planted about five years ago, *viz.*, one mile on the Chānda-Chimūr road and 1½ miles on the southern road from Warorā to the border of the District towards Wardhā. The trees in a small portion of the Chānda-Chimūr road are said to be subject to attacks of white-ants and demand especial care. The trees usually planted are *babūl*, mango, *nīm*, *siris* (*Albizzia odoratissima* and *procera*), tamarind, *kāranj* (*Pongamia glabra*) and mahuā. The Warorā-Chānda road has good shady avenues of mixed growth and pīpal. *Babūl* trees were planted on many portions of the District roads and have grown very well with almost no expenditure. These trees are useful for agricultural implements, fuel, etc., but do not make shady avenues.

MINERALS.

Coal. The Mayo Colliery.

245. The remarkable mineral wealth of the District has so far been exploited on a commercial scale in only one direction, namely, the development of its coal deposits. The west side of the District as far south as the Third Barrier of the Godāvari lies within the Wardhā Valley Coalfield, an area, the natural geological limits of which indicate a total extent of 1600 square miles, and which towards the north runs up to within 16 miles of the important cotton mart of Hinganghāt. The first traces of coal in this District[1] were discovered in October 1865 when some pieces of carbonaceous shale were picked up in the bed of the Wardhā river; these were followed up, and were found to have been washed from the Chānda bank of the river to the west of Ghūgus, a village lying due west of Chānda. A pit was thereupon sunk in that village, and coal was struck at a depth of 30 feet. The search for further

[1] The valueless coal discovered in 1848 at Kotal may be left out of consideration.

deposits was vigorously prosecuted and outcrops were discovered at Ballālpur and Lāthi. In 1869, Mr. Fryar, a Mining Engineer, was deputed by Government to make a systematic enquiry into the value and extent of the coalfield. Proper boring instruments were provided, and it was proved that the Ghūgus seam was thicker and more constant than had at first been supposed. A working pit sunk within 300 yards of the river struck an upper seam 4 feet thick at 80 feet below the surface and a lower seam 33 feet thick at 95 feet down. Although the coal was of variable quality a thickness of at least 20 feet was composed of good coal. By 1870 the Ghūgus pit had been brought into thorough working order with regular galleries, two cages, and a gin worked by hand power which raised 10 or 15 tons of coal a day. It was considered of sufficient importance to merit the patronage of a Viceroy, and in 1870 it was formally declared open by Lord Mayo, thenceforward assuming the name of the Mayo Colliery. It remained in steady working till the following year, about 70 tons being raised each month; the coal was partly consumed by the steam borer, while the rest was taken by the Great Indian Peninsula Railway. The composition of the coal was somewhat uneven, but as a whole it was good enough for steam service in dry weather; in rainy weather, however, it was found to be incapable of standing exposure, and this defect made it necessary to search for a more suitable material. An average sample of Ghūgus coal gave the following analysis:—

Carbon	... ...	45·61 per cent.
Volatile matter (including water)	...	33·49 „ „
Ash	... ...	20·90 „ „

The Warorā Colliery.

246. Many indications pointed to the probable existence of coal to the north round about Warorā within easy reach of the Hinganghāt cotton market, and search was naturally directed towards that locality when the desirability of abandoning the Mayo Colliery had become obvious. The first coal was proved in

1870 by a boring 102 feet in depth about half a mile east of Warorā. Other borings were made to ascertain the dip of the strata, and, to sum up the result of these investigations, the existence was proved of a slightly broken coalfield extending from Ghūgus to Warorā, a distance of 22 miles, the quality of the coal being found to improve in the vicinity of Warorā; it was also deemed probable that the coal extended well to the east of Warorā. These preliminary operations were in the hands of Mr. Fryar. The year 1871 witnessed the actual commencement of work at the Warorā Colliery. Many difficulties had to be overcome, the chief of which was the extraordinary influx of water, with which the pumps at first provided were not adequate to cope. The railway was as yet not in existence, and frequent changes of management still further militated against good progress. In 1873, however, on the appointment of Mr. Ness, an Engineer of considerable experience in England, the sinking of the pits was successfully completed. In all, seven pits were sunk, with a depth varying from 140 to 240 feet. An unlooked for addition to the mineral wealth of the area was given by the discovery of a second seam of superior coal below the first. Both the upper and the lower seam were worked; the former was known as No. 2 and was from 12 to 15 feet in thickness, the latter, or No. 3 seam, was between 10 and 11 feet thick, and the two seams were divided by a band of shale about 6 feet thick. Trials made by the Great Indian Peninsula Railway in 1874 gave satisfactory results, and it was found that the consumption per ton mile only exceeded that of English coal by 13 per cent. Two systems of working were at first in vogue; the 'bord and pillar' and the 'long wall' system, but the friability of the coal proved unsuitable to the latter method and it was abandoned in 1877. Under the 'bord and pillar' system which thenceforth obtained alone the seams are cut into pillars by means of galleries and subsequently the pillars are themselves extracted. From the beginning, the presence of iron pyrites in the coal rendered it susceptible to spontaneous combustion and led to frequent underground fires which were a source of constant anxiety and danger, to say nothing of the expense attendant on the work of keeping them under control and providing for the safety of the workers; towards the end there were underground fires in all the pits, which were combated by surrounding them with brick walls. It was realised that the mine would have to close down about the end of 1906; the end, however, came sooner than had been expected. On the 28th March 1906, a large subsidence took place fortunately unattended by loss of life, and an influx of water followed which the machinery of the mine was unable to pump out. A considerable area of coal was lost, and, as the remainder was not sufficient to allow of the colliery being worked at a profit, it was finally closed down on the 30th April 1906. The causes which led to the subsidence are fully set forth by Mr. Pickering, the Chief Inspector of Mines, in his report for the year 1906. The radical and fatal mistake lay in the working of both seams simultaneously, instead of working the top seam first and allowing the strata to subside before touching the bottom seam. The loss of coal due to this defective system of working was enormous. According to Mr. Pickering, a reasonable estimate of the coal in the area worked would be 12,000,000 tons. Of this 3,086,220 tons or only 25 per cent. had been raised. If the mine had been properly laid out and worked from the beginning, perhaps 75 per cent. would have been recovered. The additional six million tons would have prolonged the life of the colliery by about forty years.[1]

As mentioned above over three million tons of coal were raised from the mine during its existence, the largest output in any one year being 153,336 tons in 1902. About half the coal raised was sold to the Great Indian Peninsula Railway, and the remainder to various mills, gins and presses between

[1] It is but justice to add that the evil was done in the early years of the colliery, and that the management of the later years of the mine was entirely exculpated.

Nāgpur and Bhusāwal; the demand from these latter had towards the end completely outgrown the supply. The selling rate at the pit's mouth was Rs. 5 per ton. Until 1882 the colliery was worked at a loss, but thenceforward with a temporary and only partial check from 1892 to 1895 it paid very well indeed. The capital outlay in 1894 stood at 20·65 lakhs: by 1906 this had been written down to 12·84 lakhs by means of a sinking fund. The net profits during the whole life of the mine amounted to 30·86 lakhs, and the highest rate of interest paid in any year was just over 17 per cent. in 1902. During the busy season about 1200 people in all were employed, rather more than half of these being underground workers. Most of the coal-cutters came from the United Provinces; they were all paid by piece-work, and earned on an average from 6 to 12 annas a day; unskilled labourers were paid 4 or 5 annas a day. Fire-clay was also worked; it was found on top of the coal. Fire-bricks, floor and roofing tiles were made in large quantities and were a source of considerable profit. The following is a fairly accurate analysis of the coal:—

Fixed carbon	...	...	45·4 per cent.
Volatile matter	...	...	26·5 ,, ,,
Moisture ...	...	...	13·9 ,, ,,
Ash ...	...	...	14·2 ,, ,,

The underground working extended from the Nāgpur-Chānda road between miles 67 and 68 to the town of Warorā where the coal thins out and disappears. The boundary on the north was a fault running a little to the north of No. 2 pit to the middle of the town tank; the south boundary was also a fault which ran nearly east and west from the village of Ekarjunā.

The Ballālpur Colliery.

247. The existence of coal at Ballālpur, some ten miles south of Chānda, had been suspected as early as 1871. In that year the Public Works Department of Hyderābād had discovered coal on the opposite bank of the Wardhā near the village of

Sasti. This discovery caused boring work to be taken in hand at Ballālpur at a spot opposite Sasti, but, after several unsuccessful attempts it was concluded that the bulk of the coalfield lay across the river, and work was stopped. In 1900, however, it became imperative to find a substitute for the Warorā Colliery which was known to be approaching exhaustion, and a visit was paid to Ballālpur which resulted in the discovery of favourable indications. A small sum of money was sanctioned for exploration work, and, coal having been proved in two bore-holes in the bed of the river, more bore-holes were, in spite of considerable local criticism, commenced to the east, and as a consequence coal was proved at a depth of 550 feet a mile from the river. More boring was then undertaken nearer the village of Ballālpur. As all boring had been done by hand, progress had hitherto been very slow. A trial pit was commenced in 1903 in order to get out samples of coal for trial purposes. The work laboured under severe difficulties; there was no road to Chānda and all machinery and boilers had to be drawn by bullocks over a rough country track; firewood had to be used for fuel and whenever the supply failed water rose up in the pit and stopped work; added to this, work was impossible during the rains. When coal was reached at a depth of 200 feet, it was decided to commence a second pit and begin to open out a new colliery. This second pit was sunk in 1906 to a depth of 257 feet, and the seam of coal was found to be 50 feet thick and of better quality than Warorā coal. The actual output of coal remained insignificant until 1907, but in that year the railway reached Ballālpur and considerably assisted the work of opening out the mine. In January 1908, the daily output of coal reached 140 tons. Ballālpur is now a prosperous mining village, and the colliery has a great future before it. The capital outlay on the mine amounts to about nine lakhs, five lakhs of which represents the book value of stores and machinery transferred to it from the Warorā Colliery. The colliery is connected with the station at Ballālpur by a line about a mile long with numerous sidings.

This extensive discovery of coal at Ballālpur is a matter of considerable interest. So far from the bulk of the coalfield lying on the Hyderābād side of the river, as was previously supposed, indications at present point to the outer edge only being across stream, and the main body seems to extend a great distance into the Chānda District. All the collieries hitherto described are the property of Government. Of private enterprise there is little to record; a prospecting license was granted to Messrs. J. and N. Tata of Bombay over an area of 2 square miles in the village of Dudholi near Ballālpur, and they sank several borings and a trial pit, but operations were abandoned when it was decided that the iron resources of the District were unsuitable to form the basis of an iron and steel industry. Coal has also been proved at several other sites mostly in the riverain tract along the banks of the Wardhā in the Warorā and Chānda tahsīls. Mr. Theodore Hughes' paper on the Wardhā Valley Coalfield in Volume XIII, part 1 of the Memoirs of the Geological Survey of India, gives an exhaustive account of the researches conducted and conclusions arrived at by him. In his opinion, the greatest store of coal in the District is probably to the east of the town of Chānda, but the seams are, he supposes, too low down to be worth working. Outside the riverain tract, three seams with a total thickness of 38 feet have been proved at Bandār, and Mr. Hughes estimated the area of readily workable coal to be at least 6 square miles. This field is advantageously situated in respect to the iron ores of Lohāra and Pīpalgaon, but as there now seems no prospect of these latter being worked on a commercial scale, this fact has not the importance previously attached to it. Some coal of poor quality exists at Kotah, north of Sironchā, where boring operations were undertaken as far back as 1848. A little slaty coal and lignite has also been observed elsewhere in the Sironchā tahsīl, but there does not appear to be any deposit of value.

248. The iron ores of Chānda have long excited the interest of investigators, and, situated as they are in close proximity to the coal and limestone in and about Warorā, the question of exploiting them after modern commercial methods has frequently been mooted. The first detailed examination of the local iron deposits was made by Mr. Theodore Hughes of the Geological Survey of India in 1873, whose paper on the subject will be found in Volume XIII, part 1 of the Memoirs of that body. He formed an extremely high estimate of the value of the iron deposits of Chānda. In 1875, Mr. Ness conducted experiments with the view of testing the practicability of smelting the local iron with the local coal, but the latter was found to be unsuitable to the blast furnace, although moderately good results were obtained with a reverbatory furnace. In 1881, Herr Ritter von Schwartz, an expert of great mining experience in Austria, made a survey of the local iron deposits and formed a highly sanguine opinion of the prospects of an industry on modern lines with headquarters to be placed at Durgāpur. He contemplated an annual outturn of no less than 260,000 tons of iron and steel, and was of opinion that Chānda could not only supply the whole requirements of India in iron and steel, but would also be able to compete with the Continent in importing ferro-manganese and Brescian steel into England. Subsequent investigations have shown that these anticipations were very highly coloured. In 1900, Major Mahon, R.E., was specially deputed by the Government of India to investigate and report on the prospect of an Indian iron and steel industry, and among other localities visited this District. His opinion of its natural resources was a high one, but difficulties of fuel and communication led him to place Chānda only third on the list of possible sites for a modern iron industry. In 1902 the same authority drew up a 'Note on the Chānda Iron Deposits' which gives a complete account of the iron resources of the District. When Messrs. J. and N. Tata a

Iron.

few years ago conceived the scheme of the Iron and Steel Syndicate recently (1907) floated by them, this District was the first locality selected by them for investigation. The results of this investigation were disappointing; not only was it found that the amount of ore available had been greatly over-estimated, but there were also insuperable difficulties as to fuel and water-supply. The local coals are non-coking, and, though there was at one time some hope of overcoming this drawback by the aid of certain German and American processes, Messrs. Tata were finally induced under the advice of their experts to leave inferior coals alone and go direct to the good coking coals of Bengal. Thus, for some years to come at any rate, the hope of seeing Chānda the Middlesborough of India must be abandoned.

The most common forms in which iron occurs in this District are those of the anhydrous ferric oxides ($Fe_2 O_3$), specular ore and red hæmatite Magnetic oxide and limonite also occur. In the former iron is found in the form of ferrous and ferric oxide combined while the latter is anhydrated ferric oxide. Laterite, an impure variety of limonite, is very common. Titaniferous iron ore is found in the sand of many streams. Except in the extreme west the ore is widely distributed, but Major Mahon distinguishes five principal deposits, *viz.*, Lohāra, Pīpalgaon, Gunjewāhi, Dewalgaon and Ratnapur, which have been visited and partially explored, and four other deposits which are, as far as is known at present, of less importance at Bhīsi, Metāpur, Ogulpet and Bhānpur. Undoubtedly the most interesting deposit in the District is the so-called iron hill of Lohāra which was designated by Mr. Hughes one of the wonders of the Indian mineral world. As a matter of fact the hill is not an iron hill, but consists in the main of a massive outcrop of quartzite, through which, however, runs a lode of iron-stone of extraordinary richness which in places approaches a breadth of 30 or 40 yards. Major Mahon, in his detailed description of the hill, says that he has never seen anything to equal the massive richness of the pure black specular ore heaped up in huge rocks which constitute the lode. The lode disappears underground after a certain distance, and it was at one time supposed that it extended for several miles. Had this supposition been borne out by the facts, Lohāra would have boasted a concentrated wealth of iron not to be exceeded elsewhere in the world, but Messrs. Tata's researches have revealed that the mineral wealth of Lohāra has been very much exaggerated, and, according to their estimate, the five principal deposits of the District mentioned by Major Mahon do not collectively contain more than one and a half million tons of ore. If the quantity of the ore is disappointing, there is at least no doubt as to its quality, and samples taken from Lohāra, Pīpalgaon, Gunjewāhi, and Dewalgaon and analysed by Major Mahon gave extraordinarily rich results, the usual percentage of iron being as high as 68. Local ore is exceptionally free from sulphur and phosphorus, and therefore is eminently qualified for the manufacture both of iron and steel.

Smelting was once extensively practised by the aboriginal inhabitants of the District, but of late years this industry has been greatly on the decline. It has been more fully dealt with in the chapter on 'Manufactures.'

Limestone.

249. In addition to coal and iron, the third main essential for an iron industry, *viz.*, limestone is also found and in close proximity to the two others. Rock limestone can be obtained from Vindhyan and Lametā beds, the former yielding a purer variety of fairly uniform composition. Vindhyan limestones occur at Kandāra, six miles north of Warorā, and at Niljhā eight miles west of that town. Lametā limestone is exposed two miles south of Warorā at Karamgohan, and in the Wardhā river at Mardhā and elsewhere. Lime is also procurable in the neighbourhood of Warorā and Bhāndak in the form of the surface deposit called *kankar* which often contains a high percentage of carbonate of lime. It has

already been mentioned that fire-clay was extracted from the Warorā mine, and this too would have been of service for a modern iron industry.

Minerals of less importance.

250. Diamonds and rubies have been found in alluvial deposits and in laterite near Wairāgarh, but are not regularly worked. Gold in minute quantities is found in the sands of the Waingangā, Indrāvati and Godāvari rivers, and is washed by a wandering people called Sonjharīs, who, however, make but a bare living out of the business. Gold washing is unpopular not only because it is not lucrative but also by reason of a superstition that those who practise it will be childless. Auriferous sands are found in several other streams in the metamorphic area of the east, and Major Lucie Smith wrote that the rocks in the south-east are undoubtedly auriferous, but no serious attempt has yet been made to ascertain their gold-bearing value. Abandoned copper workings may be seen at Thānwāsana in the Chānda tahsīl, and at Govindpur in the Bramhapurī tahsīl; another mine is said to have been worked at Tanbāgarhī Mendhā near Rajolī. The story is that all these mines were closed by the Marāthā Government about the middle of the 18th century in consequence of a belief that digging copper ore would bring evil to the country. A prospecting license has recently been granted for some of these old mines. A limited quantity of manganese occurs in botryoidal masses in the red clays at Mālagarh Hill, but the content of manganese is only 44·6 per cent. as against an average standard of from 50 to 55 per cent. in other parts of the Province. An application for a prospecting license for manganese was received in 1907. Dark-green serpentine used to be extensively quarried at Jāmbulghāta by Rājā Raghujī III of Nāgpur, but after his death the excavation was allowed to silt up. A quarry of black soapstone is found at the same place, and this material has been fairly extensively used for the manufacture of household vessels, but the quarry is at present closed for lack of a lessee.

Mica is found in small quantities in the Ahīri zamīndāri. Talc and saltpetre also occur.

Building stone.

251. The sandstones of the Kāmthi group provide excellent building stones of every hue and texture. The city walls of Chānda were built out of these. Isāpur produces a pink sandstone beautifully adapted for fine tracery work. The Vindhyans also furnish good building material, which in the north of the District is at present being extensively used in the construction of railway bridges. Quartzite and quartz give good road metal. Laterite is frequently used for wells and culverts. Hornblende schist, though soft, can be used in the dry climate of these parts, and the ease with which it can be quarried and dressed causes it to be sometimes employed in construction. Granite of all varieties occurs in unlimited quantities in the east of the District, and the coarser varieties would be suitable in ornamental work. Variegated sandstones with a singularly pleasing range of colours also occur in the Sironchā tahsīl. It will be seen that the District can boast a goodly store of excellent building material, but unfortunately much of it is for the present locked up by distance and lack of communications.

CHAPTER VII.

FAMINE.

Early history of famine.

252. Chānda has, unhappily for itself, a long record of famine or scarcity, and the rice tract has been particularly unfortunate. There are no authentic records of famines prior to the 19th century, but the opening years of that century were one unbroken series of disasters. This was the period of the Pindāri incursions when every village had its fort and men tilled and reaped with weapons girt at their side. Chānda lay in the full sweep of the Pindāri raids of devastation, and suffered accordingly. Two years stand out as the worst of the series, *viz.*, 1804 and 1818. The latter was the year of the sack of Chānda by the British, when the general confusion was heightened and perpetuated by the confiscation of enormous numbers of cattle by the invaders. Of organised famine relief in these years there was none; it may rather be said that such organisation as there was in the unhappy country was directed towards accentuating the misery of its inhabitants. So great was the exhaustion of the countryside that it is said that in 1822 the population of Chānda was only half of what it had been in 1802.

The famine of 1832.

253. The next year of famine was 1832, and the cause was excessive rain accompanied by insect pests. A certain amount of relief was administered by the Marāthā Government, which was still imbued with the traditions of the British Protectorate. The Government granaries were thrown open to the poor, and the local Baniās were ordered to sell their stocks, the State undertaking to recoup them at the end of the famine.

The famine of 1868-69.

254. Chānda was one of the first Districts to feel the stress of the famine of 1868-69. In 1868, the monsoon broke unusually

early and the ground became so saturated that the *dahia* method of cultivation which then prevailed through half the area of the District became impracticable. June and July were months of heavy rainfall, but were followed by three weeks of dry weather which ruined much of the rice and seemed about to compass the destruction of every kind of crop when the heavens once more opened, and for the next six weeks the weather was all that could be wished. But then ensued another rainless fortnight, and by September it became clear that the damage to rice was irremediable, and that the outturn of the other crops was not sufficient to counterbalance its failure. The wild roots, too, to which the poorer classes resort in default of more palatable food, were this year unusually scanty, and a panic, accompanied by a general outburst of crime, began to set in. The distress was most acute in the north-east of the District which is the chief rice area, and emigration began to take place from this part. Relief works were, however, opportunely taken in hand, and checked this tendency. In September 1868, there were six such works, but in April 1869 the number was increased to nine, five of which were directed to repairing tanks, and the other four to the construction of roads. The cost of these works was Rs. 13,644, and was met out of a Pāndharī grant. Advances to the amount of Rs. 5,500 were made to traders for the importation of grain, and storehouses were established at which grain was sold at cost price. Although emaciation was general, there were only two recorded instances of death from actual starvation, and there was not, as might have been expected, any unusual epidemic mortality. Nor did any large area drop out of cultivation. But it is said that the memory of this famine lingers in the nickname 'Sixty-niner' which is still applied to anyone who 'wolfs' his food.

Bad years 1892—1895.

255. The District appears to have enjoyed immunity from scarcity thenceforward until the early nineties. With the monsoon of

1891, commenced the cycle of lean years which culminated in the famines of 1897 and 1900. Floods, followed by a rainless cold weather, reduced the total outturn of the year 1891-92 to 60 per cent. of the normal. The price of rice went up slightly and of juāri by 4½ seers the rupee, but no distress was felt except among the jungle tribes of Sironchā, who were relieved by the step taken of throwing open to them forest blocks for the collection of edible products. Road-work was commenced in certain other distressed tracts, but did not attract many workers. In 1892-93, the autumn crops, with the exception of kodon, fared moderately well, but heavy rains in the latter part of the cold weather induced rust in wheat and linseed, and the total outturn of the year was but 61 per cent. of the normal. Prices, however, remained steady. The monsoon of 1893 was characterised by a long break which seriously impeded the transplantation of rice, and was followed by a continuous downpour, the consequence of which was that the rice plants were attacked by the disease known as *gād*, and the transplanted crop was almost entirely ruined. Cloudy weather in the cold season brought about rust among the spring crops, and the total outturn of the year was only 53. Some anxiety was felt as to the situation in 1894, but prices still ruled steady and road-works, started as an experiment to ascertain the gravity of the distress, failed to attract labourers in any numbers. With the early rice harvest in October, all apprehension was set at rest. Nevertheless, the death rate of 1894 which rose to nearly 34 as compared with 27½ in 1893, and was accompained by a stationary birth rate, indicated that the prolonged deficiency of harvests was beginning to tell on the population. The year 1894-95, though not quite so unfavourable as its predecessors, was not free from misfortunes; continuous rain in the early monsoon damaged juāri and cotton, which subsequently suffered still further from a plague of caterpillars; linseed was much affected by rust, while the wheat plants were unhealthy and their ears failed to fill out satisfactorily. Rice however did well. The total outturn for all crops was 64 per cent.

256. The following year, 1895-96, was a very fair one and an average outturn of 77 per cent. of the normal enabled the agriculturist, if not to recoup the losses he had suffered of recent years, at any rate to maintain his position.

The year 1895-96.

257. The agricultural year 1896-97 opened with the brightest prospects, and up to the end of August 1896 a bumper outturn harvest was confidently anticipated. But throughout September and October the rain held off altogether, and the crops rapidly deteriorated. The same condition of affairs continued into November and caused grave anxiety as to the fate of the spring crops. Hope was to some extent revived by a fall of rain at the end of November, but the ensuing months of the cold weather were exceedingly deficient in rainfall, and this had a disastrous effect on the *rabi* outturn. The outturns of rice, wheat and linseed, were only between one-half and one-quarter of the normal, and juāri and til were the only crops which even approached the average. About the end of December 1896, reports of distress began to come in, especially from the zamīndāris, where the rice crop had altogether failed, and District works were put in hand to relieve the situation. Want of water and fodder began to be felt in April, and continued to increase till July. The people had sold the juāri and rice straw which is usually reserved as fodder for cattle, and made no attempt to replace it by collecting leaves or storing grass. The mortality among cattle, which had been under 10,000 in 1896, rose to almost 25,000. Although the District was never officially recognised as distressed, it was for a long time on the verge of being so declared, and the situation was such as to call for measures of relief on a fairly large scale, both by the agency of the District officials and by private charity. Prices rose rapidly; in March 1897 they stood at one and a half, and in July 1897

The scarcity of 1897.

at two and a half times their usual rates. The average price of rice during the period from October 1896 to October 1897 was 9·38 seers to the rupee, and of juāri 12·48 seers. The highest prices reached at any period were 7·5 and 8·6 seers respectively. But it was not found necessary to take any special measures for the importation of grain except in Sironchā, where the cultivators had recklessly sold the whole of an excellent juāri crop to traders from Hyderābād and Madras and as a result found their grain stocks entirely depleted. Even in Sironchā the importations were not on a large scale. On the other hand, exports of grain took place on such a large scale as to cause some apprehension; 59,218 maunds of grain left Warorā in 1896 and 126,555 tons in 1897, as compared with an average of between 1100 and 1200 maunds in the two preceding years. Only two relief works under the management of the Public Works Department were taken in hand. These were a road from Ambāgarh Chauki in the northern zamīndāris to Nāndgaon, and a tank at Ambāgarh Chauki. The numbers at work on these never exceeded 2700, and included many persons from adjoining Feudatory States. Tanks were also undertaken as local works in 20 other villages, and as loan works in 451 villages, the funds for these latter being provided by a grant of Rs. 48,000 under the Land Improvement Loans Act and by a special famine loan allotment of Rs. 1,15,000. Besides this, work on tanks to the value of Rs. 28,500 was done by the private enterprise of mālguzārs and zamīndārs. Gratuitous village relief, which had been commenced in the hot weather, came into full swing in July when the advent of the rains put an end to the tank work. Sixty-eight centres were formed and put in charge of non-official committees. To these centres all wanderers were sent for relief, and from them daily or weekly doles were made to indigent persons. The average number of persons thus relieved was 5836 and the maximum 8887 at the end of October. Kitchens were also established for children at various places, and the numbers attending these rose to 1652 in October 1897. Private charity was not idle, and out of a sum of Rs. 55,000 contributed from this source in cash or kind, Rs. 17,500 represented subscriptions raised in the District, a larger sum than was collected in any other District of the Province. A contribution of over Rs. 30,000 from the Mansion House Fund was chiefly utilised in advances for the purchase of seed-grain, while the equally necessary provision of funds for the purchase of plough bullocks was secured by advances amounting to over Rs. 14,000 under the Agricultural Loans Act. Mālguzārs were induced to sell grain to their tenants at favourable rates, and cheap grain shops were opened at each tahsīl headquarters and at three villages in the Lower Tāluks of Sironchā. But the most far-reaching measure, and that which undoubtedly prevented the distress from becoming terribly acute in the zamīndāris and in Sironchā, was the throwing open of the forests for the collection and removal of edible roots and fruit, grass and fuel. In this matter, and also in the initiation of tank work, an excellent example was set by Gangshā Bāpu, the zamīndār of Palāsgarh, whose lead was followed by all the other zamīndārs. No remissions or suspensions of revenue were granted by Government, and the area under cultivation not only did not contract but actually expanded by some 34,000 acres. In spite of the undoubted distress that prevailed, the statistics of mortality were not high, and were actually lower than in the preceding year of comparative prosperity. But it may be doubted whether the official returns on this head are reliable. Certain it is that there was a very general impression that the gravity of the distress was consistently minimised, and that specially in the more remote tracts, the distress was very acute.

The interval between the famines.

258. The monsoon of 1897 broke late, and the situation up to the second week of July was critical in the extreme. But the rain came in time to avert disaster, and

having once made a commencement, continued to fall seasonably so that both the autumn and spring crops were excellent, giving a combined outturn of 109 throughout the District. The year 1898-99 was not quite so favourable. There was an unusually heavy and continuous fall of 21 inches in July, which retarded weeding operations, but in September the rain ceased abruptly, and deficient rainfalls in October and November, followed by a rainless cold weather, were prejudicial to the spring crops. The combined outturn of the year was 73 per cent. of the normal.

The famine of 1900.

259. The hot weather of 1899 was characterised by abnormal showers which were read as an omen of disaster. The monsoon was rather late and very weak, less than two inches of rain being registered in July. In August there was a general and most welcome rainfall, which for a time improved prospects, but with September the rain practically ceased, and famine became assured. The total rainfall of the year was only 20 inches. Cotton did fairly well, but the rice failed almost entirely, and the total outturn for all crops was only 27 per cent. of the normal. Prices went up with a rush in October 1899, and at Chānda reached in that month the high figure of 7 seers per rupee for rice and 9½ for juāri, as compared with normal rates of 14 and 24 respectively. The Baniās held up their stocks in the hopes of a further tightening of the market, but they were promptly countered by extensive importations by Government of Bengal rice. Over half a million maunds of food-grains were imported during the famine by rail alone, while it is impossible to say how much more came into the District by other means of transit. This policy eased the markets till May, when, owing to the expected advent of the rains which would render transport a matter of the greatest difficulty, prices again rose and thenceforward continued at a high level until the new rice harvest was assured. In the interior of the District, prices were still more stringent, and in some of the more remote parts

never went below 5 seers to the rupee for rice during June and July 1900.

General course of the famine.

260. The official duration of the famine was from September 1899 to October 1900, but relief operations in this District continued till the end of the year. The scarcity was most intense in the trans-Waingangā tract. The Bramhapurī tahsīl as a whole, depending as it does almost entirely upon the rice crop, was very severely hit, but Warorā was less seriously affected, while true famine conditions can scarcely be said to have existed in Sironchā. Before the commencement of relief operations, the refusal of the Baniās to sell their grain stocks provoked several grain riots, especially in the vicinity of Talodhī, but this tendency was promptly checked by the police. Want of water and fodder began to be felt in January, and by April nearly all wells were dry. Fortunately, the network of nullahs which covers the District provided a solution of the difficulty, so far as drinking water for human beings was concerned, and this was obtainable throughout the hot weather by digging holes in their beds. In the early part of 1900, some consolation was afforded by the unprecedented flowering of the bamboos which gave an unexpected supply of food to the poorer classes, and by the fair promise of the mahuā crop. The numbers on relief fluctuated between 60,000 and 80,000 up to April, when suddenly the mahuā crop absolutely failed, a wholly unforeseen calamity, the intensity of which cannot be exaggerated when it is considered to what an extent the large jungly population of this District depends on the products of the mahuā for its food supply. The numbers on relief immediately rose with a bound, until at the end of May they stood at over 180,000. The sufferings of the cattle, meanwhile, were dreadful, as it was impossible to provide water for them. But the flood of disaster had not yet exhausted itself. In the middle of June, cholera broke out and raged furiously, and immediately

over 40,000 people stampeded from the relief camps carrying the disease to the four corners of the District. Mr. Coxon, the Deputy Commissioner, wrote of this period:— 'By the end of June every element of destruction 'appeared to have combined against the people of this 'District, and with the rains holding off, the prospects were 'of the gloomiest. The heat was something that had never 'before been experienced, and men were dropping daily 'from sunstroke. Cholera was raging to such an extent that 'it was found impossible to collect people together in any one 'place, even for the distribution of the money which was so 'urgently required for the purchase of food, while fires were 'sweeping villages off the face of the earth wholesale.' At length the monsoon broke, though late, dissipating the cholera epidemic, but even then, owing to the general poverty and the scarcity of seed-grain, pressure did not relax, and the numbers on kitchen relief went on increasing, until in September they rose to over 227,000. The nullahs were, with the advent of the monsoon, transformed from a blessing into a curse, constituting a most formidable barrier against the transit of grain, and rendering relief operations a matter of the greatest difficulty. About the middle of September, the numbers on relief began to decline, at first slowly, but in the early part of October by 5000 or 6000 a day, until by the end of that month they stood at only 77,000. Nevertheless, owing to the backwardness of the *kharīf* harvest, the famine lingered on for a period not parallelled in the rest of the Province; mortality continued high and prices obstinately refused to fall. Whereas elsewhere famine relief practically ceased after the middle of November, in this District kitchens continued to the end of that month, and the village relief list was not finally closed till the end of the year.

Mortality.

261. The mortality from September 1899 to October 1900 was, according to the official returns, 51,663 deaths or 89·75 per mille of the population, and for the calendar year 1900 the

rate of mortality was 96·62. The highest mortality for any one month was 17 per mille in June, when cholera was at its height. Over 43 per cent. of the casualties took place among children under 10 years of age, and infant mortality was, owing to an abnormal number of births in the preceding year, especially heavy. Cholera accounted for 8000 deaths, fever for 19,000, and bowel complaints for nearly 5500. These latter are supposed to have been largely induced by the use of Bengal rice. Only one death was actually attributed to starvation, but an immense amount of the mortality from other causes must of course have been due to the reduced condition of the persons attacked.

Condition of the cattle.

262. If the condition of the people was pitiable, the fate of their cattle was still more appalling. Something was done towards providing them with fodder, but the water difficulty was insuperable, and they died like flies from thirst. The exorbitant rates prevailing for cart-hire were the death of many a poor beast, driven till he dropped dead from sheer exhaustion. The sides of the road from Warorā to Chānda were strewn along its whole length with corpses of animals which had perished thus, and the scenes at the river-crossings were too ghastly for description. The privation of water was not confined to domestic animals. Tigers were shot or stoned to death in village wells. One officer, adapting himself to the circumstances of the time, sat over a trough of water in place of the usual buffalo, thus securing on one occasion two tigers in one beat. Strangest of all, during well-deepening operations in Alāpallī in the month of May, there were simultaneously found alive in one well seven monkeys, one *nīlgai*, three sāmbhar, and five bison, a collection which has the makings of no mean menagerie. When the rains came, and the starving survivors of the cattle fell upon the young grass, the mortality caused by the surfeit of food acting on their impaired digestive organs was something frightful. Altogether it was estimated by

Mr. Coxon that at least 120,000 or 25 to 30 per cent. of the entire stock of cattle must have perished. Plough cattle alone, which would naturally have been most carefully preserved and earliest replaced, decreased by 20,000 in the year.

Expenditure on relief.

263. The measures of relief taken to combat the situation were admirably organised and worthy of its gravity. In the words of one of those who were relieved 'it was all very wonderful 'and the Sarkār regarded money as *gitti*, so long as the 'people were kept alive.' The direct expenditure on the several heads of famine relief amounted to 23 lakhs, and out of this expenditure 30¾ million day units were relieved at an incidence per diem of 1·19 annas per unit. Suspensions of land revenue amounted to 2.15 lakhs, while the value of forest concessions was 1·62 lakhs. The amount of land revenue suspended represents 74 per cent. of the total demand, and in fact the only sums collected were those due from non-rice villages. Besides this, Government distributed 3·65 lakhs in taccavi loans to enable the cultivators to complete their sowings for 1900-01, while 1·86 lakhs were distributed in free gifts for the same purpose to the poorer cultivators out of the Charitable Relief Fund. Within the District itself, a sum of over Rs. 68,000 was collected by private subscription on the understanding that it should be all disbursed locally. Nearly Rs. 30,000 of it was utilised in buying clothes from local weavers, and was thus made to serve twice over for purposes of relief.

Measures of relief.

264 No poor-houses or pauper wards were established. Kitchens were organised at the commencement of the famine, but were discontinued for a time in the *khālsa* when the camps opened, although in the zamīndāris they were always a main feature. Relief camps under the management of the Public Works Department were opened in October, and formed the backbone of the operations until well on in the hot weather.

The total number of Public Works charges opened was sixteen, and the maximum open at any one time was fifteen. The largest number of workers on relief at any time was 80,895 on the 12th of May, or over 72 per cent. of the total numbers on famine relief at that time. The Forest Department, besides forming camps for the construction of two roads, with tank works annexed, took in hand extensive fodder operations for the supply of Wardhā and the Bombay Presidency; 26 grass depôts were established, and 7109 tons of grass collected. The maximum number relieved by forest works was rather over 9000 towards the end of May. Other fodder operations in the zamīndāri forests of the north were put in charge of the Manager of the Court of Wards, and, though not financially successful, gave useful relief to the neighbouring population. Tank schemes involving an expenditure of 3¼ lakhs were drawn up, and numerous tanks were taken in hand as village works. At the close of the hot weather 179 such works were in operation and the number of workers on them was over 26,000. In April, the failure of the mahuā crop necessitated special measures, and an enormous impetus was given to kitchen relief. A special staff had to be engaged, as it was no longer possible to manage the kitchens by the agency of volunteers. With the opening of the rains, the relief policy had to be modified to suit the altered conditions. Relief camps became unsuitable, as the one great object was to make the people go back to their villages, and let them work in the fields, in the meanwhile feeding them and keeping them in health. Village relief now became the order of the day, and the form which it took was chiefly the extension of the kitchen system. In July, the rush was so great that 200 subsidiary kitchens were started and put in charge of *mukaddams*. The highest number of kitchens simultaneously at work at any one time was 239, with 161,443 inmates. All inmates were required to do some service in return for their food, and gratuitous relief was confined to cripples, blind persons, and the dependants of kotwārs. Relief in return for work in villages (B list relief) was found especially necessary in the case of cultivators of small means, and was more freely resorted to than in any other District of the Province. The workers were mainly employed in carrying grain to kitchens and depôts. The numbers on B list relief reached a maximum of over 54,000 about the middle of September. The maximum number of persons on relief of all kinds at any one time was 180,673 during the open season and 224,799 during the rains. This latter figure represented 32 per cent. of the total population.

Famine works.

265. Of the sixteen roads taken in hand by the Public Works Department, none were actually brought to completion, although earth and *muram* were laid along 32 miles of the road from Warorā to Chimūr. Nineteen tanks were, however, constructed as annexes to these roads, and notably four very fine tanks were built at Naotallā. The Forest Department constructed an excellent second-class road 18 miles in length from Chānda to Moharlī and another 5½ miles in length from Alāpallī to Ahīri, besides some tanks. Altogether, as village or forest works, 4 new tanks were constructed, and 238 existing tanks were restored or improved, while seven new roads were taken in hand, of which five were completed. Ten wells were also sunk.

Attitude of the people.

266. Crime naturally received an impetus during the progress of the famine, especially in Bramhapurī, where the number of thefts and house-breakings increased by over 600. But the attitude of the people as a whole, except for the grain riots in the early days of the distress, was one of complete apathy or fatalism. Mr. Coxon describes it as one of 'absolute indifference combined with a perfect confidence in the Sarkār.' As to their appreciation of the efforts made by Government to alleviate their misery, the prevailing impression at the time seems to have been that real gratitude was conspicuous by its absence, although lip-gratitude, especially

in acknowledgment of gifts of clothing, was fairly common. Doles and wages were usually grumbled at as insufficient and the usual cry in the kitchens was for more or for a different kind of food, or a gift of clothing. But it is admitted that it is very difficult to gauge the real feelings of the people by their actions or expressions, and it is certain that the indelible impression left by the famine is always coupled in the minds of all with a profound conviction of the immense efforts made by Government to cope with an unparalleled disaster.

Casualties of the Famine staff.

267. Thirty officials, all natives, lost their lives in conducting the campaign against the famine, while many others were invalided.

The year 1900-01.

268. The monsoon of 1900 commenced late, and the period of suspense during which it was awaited was the most trying period of the whole famine. However, rain at length fell heavily, and enabled agricultural operations to commence. But in spite of all that loans from Government and private charity could do, such was the general poverty and so great had been the wastage in agricultural stock that it was impossible to avert an enormous shrinkage of the area under *kharīf* cultivation which fell by 112,000 acres. Extensive *rabi* sowings, however, adjusted the shortage. The monsoon ceased abruptly at the end of September to the general detriment of broadcast rice, but cotton gave an outturn of 80 and juāri and transplanted rice were 90 each, so that the autumn harvest was on the whole fair. But the spring crops suffered not only from a contraction of the area under cultivation but also from the entire absence of rain from October to December, followed, when the crops were ripening, by the setting in of wet and cloudy weather accompanied by a visitation of insects. Wheat gave an outturn of only 45, gram of 30, and linseed of 22. The outturn of all crops combined amounted only to 46. In April 1901 the situation looked gloomy, and preparations were in hand for further relief operations, when

suddenly the peril of famine was averted by an unexpected windfall. The mahuā crop which, owing to the unseasonable weather, had been considered foredoomed to failure, flowered with extraordinary abundance long after the normal season, and the poor were thus provided with a stock of food to tide them over the rains. No relief was necessary and the works already opened were at once closed. Prices fell in the case of juāri by 6 seers below the preceding year's figures, and in the case of rice by 1½ seers. But the effects of the famine were clearly visible in a reduced birth rate of 21 per mille during 1901.

Succeeding years.

269. The year 1901-02 was marked by the prevalence of insect pests, and though the cotton crop was good and the rice fair, the combined outturn of the year was only 59, so that the process of recovery was again retarded. The monsoon of 1902 was a weak one, but, in spite of an almost total failure of the rice crop, the total outturn amounted to 78, and the condition of the District gave no cause for anxiety. Next year, 1903-04, was a much better one, and of the important crops cotton alone gave an outturn of less than 80 per cent. The condition of the agricultural classes continued to improve, but the progress made was slow in the rice tracts, where there was a strong tendency to await the announcement of the new settlement before making really strenuous exertions to retrieve past losses. The monsoon of 1904 followed the example of most of its recent predecessors in causing grave anxiety for a period, but plentiful September rains came to the rescue, and the outturn of the year was 91. The year was a good one for cotton, and the open-field tracts, and those tracts with mixed or intermediate cultivation which lie near the best markets and trade routes may be said by this time to have fully re-established their prosperity, but the rice and the more remote intermediate tracts continued in a condition of instability. The history of the year 1905-06 much resembles that of 1904-05: juāri, cotton and

tūr all did well, but rice was again only 75. Hailstorms early in 1906 necessitated some local suspensions and remissions, but the total outturn was as high as 93. The year 1906-07 was also a good one. The current year has witnessed a check to this comparative prosperity, but the District has cause for congratulation as compared with most of the rest of the Provinces, and suspensions will be necessary only on a very limited scale.

CHAPTER VIII.

LAND REVENUE ADMINISTRATION.

Changes of area.

279. Before reviewing the history of the land revenue administration of Chānda, it is advisable briefly to recapitulate the various changes of area that have taken place in the District. Under the Gonds, the kingdom of Chānda included considerable tracts of land which are now incorporated in the Districts of Wardhā and Yeotmāl, and in the territories of the Nizām. It was not until 1803, or over fifty years after the sovereignty had passed to the Marāthās that the country on the right bank of the Wardhā and Prānhita was ceded to the Nizām. Subsequently, the Warorā, Chimūr and Bramhapurī parganas were transferred to the Nāgpur District, but they were eventually retransferred to Chānda, the two latter in 1820-21 A.D. and the first in 1837-38 A.D. In 1860-61, ten villages of the Nāgpur District were transferred to the Chimūr pargana, and in 1874 the Sironchā, Albāka, Nūgur and Cherlā *tāluks* of the abolished Upper Godāvari District were formed into the Sironchā tahsīl. In 1907 the zamīndārís of Ambāgarh Chaukī, Pānābāras, Aundhī and Korācha were transferred to the Drug District. Another change of some importance as affecting the land revenue was the confiscation in 1858 of the Arpalli and Ghot zamīndāri for the rebellion of the zamīndār and its transformation into a *khālsa* pargana. These changes must be borne in mind when comparing the present figures of land revenue with those of past years. The fiscal as well as the general history of the Sironchā tahsīl follows a different path from that of the rest of the District, and will be considered separately. For the present we shall deal with that portion only of the District, which originally formed a portion of the Gond kingdom of Chānda, fell for a hundred years under the sway of the

Bhonslā kingdom of Nāgpur, and finally lapsed to the British Government in 1853.

Land revenue system of the Gonds and Marāthās.

271. The land revenue system of the Gonds is only known to us by tradition and through our knowledge of the system of the Marāthās which was directly inherited from it and preserved its main external features, though widely departing from it in spirit. But of the system of the Marāthās as it stood in 1818, when the British Government undertook the management of the Nāgpur kingdom during the minority of the Rājā, we have a complete and interesting account drawn up by the then Resident Sir R. Jenkins. The system therein described was founded on what would now be termed a purely ryotwāri basis. Without actually asserting a definite title in the ownership of the soil, the State claimed a right to a share in its produce, and possessed a fairly elaborate organisation for the realisation of its dues. Under the Gonds, the whole of the *khālsa* area of the District had been subdivided into *killās* consisting of a varying number of villages, each *killā* being under a *killedār* or *diwān*, assisted by an establishment, the chief officers of which were the Deshmukh, Deshpānde and *sir mukaddam*, who held an intermediate position between the *killedār* and the village officials presently to be described. The Marāthās removed these intermediate officials, retaining only the general manager, who was now called *kamaishdār* and whose charge was styled a pargana, the keeper of the Government accounts, now called *phadnavīs*, and the *warār pāndia* or recorder of the village accounts. Of the village officials, the patel was the most important. Each village had its own patel, who was the agent of Government for apportioning and collecting the revenue assessed on his village and was absolutely responsible for its payment, and who also possessed a subordinate and rather undefined judicial authority. As a remuneration for this agency and responsibility, the patel received rent-free land or money

usually equivalent nominally to one-fourth of the Government demand, but actually amounting to not more than one-sixth of that demand when various customary deductions had been made. The office was not saleable nor hereditary, although in actual practice it very commonly passed from father to son. The patel was assisted by a *pāndia*, or village accountant, and a kotwār or village watchman. All village lands were held on a yearly lease, granted to the cultivators by the patel. No cultivator was entitled to hold the same fields in perpetuity, nor was it the practice to grant leases for more than one year.

Method of annual assessments.

272. The following summary of the method of assessment is reproduced from Mr. (now Sir) J. B. Fuller's 'Note on the Land Revenue Settlements of the Central Provinces':—

'The assessment was made annually and its amount was 'fixed in the first place in the aggregate for the pargana and 'then distributed amongst the villages by the pargana officer, 'or *kamaishdār*, in consultation with the patels. It is a 'curious fact to modern notions that though engagements 'were taken from the patels at the commencement of the 'agricultural year, the amount for which they were to be 'responsible was not fixed and communicated to them until 'some months later, when the character of the season became 'pretty well known. This practice undoubtedly enabled 'Government to extract a great deal of revenue from the 'people, as each person was fully rated according to his 'ability to pay in each year. At the time when the patels 'concluded formal engagements for the revenue of the year, 'they were actually in ignorance of the amount for which 'they engaged. This led to a curious device for apportion-'ing the responsibility for the revenue among the ryots. For 'the main portion of the village lands technically called the '*chāl* lands no rental was fixed, but each field was given a 'value to express its revenue paying capacity in relation to 'the other *chāl* fields of the village. This value was termed 'the *ain* of a field and was ordinarily expressed in annas or 'in cowries per rupee. The revenue was apportioned 'amongst the ryots according to the *ains* of the fields held 'by them. Thus, the ryot who held a field the *ain* of which 'was 6 pies would pay half the revenue which was payable 'by a ryot holding a field the *ain* of which was 12 pies, and 'in this way it was possible to settle at the commencement 'of each year the revenue payable by each man although the 'amount of the revenue was unknown. It must be borne in 'mind that there was nothing permanent in the *ain* valuation 'of a field, which might be different each year and render 'its holder liable to pay a different share of the village 'revenue. A further complication was introduced by the 'fact that this system did not apply to all the village lands, 'but that a certain area was commonly let each year on fixed 'money rents. The fields so let were termed *thok* fields. 'They usually included the poorer land for which the patel 'was unable to conclude engagements on the *ain* system, 'the ryots being unwilling to cultivate them except on 'limited responsibility. When the revenue of the year 'was given out the rent of the *thok* fields was first deducted 'from it, and the balance distributed over the *chāl* fields 'in proportion to their *ains*. It must be understood, 'however, that the difference between *chāl* and *thok* fields 'was by no means a permanent one, and that fields 'annually passed from one denomination to the other in 'conformity with the change in the engagements between 'the ryots and patels. The lands let under the *thok* engage-'ments bore but a small proportion to the others, and as 'the *chāl* fields paid the highest, lands in progress of deteriora-'tion passed from *chāl* to *thok*, and when advancing in 'improvement from *thok* to *chāl*. Each year a record was 'prepared called the *lāgwan*. It answered to the *jamābandi* 'of Upper India, and gave the details of the engagements con-'cluded at the commencement of each year between the patels 'and the ryots. It showed the name of each ryot, the name of 'each *chāl* field held by him and the *ain* of those fields as 'settled in the preceding year; also the same particulars for the 'current year, noting all changes whether arising from the 'transfer of fields from one ryot to another or from a transfer 'of a *chāl* field to the *thok* class, or *vice versâ* or from varia- 'tions in the *ains* of any of the *chāl* fields. So soon as the 'amount of the revenue was known the rate of its assessment 'on each unit of the *ain*, called the *dhāra*, was also inserted.'

Working of this system under the Gonds.

273. It is evident that a system like this, although not open to serious objection if carefully worked, would be liable to terrible abuse in the hands of a necessitous or greedy Government, exorbitant in its demands and prepared to farm out villages to the highest bidder. Under the Gond Rājās, however, it appears to have worked well. Owing to the destruction between 1819 and 1823 of all the records connected with the Gond assessment by one Lingopant who found them to interfere with his private ends, it is now impossible to say what was the proportion of the cultivator's profits which was taken by the State, but according to Major Lucie Smith the whole voice of the country testified that it was small and the agriculturists of his generation looked back to the Gond administration as the golden age of the country. The system of farming villages to individuals was quite unknown, and though *bargans* or special imposts were occasionally levied, they were not of an amount or frequency to distress the people.

Abuse of the system during the first Marāthā period, 1749—1818 A.D.

274. The Marāthā conquest of 1749 put an end to this utopian state of affairs. The old fiscal machinery was retained but it was worked in an oppressive and rapacious fashion. The demand was increased; many old Gond patels were dispossessed in favour of friends of the Marāthā officials or of persons who offered to raise larger sums than the old holders could promise; heavy *bargans* were yearly levied, and gave an opportunity for peculation for all

officials from the *kamaishdār* down to the patel, since each as a matter of course exacted from those below him something more than he himself had to pay. Owing to the destruction of the records prior to 1818, it is not known to what figure the administration of the Marāthās raised the revenue, but Sir Richard Jenkins mentions that the collection from the *khālsa* portion of the District during the ten years previous to the British Protectorate, averaged Nāgpur Rs. 3,91,104 per annum, (Government Rs. 3,34,277).

Reforms of the British Protectorate, 1818—1830.

275. From 1818 to 1830 Chānda, like the rest of the Nāgpur territories, came under the administration of the British, owing to the minority of the Rājā Raghujī III. A British Superintendent, Captain Crawfurd, was appointed to the charge of the District. A period of great activity set in, the fiscal policy, as sketched by the Resident, being to maintain the ancient system of land revenue management, but 'to 'strike without sparing at those parts of the Marāthā adminis-'tration which were manifest and tyrannical innovations 'and abuses.' To this end, a clean sweep was made of the numerous imposts which improperly figured in the accounts as land revenue, the levy of *bargans* was abolished, and every endeavour was made to re-people deserted villages and to repair breached tanks. Settlements were made at first for two, then for three, and lastly for five years, the allowance to the patel ranging from 13 to 15 per cent. of the total village assessment. At the three years' settlement, a system of progressive assessment known as the *tāhut bandobast* was very generally introduced into the Bramhapurī and Chimūr parganas, and probably elsewhere, although owing to the absence of documents this supposition cannot be verified. Preference was given to existing patels, provided that they offered a reasonably high rate for their villages. An important change was effected in the position of the *lāgwan*, which now became the basis for the assessment instead of being, as heretofore, a mere record of the distribution of the aggregate

village assessment. This change was fatal to the trustworthiness of the *lāgwan*, since patels had now an object in understating the rents. As a result of all these reforms, there was at first a considerable reduction of revenue from nearly 4 lakhs to 2·3 lakhs, but this reaction was succeeded by a sharp recovery, so that by 1825 the revenue had all but expanded to its previous amount, while by 1827-28 it reached high water mark at 4·85 lakhs. Sir R. O. Jenkins appears not to have been altogether satisfied with Captain Crawfurd's assessments, considering that they erred upon the side of leniency, but the figures given above support the opposite view, and the assessments were certainly not regarded as light by the people of the country.

Lingopant Dikshit.

276. Although much was done under the British règime to cleanse and adjust the machinery of administration, it was but to be expected that all traces of former misuse could not be immediately wiped out. Foremost among the influences of corruption stood Lingopant Dikshit of whom Major Lucie Smith gives the following interesting account:—'Captain Crawfurd during the 'first years of office was chiefly engaged in operations against 'rebels and in measures for putting down plundering and 'robbery, and the details of revenue management fell into the 'hands of the *sadar warār pāndia* at Chānda, Lingopant 'Dikshit, commonly called Abā Sāhib, who became a power 'in the District. With a view to prevent inconvenient references, and to afford a clear field for his schemes, he deliberately destroyed all the records of the period anterior to the 'protectorate, and he did not hesitate to compass the death of 'those, even of his own caste, who stood in his way. Numerous stories are current regarding his influence, not only with 'the Superintendent, but with the Resident; and one of these 'states that on one occasion Lingopant accompanied Captain 'Crawfurd to Nāgpur, and while there was invited to dinner by 'Nārba Kālikar, whose *maktās* in Chānda had been confiscated 'consequent upon his disaffection to the British. As Lingo-

'pant was performing his ablutions previous to dinner, Nārba 'said to him, "Well, Abā Sāhib, you are a man of great influ-'ence ; can you not manage to have my *maktās* restored?" To 'which the other replied that he would not eat until his host's 'wish had been gratified, and sitting down wrote out a *tākid* 'restoring the *maktās*. This he sent to the Resident, and within 'an hour received it back signed and sealed. He may have 'arranged the matter before going to Nārba's and led up to 'its disclosure in the manner most beneficial to himself, or 'the anecdote itself may be apocryphal, but its general accept-'ance shows the popular estimate of Lingopant's power. He 'amassed a large fortune, and became possessed of many 'villages: while for his fellow Brāhmans he obtained nume-'rous grants of free lands and pensions. His death occurred 'shortly before Captain Crawfurd's departure in 1824 A.D., 'but the system of official intrigue and oppression did not die 'with him, but grew and spread until it reached its culminat-'ing point in the latter years of the second Marāthā adminis-'tration.' Captain Crawfurd abolished the post of *pāndia*, making the patel responsible for the due submission of the village papers. The policy of short term assessments continued throughout the regency of the British, and the period was one of general contentment and prosperity, although the land tax was pitched at what would now be considered a very high rate.

The second Marāthā period 1830-53.

277. In 1830, the management of the Nāgpur territories was handed over to Rājā Raghujī III, and Chānda was thenceforward administered from Nāgpur through a resident executive officer styled the sūbahdār. He had a numerous staff of officials, who were, however, all appointed by the Rājā, and who looked for their promotion to Nāgpur. The sūbahdār had no power to punish any of them; he was surrounded by spies, and was always attended by an official whose duty was to note everything that he did in public or in private, and to forward a daily account thereof to the court.

Consequently, he was afraid of his own subordinates and was obliged to leave them a free hand. The natural results of this policy are thus described by Major Lucie Smith: 'The 'offices throughout the District were filled by Brāhmans and 'Purvoes from Nāgpur, many in needy circumstances, and 'all looking to the ministers and the courtiers of the Rājā 'for advancement and protection. Where villages were seen 'to pay well and were held by men without interest, swarms 'of officials from the sūbahdār downwards were on the 'watch to get them either for themselves or relatives, or for 'their patrons at Nāgpur. If the patel to be ousted relin- 'quished with a good grace, he was often rewarded with a 'revenue-free field, but if he remained stubborn, and persecu- 'tion and threats proved fruitless, then a larger sum than the 'village could yield would be offered for the lease. Perhaps 'the old patel, broken-hearted at the prospect of parting with 'a village his family had held and improved for generations, 'would agree to the enhanced rate offered by his rival, and 'would so keep on a little longer, but the struggle surely 'ended in his ruin, and the official bidder thereupon stepped 'in. For the first year he might pay the full demand, but he 'would then fall into arrears which would be remitted, and 'at the next settlement the village would be assessed below 'its value. Thus in many instances a patel, whose ancestors 'had founded the village, had made its tanks, and had held it 'for generations, was without pity ruined, and then ejected 'to make room for a Nāgpur or Chānda official. And then 'it happened that the official, being an absentee, could not 'work the village as the resident patel had done; so the 'receipts fell off, and the influential holder thereupon pressed 'for a reduction of *jamā*, which was rarely refused. But it 'was necessary to counterbalance these reductions by 'increasing the demand on villages whose patels were not 'men of consequence, and, as these estates could not bear an 'increase, and no stranger would take them at an enhanced 'rate, the old patels had to be intimidated into consenting, and 'so it came to pass that fetters and imprisonment were 'among the methods latterly adopted to arrange a settlement. 'The patels, on their part, combined as well as they could, 'and industriously falsified the village papers, while what 'money they possessed went to bribe the various officials. 'So grew and flourished as rank a system of corruption, 'intrigue and oppression, as can well be conceived; while 'alike from the absenteeism of influential holders, and from 'the over-assessment on resident patels, villages every-'where deteriorated. Settlements were made ostensibly on 'the old principle that the patel was to collect the revenue 'from the ryots, and to receive a certain sum for village 'expenses and a percentage on collections ; but, in reality, the 'assessment on resident patel villages was more than the 'fields could pay, and the patel made up the difference by 'any exactions he was able to enforce. The Rājā twice 'visited the District, and surrounded though he was by 'persons interested in concealing the truth, yet he learned 'something of the abuses prevailing. On the first occasion 'he fined the sūbahdār, Krishna Rao Anand, and his accom-'plices, Nāgpur rupees 1,19,072, and on the second visit he 'dispossessed the Nāgpur Chitnavīs and his relatives, 'together with other officials, of many of their villages, but 'the only result of these measures was to increase the extor-'tion of the persons fined, and to make the official class 'generally hold in the names of their agents. Some slight 'check existed, for a time, in the shape of a Chānda woman 'named Sheo Bai Joshin, who, early left a widow, devoted 'herself to public affairs, and, on several occasions, procured 'the punishment of officials by disclosures made personally 'to the Rājā. No suspicion of improper conduct attaches 'to her name, and she was feared not only in Chānda but at 'Nāgpur. Her efforts, however, could only affect particular 'cases, and at length the great officers of the court induced 'the Rājā not to receive her. The systematic misrule which 'afflicted the District could not be maintained without injur-

'ing the revenue, and consequently, although no device to 'raise money was spared, we find that, with one slight 'recovery in 1848-49, the land revenue since 1844-45 fell 'steadily year by year. In a word, the greed and fraud of 'the second Marāthā administration inflicted irreparable wrong 'on thousands of individuals, impoverished and demoralised 'the people generally, and proved to the District the darkest 'period it has known.'

Beginning of British rule, 1853.

278. In 1853, an end was put to this chaotic misgovernment by the lapse of the Nāgpur kingdom to the British Government. A British Deputy Commissioner was appointed to the District, and the task of cleaning the augæan stables was again promptly taken in hand. Extraordinary imposts were abolished, and this step was followed in 1861 by the abolition of the transit duty, at a direct cost to Government of over half a lakh a year. The District was divided into two tahsīls with headquarters at Mūl and Chimūr, a third tahsīl with its headquarters at Warorā being formed in 1857. Summary settlements were made, village by village, for terms of three years, but such was the general impoverishment that all manner of ruses had to be employed in order to obtain lessees. By 1862-63 when the regular settlement commenced, the land revenue demand had been reduced to 2·65 lakhs as compared with 3·26 lakhs at annexation, but part of this decrease was due to transfer of certain items of land revenue to other heads.

The conferral of proprietary status upon patels.

279. The most remarkable feature of the first regular settlement of the District was the conferral of the proprietary status upon the patels. The gradual growth in the power of the patel had been a noteworthy feature of the Marāthā administration. Theoretically, it would appear that the Marāthās had, to the last, maintained the ancient principle that the ryot was only liable for the revenue assessed by the State on his holding, but in practice it seems certain that even

during the first period of their rule, patels had fallen into a habit of making illicit gains out of their ryots to supplement their legal allowance. Sir R. Jenkins wrote that 'the allowance to patels had not been admitted by the Government for many years previously to our assuming charge, and the profits of the patels arose from whatever they could collect surreptitiously from the ryots, over and above the Government demand, which they often contrived to do to a considerable amount, in consequence of the system of *bargans*, and, when possessed of capital, from the advances of money and grain they made to the poorer ryots.' During the period of chaos between 1804 and 1818, when the whole countryside was harried by Pindāris and lesser freebooters, the patel doubtless greatly strengthened his position. The villages were thrown almost entirely on their own resources for self-defence, and would naturally turn to their patel for guidance. A strong patel would practically be able to constitute himself the dictator of his village, and, having piloted it through the storm, would find his position in relation to his fellow villagers enormously strengthened. The British Protectorate while absolutely forbidding the extortion of *bargans* by patels, openly recognised the right of the patel to make his own terms with the cultivators as to rent. 'The patel,' wrote Sir R. Jenkins, 'is entirely entrusted with the renting of the whole of his village, and he is at liberty to let the land in any way he may choose. There are frequent complaints from ryots against patels for depriving them of fields they have cultivated for years, the patel wishing either to cultivate the land himself, or to raise the rent. No interference is exercised on the part of the Superintendents, unless any violation of positive agreement can be made out by the complainant.' It will be seen then that even under the management of the British, the patel was recognised to have a right to fix the rents of the ryots, not merely to apportion the revenue demand amongst them, so that, although by no means recognised as the proprietor of the soil, he exercised a function usually bound up in English ideas with the status of proprietorship. The second period of Marāthā rule, with its scandalous encouragement of extortion, would tend still further to depress the position of the ryot in respect to his patel, and so render the transition to absolute proprietorship on the part of the latter more easy The final step was taken in 1860, when the Government of India formally sanctioned the conferment of proprietary rights upon patels, by this time re-named mālguzārs, a term borrowed from the North-West Provinces, and, brushing aside various restrictions proposed by the Local Administration, declared their intention of conferring 'on every 'landholder, as nearly as possible, a fee-simple in his estate 'subject only to the payment of revenue of the Government, 'and to put in his power to dispose of his interest in the land 'as he pleases, by sale, gift, mortgage, bequest or otherwise,' adding that 'though it is not desired that this policy should 'be pushed so far as to do violence to the feelings of the 'agricultural community, or to interfere with vested interests. 'yet His Excellency in Council wishes you to bear in mind 'that it is not the wish of the Government to limit the 'proprietary right any further than a due respect for such 'feelings and interest requires.' In its final form, however, the grant of proprietary right was by no means unconditional; Government reserved to itself the right to all mines and quarries and to all large forests where valuable timber existed, and furthermore retained the proprietorship of large areas of uncultivated land; it also conferred the proprietorship of their holdings on tenants of long standing, and gave occupancy rights to other tenants.

The first settlement, 1862—69.

280. The settlement which commenced in 1862 is usually associated with the name of Major C. B. Lucie Smith, the compiler of the Chānda Settlement Report, but he did not actually take over charge of the operations till towards the end of 1866. The first work was to lay down

the exterior boundaries of villages and then to take the interior measurements, a task which was accomplished with fair accuracy, although the instruments used were of an inferior character. The usual rule for defining the limits of a village was to measure up the area occupied by tanks, crops, and the fallow of the two last years, and then to allow double that area for village waste, relegating the excess to Government forest. In this way, an area of 2526 square miles of the *khālsa* was delimited as village estates, while 2255 square miles were declared to be Government forest. As each field was measured, it was roughly classified by its soil. Claims to proprietary right were meanwhile sifted, and the opportunity was taken in many instances to rectify the maladministration of the Marāthās by putting in as proprietors deserving patels who had been wrongfully ousted, or their representatives. Sometimes an absentee lessee who merely farmed his village, was superseded in favour of the leading resident ryot of the village. In this way, out of 1281 mālguzāri villages, 982 were confirmed to the existing mālguzār, 132 were restored to the old patel or his heirs, 143 were made over to the leading ryot, while 24 were either reserved to the State for special reasons or held temporarily under direct management in default of a suitable candidate for the proprietorship.

Method of deducing assets and distributing assessment.

281. The general orders in regard to assessment were that 'the true gross rental of each 'estate having been ascertained by care- 'ful enquiry, the Governor-General 'in Council would be disposed to allow 'the mālguzārs in all cases at least 40 per cent. for expenses 'of management and proprietary profits and to extend the 'limit in certain cases even to 50 per cent.' [1] The chief problem before the Settlement Officer was, therefore, to ascertain the theoretical full demand. The first step towards this

[1] Letter No. 2279 from Government of India, Foreign Department, dated 28th June 1860.

was to group all neighbouring villages of similar circumstances into an assessment circle or *chak*, and then to ascertain the existing rent-rate for each class of soil in the *chak*. The existing rent-rolls or *lāgwans*, though untrustworthy in themselves, gave great assistance in determining the relative values of the various types of soil, and could be checked by comparison with the papers of estates held on privileged tenure in which there was no strong motive to deceive. An average rent-rate for each class of soil was thus obtained, and the Settlement Officer then proceeded to construct an assumed rent-rate based on the future prospects of the circle. As it was thought to be beyond a doubt that rents would gradually rise, the assumed rent-rates for each class of soil were placed in all parganas at a figure above the average rent, though not above the highest rent, existing in such class before assessment. To check the demand arrived at by these rates, a produce rate, based on the average produce per acre of each class of soil under each description of crop and its value, was worked out. A further, but not very satisfactory, check was given by the plough rate, which was found by dividing the total cultivated area by the number of ploughs, and multiplying the quotient by the assumed rent-rate per acre. When the cultivated area had been dealt with, the assets from the waste area were estimated and 50 per cent. taken as the Government share. The theoretical demand having thus been ascertained from the average rates, the total assessment was distributed among the various villages, consideration being given to the history of the village, its appearance and management, the class of its cultivators and the incidence of the revenue formerly paid by it.

Treatment of rents and its results.

282. The actual rental demand, except in the case of privileged tenants, was left to the discretion of the mālguzār, a policy which was regarded with much discomposure by Major Lucie Smith, who considered that it delivered the unprivileged tenants bound hand and foot to the mercy of the

mālguzār. Well grounded though this fear was, it has not been actually realised, and the conferral of the occupancy status on tenants-at-will has turned the tables on the mālguzār. To quote Mr. Hemingway: 'It was expected that the 'mālguzārs would fix higher rents than those attested in the '*lāgwans*; it was suspected that the true rents were in many 'cases concealed, and in any case the mālguzārs would take 'advantage of the permission to enhance, a luxury which had 'till then been forbidden. In many Districts, the mālguzārs 'at once accepted this opportunity and did enhance; in 'Chānda that course was not generally adopted; possibly 'the tenants were too strong for the mālguzārs; but probably 'the latter found, then as now, that poor rice years had 'lowered the demand for the best land, especially in the 'more distant tracts. When once fixed, the rents were 'unchangeable during the term of settlement; all the tenants-'at-will were granted occupancy status. Therefore in many 'villages the assumed assets of settlement have never been 'reached and the revenue has been paid with difficulty.'

Treatment of proprietary plots.

283. In addition to deciding the proprietary title to villages, the Settlement Officer had in many instances to award proprietary titles to plots. Such plots might vary in size from a small field to a large area in no respect inferior to a village. The following classes of holders were given proprietary rights in their plots in the *khālsa*:—

I. In villages where the standing of the mālguzārs did not exceed 20 years, all ryots of 12 years' occupancy and over who had held their plots longer than the malguzārs had held the village.

II.—In villages where the standing of the mālguzārs exceeded 20 years, those ryots who had materially improved their plots and had held such plots longer than the mālguzār had held the village.

III.--Relations of present mālguzārs or of former patels, who were holding rent free, or at favourable and fixed rates.

IV.—Holders of privileged tenure plots.

V.—Holders of resumed privileged tenure plots.

Each plot was assessed at the suitable revenue rate, and waste was allotted to it proportionately to the quantity given for the entire village, provided that the area so allotted did not fall below one acre. Altogether 3914 holdings with an area of 107,706 acres and a revenue demand of Rs. 31,509, were thus awarded in proprietary right.

Treatment of revenue-free and quit-rent grants.

284. Besides these proprietary plots, there were various holdings to be dealt with which were held on a revenue-free or quit-rent grant. In the *khālsa* the three chief forms of such grants found in existence at the commencement of the settlement were known as *mukāsa*, *maktā*, and *tukum*. *Mukāsa* grants were theoretically absolutely revenue-free, having been granted either in charity, or for the subsistence of relatives or retainers of the sovereign, or in reward for military, religious or other services. *Maktā* grants were given at a fixed annual demand, in theory not liable to alteration, the grantee undertaking to improve cultivation or bring jungle under the plough. The *tukum* grant, one of the most ancient and admirable features of the Gond system, invested the builder of a tank with as much land as the tank could water, at a fixed demand which was in theory not open to enhancement. Under the Marāthās, *Maktā* and *tukum* grants were attached upon the death of the holder, but were usually renewed on payment of a heavy *nazrāna* by the heir. *Mukāsa* grants were usually allowed to pass to a successor without fine. In deciding claims to hold on these privileged terms Major Lucie Smith's principle was to recommend the continuation of a grant in perpetuity only where it was clearly very ancient or where the grantee could produce a royal patent conferring the grant in perpetuity. In other cases, if the grant had been held prior to annexation, it was confirmed to the grantee during the term of his life, or until the period of the settlement; if it was of more

recent date, it was resumed. Assignments to village servants were entered up as service tenures held under the proprietor, not under Government; only those held by Joshis were entered up as revenue-free grants for life. The amount of revenue thus alienated was some Rs. 30,000, of which about Rs. 8000 was alienated in perpetuity, while land worth about Rs. 4000 per annum was resumed.

Absolute occupancy tenants.

285. Turning to the tenant classes, the policy of the settlement was directed towards according them extremely high protection. Absolute occupancy rights were granted in the *khālsa* parganas to the following classes:—

(1) Ryots whose possession carried with it something of a hereditary character.

(2) Ryots who had expended such capital on their fields as to give them some special title.

(3) Ryots who were relations of present mālguzārs, or former patels.

(4) Ryots of new villages who had held their fields since the villages were founded, or since their fields had been reclaimed from the jungle.

(5) Ryots who held their fields from a date antecedent to the proprietor's connection with the village as landlord.

(6) Ryots cultivating land which had descended to them by inheritance, provided the hereditary possession had lasted not less than 20 years.

(7) Ryots of villages in which the mālguzār was an absentee and had held under 20 years.

Other tenants.

286. About one-quarter of the tenant body was comprehended in these wide definitions. It was originally intended to grant 'conditional[1] occupancy' rights under Act X of 1859 to such other tenants as had cultivated their holdings for at least 12 years, and to classify the remaining tenant body, excluding holders of service grants, as tenants-at-will, but before

[1] That is conditional on the maintenance of Act X of 1859.

the completion of settlement orders were issued to promote tenants-at-will to the occupancy class, a policy which has been confirmed by all subsequent tenancy legislation.

Financial results and term of first settlement.

287. The financial results of the settlement of the *khālsa* were as follows. The gross revenue was raised from Rs. 2,57,917 to Rs 2,62,351. This latter figure represents 64 per cent. of the ascertained or supposed assets (including *siwai*) and 52 per cent. of the gross rental as per the assumed average rates on soil. The net revenue excluding assignments was Rs. 2,42,990, a reduction of nearly 6 per cent. on the existing revenue. The term of settlement was fixed at 30 years for all the *khālsa* parganas except Rājgarh, Ghātkul, Amgaon, Wairāgarh and Ghot. For the first four a term of 20 years was proposed, while for Ghot the period of currency was fixed for only 13 years, so that the villages granted by *sanad* to the zamīndārin of Ahīri as a reward for her services in the Mutiny, might be re-assessed at the earliest date permissible in accordance with the terms of the *sanad.* As a matter of fact, however, the pargana was not re-assessed till 1889.

Re-settlement of Rājgarh, Amgaon, Wairāgarh, Ghot and Ghātkul parganas, 1886–1889.

288. The revision of the Rājgarh pargana was undertaken by Mr. Carey, I.C.S., in 1886. Existing rents were found to have risen but little, owing to the inability of the mālguzārs to enhance, but the rental demand had been largely increased by the breaking up of new land. Before framing his proposals for revenue, Mr. Carey corrected the assets according to what he considered a fair value for the land. The lines on which this was done were not dissimilar from those followed at the original settlement, but the valuation, particularly of the home-farm, was much more minute and methodical. This valuation showed that many tenants were holding at inadequate rates, and, as they resisted all attempts on the part of the mālguzārs to interfere with the rents, it was determined to announce a

revised rent-roll by official agency. In this way existing rents were raised by 10 per cent., and rents were fixed for land which tenants had added to their holdings free of rent. In 1887, Mr. Purushottam Dās effected the revision of the Amgaon pargana, following the same lines as had been pursued by Mr. Carey, the only remarkable innovation being the introduction of a factor-scale giving the comparative values of different soils in the form of a ratio; actual rent-rate reports were then submitted and rents were deduced before fixation as is now done. Rents were enhanced by 10 per cent. The revised revenue absorbed 59 per cent. of the gross assets. The same officer undertook the revision of the Wairāgarh pargana, where rents were enhanced by 9 per cent. and *mālik makbūza* payments by 25 per cent., and 58 per cent. of the gross assets were taken as revenue. In the assessment of this pargana, a fault that had to some degree marred the assessments of the other two parganas became very manifest; an abnormally large area of home-farm was classed as cane land, and was valued at a very high acreage rate without making allowance for the resting periods which this type of cultivation is locally thought to necessitate. In the case of Wairāgarh a further error was committed which had untoward results. Many rents had hitherto been paid in kind; these were now commuted to cash rents, but in this process the value of grain was taken at too high a figure, so that the commuted rent stood 25 per cent. or more above the original payment in kind. The aboriginal tenant would not pay the higher figure, and consequently a wholesale abandonment of second-class rice land took place. The re-assessment of the Ghātkul and Ghot parganas was conducted by the Deputy Commissioner, Mr. MacGeorge in 1887 and 1889 respectively. The proceedings here were very summary; rents were not touched, and the valuation of assets was rough. Fifty-seven per cent. of the recorded assets were taken in Ghātkul, and 50 per cent. in Ghot. In each case a rise of assets led to an enhancement of revenue. The valuation of home-farm in Ghātkul was distinctly low, and the occupied area expanded rapidly after re-settlement, so the assessment there proved very lenient.

Land revenue administration of the zamīndāris.

289. The fiscal system of the Gonds and Marāthās, as described in the earlier portion of this chapter, was only capable of practical working in fairly settled and accessible tracts. For the wild and forest clad regions east of the Waingangā, some more rough and ready method had to be devised. To secure comparative law and order it was necessary to use a light hand with the natural chieftains of the aborigines, whose subjugation would have been of very little profit, while their enmity would have been a source of continual annoyance. Both Gonds and Marāthās were, therefore, content to recognise the petty chiefs who were the ancestors of the present zamīndārs, and by this policy of moderation to glean a certain amount of revenue in the shape of the zamīndār's tribute or *takolī*, leaving the management of the internal concerns of the zamīndāris in their hands. When the District came under British management in 1818, the total *takolī* of the zamīndāris stood at 3424 Nāgpur rupees. This sum Sir R. Jenkins reduced to Rs. 415, remarking that 'the tribute due 'by these zamīndārs was scarcely an object to Government, 'whilst it bore hard upon their slender means and irregular 'habits.' It was even remitted altogether in some cases, and this sympathetic policy had the result of conciliating the chieftains and curbing their tendency to make border forays on the *khālsa*. When settlement operations were undertaken in 1862, the *takolī* demand stood at Rs. 339. It was raised by Major Lucie-Smith's settlement to Rs. 2205, but the principles of Sir R. Jenkins' policy were still maintained, enhancements, and those of a moderate nature, being made only when the forests were of a peculiar value or the income and position of the zamīndāri favourable; in other cases, the

demand was slightly changed, merely to assert the principle that the *takolī* is subject to revision.

The regular settlement of the zamīndāris expired in 1888, when a summary settlement was undertaken. At this summary settlement rents were not touched, but the *takolī* payments were simply revised. The total *takolī* payable by all the estates was raised very slighty to Rs. 2292, and fell at from 3 to 11 per cent. of the assets, the higher percentages falling as a rule on the smaller estates. In 1892, the *takolīs* were again altered, an addition being made to them to cover the cost of the patwāris, who till that year had been paid by the zamīndārs themselves, but who were thenceforward paid by Government. Forest *takolīs* were revised at the same time and the land revenue and forest *takolīs* and payments on account of cesses were consolidated into one lump sum.

Land revenue administration of the Sironchā tasīl.

290. Little or nothing is known about Sironchā prior to the 17th century, when the tract formed part of the Nizām's territory but was held in immediate management by the Velamā family of Sardeshmukhs who are still the superior proprietors of the tahsīl. This family seems to have held the tāluks on a quit-rent tenure under obligations for military service. In 1822, an unsuccessful rebellion led to the resumption of their fief by the Nīzām's Government, but in 1829 they were restored to it, though with much curtailed authority: in course of time, however, they appear to have recovered most of their former privileges, and their position at the time of the cession of Sironchā to the British was deemed such as to warrant their being recorded as superior proprietors. As the proprietors had been in the somewhat curious habit of redistributing circles of villages periodically, so that the same tāluks never remained in the possession of one of the sharers more than twelve years, each Sardeshmukh was shown as having a share in each of the tāluks. All the tāluks, with the exception of Sironchā, had at various times been leased out by the

proprietors to lessees known as *dhorwās*, and the lessees who were found in possession in 1860 were granted the status of inferior proprietors. In the Albāka and Cherlā tāluks the inferior proprietorship subsequently lapsed for want of heirs, but Nūgur is still held in that right. In Sironchā, as there was no inferior proprietor, the Sardeshmukhs were recorded as absolute proprietors.

Revenue system prior to cession.

291. The revenue system obtaining at the time of the cession bears traces of Muhammadan influence. The regular revenue assessment went by the name of *ain kaul*. Except in the case of irrigated land which was assessed by the *bīgha*, the assessment was calculated upon the plough; at the beginning of the season the cultivator had to state to the revenue authorities how many ploughs he intended to use, and was then assessed accordingly, being afterwards at liberty to bring as much land under cultivation with that number of ploughs as he could. In hilly tracts where *pord* or *dahiā* cultivation was carried on, the unit of assessment was the axe Besides the *ain kaul* there were numerous arbitrary charges called '*akhīra-chat*' which varied every season according to the paying capacity of the cultivator, and ranged from 5 or 10 to 100 per cent. on the *ain kaul*. The amount of these was fixed upon the report of the patwāris after a field to field inspection shortly before harvest. To secure payment, the crops were not allowed to be removed from the fields until all claims were settled. The exact amount of revenue obtained by this system is not ascertainable, but it must have been very considerable, and balances should have been practically impossible.

Summary Settlement of 1861.

292. As soon as Sironchā became British territory, a Summary Settlement was effected for four years by the Deputy Commissioner, Captain Glasfurd. The tract at this time was incorporated with two other tāluks since transferred to the Madras Presidency—forming with them the Upper Godāvari

District, but for the purposes of this section these tāluks have been excluded from consideration. As the existing assessment was found to press heavily on the people, especially in the Sironchā tāluk, Captain Glasfurd reduced it, and pitched the lease money payable by the proprietors at a low figure. During the currency of the summary settlement the rent-roll of the proprietors substantially increased, especially in the Sironchā tāluks, where the security afforded by British rule led to the clearance of large areas of waste land. When, in 1863, orders were issued to effect a regular settlement, it was obvious that a considerably higher revenue might fairly be levied from the proprietors. Not only was this justified by the fact that the settlement was for a long term during which great advances in cultivation were to be expected, but also it was anticipated that the proprietors would take full advantage of the power to revise rents annually which was still vested in them; it was, in fact, apprehended that this power would be exercised too freely, as the peasants of Sironchā were particularly abject in their attitude towards their landlords, and had come to look upon enhancement in favourable years as a matter of course.

Regular settlement, 1863—1866.

293. The methods of the regular settlement were much the same as have been described in treating of Major Lucie Smith's Settlement; that is to say, assumed rent-rates were calculated from the existing rates and checked by plough and produce rates. Waste land was allowed to each village in a proportion of from 100 to 200 per cent. of the occupied area, but even so the unoccupied area of the District was so large that no less than six-sevenths of it became Government property. The revised revenue was fixed at Rs. 14,087, an increase of 46 per cent. It absorbed nearly 91 per cent. of the rental as it existed previous to assessment, and fell at the rate of 11·3 annas per cultivated acre. With regard to rents, the people were made to understand that adjustment was a matter which

was left entirely to themselves, and that the rents as adjusted were not necessarily to be considered fixed for the term of settlement: the Settlement Officer, however, gave them his opinion as to what he considered a fair rent and used his influence to settle disputes. As a consequence of this latitude of enhancement, rents were raised so freely that the Government demand after their adjustment only amounted to 63 per cent. of the total rent-roll.

Summary re-assessment, 1887.

294. Captain Glasfurd's Settlement was sanctioned for a term of 20 years, and came into force in 1867. On its expiry in 1887, the tahsīl was very summarily re-assessed by Mr. Rangiah and the revenue was revised without touching the rents. Assets were found to have risen by 37 per cent. and the revenue demand was accordingly raised to Rs. 19,300, but this was subsequently reduced to Rs. 18,400 on the representation of the proprietors, conditionally upon their undertaking tank repairs and managing their villages better. Although the proprietors did not fulfil these conditions, only the lowered revenue was collected during the term of this settlement.

Evolution of the Land Record Staff.

295. Administratively the most important feature of the period between the original and the recent settlement is the evolution of the Land Record Staff and more particualrly of the patwāri or village accountant. This official had existed from ancien times in the zamīndārs, but in the *khālsa* he had (under the name of *pāndia*) been abolished by Captain Crawfurd during the British Protectorate, and the patels had been made responsible for the due submission of the village papers. With the creation of varying rights at the first settlement, the institution of a recording agency independent of the mālguzār became a practical necessity, and soon after settlement regular patwāris were enrolled for groups or circles of villages, and it was laid down that they should be remunerated by the village communities. In the year 1885, these patwāris were formed into a regular land record staff, the

khālsa being divided into 145 and the zamīndāris into 19 circles. The number of circles was increased in 1899 and again during the recent settlement, and now stands at 161 in the *khālsa* and 59 in the zamīndāris. Concurrently, the system of paying patwāris has been radically altered. From payment entirely by the village community it has evolved through part payment by tenants and part payment by Government, to payment by the latter alone. Patwāris are now Government servants pure and simple.

Survey.

296. A regular survey of the District was commenced in 1889, and was completed in the *khālsa* in 1894. From 1895 to 1899 a survey was made of the more important villages of the zamīndāris in which the rental demand exceeded Rs. 105. Only one zamīndāri—that of Ambāgarh Chauki—was completely surveyed. In the rest of the tract, 755 out of 1221 villages remained unsurveyed, besides a very large area of hill and forest. At present it is inadvisable to complete the survey of this tract, since in the wilder zamīndāris villages spring up and disappear like mushrooms. In the survey of the *khālsa* points on the village boundaries and subtraverse lines were fixed by a professional traverse party: the interior survey was then carried out by the patwāri staff by triangulation. Unluckily, the intervention of bad seasons between survey and settlement rendered the survey maps of little value in the later operations, and corrections were very numerous.

Procedure of the settlement.

297. Settlement operations proper began in 1897, when Mr. Hallifax, I.C.S., was posted to the District as Settlement Officer. After completing the attestation and inspection of the Warorā tahsīl, and the attestation and part of the inspection of the Bramhapurī tahsīl, he was succeeded in the direction of the settlement operations by Mr. P. Hemingway, I.C.S. His principal assistants were Mr. Chamberlain, I.C.S., and Mr. Lancaster who conducted the settlement of the zamīn-

dāris under the general supervision of the Settlement Officer, and Messrs. Chhote Lāl and Mahmūd-ul-Hasan. In the *khālsa*, the method of assessment was that now prescribed for the Province as a whole, and included the elaborate classification and valuation of soils by relative factors, generally known as the soil-unit system. This system is too sophisticated for the primitive conditions of the zamīndāris, and here valuation was calculated on the local plough rate or all-round ryoti rate. In the *khālsa*, a general revision of rents was an essential condition of the work of reassessment, but in the zamīndāri, owing to the general depression consequent on the famine, rents were not touched except in a few cases where they were excessively low or where land had been held without rent by encroachment or otherwise. Settlement work had to be altogether abandoned during the famine of 1899-1900, and for a whole year the settlement staff was employed on famine duty. Work re-commenced in January 1901, but conditions had been so altered by the famine that much that had already been done had to be done over again. Attestation was very troublesome and tedious owing to the large number of changes which were found in all groups, and was not completed in Bramhapurī till December 1904, while inspection work lasted till the end of February 1905.

Rental enhancements.

298. In effecting his rental enhancements the Settlement Officer had to balance two main considerations against each other. On the one hand, although the general rise of prices during the currency of the previous settlement, a rise which was nowhere less than 50 per cent., and in some tracts was fully cent. per cent., justified considerable freedom in enhancement, it was manifestly impossible, in view of the depression caused by the recent bad seasons, to press the theoretical consideration to a practical issue without disastrous results. On the other hand, the District stood on the threshold of a great development of communications, and, given average seasons, it was obvious that recovery should be rapid: therefore, since no rents

can be raised except at settlement, and existing rents were very low, the interest of the mālguzārs and of Government demanded that they should be enhanced wherever possible. Careful differential treatment according to the past history of each village and a short term of settlement were the two chief remedies prescribed. In the upshot, the rents of absolute occupancy and occupancy tenants were raised at announcement by 17 per cent. over the District as a whole. The revised rents sanctioned gave an enhancement of 15 per cent. only in the case of occupancy tenants; the increase of 2 per cent. is due to the breaking up of waste land between rental fixation and actual announcements, as well as to some small raising of rents by the mālguzārs with the consent of tenants. In Warorā, where the rents were revised immediately after the famine and the tenants' powers of recuperation under-estimated, the revision erred somewhat on the side of leniency. Elsewhere, enhancement was more freely imposed, but much of it was due to the raising of purely nominal rents which the strong positions of tenants had hitherto prevented the mālguzār from enhancing, and to the fixation of rent for the first time on large areas of encroachments or of newly cleared land hitherto held absolutely free of rent.

Differential treatment was the more necessary from the circumstance that the rents of the District are extraordinarily uneven from village to village, and—a fact of even greater importance—from tract to tract. In illustration of this, the soil unit incidences of a few groups may be quoted. By soil-unit incidence is meant that fraction of an anna which is paid by each unit of soil in the rent paying area. In the Warorā tahsīl, with the exception of two groups, this incidence fell at between ·28 and ·37 prior to re-settlement: in the less wealthy Chānda tahsīl, excepting the Ghātkul and Ghot groups where the incidence was exceptionally low, it varied from ·45 to ·64, while in Bramhapurī rates varied between 31 and 1·02. This unevenness of rents in villages contiguous to each other rendered the formation of groups a very difficult matter. Theoretically all the villages of a group should be rated by the same standard, but it was almost impossible to do this in a satisfactory manner, and the course of the settlement showed that it was advisable to differentiate the villages of each group into minor classes, according to their types of cropping, and to take a different standard rate for enhancement of each class. This experience was, however, gained too late to allow of this principle being put into practice, save in the Bramhapurī tahsīl. In that tahsīl the villages of each group were divided into three classes: A—high class rice villages with excellent irrigation, B—villages with good *rabi* crops to help out the rice and C—inferior and depressed pure rice villages; and separate standard rates were laid down for each class of each group.

The total rental payable by the tenants of the whole *khālsa* portion of the District was raised from Rs. 3,76,356 to Rs. 4,40,863, or by 17 per cent., exclusive of revenue paid by *mālik makbūzas*. The percentage of all-round enhancement and the unit incidence of rentals after enhancement is shown below for each tahsīl as it stood at re-settlement:—

Tahsīl.	Percentage of all-round enhancement.	Unit incidence.
Chānda	16	·54
Warorā	14	·41
Bramhapurī	17	·56
Sironchā	19	·80

The total revised rental demand of the District is roughly calculated by Mr. Hemingway to be equal to one-fourteenth of the total gross value of its produce. This shows that the rental is exceptionally light: it is especially so in the open tracts, but even in the rice villages where rents rule most high, the rental is seldom equivalent to as much as one-ninth of the produce. This light rental is very largely due to the large number of nominal rents which result from the mālguzār's disability to enhance, and which could not be raised to a fair figure at settlement without involving too large a *per saltum* increase. The disability to enhance not only entails heavy loss of revenue to Government and to the mālguzār, but it makes the tenant value lightly the land that he holds upon such light terms, and it is, Mr. Hemingway thinks, a matter for regret that Government officers are not invested with powers to enhance at the suggestion of the mālguzār during the currency of the settlement.

Miscellaneous income.

299 *Siwai* or miscellaneous income was more strictly dealt with than at the first settlement, when assessment had been based merely on a rough calculation of the probable income to be derived from the village forest. At the new settlement, several new items were included under this head, the most important being water dues for cane and rice, the value of which was calculated by striking an average of the realisations of the previous ten years. The tanks also supply an income from fishery and the cultivation of the *singhāra* or water-nut, *khamori* and *wandu* were rated as miscellaneous income instead of being included under the rental demand: the former is really payment for the forest that is felled and burnt to manure the land, while the latter is the fluctuating income from the silt deposited in the bed of the Godāvari and in neither of these cases is the cultivator's tenure permanent, and it would therefore be useless to survey the plots and treat them as held in occupancy right. The actual receipts at the time of settlement amounted to Rs. 39,400 and the assumed annual average income was Rs. 33,700.

Exemption for improvements.

300. Very little revenue or rental had to be reduced on account of improvements effected during the term of settlement. In this District mālguzārs rarely effect improvements and in only seven cases was revenue lowered from this cause.

Tenants' improvements usually take the form of small irrigation *borīs* and embankments. Four thousand acres of land were thus improved, the annual value of the improvements aggregating Rs. 1897. The rents assessed on this area, amounted to Rs. 2372 below the deduced rent : thus the reduction granted was more liberal by Rs. 475 than required by rule.

Assessment of land revenue.

301. By the end of the thirty years' settlement, the revenue demand had become very unevenly distributed, and the assessment proposals of the new settlement to a great extent amounted merely to a redistribution of the existing demand. It has been previously pointed out how the revenue proposals of 1868 had largely been framed on a consideration of prospective assets, and indeed often absorbed all the recorded assets. In many villages, thanks to bad seasons, bad communications, lack of tenants and the prohibition of enhancement which was introduced by the first Tenancy Act and confirmed by all its successors, assets did not rise at all, and mālguzārs experienced the greatest difficulty in paying their dues. Some tracts on the other hand were far too lightly assessed. Reviewing the District broadly, it was found that at re-settlement the revenue demand was very light all over the Warorā tahsīl except in the Warorā group, in the best northern groups of the Bramhapurī tahsīl and all over the Sironchā tahsīl except in the Cherlā group: in most of Chānda and in the rice tracts of Bramhapurī, the demand was high : it was a good deal too high in comparison with existing assets in all those groups which had been summarily re-settled except Ghot and Ghātkul, while in Wairāgarh and part of Murjhā it was frankly oppressive. Thus the richest tracts were paying the lightest demand, and the poorest tracts were paying the heaviest demand. The chief principle followed in the revision of the assessment was to adopt a low fraction in remote tracts where assets were unstable, and a higher fraction in the stable tracts where assets must rise : this

principle was followed irrespective of the existing revenue and no attempt was made to maintain the latter in unstable and deteriorated tracts by taking a high fraction of the assets. A remote tract with poor communications and markets must, it was felt, have strong local managers as a backbone to its tenantry, and it was impossible to obtain these without a lenient assessment. The revised *kāmil-jamā* as announced amounted to 3·56 lakhs, as compared with a *kāmil-jamā* of 3·00 lakhs prior to announcement, and absorbed 55 per cent. of the revised assets. Allowing for fairly numerous revenue assignments on account of the construction of tanks and to Deshpāndes, Deshmukhs and the Bhonsla Rājās of Nāgpur, the net realisable revenue amounted to 3·36 lakhs. In a few instances where mālguzārs were called upon to pay a considerable extra sum over and above what accrued to them in increased rents, they were accommodated by progressive assessments up to a maximum term of five years. The amount thus alienated in the first year was about Rs. 5,600.

Zamīndāri assessment.

302. The zamīndāri area, as has been remarked above, was not completely surveyed, and settlement operations were mainly confined to a revision of the *takolī* demand, rents being touched only in a few cases where they were exceptionally low, or where land had been held free of rent. In the revision of *takolīs*, the general principles laid down for the Raipur zamīndāris were followed, but a lower percentage was taken. This lower percentage was necessitated by the general depression and the generally smaller size of the estates, and by the fact that at the original settlement a far lower percentage had been taken than in Raipur. The *kāmil-jamā* was fixed at 55 per cent. of the village assets and 50 per cent. of the forest income. The standard *takolī* was fixed at 10 per cent. of the *kāmil-jamā*, but this principle was departed from when adherence to it would have reduced the zamīndār's profits below the figure at which they stood at the previous re-settlement in 1889. As a result of the revision, the total *takolī* demand

was fixed at Rs. 4300 in addition to which Rs. 1890-9 were payable on account of cesses.

Inferior proprietary rights were granted in 56 villages in the Ahīri zamīndāri, but in all these cases the right to hold at the privileged rates was made resumable at the pleasure of the zamīndār. Inferior proprietary rights were also granted in 51 villages of other estates.

Expenditure.

303. The total expenditure on survey and settlement amounted to 5·25 lakhs, and was spread over sixteen years, from 1889 when survey commenced, to July 1905 when assessment proposals were completed. Of the whole sum 1·70 lakhs were spent on survey alone, prior to the commencement of settlement work proper. Of the balance, 2·91 lakhs were spent on settlement work in the *khālsa* and Rs 64,000 on work in the zamīndāris. This expenditure falls at Rs. 109 per square mile of the mālguzāri estate, and at Rs. 13 per square mile of the total zamīndāri area. Considering that the whole of the work, including mapping and preparation of *misals*, had to be done twice for the Warorā and Bramhapurī tahsīls, where operations were stopped for a whole year by famine, the cost is not excessive, but on the other hand it is very heavy as compared with the additional revenue accruing to Government as the result of the revision.

Ryotwāri.

304. The ryotwāri estate of Government in this District at present consists of 533 villages classified as follows :—

213 regularly settled.
168 summarily settled.
131 patch cultivation.
21 rice rule.

No fewer than 255 of these villages, including all of the patch cultivation class, lie in the Sironchā tahsīl, which has almost as many ryotwāri as mālguzāri villages. In this tahsīl there are 106 regularly settled ryotwāri villages, 18 summarily settled, and 131 patch cultivation villages. A few of the villages lie in the fertile tract along the river bank and these are well taken up, but the great majority are situated in the forests of the interior and are of inferior soil. The ryots are naturally mainly Gonds, Koyās or Mārias. The occupied area is gradually spreading and the good land of the tahsīl has almost all been taken up already. The total area of the villages or patches in this tahsīl is about 64,000 acres and the land revenue amounts to nearly Rs. 7000.

Different classes of ryotwāri villages.

305. Turning to the ryotwāri estate of the rest of the District, 32 of the villages date from a period anterior to the settlement of 1886, when, whether directly managed or leased to *thekādārs*, they were brought under regular settlement. The vast majority of the remaining villages owe their origin to the policy of excision of culturable lands from Government forest which was formulated at a conference at Pachmarhī in 1891, when 1100 square miles of the District area were ear-marked for this purpose. Up to date, over four and a half lakhs of acres of culturable waste have been excised, and out of this 243 villages with an area of 230,000 acres have been formed. Of these 243 villages 72 are regularly settled, 150 are summarily settled and 21 are rice-rule villages. The summarily settled villages were formed during the survey operations of the last settlement in 1893: many of them are only small patches, and very many have gone entirely out of cultivation owing to the ryots absconding during the famines. A very large portion of the excised area remains to be taken up, especially in the Ghot and Wairāgarh ranges: much of it consists of land which is unculturable unless irrigated. Leases under the rice-rule system have been granted in 47 cases in all: in 15 of these the lessees fulfilled their agreements, and the villages were regularly settled: in 11 cases the lessees failed to establish the villages, which were thereupon settled summarily. The 21 villages still held under the system will in due course be surveyed and assessed regularly when the leases expire. Few

of them are in a flourishing condition. Of non-rice rule villages there are two, one in the Warorā, the other in the Garhchirolī tahsīl; these were granted revenue-free for a period of three years under promise of conferring *watandāri* status on the grantees if they should succeed in bringing two-thirds of the whole area under cultivation. There are also three villages, Kunghāra, Nawegaon and Paunpār, possessed of large tanks repaired at heavy cost by Government; these villages have recently been purchased by the State.

Management.

306. In all the regularly settled villages a regular cadastral survey has been held and the survey numbers are demarcated with stone boundary marks. Areas are reserved for grazing, forest user, roads and village sites. Originally the management of the forest areas was left to the Forest Department, but the attitude of the forest subordinates was found to be oppressive, and their powers of interference have been curtailed. The ryots are allowed to graze their cattle free of charge in the village forest, save in cases where one ryot keeps so many animals as to interfere with the due exercise of grazing rights by the remainder. Ryots are also allowed to collect mahuā free, and they may cut all kinds of wood except teak without charge. Summarily settled villages are for the most part unsurveyed. Ryots are given the same privileges that are granted to ryots of regularly settled villages, but in waste villages the power of control over the forest area is still vested in the Government Department, and licenses have to be taken out for grazing and cutting timber. A few of the villages are cadastrally surveyed, but they have not been regularly assessed: in such villages as well as in unsurveyed villages, the area actually brought under cultivation by a ryot is assessed at patch rates fixed by the Settlement Officer. These patch villages require good irrigation as an essential preliminary to their development.

Until 1907, the supervision of the ryotwāri estate of Government lay with the Settlement Department, but since that date direct management has been transferred to the Tahsīldārs, and a special ryotwāri Naib-tahsīldār has also been appointed for the whole District except Sironchā. But the estate is too unwieldy for supervision by one man, and a much larger and better-paid special staff will be necessary to its proper management. An allotment of Rs. 6,000 a year is granted for the construction of tanks and wells. Nearly all the villages in the Warorā and Bramhapurī tahsīls and those of the Dābha group in the Chānda tahsīl are in a fairly flourishing condition. Soils, however, are as a rule of inferior class and irrigation is also very poor except in a few villages where tanks have been provided by Government. Except in the rice-rule villages, juāri is the principal crop grown. The total area of regularly settled villages in the District (excluding the Sironchā tahsīl) is 160,000 acres, and of summarily settled villages 108,000 acres: the occupied areas are 64,000 and 17,000 acres respectively.

CHAPTER IX.

GENERAL ADMINISTRATION.

Administrative Staff and Subdivisions.

307. The District forms part of the Nāgpur Division and is administered by a Deputy Commissioner who is also District Magistrate and District Registrar. There are four executive Assistants of whom one is generally an Assistant Commissioner or member of the Indian Civil Service. The District is divided into five tahsīls each of which has a Tahsīldār and Naib-tahsīldār. There is a special Naib-tahsīldār in charge of ryotwāri work which is growing in importance. At the time of the old settlement the District was divided into three tahsīls, Mūl, Warorā and Bramhapurī. But in 1874 consequent on the abolition of the Upper Godāvari District a part of its territory consisting of four tāluks was added to the Chānda District and was formed into the Sironchā tahsīl. A further readjustment of the boundaries of the tahsīls took place in the year 1905 when the Ahīri zamīndāri was transferred to the Sironchā tahsil, and a new tahsīl was formed at Garhchirolī containing the zamīndāris of the Bramhapurī and Chānda tahsīls except Ahīri, with a strip of non-zamīndāri area. On the 1st October 1907 four zamīndāris of the Garhchirolī tahsīl, Ambāgarh Chauki, Pānābaras, Aundhi and Korācha were added to the newly formed Drug District. The transfer to the Madras Government of the tāluks of Nūgur, Albakā and Cherlā of the Sironchā tahsīl covering an area of 593 square miles and containing 142 villages with 20,218 persons has been under consideration for several years and is likely to take place in the near future. This tract is separated from the administrative centre of the District by many miles of forest and from the Upper Tāluks of Sironchā by a

strip of the Bastar State about 20 miles broad. It is more easily accessible from the southern side by the waterway of the Godāvari river which forms the western boundary of its whole length. According to the village lists the Chānda tahsīl contains 401 villages, Warorā 574, Bramhapurī 389, Garhchirolī 997 of which 629 are zamīndārī and Sironchā 773 of which 671 are zamīndāri.

The civil judicial staff ordinarily consists of a District Judge and two munsiffs at the headquarters and a munsiff at Warorā and Bramhapurī. The Tahsīldārs are appointed as additional judges to the munsiffs for civil work. Benches of Honorary Magistrates exist at Chānda and Warorā, while third-class powers have been conferred on the Manager of the Ahīri zamīndāri under the Court of Wards and on the Engineers of the Irrigation Department in order to facilitate the disposal of cases under the Workman's Breach of Contract Act. The Divisional and Sessions Judge of Nāgpur has jurisdiction in Chānda. Owing to the extent and importance of its forests the District has two Forest Officers both generally of the Imperial Service. The office of the Civil Surgeon is held by an officer of the Indian Medical Service. Chānda is an independent Public Works Division in the Roads and Buildings Branch. In 1905 the South Waingangā Subdivision was formed into a separate Division, the Mūl Irrigation Division, under an officer of the rank of an Executive Engineer.

Land Record Staff.

308. The Land Record Staff consists at present of a Superintendent, 3 Assistant Superintendents, 13 Revenue Inspectors and 199 patwāris. The Revenue Inspector's circles are Mūl and Kothāri in Chānda tahsil; Nandori, Chimūr and Segaon in Warorā; Talodhi and Mendki in Bramhapurī; Palāsgarh, Dhanorā and Ghot in Garhchirolī and Ahīri and the Upper Tāluks in Sironchā. On an average each Revenue Inspector has 15 patwāris' circles to supervise. This gives 246 villages to a Revenue circle, the average for a patwāri circle being 16.

The patwāris are mainly Brāhmans and Kunbīs with a sprinkling of Muhammadans and other castes. At the time of the 30 years' settlement no patwāris were appointed and the mālguzārs were held responsible for the rendition of *lāgwans* or village papers showing the names of tenants, the area under each crop and the rents collected. The *lāgwans* were written by village scribes on contract and were compiled from superficial enquiry from the people without actual observation or inspection. Their utility as a record of collected rents was therefore small and untrustworthy. The patwāri system was for the first time introduced in 1885. One hundred and forty-four patwāris were appointed for the *khālsa* only. In 1899 the system was extended to the zamīndāris and 44 patwāris were added. A patwāri cess at 6 per cent. of the land revenue was collected; while a *merh kuro* at the rate of 1 *kuro* (20 lbs. of cleaned grain) was contributed by each tenant. Both the patwāri cess and the *merh kuro* were abolished during 1906 and the pay of the patwāris was increased, the minimum pay being fixed at Rs. 10 and the maximum at Rs. 15 per mensem. At the recent settlement the number of 'Patwāri Halkābandī' was increased from 188 to 225, but owing to the transfer of four zamīndāris to the Drug District 27 patwāri circles were also transferred and a new circle was formed making a total of 199 for the District.

The receipts and expenditure of the patwāri cess are shown below:—

Year.		Receipts.	Expenditure.
		Rs.	Rs.
1903-04	...	17,820	29,284
1904-05	...	24,017	29,289
1905-06	...	21,383	32,578

The patwāris in the northern and more civilised portion of the District are a fairly intelligent lot of officials. But the backward tracts in the east and south of the District have always been shunned and dreaded by officials of all ranks and it has been a considerable difficulty in the administration of the District to maintain even an average standard of intelligence and honesty among the patwāris of these tracts.

Litigation and crime.

309. Considering the size of the District crime and litigation are small. The total number of civil suits instituted during the last ten years is 35,850, and the number of suits between landlord and tenant is 3414, which gives an average of 341 cases yearly. Suits affecting land and mesne profits are not many and the bulk of the litigation is based on simple bond cases for grain or money. The *sāhukāri* system is prevalent throughout the District and in Sironchā the cultivator has for years been the slave of the local Komtī; but as a rule the last thing the debtor desires is to be brought into court and so long as the larger portion of his profits is paid in annually to his *sāhukār* the latter abides content.

The number of cognisable and non-cognisable offences dealt with by the criminal courts in the decade ending in 1906 was 6595 and 3252 respectively. House-breaking, ordinary theft and cattle-thefts are the most common forms of crime. The cycle of bad years has doubtless caused some increase in indigenous petty offences against property, but by far the greater portion of serious crime can be ascribed to the gangs of Waddars, Kanjars, Kaikāris, Māng Gārorīs and others, who are continually passing through the District on the way to or from the Mughalai or the Bastar State. The average number of persons annually convicted for house-breaking and thefts during the decade was 426, for cattle-thefts 108, for robberies and dacoities 8. Serious offences against the person are not common considering the size and population of the District. The statistics show an annual average of 14 persons convicted of offences against human life, 12 of rioting and 7 of grievous hurt. Interesting cases occasionally come up from the Māria Gond country in the zamīndāris indicating the survival of such ancient customs as marriage by capture and trial by ordeal. Except in the more civilised tracts of the Chānda and Warorā tahsīls, where petty complaints and false charges are fairly common, trifling disputes and assaults are not brought into court. Cases of fiscal offences of the Excise and Forest Departments are increasing in number with improvement in supervision. There were as many as 805 excise cases during the decade.

310. The office of District Registrar was vested in the Deputy Commissioner from 1904. There are five sub-registration offices, one at the headquarters of each tahsīl, all presided over by salaried sub-registrars except at Sironchā where the Tahsīldār is ex-officio sub-registrar. The sub-registrar at headquarters has certain special powers. The average number of documents registered in the decade ending 1906 was 850. The number in 1902 was 766. Thereafter the number fell slightly and in 1906 was 679. Average receipts for the decade were 2780. They reached their highest (2904) in 1906.

Registration.

311. The following statement shows the revenue under the principal heads in the last years of the last two decades and in 1904-05 and 1905-06:—

Statistics of revenue.

Year.	Land revenue and cesses.	Forest.	Stamps.	Excise.	Income-tax.	Registration.	Other receipts.	Total.	Remarks.
	Rs.	Rs.	Rs.	Rs.	Rs.	Rs.	Rs.	Rs.	
1889-90	3,07,653	1,82,186	60,684	1,82,944	6985	2794	18,881	7,62,127	
1899-1900	81,035	1,17,973	42,241	1,63,201	7941	1969	13,027	4,27,387	Famine year.
1904-05	3,39,363	1,23,946	51,849	2,21,722	8864	2389	12,479	7,60,612	
1905-06	3,53,547	1,53,399	57,263	3,52,313	9595	2436	23,147	9,41,690	

Excise.

312. Up to the end of the financial year 1906 country liquor was supplied in Chānda and Warorā from Sadar distilleries situated at the headquarters of each tahsīl and supplying an area of 273 and 590 square miles respectively. The remainder of the District was supplied by outstills. In the Sadar distilleries a still head duty of 2 annas per seer was levied on the mahuā used in distillation and the contracts were disposed of on tenders. In 1904-05 there were 32 and 84 shops respectively supplied from these two Sadar distilleries, giving an average area of 8·5 and 7·0 square miles per shop. In that year there were in the District 676 permanent and 34 temporary shops for the sale of country liquor, the average area per shop being 13·1 square miles and the average population 749. The average revenue from the country liquor for the ten years ending on the 31st March 1908 was 1·9 lakhs. The contract supply system was introduced into the Chānda, Warorā and Bramhapurī tahsīls in 1906-07. Liquor was supplied by Messrs. Parry and Co., who received R. 0-15-0 per proof gallon. Warehouses were opened at the headquarters of each of these three tahsīls and retail vendors paid beside the price of the liquor a duty of R. 0-15-0 per proof gallon. In 1907-08 this duty was raised in the Chānda and Warorā tahsīls to R. 1-14-0 per proof gallon. Retail shops are in all cases sold annually by auction. The revenue rose from Rs. 3,00,211 in 1905-06 to Rs. 3,2,5946 in 1906-07, the increase being chiefly due to the introduction of the contract supply system. In that year the number of permanent shops in the District was reduced and there were in 1907-08, 212 shops under the contract system and 310 under the outstill system. The average income from *tāri* during the ten years ending in 1908 was Rs. 2351. *Tāri* is largely consumed by the aboriginal population of the Ahīri zamīndāri and the Sironchā tāluks, but little revenue is realisable from these remote and backward people and the bulk of the income from *tāri* comes from the Warorā

tahsīl. There are two foreign liquor shops, one at Chānda and the other at Warorā. The average revenue from opium in the decade was Rs. 29,000, the highest figure being Rs. 38,845 in 1905-06. In 1907-08 there were 53 shops. *Gānja* is obtained from Khandwā and was sold in 53 shops in 1907-08, the average revenue for the decade being Rs 7,000. *Bhāng* is obtained from Indore and is sold by *gānja* contractors. It is chiefly consumed by Mārwāris. There is no consumption of *mājum*. The income from excise in the zamīndāris was formerly enjoyed by the zamīndārs, who gave out their own contracts and controlled their own excise arrangements. The consequence was a practically unlimited supply of cheap bad liquor in a country inhabited by an aboriginal population especially addicted to strong liquor. In the year 1893 Government assumed the control of the zamīndāri excise arrangements and the revenue therefrom. Compensation amounting to Rs. 41,470, representing the capitalised value of the annual income from excise, was paid to the zamīndārs. Since that year zamīndāris are supplied from outstills given on contract by Government in the same manner as in the *khālsa* portion of the District. The Excise staff of the District consisted up to the year 1906 of two Inspectors and a clerk in charge of the accounts of each of the Sadar distilleries. In connection with the strengthening of the excise establishment throughout the Provinces in 1906 15 Executive Sub-Inspectors were in that and the subsequent year posted to the Chānda District giving the average of three Sub-Inspectors to each tahsīl. A Sub-Inspector was also put in charge of each of the three warehouses and a District Inspector of Excise appointed for the general control of the District staff of Sub-Inspectors and the excise arrangements generally under the Deputy Commissioner.

District Council and Local Boards.

313. There are three distinct District funds in the Chānda District, *viz.*, the Chānda District fund, the Sironchā District fund and the zamīndāri District fund. The

hānda District fund is controlled by the Chānda District Council which administers the cesses and other income of the Chānda, Warorā and Bramhapurī tahsīls and the *khālsa* portion of the Garhchirolī tahsīl. The Council is composed of 14 elected and 5 nominated members nearly all being non-official gentlemen. The average income of the District fund, Chānda, for the decade ending 1901 was Rs. 33,000, the principal sources of receipts being local rates Rs. 11,000 and cattle pound receipts Rs. 4500. The fund was assisted by a large grant of Rs. 11,000 from Provincial funds. The chief items of expenditure were education Rs. 14,000, civil works Rs. 5000 and medical Rs. 4500. In 1904-05 the income went up to Rs. 54,000, local rates having increased to Rs. 14,000, and the Provincial grant being raised to Rs. 22,000. The incidence of taxation in this year was 5 pies per head of population. The expenditure was Rs. 54,000, education Rs. 18,000, civil works Rs. 5000 and medical Rs. 13,000. In the subsequent year the income still further increased to Rs. 66,000, the Provincial grant being further raised. The expenditure in 1906-07 on education amounted to Rs. 29,000 and the expenditure on civil works to Rs. 32,000. Local Self-Government has made little advance in the Chānda District. Owing to the great size of the District members find it difficult and irksome to attend meetings at headquarters, where they may only have to discuss and decide questions in which they have no local knowledge or interest. The member for Dābha probably knows as little about conditions in Wairāgarh as he does about Jubbulpore and public interest at present awakens with difficulty in Chānda where personal interest and knowledge are not involved. The number of really wealthy men in the District is small, private subscriptions are inconsiderable and in all matters of public interest the people are with some exceptions as yet backward and self-centred. There are under the District Council four Local Boards one at the headquarters of each of the tahsīls in the northern portion of the District. They are constituted as follows: —

				Elected.	Nominated.
Chānda	Local Board		...	12	3
Warorā	do.	do.	...	14	4
Garhchiroli	do.	do.	...	9	3
Bramhapurī	do.	do.	...	12	3

Large powers have recently been delegated to these Local Boards and the future of Local Self-Government in Chānda rests largely in these bodies, whose members can meet and discuss questions which are within their knowledge and devise projects whose completion they may themselves assist. The extension of education, the construction of good school houses and the improvement of village sanitation are all objects affording a large scope for the efforts of the local bodies of the District, while there is a programme of useful roads for construction by the engineering staff which has recently been strengthened and placed under better control. The Sironchā District fund was constituted in 1885 and is administered by the Tahsīldār of Sironchā with a small advisory committee of three local members, the Deputy Commissioner being President of the fund. The average income of the fund for the decade ending 1901 was Rs. 2700 and the expenditure Rs. 3000. In 1906-07 the Provincial grant was increased to Rs. 10,205 and with that and the enhanced rates of the new settlement the income went up to Rs 14,000. The fund finances the local schools and pounds of the Sironchā tahsīl including the Ahīri zamīndāri and is now assisting in the opening out of new markets and the construction of local roads in the Sironchā tahsīl. The zamīndāri

Local fund was constituted in the year 1903. It receives the local rates of the zamīndāri areas of the Garhchirolī tahsīl. It is administered by the Tahsīldār of Garhchirolī as Secretary, the Deputy Commissioner being President. It is proposed to constitute a committee of zamīndārs to assist the Tahsīldār in administering the fund. The average income for the three years ending in 1906 was Rs. 3400, the principal heads of receipt being local rates Rs. 1000, receipts under Cattle Trespass Act Rs. 400 and contribution from Provincial revenue Rs. 1800. The average expenditure during the period was Rs. 2700, the chief items being education Rs. 800, medical charges Rs. 500 and cattle pound charges Rs. 300. In 1906-07 the income increased to Rs. 9000 chiefly owing to increased realisations under local rates and an enhanced contribution from Provincial revenue. The total expenditure during this year was Rs. 8900, the chief items being cattle pound Rs. 900, education Rs. 2600, medical charges Rs. 500 and civil works Rs. 3500. The north-east zamīndāris provide a large field for the extension of education and the opening out of roads and markets.

Municipalities.

314. The District contains two municipal towns, Chānda and Warorā. Both municipalities were constituted in the year 1867. The Chānda municipality has a population of 17,803 and the committee consists of 16 members of whom 10 are elected and 6 nominated by Government. The average income of the municipality for the decade ending 1901 was Rs. 31,000, the average expenditure being Rs. 30,000. The income in 1905-06 was Rs. 44,000 and the expenditure Rs. 41,000 while in 1906-07 the income rose to Rs. 48,000. The receipts are principally from octroi, market-dues and conservancy and the expenditure includes conservancy, roads, education and hospitals. The incidence of taxation per head of population in 1906-07 was R 1-11-3 and of income Rs. 2-6-9. The municipality has contributed to the upkeep of the Government High School and maintained the primary

schools in Chānda. Schemes for drainage and water-works are in contemplation. A fair is held annually in the month of May near the Mahākāli temple within municipal limits. The municipality spends about Rs. 1000 on this fair and most of the shops are moved from the town to the fair. Warorā with a population of 10,626 has a committee consisting of three nominated and five elected members. The Tahsīldār is usually President and the Naib-tahsīldār Secretary, a non-official Vice-President being elected. The committee had an average income of Rs. 21,000 in the decade ending in 1901. The income in 1905-06 was Rs. 35,000 and the expenditure Rs. 30,000. The position of the municipality which had been growing in prosperity was adversely affected by the closing down in 1906 of the colliery at Warorā and the removal of the colliery population to Ballālpur. With the completion of the Great Indian Peninsula Railway line to Ballālpur, Warorā also loses its advantageous position as a railway terminus. Octroi, market-dues and conservancy form the chief sources of income and the expenditure which in the year 1906-07 was Rs. 33,000 is chiefly devoted to education, conservancy, roads, markets and water-supply. So long as the colliery was open at Warorā the town was served with a fair supply of water pumped from the Bordā well. The incidence of taxation per head of population is R. 1-15-1 and of income Rs. 2-11-1.

Village sanitation.

315. The Village Sanitation Act has been in force at Mūl, Armori, Chimūr, Bramhapurī and in Sironchā, where it was introduced in the year 1906-07. The income is derived from a local rate the assessment of which is made according to a scale fixed by the Deputy Commissioner, the maximum amount assessed on any individual being Rs. 36 per annum. The funds are spent on the construction and repairs of roads and wells and the sanitation of the villages. The average income and expenditure of the sanitation *panchāyats* for the last three years are—

	Average income.	Average expenditure.
	Rs.	Rs.
Mūl	455	427
Armori	894	759
Chimūr	925	834
Bramhapurī ...	1413	1384

During the last three years Rs. 540 have been spent by the *panchāyats* for the construction of wells. The District Council also expends a fair amount annually on the construction of wells and in the matter of water-supply local enterprise is fairly developed. This cannot be said to be the case in respect of village sanitation to which little attention is paid by the people themselves.

The Mukaddam rules are in force in the villages of Bhāndak, Neri, Nāgri, Garhchirolī, Segaon, Chāmursi, Bhīsi, and Dābha. The sums raised annually are spent in the manner already specified in the case of villages under the Sanitation Act.

Public works.

316. The value of the buildings under the charge of the Public Works Department is Rs. 6,67,174 and the annual maintenance charges amount to Rs. 7000. The District court house was built in the year 1867 at a cost of Rs. 21,747, and the church in 1870 for Rs. 6173. The cemetery was opened in 1869 at a cost of Rs. 3774, and contains some interesting old grave stones. The circuit house was built in 1869 and enlarged in 1904, the total cost being Rs. 7022. There are few private bungalows in Chānda. The Deputy Commissioner's house which is situated on the ridge to the north of the civil station was built in 1852, and was acquired by Government in 1892. The bungalow which was originally built by the Bhonsla Rājā and was for some time used as an officers' mess was long occupied by the Forest Officer. Bungalows have now been built by Government for the District Superintendent of Police, Forest Officers,

Civil Surgeon, Assistant Commissioner and Extra Assistant Commissioners and for the Executive Engineers and Assistant Engineers of the Public Works Department in the Roads and Irrigation Departments. The total number of residential quarters is 19. Chānda is connected with Warorā which, till lately, was the terminus of the Great Indian Peninsula Railway by a first-class road 28 miles in length. To the west of Warorā is the Wūn road connecting the District with Berār. Another first-class road connects Chānda with Mūl 27 miles to the east, while the southern road from Chānda to Sironchā is under construction and will shortly be completed as far as Alāpalli, 72 miles south of Chānda. There are in all 101 miles of first-class road and 286 miles of second-class *muramed* roads in the District, the northern portion of which is well connected with the neighbouring Districts of Wardhā, Nāgpur and Bhandāra. There are three dâk bungalows at Warorā, Chānda and Sironchā and 12 inspection bungalows on the principal lines of roads. Till 1905 the Chānda District formed part of the Nāgpur-Wardhā Chānda P. W. D. Division. In that year the District became a separate P. W. D. Division and was put under an Executive Engineer who usually has under him an Assistant Engineer and four Subdivisional Officers.

Irrigation.

317. The south Waingangā subdivision formed in 1903 with headquarters at Chānda developed into a separate Division, the Mūl Irrigation Division, in 1905. The Division is in charge of an Executive Engineer with Executive Subdivisional Officers. The three large works under construction are:—

Name of work.		Estimated cost.	Probable year of completion.	Area to be irrigated.	Area commanded.
		Rs.		Acres.	Acres.
Asolā-Mendhā Tank	...	10,37,924	1911	20,000	40,000
Ghorājhari Do.	...	8,32,784	1909	26,000	39,656
Khairi Do	...	1,[illegible]7,4[illegible]2	1909	2000	2,550

The progress on these works has been much retarded owing to the paucity of labour in the District and to their being situated in the reserved forest. No irrigation has yet been done from these tanks, their construction not being sufficiently advanced, but the Ghorājhari tank has now been closed and filled and some irrigation may be possible from it in 1908-09. Large projects at Naleshwar and Bhainskhandī are also on the programme. In regard to minor works the ryotwāri village tanks of Janāla, Tekrī, Maregaon, Kunghāda, Junonā, Mahābāra, Ghorpeth and Itolī were improved or remodelled at a cost of Rs. 75,786, while those of Paunpār, Kachapār and Rudrapur as also the 'Distributaries' to the Tekrī tank at an estimated cost of Rs. 61,973 have been lately completed. The construction of Chindi tank and of the Maregaon tank irrigation channels and Kunghāda tank distributaries is now going on. The area brought under irrigation by these minor works is 2005 acres, the Kunghāda tank contributing as much as 960 acres of rice; the irrigation from this tank will still further increase when the 'Distributaries' are completed. Sugarcane which forms a feature of the more prosperous mālguzāri villages of the Bramhapurī tahsīl is at present only cultivated at Kunghāda, Paunpār, Janāla, Ghorpeth and Tekrī, but there is every prospect of the area of this crop increasing largely. Some 31 acres of wheat were irrigated from the Paunā tank in 1907, but elsewhere cultivators of Chānda do not seem to take readily to *rabi* irrigation at present. The general prospects of irrigation are very encouraging. The Kohlīs and Kunbīs are naturally clever at designing storage tanks and the rice areas are studded with fine tanks which, built years ago by unskilled labour, have at a very small cost, year by year, irrigated and protected the large area of rice and cane below them. There is always a demand for water from the Government tanks and the land irrigated by each tank increases in area every year. When the projects on the present programme are completed practically the whole rice area of the Chānda and Bramhapurī tahsīls will be protected.

Under the grant-in-aid system six private tanks have been repaired and improved at a cost to Government of Rs. 9325, the other half of the cost being paid by the owners who have in all cases taken taccāvi for the purpose. Mālguzārs of this District are, as a rule, jealous of any interference with their tanks and the grant-in-aid system has not been widely popular.

The rates usually charged for water are at present—

		Rs.	a.	p.		
Staple grain crops at	...	1	12	0	per acre	
Garden crops ...	...	2	0	0	"	"
Sugarcane ...	...	7	0	0	"	"

A reconnaissance has recently been made in the Sironchā tahsīl and sites have been discovered in the northern tāluks where useful protective works can be constructed.

Police.

318. The total sanctioned strength of the police force is 663 officers and men, including 24 officers and 3 mounted constables. The District has a District Superintendent, 7 Inspectors and 17 Sub-Inspectors. A Deputy Superintendent has recently been appointed and an Assistant District Superintendent of Police is occasionally posted to the District during the camping season. There is a small body of railway police. There are 15 Station-houses and 31 outposts, the Station-houses being located as follows:—Chānda, Mūl, Dābha (Chānda tahsīl); Warorā, Segaon, Chimūr (Warorā tahsīl); Bramhapurī, Talodhī (Bramhapurī tahsīl); Garhchirolī, Chāmursi, Murumgaon, Armori (Garhchirolī tahsīl); Sironchā, Venkatāpur, Ahīri (Sironchā tahsīl). The cost of the police in the last three years was Rs. 1,01,848 in 1905, Rs. 1,16,317 in 1906, and Rs. 1,22,662 in 1907. Of the officers 5 are Brāhmans, 9 Muhammadans and 10 of other castes. In 1907 there was one policeman to 95 square miles of area and 837 persons. Recruitment always presents a difficulty. Though the majority of the men are recruited within the District, the class obtained is not high. The life is not an easy one in a District

where the distances are great and the people often timid and unfriendly, and the possibility of transfer to some remote and jungly outpost, while it perhaps makes for good behaviour within the force deters many outsiders from enlisting. Up till 1893 the police in the zamīndāris were appointed and paid by the zamīndārs, though under the general control of the District Superintendent of Police. This arrangement terminated when the excise rights of the zamīndārs were assumed by Government in 1893. The control of the subordinate police in some of the remoter parts of the District has of late been rendered more efficient by the increase in the number of inspecting officers. One of the most important duties of the police is to watch the many criminal tribes that move through the District on their way to and from the Native States on the borders.

Kotwārs.

319. The kotwārs in the District are principally Mahārs with a few Pardhāns. The office is hereditary subject to good conduct and general fitness. The remuneration of kotwārs at the 30 years' settlement consisted of fees in grain from the tenants, hides of cattle dying within the village and a plot of land given rent-free by the mālguzār. The kotwārs now get a fixed cash remuneration varying from Rs. 30 to Rs. 36 per annum assessed on the rents of the tenants and the profits of the mālguzārs. In some villages the whole or a part of the mālguzār's share is given in the form of rent-free land. Though the right of hides of village cattle in most cases accrues either wholly or in part to the kotwār, it has not now been taken into account in assessing his remuneration. The kotwārs as a body are hard-working and honest, and excep ton the main lines of communication where they are subjected to continual calls from passing travellers the appointment is popular and sought after. The kotwār can usually get a free drink of *ambil* at the mālguzār's *bāra* whenever he goes, and on holidays and feast days he is generally remembered by those at least of the villagers to whom he has been able

to do a good turn either in the way of commission or of omission. The following is the number of kotwārs in the tahsīls of the District:—Chānda 288, Warorā 417, Bramhapurī 368, Garhchirolī 568 and Sironchā 357. In the richer tracts of the District the Mahārs have, owing to the high value of skins, become in many cases an exceedingly prosperous community and the kotwārs have had their share in this prosperity. On the other hand the kotwārs of the backward zamīndāri areas are poor and badly paid and live practically from hand to mouth.

Jail

320. Chānda has a third-class jail under the management of the Civil Surgeon with accommodation for 148 prisoners including 13 females. In 1907 the number of prisoners admitted was 120 of whom 94 were illiterate. Of this 120, 13 were in the employment either of Government or of some local body. The cost of maintenance per head was Rs. 21-10-0. The average earnings per head of those engaged in work was Rs. 81-13-0. The total amount of expenditure including the pay of the establishment was Rs. 7220. The recognised industries of the jail are stone-breaking, aloe-pounding, dyeing, *newār* (tape-weaving) and grain-grinding and work in the jail garden always occupies a considerable number. The daily average number of prisoners in the last five years has been—

	Males.	Females.
1903	51·48	3·22
1904	56·65	4·04
1905	45·35	5·54
1906	55·85	6·34
1907	53·48	3·58

The total receipts in 1907 were Rs. 1106, from manufactures Rs. 924 and from the garden Rs. 182. The health of the prisoners is generally good. The fine old fort situated within the walls of the Chānda city on the banks of the Jharpat river makes a strong roomy and picturesque jail. Sironchā has at present a sub-jail under the charge of the local hospital assistant. The average number of prisoners yearly for the last five years has been 4·78 including females, and the average annual expenditure Rs. 990.

Education.

321. Chānda has always been regarded as the chief seat of learning in the Nāgpur country, and in the early seventies the schools opened by the Educational Department made a very satisfactory progress. The English middle school examination of 1867 then known as Scholarship examination showed the Chānda Zila school to be very considerably the best and most advanced school of its class, and more than 800 scholars attended it and its affiliated branches. There was said to be a strong active desire for High school education, and to meet these wants a scheme was therefore put forward for establishing three new High schools. They were to be at Hoshangābād, Raipur and Chānda. Three such schools in addition to the school at Saugor would, it was thought, provide more adequately for high class education. On a full consideration of the proposal it was determined that a single High school would meet existing wants and Chānda was considered to have a superior claim to either Raipur or Hoshangābād. Accordingly a High school was opened on 1st October 1868. It made a good beginning, but before the close of the next year it was deserted owing to the admission of certain Dher boys who had passed the examination qualifying for admission to the High school. Nearly all the scholars and the indigenous Chānda teachers simultaneously withdrew. The prejudices of the Brāhmans remaining unchanged, the High school department ceased to exist and the school reverted to its former status. After a sleep for three decades a private High school was opened in 1898 and was financed by fees and local subscriptions until it was once more constituted a Government High school in 1906. There are 229 scholars attending it and it has attached under it 8 branch primary schools, which are maintained by the municipality and include an Urdū school and a Dher school.

These branches are attended by 741 pupils. The schools in the District besides the High school in 1907-08 were 1 second grade middle school, 6 vernacular middle schools, 99 primary boys' schools, 5 aided mission boys' schools, 4 unaided primary boys' schools, 8 Government girls' schools, 1 Local fund girls' school and 2 aided mission girls' schools. The progress of education in the District is shown by the following statistics. In 1897-98 there were 131 schools and 7245 scholars. In 1899-1900 the number sank on account of the famine to 100 schools and 5668 scholars. Thereafter the numbers gradually rose, till in 1903-04 there were 112 schools and 6081 scholars; in 1905-06, 123 schools and 8615 scholars; and in 1906-07, 133 schools and 8364 scholars. Statistics of the total number of pupils under instruction in the beginning of the past four decades have been as follows:—1870-71, 3745; 1880-81, 3670; 1890-91, 5495; 1900-01, 5278. Out of 136 schools 9 are maintained by the Government, 107 by the District Council and 9 by the municipalities; the remaining 11 are private schools. The 8 Government girls' schools are located at the headquarters of the 4 northern tahsīls and at Mūl, Bhāndak, Chimūr and Neri and the girls' school at Sironchā is maintained by local funds. The 7 mission schools contain 258 scholars of whom a considerable number belong to the Dher community. Out of the total number of 8364 scholars in the year 1906-07, 897 were in receipt of secondary and 7467 of primary education. Educational facilities have been largely extended in late years to the zamīndāri areas; and in Sironchā middle school Marāthī is now being taught. Good school houses are being erected by the local bodies to replace the inadequate and unsuitable buildings which have served for school houses, and the number of trained masters is increasing every year. The expenditure on education was Rs. 23,327 in 1891-92. In 1907 Rs. 51,428 were spent on schools outside Chānda and of this Rs. 8064 came directly from Provincial funds and Rs. 43,364 was contributed by the local bodies of the District. Besides this in that year Rs. 13,555 were spent on the Chānda High school and the branch schools. At the census of 1901, 40 per thousand of male population were returned as literate. In the whole District there were only 200 literate females. The District is under the Inspector of Schools of the Nāgpur circle and is divided into three ranges, Chānda, Bramhapurī and Sironchā, each under a Deputy Inspector. There are no printing presses in Chānda.

Medical relief.

322. The District has in all 13 dispensaries, two at Chānda, one being the police hospital, one at each of the following places—Warorā, Mūl, Bramhapurī, Garhchirolī, Armori, Sironchā, Venkatāpur, Chimūr, and Ahīri, one under the Forest Department of Alāpalli and one in connection with the colliery at Ballālpur. In addition to these there were in 1907 five temporary dispensaries, three in connection with P. W. D. roads and two on irrigation works. In 1907, 621 indoor and 78,989 outdoor patients were treated, the daily average being 12·06 indoor and 317·90 outdoor patients for all charitable dispensaries. The dispensaries are maintained out of funds raised by contributions from Government, local bodies and private persons. The Chānda Victoria dispensary was built in 1906 and has accommodation for 12 resident patients. Warorā dispensary can accommodate 5 patients, Bramhapurī 4, Sironchā 12 and Mūl 1. Midwives are attached to the dispensaries at Chānda and Warorā. The Vaccination Department consists of a native Superintendent and 15 vaccinators. The cost of operations in 1906-07 was Rs. 2,611-4-0. In that year 22,493 persons or 3·90 per cent. of the population of the District were successfully vaccinated as compared with 2·59 per cent. in 1900-01. Very few adults will submit to vaccination, and in certain parts of the District all vaccination at once stops as soon as an outbreak of small-pox declares itself, as vaccination is supposed to anger the deity who presides over this disease. There is a veterinary dispensary

at Chānda under the management of the District Council. The average daily number of patients treated in 1907-08 was 11·18.

APPENDIX.

GAZETTEER OF TAHSILS, ZAMINDARIS, TOWNS, IMPORTANT VILLAGES, RIVERS AND HILLS.

APPENDIX.

GAZETTEER OF TAHSILS, ZAMINDARIS, TOWNS, IMPORTANT VILLAGES, RIVERS AND HILLS.

Ahiri Zamindari.—See **Zamindaris.**

Amgaon.—22 miles to the south-east of Mūl. Here are two temples dedicated to Siva standing side by side. They are built in the Hemādpanthī style.

Andhari river.—A river which has three main branches, the first known as Bokardoh rising in the eastern slopes of the Phersāgarh hills; the second rising in the trap country near Bhīsi known in its first course as the Pātalgangā, Chimūr and Neri rivers and finally as Gondni; and the third rising in the Chimūr hills known as Purāna Andhāri. The first and second unite at Kuramgaon and are joined by the third near Jāmb and the river which is eventually known as Andhāri falls into the Waingangā a little south of Ghātkul after a course from north to south measuring in a straight line of 65 miles. That portion of the river from Kuramgaon until it is joined by the third branch near Jāmb is also known as the Mūl river. During the rains the Andhāri has a large body of water running with much violence and in the summer there is a chain of pools along its entire course. Several nullahs contribute their quota to the river which passes through stretches of Government forest of valuable bamboo and other timber.

Ankisa.—A large and exceptionally fertile village of the Upper Tāluk of the Sironchā tahsīl lying on the left bank of the Godāvari river, 17 miles south of Sironchā on the road to Dumagudiam. Population in 1901, 3029 against 2375 in 1891. The best land is the low-lying *gadda* land which receives the silt of the river, and grows exceptionally heavy crops of juāri and chillies. The central belt of the village consists of *regorde* land, on which wheat is cultivated. To the north lies an area of poor soil in the vicinity of forest, and in this the cultivation consists of small patches of rice and *bāris*. In this last area there are two tanks one of which irrigates about 20 acres of rice land, while the other is reserved for drinking purposes. Most of the resident tenants are Arewārs. The village is purely agricultural, and its only trade is in juāri, til, mūng and gram which it exports to Rājahmundry and to the Nizām's dominions. A weekly market is held on Thursdays. The only public institution is a primary board school for boys.

Arher Nawargaon.—A village situated on the plain that lies between Bramhapurī and the Waingangā in the Bramhapurī tahsīl. It is two miles from Bramhapurī and about one mile from the river bank. Some 50 years ago the village was purchased by the present mālguzār Dāji Rāghav for Rs. 2000 (Nāgpur coin). The people have the reputation of being very well off. 'Even the Mahārs are money-lenders' is said of the village. The population in 1901 was 2231. The villagers belong chiefly to the Kunbī and Mahār castes and are nearly all tenants, and the mālguzār is a Brāhman. The chief crops are juāri and broadcast rice. There is a small school with some fifty pupils on the roll.

Armori.—A large slatternly looking village lying on the road connecting Bramhapurī and Garhchirolī, and distant 15 miles from the former and 21 miles from the latter. It is also connected with Mendkī by a good second class road which will ultimately be extended to Talodhī. The population of the village is 4802 and consists mainly of Koshtīs, Kunbīs, Telis and Dhīmars. Situated as it is within eight miles of Wairāgarh and little further from the western border of the zamīndāris, Armorī has naturally become the most important mart of the eastern half of the District, and the weekly bazar held on Fridays is a very considerable one, the traffic in cloth and cattle being particularly heavy. Formerly also this was the great *entrepôt* for the disposal of the iron smelted in the east of the District, but of late years the output of this has much declined. A good deal of forest produce is brought here, and the village is the headquarters of the Wairāgarh Forest range. The Waingangā river passes two miles to the west, and during the rains carries a small boat traffic. The manufactures of the place are coarse and fine cotton cloth, country carts, and tasar spinning and weaving. About 40 families of Dhīmars are engaged in rearing tasar silk worms, while there are 23 families of spinners, but out of some 100 families engaged in weaving only four men now weave in tasar. Some of the patterns locally produced are of more than usual merit. The type of country cart for which the village is chiefly noted is the *dhamnī*, and the *dhamnīs* of Armorī command a very good market, particularly among the local zamīndārs. A Public Works inspection bungalow, a police station-house, a dispensary, school and pound constitute the public buildings of the place. The only surviving building of any archæological interest is an old triple shrined Sivite temple which Cunningham assigns to Rājā Hara Chandra Gond, but there was no Gond king of that name, and he probably means Hīr Shāh, who during a prosperous reign adorned his country with several fine buildings. North-west of the temple lies a large tank, which considerably enhances its beauty. Fragments and sculptures lie about in its neighbourhood which point to the probability of there having been other temples at one time. The village belongs to the Bhonsla Rājā Raghujī Rao of Nāgpur. There is only one tank, and irrigation is effected from small *borīs* of which there are 25. The village suffers difficulties in respect of water-supply in the hot weather.

Asaralli.—A large village in the Upper Tāluk of Sironchā lying about 19 miles to the south of Sironchā on the left bank of the Godāvari. In 1901 its population was 3128 persons. Asaralli is in the main an agricultural village, and the conditions of cultivation precisely resemble those of Ankisā. But it is remarkable as having for long possessed the only open bazar in the Upper Tāluk. This is held each Friday and is known as the Marriott Market: it attracts visitors from the Lower Tāluks, from Bastar and from the Nizām's dominions. The existence of this bazar has induced a fairly large trading community to settle in Asaralli, which, with the exception of Sironchā itself, is the only village in the tāluk which is not purely agricultural. Rājus and Komtīs form quite a large community: the *kāmdār* of the superior proprietor is himself a Rāju, and a man of much substance and influence. Needless to say, the pernicious relation between *sāhukārs* and agriculturists for which the tahsīl is notorious here flourishes in its most rank form, and *sāhukārs* have absorbed much of the cultivation of the village. Most of the tenants are Arewārs. A police outpost, a primary school and a post office complete the tale of public buildings. The population at the last census numbered 3128.

Ballalpur.—This ancient village stands on the bank of the Wardhā about eight miles south-east of Chānda. In 1901 it had a population of 534 persons as against 582 in 1891. Though lately but an insignificant village in ancient times it was a royal city, and, in the ruins of its fort and palace, still retains memorials of its past greatness. It is said to have been founded by the Gond King Khandkia Ballāl Shāh (1437-62 A.D.) who was also the founder of Chānda. This King was so afflicted with tumours and boils that he was an offence to his wives and court, only the wise and beautiful Hiratālni, his queen, remaining faithful to him and bearing him company. She induced him to leave Sirpur and build a fort and palace on the opposite bank of the Wardhā, where in retirement she tended him till his happy recovery (see History Chapter para. 33). Round the fort grew up Ballālpur, (the city of Ballāl). Though a new royal palace was completed in Chānda in the reign of Khandkia's successor, and the seat of Government transferred there, Ballālpur appears to have been a secondary royal residence for several centuries. Here in 1751 A.D. Nīlkanth Shāh, the last Gond King, was imprisoned and died, and in 1790 the palace was repaired by Nāna Sāhib Bhonsla, so that much of the existing ruin is comparatively modern. The gateway is very picturesque and inside the fort the outlines of the ancient palace can be traced with ease. Within the palace are two tunnels with entrances a few feet apart, which, branching off in opposite directions, lead each to a set of three underground chambers: one of which communicates with the entrance from the river or watergate. When these chambers were explored in 1865 A.D. some ancient copper coins and rusted iron rings were found. There is also a perpendicular shaft the object of which has not been ascertained. The usual legend concerning two adjacent forts is told of this, *viz.*:—that it communicates with the palace in Chānda, now the District Jail, by a tunnel, the entrance to which is said to be in the well wall in the jail courtyard. The foundations of the ancient city can still be traced for a considerable distance in the surrounding jungle, indeed as far as the ruined palace on the tank band at Junonā remains of old stone buildings are found. North of the village is a large and elaborately constructed tank, which probably owing to the falling in of its under channels does not retain water: any that does collect, sinking through the ground, appears as a small stream a little lower down. On an islet in the Wardhā is Rāma Tīrtha, an exceedingly curious rock temple, which, during several months of the year, is fathoms under water. In 1866 A.D. it was thoroughly cleaned and explored. In Sasti a village in the Nizām's dominions opposite Rāma Tīrtha are three caves cut in the rock, each of which contains a *lingam* of Siva. A leaden image of Keshavanāth, plated with gold, formerly stood in a small house under a *nīm* tree in front of the palace. In 1818 during the wars of the British with Appa Sāhib this idol was stolen. Four years later a Kamaishdār named Pungpatel More presented the village with a stone image in place of the stolen metal one, and Mr. Crawford who was Superintendent sanctioned a *nemnuk* for the temple. This *nemnuk*, now converted into promissory notes, yields an annual income of Rs. 24 which is drawn by the family priest of the Gond kings. East of the village stands the temple-tomb of Khandkia Ballāl Shāh locally called the temple of Kharji. In front of it at his feet, as is meet, is the tomb that encloses the ashes of his wife, the loving and faithful Hiratālni, noblest and wisest of the queens of Chānda. Near her lowly and unpretentious tomb is a stone on which are carved the representations of 84 feet arranged in pairs. These are said to be the memorials of the 42 wives of Khandkia, who redeemed their neglect of him in life, by performing *satī* at his death. Behind the monument is an unnamed tomb said to be that of a 44th wife. Alongside the tomb of Khandkia is a plain platform without superstructure or ornamentation. It is the tomb of Nīlkanth Shāh, the nineteenth and last Gond king who ruled in Chāndā. Thus, here, side by side in death lie the founder of Chānda and his degenerate and dishonoured descendant from whose unworthy grasp the sceptre of the Gond kings fell. The existence of coal at Ballālpur was suspected in 1871. In that year borings were undertaken, but after several unsuccessful attempts it was concluded that the bulk of the coalfield lay across the river and work was therefore stopped. In 1900 it became imperative to find a substitute for the Warorā Colliery, which was then approaching exhaustion, and a visit was paid to Ballālpur which resulted in the discovery of favourable indications. In 1903 a trial pit was sunk and coal was found at a depth of 200 feet. In 1906 a second pit was sunk to a depth of 257 feet and the seam of coal was found to be 50 feet thick and of better quality than Warorā coal. A colliery has now been opened to work the coal. In 1907 the extension of the Wardhā-Warorā branch of the G. I. P. Railway *viâ* Chānda reached Ballālpur and the colliery is connected with the Railway station named Ballāl Shāh by a line of about a mile long with numerous sidings. Ballālpur is now a prosperous mining village and the colliery

Bemrose, Collo., Derby.

INTERIOR OF OLD TEMPLE OF TAṆKA TALAO, BHANDAK.

has a great future before it. The mālguzār of the village is a Brāhman.

Bandia River.—A considerable river which drains 750 square miles of the zamīndāri country of this District. It rises in the eastern highlands in the Aundhi zamīndāri and flowing due south through Jhārapāpra and Ahīri zamīndāris in a wide channel of coarse sand with granite and hornblende rocks falls into the Indrāvati after a length of 76 miles. In the rains it has a large volume of water but ceases to flow in the hot weather, though it always retains several large pools from which the cattle of neighbouring villages are watered.

Bhandak.—A large and flourishing village in the Warorā tahsīl situated 16 miles north-west of Chānda and 12 miles from Warorā on the main road to Chānda. It occupies the top of a low broad plateau of rock thinly covered with soil. The population in 1901 was 3188 against 3228 in 1891. The village is long and straggling, extending over a mile in length, and now contains only 740 houses, but in former days it must have been a very large place extending about two miles from north to south and one mile from east to west. It is supposed to be identical with the great city of Bhadrāvati mentioned in the Mahābhārat extending from Bhatāla on the north to the Jharpat on the south and the scene of the battle for the Shyāmkarna horse, which eventually was borne away by the demi-god Bhīm for sacrifice by Dharm the king. This sacrifice has been described at length in a separate work devoted to the subject named Jaimini Ashwamedha. The architectural remains in and round the town are of remote antiquity and great interest. Among the principal of these are the old fort, which is on the west side of the village and is partly ruined. The temple of Bhadranāth or Bhadranāg, a short distance to the south of the village, is a structure recently rebuilt partly from the materials of an old temple and partly with fresh materials. A small courtyard and *dharamsāla* are attached to it, the latter having been built by Hayagrīva Swāmi of Chānda. Many old sculptures are built into the front wall of the temple, and lie loose about the courtyard, such as Ganpati, Vishnu, Lakshmī-Nārāyan, Siva-Pārvati, Varāha, etc. The object of worship is the Nāg and people believe that a live white serpent makes its appearance at the time of the fair. Lying beside the temple is an inscription slab and another in a very curious character was recently discovered. It has not yet been deciphered. On the south of the village, and adjoining it, is a cave in the rock which is now partly filled in with earth. It is unfinished and consists of a long verandah supported outwardly by two heavy, massive, octagonal pillars. Off the back wall are three unfinished cells. In the cell at the north end has been placed a ten-armed Devī. About a mile and a half to the south-west of the village, in the hill of Wijāsan, is a very curiously planned Buddhist cave. A long gallery is driven straight into the hill to a distance of 71 feet at the end of which is a shrine containing a colossal Buddha seated upon a bench. On the right and left of the entrance to this gallery other galleries, one on either side, are driven in at right angles to this first one, and each of these has a shrine and colossal Buddha. Local legend has it that the central Buddha is the image of king Pāndu—the image in the right gallery his son—that in the left his nephew. On the scarped side of the approach to the entrances to these galleries is a very much worn inscription in cave character. Another one belonging to the 9th century has been removed to the Nāgpur Museum and has been referred to at length in the History chapter. To the east of the village near the main road is a tank in which is an island. Connecting the island with the main land is an old Hindu bridge constructed of massive columns in two rows with great heavy beams spanning the tops of these both transversely and longitudinally. Its total length is 136 feet and its width over all 7 feet 2 inches. There are numerous images lying about, among them a collection of beautiful Jain images, the Sesha or the serpent on which Vishnu lies and a very interesting image of the skeleton goddess Mahākāli lying at the old ruined temple of Chandikā Devī, which is represented with three heads and six hands. This is a most unusual representation.

The village is surrounded except on the west by *pān* gardens, tanks, old groves and jungle; towards the west the country is bare, but the barrenness is redeemed by the picturesque temple-crowned hill of Wijāsan. The village has made good progress since the 30 years' settlement; 65 per cent. of the area is occupied, most of the remainder being rock and scrub jungle. There is a large community of Barais and Dhīmars here who take a special interest in the cultivation of *pān* (betel leaves) and *haldī* (turmeric) respectively. All the trade of the village is in the hands of one or two families of Komtīs who deal in grain and local products but their dealings are purely local. An annual fair is held in the month of Māgh (February-March) in honour of Bhadranāg Swāmi and lasts about three weeks. This formerly ranked next to the Mahākāli fair at Chānda, but its commercial importance has declined owing to the competition of the fair at the Berār town of Wūn about 15 miles away, which is held about the same time. The Bhāndak fair now is largely religious, and is attended by about 20,000 persons, including the usual traders who sell provisions to the pilgrims. A weekly bazar is held on Wednesdays. Since the opening of the Warorā-Chānda line in February 1908 Bhāndak has become a railway station. It possesses a vernacular middle school and a girls' school, the number of pupils on the roll being respectively 124 and 42. The Chānda Mission has also an out-station here and a small school with 40 pupils, mainly Musalmāns and Mahār children, on the roll. A branch post office also exists. The village has been brought under the Mukaddam rules and an annual cess of Rs. 355 is raised from a house-tax for sanitary purposes. The proprietors of the village are well-to-do Komtīs.

Bhatala.—Ten miles north of Warorā, is supposed to have formed part of the ancient Bhadrāvatī. On a long hill near the village are the remains of a very fine ancient temple, lofty and in good preservation. The outer walls are severely plain, the only ornamentation being three large images in inches around the shrines and one on each side of the antechamber. They contain the images of Siva, Pārvatī, Kārtikeya upon his peacock, Siva standing and Mahākāli or the Tāndava. Until lately in the four quarters of the village four ancient temples of Makardhwaja (the warden of the boundaries) could be distinguished. The whole hill bears traces of having been fortified. There is also another temple at Bhatāla into the front walls of which are built a lot of images, but it is not of much account. The population of the village was 790 in 1901 against 1190 in 1891. The mālguzār is a Marāthā. There is a primary school in the village.

Bhezgaon.—Five miles south of Mūl. Contains a temple of Mahādeo, built in Hemādpanthī style; it is now in a much dilapidated condition.

Bhisi.—A village in the Warorā tahsīl about 11 miles north of Chimūr, the population of which fell from 3154 in 1891 to 2586 in 1901, the decline being due to cholera and to migration to Berār. The village has passed through various hands in the past few years and is at present owned by a Sonār. Only one half however of the village is in the true mālguzāri area, the remainder being in the possession of three *tukums*. The village lands are well irrigated and the principal crop is rice. The institutions include a police outpost and a primary school. The Mukaddam rules are in force and the annual income is about Rs. 550.

Bramhapuri Tahsil.—Occupies the centre of the northern parts of the District, being bounded on the north by the Bhandāra District, on the west by the Warorā tahsīl, on the south by the Chānda and Garhchirolī tahsīls, and on the east by the Garhchirolī tahsīl. It is situated between 20° 9′ and 20° 44′ N. and 79° 25′ and 79° 59′ E. Until 1905, it included within its limits fifteen zamīndari estates

Bemrose, Collo., Derby.

OLD TEMPLE FROM SOUTH-EAST, BHATALA.

Bemrose, Collo., Derby.

FRONT OF SMALL TEMPLE. BHATALA.

and covered an area of 3324 square miles, but on the formation of the Garhchirolī tahsīl in that year, 2527 square miles including the whole zamīndāri area was handed over to the new tahsīl. At the same time 100 square miles of *khālsa* territory was transferred from the Chānda tahsīl to Bramhapurī. As a result of these changes, the tahsīl is now the smallest in the District, having an area of only 897 square miles. There are no well-defined hills in the main body of the tahsīl, though the Phersāgarh hills lie on its western border and the Mūl hills commence towards the north. But there are numerous small hills dotted about in the Garbori pargana which have an important effect on its agricultural economy in providing excellent facilities for the construction of tanks. The soil of the main part of the tahsīl is rather sandy, but good irrigation has rendered it ideal for rice and sugarcane. Towards the north in the Bramhapurī pargana there is a comparatively open and level stretch of black soil lying along the right bank of the Waingangā and much resembling the 'Chaoras' of the Bhandāra District : and this is an open-field tract. The Waingangā forms the eastern boundary of the tahsīl, and the only other important stream is the Bokardoh nullah, which, flowing almost due south from the Sāt-Bahini hills until it empties itself into the Mūl river, waters the west of the Garbori pargana.

Population.

The population of the tract in 1901 numbered 115,049 or 128 per square mile, and it is thus the most densely populated tahsīl in the District. Changes of area preclude a comparison with previous statistics, but there can be no doubt that there has been a heavy drop in the population as a result of a series of bad years, and recovery in the rice tracts is still proceeding but slowly. There is still however a very heavy pressure of population on the best of these tracts : thus, in Garbori after a drop of over 20 per cent. between 1891 and 1901 there are still over 700 souls to the square mile of actual cultivation. The population is almost entirely agricultural, Kunbīs, Kohlīs,

Telis, Marārs and Mānas being the chief cultivating castes : Gonds are numerous, but generally figure as field-servants only. Local manufactures are of little importance : Mahārs make coarse cloths, Dhangars blankets, a few Koshtīs in the villages to the north-west make silk-bordered *dhotīs* and *sāris* of the Umrer stamp, while a certain amount of *kosā* is also produced. In the matter of communications, the rich tracts of the north are 50 miles from the nearest railway at Nāgpur, and the heavy rice tracts of Garbori are separated from Warorā by 40 miles of bad tracks. The railway now under construction from Chānda to Gondia with a branch to Nāgpur will, however, entirely revolutionise the existing state of affairs. As regards road communications the tahsīl has hitherto been the best served part of the District. An excellent road links up Nāgbhīr with Mūl on one side and Umrer on the other, with a branch thrown out to Bramhapurī : Bramhapurī is also connected with Garhchiroli *viâ* Armori by a made road and Mendkī is similarly joined up with Armori. The chief trade centres are Bramhapurī, Talodhī, and Nawargaon. Nearly all the traffic of the Bramhapurī pargana and of the upper portion of Garbori is with Nāgpur, that of the rest of the tahsīl is with Chānda. Food-stuffs, country-cloth, iron and carts of local manufacture are the chief exports : salt, foreign cloth, brass vessels, kerosene oil, groceries and *gur* are the chief imports.

Agriculture.

Bramhapurī is almost wholly a rice country and contains a number of fine irrigation tanks in the large villages. Generally speaking the soils are deep and rich in Bramhapurī pargana and shallow and poor but well irrigated in Garbori. In this tahsīl the soil is better than in Chānda ; 10 per cent. of the cultivated area is first class, *kāli* or *kanhār*, against a District figure of 10 per cent. Twenty-two per cent. is *bersī* against the District percentage of 32, and 43 per cent. is *morand* against a District figure of 40 per cent. The better-class soils of this tahsīl are found in the northern portion. There is little *khardī* but

24 per cent. is *wardī*, that being the principal soil in the heavy rice tracts. An area of 444 square miles or 49 per cent. of the total consists of Government forest. The increase in the occupied area since the 30 years' settlement was nearly 13 per cent. or almost the same as that of the Warorā tahsīl. In 1906-07 the occupied area was 44 per cent. of the village area and had increased by about 55,000 acres since the attestation of the recent settlement: 251 square miles or about 43 per cent. of the village area consists of forest or grass land in private hands. The following statement shows the statistics of cropping for the years 1904 to 1906. Owing to the changes in the tahsīl figures for previous years cannot be compared:—

Year.	Rice.	Juāri.	Gram.	Wheat.	Linseed.	Til.	Total cropped area.
1904-05 ...	60,860	28,579	5367	5399	4213	816	136,720
1905-06 ...	56,686	27,516	5439	6980	6296	928	142,274
1906-07 ...	57,121	22,276	6061	8647	9916	584	139,977

It is stated that there has been since the 30 years' settlement a gradual but steady improvement in the cropping; even after a series of exceptionally poor years the area occupied by the better class of *rabi* crops is as large now as it was at settlement. In Bramhapurī the tenants are far more enterprising than they are in other tahsīls of the District and agricultural improvements are the rule instead of the exception in the open *rabi* villages; almost every village in Bramhapurī pargana has some land embanked for wheat or gram and the embankments are in many cases of large size; in poor agricultural years tenants cannot afford to grow the better class of crops and with high prices they make respectable profits from crops that they despise in more prosperous times; but when the land has been once embanked for the better class of crop they will revive that crop as soon as they get a series of better agricultural years.

Land revenue.

The land revenue demand of the tahsīl as constituted at present was Rs. 63,905 at the 30 years' settlement and at the time of attestation for the recent settlement was found to be Rs. 65,861. The demand fixed at the recent settlement for the tahsīl was Rs. 87,639 and cesses Rs. 5338; the increase in the land revenue thus being Rs. 23,734 over that of the figure at the 30 years' settlement. The net demand of land revenue in 1906-07 was Rs. 87,621, the demand for cesses in the same year being Rs. 5335. The old Bramhapurī tahsīl consisted of three parganas, *viz.*, Bramhapurī, Garbori and Wairāgarh, and for assessment purposes at the recent settlement these were divided into eight groups; of these only five remain in the reconstituted tahsīl; they are as follows, the number of villages belonging to each being shown in brackets against each:—Arher Nawargaon (46), Bramhapurī (58), Talodhī (56), Garbori (65) and Gunjewāhi (56). Talodhī is the most highly assessed group with an acreage rate of R. 1-8-1. Next to this comes Gunjewāhi R. 1-5-1, Garbori R. 1-4-7, Arher Nawargaon R. 0-14-9 and Bramhapurī R. 0-11-5. It was found impossible to propose any truly uniform treatment for this tahsīl in the form of rental enhancement, but in open villages where much of the land is embanked for wheat and where in fair years *rabi* crops of high quality cover large areas and in rice villages which possess really first class sources of irrigation rates have been taken which will allow an enhancement of just over 20 per cent. in rents while in the really depressed rice villages with only second rate irrigation or no irrigation at all rates have been taken which will simply level the existing demand.

Miscellaneous.

The tahsīl has two police station-houses at Bramhapurī and Talodhī. It has two Revenue Inspectors' circles with headquarters at Talodhī and Mendkī and 39 patwāris' circles.

Bramhapuri Village—Is situated in the north-west of the tahsīl to which it gives its name. It is 77 miles from Chānda to the north-east. As a centre of administration for the Bramhapurī tahsīl, it is geographically almost as badly placed as Chānda is as the headquarters of the whole District, and the desirability of shifting the tahsīl headquarters elsewhere has frequently been mooted. Its natural disadvantages have, however, been greatly counterbalanced by good communications, and, now that the railway is to pass through it and place it within easy reach of the most remote villages of the tahsīl, the objections urged on the score of distance will shortly become obsolete. At present Bramhapurī is linked up to the west with Nāgbhīr and so with the main artery of the tahsīl, the Mul-Umrer road, and southwards with Armori and Garhchirolī. The town itself is pleasantly situated on red gravelly soil, through which the rock frequently appears, and is a favourite residence for the well-to-do people of the neighbourhood. The closeness of the rock to the surface ensures rapid drainage, and sanitation is good, the streets presenting an unusually clean appearance. The tahsīl buildings together with the dispensary, police station-house, municipal office and school stand in a very congested group on the site of what used once to be the town fort, no longer, as when Major Lucie Smith described it, 'a spacious square 'from which the whole of the surrounding country is seen 'stretched out.' There are four tanks, the Kot talao, the Lendhā, Korelia and Barai tanks, from which 233 acres in all are irrigated. The embankment of the Kot talao consists of solid rock. Several of the manufactures of the town have acquired a considerable celebrity. Its brass and copper ware, its cotton fabrics, and shoes are widely known outside the District. Good driving carts are also turned out here. A large weekly bazar, which is attended by more than a thousand people, is held here on Fridays. One sign of prosperity is the existence of a small local Bar. Of schools there are two, a vernacular middle school and a girls' school: once there was an English school, but it died of inanition. Of late years, however, interest in English education has revived: there is a small English class conducted by one of the residents, and English is soon once more to be officially taught.[1] There is a combined post and telegraph office and a Public Works Department inspection bungalow. The population of the town at the last census amounted to 4328 persons. Besides the main *abādi* area, there is a suburb known as 'Peth' some quarter of a mile distant. The mālguzār of the town is Mr. Vithal Vināyak Kālikar Brāhman, a munsiff at Nāgpur. The new railway station is about half a mile to the south of the village.

Chamursi.—A name which the philologists of neighbouring villages spitefully derive from Chamār-wāsi, 'abode of Chamārs,' is one of the more important villages of the Garhchirolī tahsīl. It stands near the left bank of the Waingangā about a mile to the south of the curve which that river takes to the northward at Mārkanda, and is 44 miles east of Chānda and 24 miles south of Garhchirolī. The population is now given as 2449. Formerly it was larger but the village has never recovered from the famine of 1900, when about one-fifth of the inhabitants died or left the village never to return. Fully half the villagers are cultivators of the Sao Teli caste, and the stout brushwood fences round their homes give the village the air of squalid bucolic prosperity that seems associated with the Sao Teli. Komtīs, Gāndlis and Koskātis form the bulk of the remaining population. The village site is on low-lying ground and during the rains becomes converted into a veritable quagmire: it is also extremely congested, as rice fields lie all around it and prevent expansion. The total area of the village extends to over 8000 acres, 4000 of which are cultivated. The land is well irrigated, but although there are 6 tanks and 56 *borīs* within the village bounds, the cultivators complain that there is not sufficient water for sugarcane. The water of Chāmursi is deemed peculiarly good and there are no fewer than

[1] An English school has since been established.

50 wells in the village, four of which are lined with stone masonry, the remainder with a special tile prepared by the Kumbhārs of the village. The numbers of the trading community are fairly large, and in the last generation the Saturday bazar of Chāmursi was the most important market in a large locality, being attended by traders from considerable distances. The bazar still continues but its fame has waned before the rising fortunes of the Talodhī bazar. Talodhī is a small village, four miles distant and owes its rise in the world to some far-seeing forefather of the hamlet who planted a spacious and shady mango grove on the edge of the tank—thus placing side by side the two indispensable requisites for a successful Indian bazar—cool shade and plenty of water. The superior attractions of Talodhī have supplanted Chāmursi in the affections of the public, but Chāmursi still does a considerable trade in tobacco and groceries. The tasar silk industry of the place, which is in the hands of Koskātis, has some local reputation, and has been dealt with in the section on 'Manufactures.' Cotton fabrics are also woven by Sālewārs. The four temples of the village present no antiquarian interest, but there used to be a group of twenty Kistvaens or cromlechs, which have, however, disappeared within the last fifty years. The people here say that they will not have a good season till the old ruined temple of Siva on the tank *band* is repaired, but nevertheless it remains unrepaired. A primary school with about 80 pupils, a post-office and a police outpost under the charge of a Sub-Inspector with twelve constables, constitute the public buildings of the place. Sanitation is provided for under the Mukaddam rules, but the natural disadvantages of the village site prevent any very effectual measure of cleanliness.

Chanda Tahsil—(19°31′ to 20°17′ N. and 79°6′ to 80°0 E.). As at present constituted comprises an area of 1174 square miles, and occupies the centre of the western or cis-Waingangā portion of the District. Previous to 1905, the tahsīl was much larger, having an area of 5058 square miles, but in that year 2603 square miles, consisting mainly of the Ahīri zamīndāri, were handed over to the Sironchā tahsīl and 100 square miles to the Bramhapurī tahsīl and 1181 square miles, including other zamīndāris, to the Garhchirolī tahsīl. Until 1895 the tahsīl went by the name of the Mūl tahsīl, and had its headquarters at the village of that name, but in that year a move was made to Chānda and the name of that city adopted to designate the tahsīl. The tahsīl is now of a rough and blunt triangular shape, the north side forming the base and being bounded by the Warorā and Bramhapurī tahsīl, the west and south by the Wardhā river across which lies the Nizām's dominions and the east by the river Waingangā which separates the Chānda and Garhchirolī tahsīls. The extreme length of the tahsīl is about 60 miles and its extreme breadth 62 miles. Geographically considered, the tahsīl falls into two divisions, the western forming part of the valley of the Wardhā and the eastern belonging to the valley of the Waingangā: between the two runs a watershed, here lower and more broken than it is further north. These two tracts have very different agricultural conditions: the western one consists of fertile black soil and is essentially an open-field tract; in the Waingangā valley the prevailing soil is a yellow sandy loam devoted almost entirely to rice. Along the river banks the villages lie close to each other in an open fully cultivated plain, but inland there are wide stretches of forest much more sparsely inhabited and tilled. Both of the main river valleys are supplemented by the subordinate valley of a tributary: on the west the Erai falls into the Wardhā, on the east the Andhāri flows into the Waingangā: both are small streams which contain but little water in the hot weather, but they both drain considerable areas.

Population.

The population of the tahsīl in 1901 was 121,040 persons, representing a total density of 103 to the square mile. In 1891 the population numbered 132,477: there was thus a decline of 8·6 per cent. during the decade. The loss of population was a little heavier than in the Warorā tahsīl, but a good deal lighter than in the Bramhapurī tahsīl, and it fell almost entirely upon the rice tracts; in the open field Ghātkul pargana the population even expanded by as much as 27 per cent. between 1891 and 1901. As compared with the figures of the first settlement there was a total decline of five persons to the square mile. The incidence of population on each square mile of cultivation is a good deal heavier than in Warorā, as calculated for the *khālsa* area of the tahsīl at the recent settlement, it amounted to 459 persons, as compared with 266 in Warorā. According to the census village lists the tahsīl contains one town and 401 villages.

Agriculture.

Except along the bank of the Wardhā and in the south of the Ghātkul pargana, soils are generally poor: *kālī* is never found away from the Wardhā valley, and *kanhār* only occurs in a few depressions. Only 3 per cent. of the cultivated area falls under either of these classes, and less than 19 per cent. is *bersī*, over 51 per cent. is *morand*, 10 per cent. is *khardī*, and 15 per cent. *wardī.* Until the recent years of short rainfall, rice was the principal crop, and in 1895 over 60,000 acres were under it. This area has now sunk to 26,000 acres, and juāri has become by far the most important crop. This is solely the result of unfavourable rice years, as the tenants of this tahsīl have a decided preference for rice cultivation and only take up their *wāwar* land when shortage of rain compels them to do so: as a result, rents for very fair open field soil have ruled absurdly low. Doubtless now that communications are being more fully opened up, more attention will be paid to open crops, more particularly to cotton. Of garden crops sugarcane is the chief and most valuable. Statistics of cropping are given on the next page for the years 1904-05, 1905-06 and 1906-07: figures of previous years for the present area of the tahsīl are not available, while changes of area would vitiate any comparison with the figures of preceding years:—

Year.	Rice.	Juāri.	Gram.	Wheat.	Linseed.	Til.	Total cropped area.
1904-05 ...	24,223	76,385	2792	3801	14,029	12,875	161,192
1905-06 ...	22,622	74,913	2888	4156	16,225	17,063	165,736
1906-07 ...	26,184	72,896	2892	4050	19,310	12,294	162,639

Land revenue.

The land revenue demand of the tahsīl (as at present constituted) at the thirty years' settlement was Rs. 63,366, and at the time of the recent settlement it was found to be paying Rs. 72,061. The land revenue demand fixed at the recent settlement according to the *kistbandī* was Rs. 66,232 and cesses Rs. 4021. The proportion of assets taken as revenue was 58 per cent. The net demand for land revenue in 1906-07 was Rs. 66,248, the demand for cesses in the same year being Rs 4023. At the recent settlement the tahsīl has been divided into the following groups for assessment purposes, the number of villages contained by each being shown in brackets against each:—Chānda (61), Kothāri (26), Ghātkul (79), Keljhar (63), Mūl (55), Rājgarh (52) and Vihar (68). The most highly assessed group is the Keljhar, a part of the rice tract of the tahsīl, with an acreage rate of R. 0-15-10. In this group, rents are paid partly in cash and partly in kind and the valuation of grain payments which are now commuted into cash is of great importance. It is due solely to the higher valuation put on the grain payments that, in some cases, the rent rates show a high rise, but there has been no general enhancement of rents in this group. Next to this come the Mūl group R. 0-14-0 and Vihar R. 0-12-0, while Ghātkul is the least assessed with a rate of R. 0-4-9.

Miscellaneous.

The tahsīl has four police station-houses at Mūl, Chāmursi, Dābha, and Chānda. It has two Revenue Inspectors' circles with headquarters at Mūl and Kothāri and 35 patwāris' circles.

Bemrose, Collo., Derby.

PILLAR AT BABUPETH.

Chanda Town—The capital of the District and its largest city, is situated 761 feet above sea-level, in 19°57′ north latitude and 79°22′ east longitude, only a few miles from the eastern border of the Nizām's dominions. It lies in the angle formed by the junction of the Erai and Jharpat rivers, and is surrounded by a continuous line of battlements over seven miles in length which constitutes the most striking example of Gond methods of fortification which has come down to the present age. The walls are surmounted by a heavy looking crenellated parapet, they are ten feet in thickness, and within runs a broad rampart broken down in places but on the whole in fair preservation. The legend attached to the building of these walls has been recounted in the chapter on History. Four gates pierce the circuit, one to the north called Jatpurā, Vinbā or Ghormaidān towards the west, Achaleshwar to the east, and Pathānpurā to the south: in addition to these are five wicket gates or *khirkī* named Chor, Vithobā, Hanmant, Masān and Bagad. The walls help to facilitate the collection of octroi dues, and are also of use in times when the Erai overflows its banks. Outside the walls lie the suburbs of Bābupeth, Lālpeth, Golpeth Bhiwāpur, Hiwāpur and the civil station The population of the town, in 1901, was 17,803 against 16,175 in 1891, showing an increase of 10 per cent. The principal residents are Hindus, who number 15,824. The name of the town is a corruption of Chandrapur, 'the city of the moon.' Viewed from within, the city presents a pleasing appearance, giving a general impression of cleanliness, space, and verdure. The Victoria road, ruled in a mathematically straight line from the Jatpurā to the Pathānpurā gate, bisects the city from north to south, and forms an airy and moderately well-shaded main thoroughfare such as few, if any other, towns in these Provinces can boast. Various other well made and drained roads of bright red *muram* link up the various gates, wickets and main lines of traffic with each other, but there is no main thoroughfare from east to west corresponding to the Victoria road. Fully one-third of the space within the city walls lies vacant: vegetables and juāri are grown on such unoccupied spots, but rice cultivation has from sanitary considerations been prohibited. It is these open spaces, and the many winding paths overshadowed by magnificent trees, whose verdure seems all the greener in contrast to the bright brick colour of the *muram* roads, that constitute the chief charm of Chānda. This phase of the city and its surroundings is seen at its best along the Ballālpur road for a distance of a mile beyond the Achaleshwar gate. Here the road runs through jungle studded with countless majestic tamarinds, and the view deserves the much-misused epithet 'park-like' as fully as Indian plain scenery, with its lack of the velvety turf of England, can do so. It is much to be hoped that this refreshing greenery will not be sacrificed to the commercial interests of merchants who may wish to plant their gins and factories in close proximity to the railway. The appearance of the city from the outside has consistently been described by observers as picturesque in the extreme. Major Lucie Smith's description, often reproduced, is as follows:—'Dense forest, 'stretches to the north and east; on the south rise the blue 'ranges of the Mānikdurg, and westward opens a cultivated 'rolling country with distant hills. Set in this picture, sweep 'the long lines of fortress wall, now seen, now lost among 'great groves of ancient trees: in front glitters the broad 'expanse of the Ramāla tank; and the Jharpat and the Erai 'gird either side.' It is difficult to quarrel with the details of this picture, but the general impression given is, to the mind of the present writer, somewhat exaggerated. The picturesqueness of Chānda lies in no *coup d'œil* of the city as a whole, but in its details. The city wall, for instance, seen from the north-west whence the most comprehensive view of it may be obtained, is lost in insignificance amid a vast expanse of flat and usually bare plain to which the extremely distant ranges of the Mānikdurg provide but a poor foil, while by the ordinary approach to it along the Warorā road it is not visible at all until the spectator has swung round a bend within a stone's throw of the Jatpurā gate and then he only sees a small section. The new approach by the railway, which gives a good view of the Ramāla tank and the city wall behind it, is more favourable, but not, after all, calculated to stir any great measure of enthusiasm. But while she may waive her claim to any particular pretensions to beauty when considered from a bird's-eye point of view, Chānda need yield to no place in this part of India in the charm of her street scenes, her buildings and the forests which reach up on the east and south to her very gates.

Within municipal limits there are six fair-sized tanks known respectively as Ramāla, Lendhāla, Ghutkāla, and the Gaori, Lāl and Koner talaos. The chief of these is the Ramāla tank which runs along the north-east section of the city wall, and the embankment of which provides an excellent promenade popular with those citizens who have acquired the fashion of taking the air. Once this tank was used for drinking, and the water was brought into the town in pipes which were constructed by the Gond Rājās. The water is now no longer generally used for drinking purposes as *singhāra* is cultivated in the tank by Dhīmars, but the round towers or *hathnīs* which occur at intervals along the pipe-line and serve as stand-pipes, as well as affording means to divert the water to small reservoirs, may still be seen dotted about at intervals in the city. The area of the Ramāla tank is 158 acres, and it was built at the same time as the city wall. The city at present depends on numerous wells for its drinking water, but is not without hope of attaining to the dignity and convenience of water-works in a not distant future.

The city possesses several architectural features of interest. Its walls have already been described at some length, and it only remains to add in regard to them that they were founded probably about the 15th century by the Gond Rājā Khandkia Ballāl Shāh, although legend would assign a date two centuries earlier to him, and avers that three hundred years elapsed before the completion of the work: that they were kept in repair by the Marāthās, and, after long neglect by the British, have of recent years been extensively restored by the Public Works Department, and are in future to be preserved as an example of Gond fortifications. The gateways offer good specimens of Gond art. Close to the Achaleshwar gate, and standing in a separate walled enclosure forming a kind of inner fort, stand a group of buildings known as the Gond Rājās' tombs. These are at present eight in number, but a ninth is in course of construction to commemorate the recently deceased Rājā. The largest and best tomb is that of Bīr Shāh, reputed the 17th of the line. The building is generally criticised as too heavy in appearance but it does not fail of a very pleasing effect, and is a welcome sight to the eye wearied of the constant reiteration of the Hemādpanthī style of temple. In the same outer enclosure, but separated from the tombs by a partition wall, is the Achaleshwar temple, the walls of which are covered with multitudinous small sculptured panels. The legends relating to the founding of this temple are recorded in the chapter on History. What is now the jail was formerly the citadel; it contains a large many-galleried well and an underground passage which is popularly supposed to emerge in the fort of Ballālpur eight miles distant. Behind the present municipal office stands a temple of Vithobā, which is pleasingly carved with elaborate designs in pink stone. About a mile to the south-east of the city and surrounded by dense jungle, stands a group of large stone figures locally called Rāwan and commonly known as the Lālpeth monoliths. These are more remarkable for their size than for their artistic excellence. Sixteen in number, they lie upon the ground arranged in a sort of rough circle around a *linga* of Siva. They must have been carved *in situ* out of the living rock, as many of them are much too heavy to be moved; the largest, a ten-headed Durgā, measures 25 by 18 by 3 feet and is calculated to weigh 57 tons. The bull Nandī and Vishnu's fish and tortoise incarnations are among

Bemrose, Collo., Derby.

GENERAL VIEW OF MONOLITHS FROM SOUTH. CHANDA.

the more prominent of the other figures. The popular legend about these sculptures is that in the reign of Dhundia Rāmshah there lived a wealthy Komtī named Rayappā, who conceived the idea of doing some memorable act; he accordingly had these monoliths carved intending to place them in a temple of Siva, but he died before he could build the temple, and the monoliths are lying where he left them. Between these monoliths and the town is a well, in the interior of which are built in some rather good sculptured stones. Close to Lālpeth is Bābupeth in which there are some temples, one of which contains some uncommon statues of various gods and goddesses such as Indra, Agni, etc., but the most noteworthy is a three-legged figure placed in a niche, which may be meant either for a Vedic god Tripād or for a fever demon, a *Gan* or attendant of Siva. The only other antiquarian feature which requires notice is an old well in the shape of a conch shell (*sankha*). In the reservoir there is a temple of Panchāyatan. It was built by one Bāpuji Vaidya, the Dīwān of Hīrabai, or by one of his predecessors about 500 years ago.

Of modern buildings, Chānda possesses none of any particular interest except perhaps the Kotwāli, which used, in the days of native rule, to be the *killedār* of Chānda's residence and is the only dwelling house which survived the sack of Chānda by the British. There are the usual Government offices, which have been considerably enlarged of late years, and the new block of buildings for the accommodation of the civil staff, erected in 1905, is an excellently designed if somewhat prosaic looking structure. Of dispensaries there are two, the police dispensary and the main dispensary. Education is provided for by an English middle school, five branch upper primary schools, one upper primary girls' school, and a High school with two classes, which was opened in 1897 and was supported by private subscription, but has now been converted into a Government High school with a complete staff. The Scottish Episcopalian Mission with a staff of five Europeans keeps up two orphanages, one for boys, the other for girls: an industrial class is attached to the boys' orphanage. The same Mission has erected a fairly large church in the Victoria road. The only other building that need be mentioned is the Town Hall, which was built in 1888, at a cost of Rs. 6000, from the funds of the Municipal Committee and the District Council: it is a mean-looking building unworthy of the town. The Victoria Memorial dispensary, opposite the Mission church, has taken the place of the old dispensary. Chānda was constituted a municipality in 1867, and the average municipal receipts for the decade ending 1901 were Rs. 32,000. The income has largely expanded in recent years and in 1903-04 amounted to Rs. 48,000, being chiefly derived from octroi. In 1906-07 the income amounted to Rs. 48,634. The trade of the town is now much less than it was, but Chānda is still the commercial centre of the District. It has also several hand industries, among which may be mentioned cloth weaving either of silk or cotton with silk borders by Koshtīs, who occupy about 400 houses in the town. There are about 250 houses of Mahārs, who weave cotton cloths in checked and striped patterns with coloured threads. There is also a dyeing industry which is carried on by Rangāris numbering about 75 families. Ornamental slippers are made in various patterns with silk thread stitched on leather by about 55 houses of Chamārs. Bamboo work is also done by about 20 or 25 houses of Burads who make fans, boxes and baskets in fancy colours. Gold and silver ornaments, made here of a peculiar pattern, are of some repute.

A large annual fair, known as Mahākāli fair, is held just outside the Achaleshwar gate in the month of April. It is supposed to begin on Chaitra Sudi Paurnimā, but as a matter of fact it is held from 15th April to 15th May. The total attendance is estimated at 75,000 persons. Cattle, grain, cloth, salt and *kirāna* are the principal articles sold. The total sales are estimated at about 8 or 10 lakhs of rupees. About

Rs. 80,000 worth of cattle are sold. There is also a weekly market on Wednesdays at which cattle are sold.

Chandala Zamindari.—See **Zamindaris.**

Chandapur.—Five miles south-east of Mūl, has a temple of Mahādeo in the Hemādpanthī style, but it is now in a dilapidated condition.

Chimur Hills.—A range of hills which enter the Warorā tahsil in the north, at a point where the Umrer and Hinganghāt tahsīls meet. Near this point lies the first peak of the range known as Lingā, 1341 feet above sea-level. From this peak the range runs due south and then disappears for about five miles, leaving a sort of strait to connect the two main divisions of the tahsīl. After its re-appearance it grows broader and lower dwindling away near Moharlī, a village 17 miles to the north of Chānda. The range is 20 miles in length with an average breadth of six miles and a height of 450 feet above the plain. Both slopes and summits are covered with thick forest, and all along the foot run numerous springs which never fail. The whole range is under the Forest Department. In a basin at an elevation of three or four hundred feet above the plain, lies a magnificent lake called Tāroba much visited by Europeans both for scenery and sport, and by natives (chiefly Gonds) for religious purposes. The lake takes its name from Tāroba, a Gondi god who is worshipped here. Tradition is that a Gond by name Tāru was killed here by a tiger and afterwards deified. People seek its waters for their supposed virtue in causing child-bearing in women, healing sick persons and removing diseases from crops. In taking and carrying the water only the right hand is used. Though the lake is artificially embanked at one point, it has all the appearance of a natural lake. The embankment is 401 feet long, 95 broad at the top and 60 high, composed of earth and boulders so strong and compact that it is difficult to distinguish the dam from the two hills which it connects. Under the bottom of the dam, and 180 feet above the plain, flows out unceasingly a strong, clear stream of water, which passes down the narrow valley to the south, and then enters the plains, where it irrigates the rice and sugarcane of several villages. The surface area of the lake averages 158 acres, and the depth is probably over 70 feet in the centre and by the embankment. In the early ages, so runs the legend, a marriage procession of Gaolīs was passing through these hills from the west. Hot and thirsty, they sought for water and found none, when a weird old man suggested that the bride and bridegroom should join in digging for a spring. Laughingly they consented, and with a few spadesful of earth a clear fountain leapt to the surface. While all were delightedly drinking, the freed waters rose and spread into a wide lake, overwhelming bride and bridegroom and procession; but fairy hands soon constructed a temple in the depths, where dwell in peace the spirits of the drowned. Afterwards on the lake side a palm appeared, which, from dawn to noon, shot up to meet the sun and with the sun sank down, disappearing into the earth as twilight closed. One morning a rash pilgrim seated himself upon the palm top, and was borne into the skies, where the flames of the sun consumed him. The palm then shrivelled into dust, and in its place appeared an image of the spirit of the lake which is worshipped under the name of Tāroba. Formerly, at the call of pilgrims all necessary vessels rose from the lake, and after being used were washed and returned to the waters. But at last one evil minded man took those he had received to his home; they quickly vanished and from that day the mystic provision wholly ceased.

In quiet nights the country folk still hear faint sounds of drum and trumpet passing round the lake; and old men say that in one dry year when the waters sank low, golden pinnacles of a fairy temple were seen glittering in the depths.

Chimur Village.—A large and thriving village in the Warorā tahsīl 48 miles to the north of Chānda and 33 miles from Warorā, situated on a tributary of the Andhāri river known as the Pātalgangā. The town stands high and has a great attraction for all the wealthy families in this portion of the tahsīl. It ranks next in importance to Warorā. Its population, however, declined in 1901 to 4085 from 5096 in 1891. The inhabitants are mostly Marāthās, with a sprinkling of Telugu traders and artizans. There is also a strong body of Brāhmans attracted hither by the religious associations of the place. Though not very old, the Chimūr temple has a great reputation. The image of Vishnu known as Bālajī, was found on the spot where it is now by a Kunbī, who entrusted its worship to a poor Brāhman, Devāji Chorghode, who finally rose to a high rank in Bhonsla's service and this he attributed to the favour of Bālajī. He caused a temple to be erected over the statue, and instituted what is known as the *ghodā* ceremony which is held in connection with the annual fair on the 15th day of the light fortnight of Māgh (February-March). Two days previous to the fair Bālajī's horse, which is of wood, with his image on it is taken round the town and then back to the temple. The fair lasts for 15 days, and the daily average attendance is 2000 persons. Its importance is now rather commercial than religious, and a number of traders attend from long distances; a considerable trade is done in *rengīs* (carts) and cart-wheels and cattle are also brought for sale. There is a good weekly bazar held on Fridays and the trade is principally in cotton, grain, cotton cloths, carts and oil-seeds. A good deal of cotton cloth is manufactured by the Koshtīs of Chimūr itself, and has a local reputation for durability. There is also a fairly large community of Barhais here, who prepare carts for carriage of goods and *rengīs* for travelling purposes which are well known all over this portion of the Province.

Chimūr is under the Village Sanitation Act, and an annual cess amounting to Rs. 1324 is raised from a house-tax and expended on sanitation. Chimūr contains a dispensary, police station-house, post office and inspection hut, and a vernacular middle school. The buildings stand on a handsome square cleared on the raised area of the old fort facing the river. There are some fine groves in the vicinity together with several temples worth visiting. The proprietor is a rich Kunbī widow by name Musammāt Gangābai.

Churul or Surla.—A village in the Chānda tahsil divided into two hamlets, about one mile apart, called Jūna Surla and Garhī Surla. The hamlet of Jūna (old) Surla lies eastward on the wide plain that stretches to the Waingangā river, which flows past at a distance of one mile from the village. Garhī Surla clusters round the base of a lofty flat topped eminence, on which stood the ancient *garh* or fort from which the hamlet takes its name. There is now no trace of the fort save the remains of the parapet wall, but the mound is still smoothed and the sides of the escarpment steep and difficult of ascent, save by the one sloping path on the north. The aged *kāmdār* of a neighbouring hamlet still remembers the attack of Bāpu Rao on the village in 1857, when the inhabitants all betook themselves to the ruined fort, and broke the charge of Bāpu Rao's horsemen, as they attempted to ride up the steep escarpment, by rolling down cart-wheels fixed on their axles, which frightened the horses and broke their legs. There are a number of ruined temples, one of which contains a pillar with the name of the ubiquitous 'Magardhwaja Jogi 700' carved on it. The old road from Mūl to Chāmursi passes through the village and the 'Jūna Churul Ghāt' is still a ford over the Waingangā where a good deal of traffic passes. The population in 1901 was 2227 against 3044 in 1891.

The tank which lies at the foot of the mound is large and well kept, and waters a wide area. The staple crops are transplanted rice and winter wheat and juāri.

There is a large colony of Kurumwārs in the village who feed their flocks on the uplands and wide plains in the Waingangā valley and, during the rains, manufacture large quantities of *kambals* or woollen blankets. There is a small school in the village and a police station-house.

Dabha—Is a village of 2320 inhabitants, lying about 40 miles south-east of Chānda. It is pleasantly situated in a broad fertile valley shut in by low forest-clad hills. Down the valley winds a wide shallow stream, a tributary to the Wardhā river, called the Dābha nullah. The village is built on both sides of this stream, and is surrounded by shady groves of ancient mango trees. Appa Sāhib, the Bhonsla Rājā, granted the villages of Dābha and Talodhī to Rāmchandra Venkatesh, a Brāhman, in recognition of his services as *kāmdār*. Anand Rao, the present mālguzār, is the son of Rāmchandra; he is a man of about 80 or 90 years of age and remembers the vicissitudes of life in Dābha before the advent of the British Government. He can still recall the inroads of dacoits from the Mughalai, and how their practice was to smuggle their emissaries into the service of *sāhukārs* in order to ascertain where the latter had buried their hoards: this knowledge gained, a message was sent to the leader of the band, who immediately dashed across the river and readily effected his loot. The moral effect of these raids has survived almost until the present day. Instead of the usual bazar, the town is dependent on three large general shops for all its supplies, and it is only of very recent years that the shopkeepers have had heart of grace to expose their goods. This timidity and this absence of a bazar are simply the survivals of the general feeling of insecurity created by the dacoities of former days. The three shops mentioned attract custom from villages twenty miles round, and serve as *entrepôts* for the export trade to Hyderābād, which all comes *viâ* Dābha as the direct road from Chānda to the Mughalai is in very bad condition. A thinly attended vegetable market is held weekly, but cannot claim the status of a full-grown bazar.

When the grant was made, Dābha and Talodhī were little more than hamlets in the jungle of 10 to 15 huts each. It is mainly due to the care and energy of the present mālguzār that both villages have now over 2000 inhabitants, and ten other villages have been founded in the valley and plain to the south and east. The village is almost entirely agricultural. The main crops are now juāri and oil-seeds, these having been found more profitable than rice. Some trade in salt and groceries is also carried on, but Talodhī, owing to the circumstance that the main road to Sironchā passes near it, is now resorted to for these commodities. A colony of silk weavers and a colony of Sonārs were invited to the village and induced to settle by the father of the present mālguzār, and a generation ago Dābha was famed for its silk stuffs and its silver work. Handsome woollen rugs and carpets used also once to be produced. The silk weavers' colony has diminished to three households. There are still some fifteen households of Sonārs, but only six or eight of these engage in silver and gold work, the others having taken to working in baser metals ; but Dābha is still famed for its silver snuff boxes and belts. There are five temples in the town, of which four are dedicated to the worship of Siva and one to Vitthal-Rukmini. All the temples have been erected within he last sixty years, and the curious errors in the sculpture of the carved figures show how great is the gulf between the temple builders of the present generation and the pious founder of Mārkanda.

About three-fourths of the population are of Telugu race and speak Telugu : the rest belong to Marāthā castes. There is a vernacular school with three teachers and 103 pupils. The village has a sub-post-office and a police station-house to which twelve officers and men are attached, and a dispensary is being built. About 30 years ago there was a girls' school in the town, but after the departure of Colonel Lucie Smith it seems to have died.

Deotek—(The hillock of gods). 4 miles north-east of Nāgbhīr in the Bramhapurī tahsīl ; has a small temple, and the remains of a second. There is a slab containing two distinct inscriptions, the characters of one being of the kind known as those of the Asoka edicts and those of the other belonging to the Gupta period. Both of them are fragmentary but mention a name Chikambari, which Mr. Hīra Lāl identifies with Chikmara, a village close to Deotek. Chikmara may thus boast of being 2000 years old. At Chikmara and Panori both of which are about 2 miles from Deotek, there are old statues and other ancient remains like those at Deotek. It is possible all these formed one city in ancient times.

Devalvada.—The hill of Devalvāda is situated six miles and a half to the west of Bhāndak. On the top is a small square fort, now in ruins, with four pillars and an old temple standing within. There is also a dry tank to the east of which is a natural mark in the rock, 15 inches long by 6 inches broad, which is called 'Bhīmsen's charan' or footprint. In the side of the hill are several caves, of which the largest is named Narsinha.

Dhanora Zamindari.—See **Zamindaris.**

Dhudhmala Zamindari —See **Zamindaris.**

Erai River.—The river rises in the extreme north of the District and, after flowing along the western slope of the Chimūr hills for some miles, follows a course almost due south through the centre of the Warorā tahsīl and the extreme west of the Chānda tahsīl. It debouches into the Wardhā a short distance below Chānda city. It forms a valley some ten miles in width, with good black wheat and cotton growing soil in its upper course; further south, the country on its banks is more undulating and rice is more common than wheat. When the Wardhā is full, from bank to bank, the waters of the Erai are thrown back on the walls of Chānda and 'at such a time there 'stretches from the southern ramparts what seems a vast sea of 'tawny water, bounded only by the distant ranges of Mānik-'garh, while the current drifts against the walls great logs 'and trees swept from the forests on the north.' The Erai is crossed by a girder bridge of eight spans on the Great Indian Peninsula Railway some three miles above Chānda.

Gaorara (or Gavarara)—Is a small village situated one mile and a half to the south of Bhāndak. To the west are several fine tanks, beyond which is a low hill crowned with the remains of several temples. There are also many detached rocks, several of which have been hollowed out to form caves and niches. The principal temple is called Yauvanāshwa's palace, and the two chief caves are called his big and little fowl-houses. The bigger one contains statues of Vishnu on the serpent and in his dwarf and boar incarnations, but their small size would argue that they are not the original objects of worship. From the presence of eight socket holes for the reception of statues in a raised platform running round three walls of the cave, Cunningham conjectures that the cave may have been a Buddhist one, and in favour of this theory he advances the existence of a draped figure of Buddha which lies at the bottom of the hill, and the fact that the 'Little Fowl-house' was almost certainly a monk's cell. In the Yauvanāshwa's temple there is an inscription on the left jamb dated in the Samvat year 1166 or 1109 A.D. There is also a small side temple containing a large statue of Ganesh. Traces of several other temples are visible in the vicinity.

Garhchiroli Tahsil.—A tahsīl in the north-east of the District lying between 19° 23′ and 20° 50′ N. and 79° 56′ and 80° 37′ E. It was formed in 1905 by taking the zamīndāri estates of Bramhapurī tahsīl and those of Chānda, with the exception of Ahīri, together with 1457 square miles of the *khālsa* or land held in ordinary proprietary right from the east of the Chānda and Bramhapurī tahsīls. The total area of the tahsīl was 3708 square miles. At its constitution it originally included 19 zamīndāri estates lying to the east and south of the Waingangā river containing an area of 2251 square miles. But in October 1907, four of the north-eastern zamīndāris with an area of 838 square miles, were transferred to the new Drug District, while an area of 13 square miles belonging to the Sironchā tahsīl was added to the tahsīl. Thus; the total area of the tahsīl at present is 2883 square miles. The tahsīl is an irregular oblong towards the north, with a heart-shaped strip of country running parallel to the Chānda tahsīl in the south-west corner. The Waingangā river separates it from Chānda and Bramhapurī tahsīls. It is bounded on the north by the Bhandāra District, on the east by the Drug District, on the south by the Sironchā tahsīl and on the west by the Chānda and Bramhapurī tahsīls. The headquarters of the tahsīl is at Garhchirolī a village of 2077 persons, 51 miles from Chānda by road. Most of the area of the tahsīl is hilly and thickly forested. The hills are nowhere of any height. The northern portion of the tahsīl is drained by the river Gārhvi intersecting it from the north and taking a southerly course until it joins the Waingangā below Armorī, while the Kophrāgarhī with its affluents crosses it from east to west past Wairāgarh Khās. This portion is a very jungly tract, and the only villages that are found contiguous are along the banks of the rivers. It possesses many fine tanks and an excellent soil, brown and yellow in the immediate vicinity of the rivers and red and sandy away from them. It is essentially a rice growing tract. Across the centre and southern portion of the tahsīl two rivers flow from the zamīndāris and join the Waingangā; of these the Katnī is of importance since it holds some pools of water in the hot weather and there is some irrigated *marhān* along its banks; the other, Patpuri nullah to the south, is a much smaller stream. There is a good stretch of open country in this portion of the tahsīl towards the left bank of the Waingangā where *rabi* crops are principally grown. Towards the east the villages are somewhat isolated, being separated from each other by strips of scrub-jungle of no great value. In the extreme southern strip of the tahsil the villages are as a rule completely isolated in the midst of the Government forest, and many of the villages which have some cultivation are no better than forest clearings. Rice is the principal crop here. This tract is drained by the river Dina which, rising among the hills in the east, joins the Prānhita in the southernmost corner.

Population.

The population of the tract in 1901 was 108,315 or 20 per cent. of that of the District. Of these 35,222 were the inhabitants of the zamīndāris and 72,993 belonged to the *khālsa* portion. In 1891 the total population was 150,212; of these 97,920 belonged to the *khālsa*, while 52,292 were the inhabitants of the zamīndarīs. During the decade ending 1901 there was thus a fall of about 28 per cent. The zamīndāris suffered severely losing 32½ per cent. of their population as against a decline of 25½ per cent. in the *khālsa* tract. The depression is most marked in the eastern portion of the tahsīl where the majority of the population is aboriginal, and the series of bad years which culminated in the famines of 1896 and 1899 during the decade is for the most part responsible for this loss. In 1901 the density of population was 38 per square mile, being 50 for the *khālsa* and 25 for the zamīndāri area. Roughly speaking, the population of the tahsīl is aboriginal. But in large villages and tracts nearer to the Waingangā better-class Kunbīs and Kohlīs are found with a large number of Marārs and Telis, and below Garhchirolī to the south the Madrāsi cultivating castes such as Kāpewārs, Gurdis and Gāndlis are settled in some numbers. The Marārs are principally found in the tracts adjoining the zamīndāris. Gonds are very numerous; they are excellent field servants but poor tenants as a rule. There are 997 villages in the tahsīl, of which 629 belong to zamīndāris and 368 to *khālsa*; of the *khālsa* villages 65 are uninhabited, while of zamīndāris 200 are uninhabited. The tahsīl has no towns. The principal villages are Armori (4802), Garhchirolī (2077) and Chāmursi (2449). There are six other villages which have a population of more than 1000 persons.

Agriculture.

There is a good stretch of *wāwar* land in the riverain tracts where the soil is occasionally *kanhār* and is seldom inferior to *morand*, but outside this belt of land the soil is sandy; it is not full of stones but it is shallow and fit for little besides rice. The land classed as wheat-growing *bandhia* and *bandhān* in this tahsīl generally grows a crop of light rice in the rains; this is sown broadcast and the land is ploughed up before it receives the second crop of valuable *rabi* seed. In this case rice is the catch crop, the *rabi* being really the more important ; where the rice is transplanted and the second crop is *uterā* thrown into the mud while the rice is standing, the rice is the chief crop and the land is classed as rice land. The soil of the riverain tract is too heavy to grow *kharīf* juāri especially when embanked. Tenants have, therefore, never liked the crop and prefer to grow more paying *rabi* varieties. The *morand* is very good soil for rice followed by gram and linseed. Except on the riverain tracts the soil elsewhere is generally poor, shallow and of light colour, and some of the villages which have good tanks make up the deficiency in the soil by irrigation. Of the total area of the *khālsa* portion of the tahsīl 905 square miles, or about 62 per cent. were recorded as Government forest in 1906-07, and 289 square miles or 19 per cent. consisted of private forest or grass land in the hands of mālguzārs ; of the village area the proportion of the occupied area was 33 per cent. Since the formation of the tahsīl in 1905, there has been no improvement in cropping and the cropped area dropped by about 2000 acres in 1906-07. The following statement shows the statistics of cropping during the years 1904—1906 :—

Year.	Rice.	Juāri.	Gram.	Wheat.	Linseed.	Til.	Total cropped area.
1904-05 ...	40,442	17,279	3175	1582	2685	1631	83,103
1905-06 ...	40,443	16,879	2989	2032	2893	1530	83,001
1906-07 ...	41,297	13,530	2898	2190	4217	941	81,213

Rice is the chief crop of the tahsīl and next to it is juāri. The riverain tracts are far more stable than the rice tracts in point of cropping, but several of them have fallen away seriously in the late bad years : in some of them wheat used to cover large areas ; that wheat land, much of it embanked, is now either fallow or devoted to very inferior crops ; in some cases this is due to the appearance of *kāns* ; in others it is owing to the inability of tenants to sow crops that require outlay. In 1904-05 the double-cropped area was 6368 acres, and in 1906-07 it increased to 9612 acres.

Land Revenue.

As this tahsīl was formed from portions taken from Chānda and Bramhapurī tahsīls subsequent to the settlement, no figures of revenue at the previous settlement and at attestation for this tract can be given with correctness. The land revenue demand of the tract according to the *kistbandī* for 1906-07 was Rs. 43,512, the demand for cesses being Rs. 3479. Of this amount Rs. 2275 and Rs. 1060 represent the zamīndāri *takolī* and cesses respectively. Thus, the land revenue demand of the *khālsa* portion of the tahsīl was Rs. 41,237, falling at 55 per cent. of the estimated assets. The average rent-rate of the tenants' payments falls at R. 0-10-9 per acre. This tract consists of six assessment groups, *viz.*, Ghot, Amgaon, Garhchirolī, Kurul, Murjhā and Wairāgarh. Murjhā is the most highly assessed group with an acreage rate of R. 0-14-5, next come Garhchirolī R. 0-11-9, Kurul R. 0-11-8, Wairāgarh R. 0-10-11, Amgaon R. 0-8-3 and Ghot, the most lightly assessed, R. 0-7-8.

Miscellaneous.

The tahsīl is divided into three Revenue Inspectors' circles with headquarters at Ghot, Dhanorā and Palāsgarh and 47 patwāris' circles which include 20 circles for zamīndāris. It has 3 police Station-houses with headquarters at Armori, Garhchirolī and Muramgaon.

Garhchiroli Village.—The headquarters of the tahsīl of that name, only blossomed into the dignity of a tahsīl town in 1905, but had long been the largest trading mart in the Amgaon pargana. It lies one or two miles from the left bank of the Waingangā river which, at this point for the first time in its course through this District, begins to be difficult of navigation. Formerly the village had no made roads, but since the project was formed of constituting it a tahsīl headquarters, it has been linked up by good roads, with Mūl 23 miles to the west, and also with Bramhapurī to the north *viâ*

Armorī and with Chāmursi southwards. The Mūl road has been continued eastwards as far as Dhanorā, while earthwork has also been done from Dhanorā to Muramgaon, but this is absolutely the only made road into the zamīndāris which form the bulk of the Tahsīldār's charge. The village is of the usual type, congested save where a few open spaces have been created by the destruction of houses. Buildings of antiquarian interest there are none, the ruins of an old fort being the most that the place can show. The new tahsīl buildings have been laid out about a mile to the east of the village in Rāmpuri Tukum. The population at the last census was 2077, and consists chiefly of Koskātis, Gāndlis, Kāpewārs, Dhīmars and Mahārs. A certain amount of tasar silk worm rearing is carried on, and tasar silk is also spun, but this last industry suffered severely during the famines. Twelve families find employment in the former occupation and thirteen in the latter. Agriculture is the principal resource of the inhabitants, and rice their principal crop: sugarcane used also to be grown, but has received a severe set-back from the recent bad years. One moderately good tank and 12 *borīs* are the sources of irrigation. The tank is also used for drinking purposes, in preference to well-water which is here very brackish. There are only two wells in the village which yield good drinking water, and the water-supply is so bad that it was one of the most serious objections urged against the location of the tahsīl headquarters at Garhchirolī. A weekly bazar is held on Sundays: there are also three shops which deal in *kirāna*. The timber of the zamīndāris passes through Garhchirolī on its way to Chānda. The tahsīl buildings, an inspection house, a dispensary, a police station and an upper primary school are the chief public buildings of the place. Mr. Gangādhar Mādho Rao Chitnavīs of Nāgpur is the sole mālguzār of Garhchirolī.

Garhvi River.—A river which rises in the highlands of the Sākoli tahsīl of the Bhandāra District, and, draining the south-eastern portion of that tahsīl, enters the western half of the Wairāgarh pargana of the Chānda District, and flows south for 24 miles nearly parallel with the Waingangā. It then changes its direction to the south-west and soon meets the larger river, a few miles below Armorī. It is of considerable size with low clay banks, and in the rains has a wide stretch of water, long pools of which remain during the hot months and are used for irrigation by the villages along its course. The legend runs that the Gārhvi issued from the earth at the prayer of Garga Rishi, but the waters flowing sluggishly, the holy man grew irate and shouted in a rage, 'Begone thou she-ass (Gārhwi)'; so ever afterwards the river has borne the names alike of Gārhvi and Gārgi—a combination which would doubtless disturb the choleric saint if he only knew it.

Gewardha Zamindari.—See Zamindaris.

Ghorpet.—A village 5 miles from Bhāndak on the road to Chānda. It is said to derive its name from the royal stables which were located here, when Bhāndak was the capital of the country. Here there was once a fine temple which has been utterly destroyed by a gigantic pīpal tree, the roots of which formerly held together a portion of its walls together with one pilaster and several mouldings complete. This pīpal tree has now fallen, and the pilaster is broken in pieces. The pilaster was remarkable for being built up in regular courses of stone with the walls, instead of being a monolith. The remains were formerly much more extensive, but the stones are said to have been carried away by a road officer to build a bridge. The pilaster was a very fine example of the style of mouldings of mediæval temples of this part of the country. The building probably dates from the 11th or 12th century.

Ghosri.—Twelve miles south of Mūl, has a temple of Mahādeo in the Hemādpanthī style in a dilapidated state and threatened by the roots of a tree.

Ghugus.—Thirteen miles west of Chānda, has three cave temples. These are in the rocky ground near Ghugūs. There is an idol of Bhairavadeva in one of them with broken legs.

The local tradition regarding this is that in former times while thefts and dacoitics used to take place elsewhere none could be committed at Ghūgus, and consequently the thieves and dacoits cut off the legs of the idol. In front of the idol at a distance of about 5 or 6 cubits, there is a stone standing erect called Bāhi (the sleeve of Sīta). Not far off there is another small cave which contains a stone, which the people say is the mother of Bhairavadeva. The idol of Bhairavadeva was said to be increasing in height. His mother, therefore, put a stone on the idol's head. Between these two caves are two stones where a fight between a tiger and a wild boar is said to have taken place. From a more modern point of view Ghūgus is interesting as the first locality in which coal was discovered in this District. The Mayo Colliery here was opened by Lord Mayo in 1870, but ceased working the next year.

Gilgaon Zamindari—See **Zamindaris**.

Godavari River.—The Godāvari river has its source in the Western Ghāts near Nāsik in the Bombay Presidency, and it is not until it has flowed in a south-east and easterly direction for some 650 miles that it touches the borders of this District at its confluence with the Prānhita just below the town of Sironchā. The only important affluent which it receives from the British bank during its course past this District is the Tāl or Tālpir, which flows into it in the Cherlā tāluk. It has a broad sandy bed which, in the rainy season, is full from bank to bank, but in the dry weather the volume of water is reduced to a narrow and shallow stream. Two upheavals of rock, the First and Second Barriers of the Godāvari Navigation Scheme, interrupt the navigability of the channel for several miles, the latter at a point close to its junction with the Indrāvati, and the former at Enchampallī in the Madras Presidency. An account of the Navigation Project has been given in the section on Communications. As a means of communication and trade the river is of no value to the District as a whole, but to the Lower Tāluks of

Sironchā it affords the only outlet they have towards the outer world, and a good deal of trade is carried on with Dumagudiam. Timber is also floated down to that place from the forests of Ahīri. The river has a regular habit of depositing silt on its banks; and this silt, which is of great fertilising power, makes Sironchā the most secure and productive region of the District. The Godāvari empties itself into the Bay of Bengal near Cocanada, after a course of 900 miles. In its lower courses the scenery on its banks is superb, and has been justly compared to that of the Rhine.

Indravati River.—A river which rises in the highlands of the Kālāhandi State and, flowing due west through the Jeypore State of the Madras Presidency for some distance, enters the Bastar State. After passing right through the middle of that State it touches the Ahīri zamīndāri at its south-east corner, and then flowing due north as far as Bhāmragarh where it is met by the Kothāri and the Palmagotam rivers from the north and Paralkot from the east, it takes a sudden turn southwards dividing the Ahīri zamīndāri and the Upper Tāluk of the Sironchā tahsīl from Bastar State, and eventually falls into the Godāvari near Somnūr. Little of this stream is seen in this District; it is a boundary only and passes through a very distant and unprofitable tract of country. It is a true mountain torrent and during its course by this District, it winds among forest-clad lonely hills in frequent rapids and over a broad bed of rock and coarse red sand forming scenery of wild and striking beauty, but hopeless as a navigable river. It is used fairly extensively for floating timber; but apart from that and its fishing, it has little to commend it except the picturesque. Its tributaries from this District are all on the right bank, the principal being Bandia, Vatirangā, Palmagotam, Paralkot and Kothāri. The total length of the river is 169 miles.

Ingara.—In the Rāngi zamīndāri, about four miles north of Rāngi. Here is an ancient temple, on which there is a carving of a warrior with a short straight sword and a shield. It contains images of Mahādeo, Rādha, Krishna,

Ganpati and Annapūrna. The temple fell down about 30 years ago but the pillars are almost all standing.

Jambulghata.—A village of fair size in the Warorā tahsīl situated about 8 miles north-east of Chimūr and 41 miles from Warorā town. The population in 1901 was 499. One of the best markets in the District is held here every Tuesday, and during the open season becomes a regular fair, being patronised by dealers and tenants from Umrer, Paoni and other places outside the District. The extent of the trade done may be estimated from the fact that on one bazar day in the year 1903-04, the traders raised a subscription of Rs. 83 for the repair of the bazar well at the rate of one anna per cart. A considerable trade is done in cattle; two varieties of bullocks are brought, the heavy bullock from Nāgpur for use in black soil and the small hardy breed from the eastern jungles of the District suitable for rice country. Agricultural produce is also largely dealt in. About a mile from the village are found extensive quarries of soapstone, and close to these are found others of black serpentine. From this stone cups, pestles, mortars, etc., are made. For want of bids the quarry is at present closed. It is stated that these quarries were once regularly worked for three years by Raghujī III, Rājā of Nāgpur, who employed on them for eight months out of the twelve on fixed wages about 250 persons, the stone being principally used in the construction of a temple at Nāgpur. The village contains a primary school and a forest post. The proprietor is a Musalmān, and the tenants, with a market at their doors for their surplus produce, are well-to-do.

Jharapapra Zamindari.—See Zamindari.

Jharapapra Village.—The capital of the zamīndāri of that name, contains some interesting caves in a hill: the larger of these are natural.

Junona.—A ryotwāri village 7 miles east of Chānda, possesses a very fine tank, on the stone embankment of which stand the remains of an ancient palace, said to have been built by Dhundia Rām Shāh (1597—1622 A.D.) and in its rear are traces of a wall four miles in length. In communication with the tank is an elaborate system of under-channels. The tank has recently been taken in hand by the Irrigation Department and is now a very fine sheet of water. Junonā is a picturesque spot and has a pleasant camping ground, and ducks are always to be found on the tank.

Katni River.—A small river which takes its rise in the highlands of Muramgaon zamīndāri, and, taking a westerly course through the Dhanorā and Dudhmāla zamīndāris, falls into the Waingangā two miles north-west of Garhchirolī. It has a wide channel and a bed of red sand with much granite and gneiss rock. A night's heavy rain in the hills will flood it into a broad rapid stream but during the hot season no continuous flow exists. It is an important river in the tract between Garhchirolī and Arpallī, since it retains some pools of water in the hot weather and there is some irrigated *marhān* land along its banks.

Keljhar.—A village some 17 or 18 miles from Chānda on the Mūl road. Here Sir A. Cunningham found two small cromlechs or dolmens, which he at first took for kistvaens that had been broken open: but on further enquiry he concluded that they were small shrines raised by the Kurumwār shepherds to Mallāna Deva and Mallāni Devī, at which goats are sacrificed to avert tigers and murrain from the flocks. These cromlechs seem now to have disappeared.

Khatora.—A village about 26 miles north of Chānda. Here are the remains of a considerable stone fort with a moat and double lines of defence. Near one of the bastions is the tomb of Chānd Khān, who is much venerated by the Musalmāns of the District.

Khutgaon Zamindari.—See **Zamindaris.**

Kophragarhi River—The largest tributary of the Waingangā rises in the Kophrāgarh hills of the Palāsgarh zamīndāri and, flowing south-west, is joined by the Tīpāgarhī from the Tīpāgarh range of Muramgaon zamīndāri flowing north-west, and the united stream then changes its direction to the west. Near Wairāgarh it receives the Sāt river coming from the north, and, known sometimes as the Kophrā-garhī sometimes as the Wailochani, it falls into the Waingangā a mile below the mouth of the Gārhvi river after a course of fifty miles. It is a river of magnitude in the rains, but in the summer months it dwindles into a slender thread of water in a broad bed of sand.

Kotgal Zamindari.—See **Zamindaris.**

Kunghada.—Is a large village in the Garhchirolī tahsīl, lying about 50 miles due east of Chānda and about 1½ miles to the east of the Waingangā. Its lands border the zamindāris of Gilgaon and Murandā. The village has a population of 1339 who, with the exception of about 30 households of Dhīmars and Kewats, are entirely engaged in cultivation. There is a large tank to the north of the village from which its extensive rice fields are irrigated.

Formerly the village was mālguzāri, but the mālguzār having allowed the irrigation channels and the tank to fall into disrepair, was unable to collect his rent from the tenants and was losing money on the village. He, therefore sold it to Government and since 1906 the village has been ryotwāri. The Government has repaired the tank and irrigation channels and the village is now a prosperous one. Sugar-cane cultivation is being introduced.

The vast majority of the villagers are Sao Telis. They are industrious and have the reputation of being close-fisted. There are only one Brāhman and one Musalmān, and, as a Sao Teli is a very unlucky person to meet in the morning, their lot cannot altogether be a happy one. The village itself is straggling and mean and the houses—or rather huts—are shabby and dirty looking. In another land the proverbial expression for landward peace and prosperity was, that each man should dwell under his own vine and fig-tree. In Kunghāda it well might be, that each man should sit under the shadow of his own *dhān* store and dung heap. The house of every cultivator in the village is enclosed in a stout brushwood fence, within which, close packed cheek by jowl, are the grain *dholīs*, the dung heaps and the dwelling house. There is only one public temple in the village and it is dedicated to Siva. It too is shabby and mean. Should another temple be erected the mind of the tormented alien, if he camps in the village, turns to Beel-zebub, the god of flies as a suitable dedication. But the Sao Teli is not devout. In these days of State proprietorship and experimental farms, he sees that the agriculturist is not so dependent on Providence as he used to be, and so the shrine of Siva falls into decay, and the Sao Teli worships the image of the King's Majesty on the coin of the realm.

The village has a school and post office and a new school-house is being built. The new Garhchirolī-Chāmursi road passes to the west of the village, and will be of great benefit to it when completed.

Madheri.—A large and flourishing village in the Warorā tahsīl lying on the Warorā-Nāgri road 8 miles to the north-west of Warorā town. The population in 1901 was 1412, against 1493 in 1891. Madherī is one of the chief trade centres of the tahsīl and is the headquarters of an increasing commercial community composed principally of Mārwāris. A large weekly market is held on Mondays, grain and cattle being the principal articles dealt in. The cattle sold are usually of the fine Berār breed. The proprietor of the village is a Brāhman of Badnerā, but about 15 years ago Rājā Gokul Dās obtained possession, in lieu of debt, on a 99 years' lease. The village is held *mukāsa* on three-quarters revenue. A school and branch post office are the public buildings.

Markanda.—A village in the Garhchirolī tahsīl situated on the left bank of the Waingangā river about 40 miles east of Chānda. Once a large village, it is now a hamlet with but a score of houses: frequent inundations have driven away the bulk of its former inhabitants. Mārkanda derives its name and its fame from a beautiful group of temples built in rich purple-coloured stone, and finely situated on a high

Bemrose, Collo., Derby.

LARGE TEMPLE, MARKANDI.

bluff overlooking the river. The pious fancy of Hindu worshippers here pictures Waingangā as chafing uneasily in her bed and meditating the last despairing sweep northwards to join the waters of holy Mother Gangā. For some miles the river has its will, but then relentless fate is too strong for it and hurries it southward away from the haven where it would be. *Victrix causa deis placuit, sed victa Catoni*: and man, honouring the river's unavailing yearning after purity, has raised a group of noble temples to mark the spot at which it begins its effort to force its course for the last time to the north. The temples, over twenty in number, are enclosed in a quadrangle measuring 196 feet by 118, with entrances from the riverside in front and in the two side walls. Some are in complete ruins, and others are very small, but the general effect is impressive; 'the whole taken together,' wrote Sir Alexander Cunningham, 'forms perhaps the most pic- 'turesque group of temples that I have seen. There are no 'inscriptions to tell their age; but their style is so similar to 'that of the Chandel temples of Khajurāha and other places, 'that there can be little doubt that they belong to the same 'period of the 10th and 11th centuries A.D'. Popular tradition says that they were built in a single night by Hemādpanth, but this is the stock story retailed about all temples in Nāgpur and Berār. Undoubtedly they are of great antiquity.

By far the largest and most elaborately sculptured temple of the group is that of Mārkand Rishi, which is dedicated to Siva. In general style this resembles the Khajurāha temples. The whole surface is literally covered with statues and ornaments, human figures, geese and monkeys. Sir A. Cunningham counted over 400 such figures, and there are about half as many sculptures of lions and elephants forming divisions between the human figures. About half of the panels are given up to representations of Siva and Pārvatī in various forms, the former being frequently represented in a state of nudity. Nude female figures also abound, but these are not represented indelicately. The attitudes of all the figures are easy, but the features are void of all intelligent expression. About 200 years ago, the temple was struck by lightning, and the upper part of the massive spire was hurled down on to the roof of the Mahā Mandap which was broken in, and at the same time a small temple was utterly destroyed. The roof of the hall was repaired some 150 years ago, but in a very rude fashion, by one of the Gond Rājās whose architect introduced huge piers with radiating arches inside the principal room. The upper part of the temple now bears the appearance of threatening to topple over at any minute, but the stones are said to have hung in their apparently precarious position for two or three generations. On the jambs of the south door is inscribed the name of 'Shrī Magardhwaj Jogī 700'. Similar inscriptions have been found in several other places and long puzzled archæologists, who presumed the figure 700 to indicate a date but could fit it in with no known era. The explanation now accepted, the credit of formulating which is due to Mr. Hīra Lāl, is that the figure indicates the number of disciples who formed the following of Magardhwaja. Facing the Mārkand Rishi temple and nearer the river stands the pavilion of Nandikeshvar, which was a shrine for the bull Nandi, such shrines being regular adjuncts to temples dedicated to Siva; it has now fallen down. The second largest temple of the group is named after Murkand Rishi who is said to have been father of Mārkand. The roof of the hall of this temple is supported by four richly carved pillars, and over the shrine rises a lofty spire, which is nearly perfect, and is a very graceful specimen of its kind. This temple is dedicated to Siva and has his *lingam* in the shrine. Unique of its kind is a temple dedicated to Yama Dharmrāj or the god of death. Faced as it is by one dedicated to Siva as Mrityunjaya or the conqueror of death, it would appear that the intention of the builder was to represent Siva in a two-fold capacity as Yama or death and as Mrityunjaya, the conqueror of death by reproduction. The only other building requiring detailed notice is the temple of the Das Avatāra or ten incarnations of Vishnu. This is an open cloister 75 feet long by 7 feet wide within, which runs along the western wall of the enclosure. It is divided by pilasters into twelve compartments, two of the divisions being probably intended for statues of Vishnu, and the remaining ten for the *avatāras*. In each division there is a pedestal, but several of them are now empty. These temples are probably the oldest in the whole group and apparently belong to the 6th or 7th century A.D. An inscription carved on a broken pillar which has not yet been deciphered is believed to belong to that date. There are also several curious square pillars which seem to be much more ancient than any of the temples: nearly all of them are sculptured, and some have inscriptions: the chief figures are soldiers wearing anklets and armed with battle-axe, bow and arrow-laden quiver, and depicted in an attitude of attack.[1]

The quiet of this holy spot is seldom broken save once a year, when a fair is held to which the pious resort in order to wash away their sins in the waters of repentance This fair, which, usually held in February, used to attract some 30,000 visitors, has greatly decreased of late years and the attendance of 1908 was not more than 4000.

Maroti (of Fadnavis).– Four miles north-west of Mūl. Here there is an old Hemādpanthī temple, which, though small in size, is interesting in its details. It contains a *linga*.

Mul Hills.—These are situated three miles west of Mūl and measure 18 miles from north to south, and 13 from east to west, with a height above the plain of 400 feet. They are covered with forest, among which there is a good deal of large *beulā*; and under the southern slopes, near Pipalkot, teak is springing up in greater profusion than is found in any other *khālsa* tract in the District; while numerous perennial streams

[1] Most of the account of the temples of Mārkanda is taken from Sir A Cunningham's description of Mārkanda, in Volume IX of the Reports of the Archæological Survey of India. The volume contains a ground plan of the temples and several plates illustrating details of the architecture

abound along the foot of the range dotting the forest with patches of sugarcane. The valleys of Doni and Jhari on the south, and Kolsā on the west, were once immense artificial lakes, with large villages on the slopes of the hills, at which extensive markets met. Now, there are a few Gond huts on the site of the lakes, and thick forest on the hillsides; but in the very driest weather the grass in these valleys is brilliantly green, and the streams running through them bright and limpid The Doni valley especially is worthy of a visit during the summer months, but the visitor should be careful to boil the spring water before using it. On the hills is found a species of snow-drop, the leaves of which are eaten by the Gonds as a vegetable; and under the southern slopes is a large excavation into which the elephants, that once abounded in this part of the country, were driven by the Gond hunters and there captured.

Mul Village.—The largest village in the Chānda tahsīl. Formerly, it was the headquaters of and gave its name to a large tahsīl embracing the old Havelī, Rājgarh, Ghātkul, Amgaon and Wairāgarh parganas, and including the city of Chānda within its limits, but in 1895 the headquaters was shifted to Chānda, and at the same time the name of the tahsīl was changed from Mūl to Chānda. The village lies at the trijunction of the Chānda-Mūl-Umrer and the Mūl-Garhchirolī roads, 27 miles to the north-east of Chānda and well within the heavy rice tract. This position constitutes it an important feeder market to Chānda, and it is as it were the neck of the bottle through which all cart traffic between Chānda and a large part of the interior of the District must pass. The Gondia-Chānda line is, however, about to pass through Mūl, and will divert much of this through traffic to itself. Mūl is pleasantly and picturesquely situated in the neighbourhood of the hills named after it; a river, which also bears its name in the maps but is locally called Huma, flows in a shallow bed a mile or two to the east of the village site. Mahārs and Dhīmars form the majority of the population, but there is also a considerable Telugu element. The famine has told badly on its numbers, which sank from 3811 to 2847 between 1891 and 1901. Mūl and the neighbouring village of Marorā boast several shops, but the trading community is small as compared with the number of those dependent on agriculture. Sugar-cane is extensively cultivated, and there is one large tank which gives full irrigation to 450 acres of rice, its distributaries running through the heart of the *abādi* which lies between the tank and the wet cultivation. Mūl belongs to the Marāthā family of Fadnavīs, who own four other villages close by. The estate is at present under the management of the Court of Wards, owing to the minority of the two boys to whom it belongs. Unfortunately, the funds of the estate are in a very unsatisfactory condition, and the most careful management has not yet succeeded in clearing the estate of liabilities incurred previous to its assumption. The wards live at Nāgpur in the charge of their grandmother, and the estate is immediately superintended by an old *kāmdār* who has long been in the service of the family. Some 300 houses were destroyed by fire in 1894, and 300 more were burnt down in 1903 by a fire originating in a stroke of lightning. The village has been under the Village Sanitation Act since 1892: its Government buildings are a dispensary with a mortuary, a police station-house, a school for boys and girls, and a post office. The only antiquarian remains in the village are some cromlechs which are now used by Kurumwārs as shrines for their gods.

Mundipur.—In the zamīndāri of Gewardhā, contains a *kot* or wall built of stone without mortar, but no local history or tradition is a certainable in connection with it.

Muramgaon Zamindari.—See **Zamindaris.**

Nagbhir—Is situated in the north-west of the Bramhapurī tahsīl and is the first considerable village which the traveller from Umrer to Chānda arrives at after entering the confines of this District. It is 65 miles to the north-east of Chānda. It is as usual a straggling village which has grown up without any conscious plan, and the confusion of its houses and the tortuousness of its lanes are brought into strong contrast by the Government high road, which cuts a ruthlessly straight line undeviatingly through the *abādi*. Two roads meet here, the high road from Chānda to Umrer and so ultimately to Nāgpur, and the branch road to the tahsīl headquarters at Bramhapurī 14 miles distant. To these important routes of traffic will shortly be added a rail-road. The Gondia-Chānda Railway is to pass through Nāgbhīr, throwing out at this point a branch line to Nāgpur, and Nāgbhīr junction should, in the near future, be a busy and important station. The population in 1901 was 2940, against 3896 in 1891. At present the village is chiefly celebrated for its tasar spinning industry, the yarn produced here being of a particularly fine quality. When plague raged at Umrer a few years ago, the well-known spinners of that place emigrated to Nāgbhīr, and there tided over the time of trouble. A weekly bazar is held here on Thursdays and an annual fair takes place at Mahāshivarātra about a mile from the village, and conspicuous for miles as a white spot against a dark background of hill is a temple, by which abides a *fakīr* who obtains his living from the offerings of the pious. Behind the temple is a small natural cave. An inspection bungalow has recently been built on the camping ground—a somewhat eerie spot tenanted by the tombs of dead and gone Musalmāns. There is as usual a school, into which the fairly large Muhammadan community of the place are ever wishful to introduce the study of Urdū, and at last their efforts have been crowned with success—an Urdū teacher was, in 1908, appointed to the school as assistant master. There is also a branch post office The mālguzār of the village is a Muhammadan.

Nagri.—A village on the railway between Hinganghāt and Warorā. Between it and Wāghnāk two miles away are found stones set up in circles such as are often seen elsewhere.

Naleshwar.—Twenty-four miles north-east of Chānda. There is here an old temple built in the Hemādpanthī style and dedicated to Siva. It is situated in a picturesque mango grove, where water from a perennial spring emerges from the rock which is carved into the shape of a cow's mouth. The place is known as Gaimukh.

Nawargaon Buzurg.—A village in the Bramhapurī tahsīl lying some little distance to the west of the Mūl-Bramhapurī road, and about midway between the two places. It is built in the middle of an open undulating plain which stretches away to the forest-clad hills of the Mūl range. The flat lands near the town are well cultivated and irrigated and interspersed with neat little vegetable gardens, which make the approaches to the town rather pretty. To the east and west of the village are mango groves. The village is divided into two parts called Dhūman Khedā and Dewalwādi, and between them lies a small tank which, during the rains, is sometimes so flooded as to divide one part of the village from the other. A large bazar, attended sometimes by 5000 people, is held every Thursday on the spacious bazar site on the south bank of the tank. There are four large permanent shops for general trade in cloth, groceries, metal, etc., in the town, and a considerable export trade is done in grain and bamboo matting, which goes to Umrer and Nāgpur. The bazar attracts people from distant towns, like Umrer and Bhisi. The village has a population of 4100 against 5086 in 1891, and is mainly agricultural. The cultivators are mainly of the Kohlī caste who grow rice (transplanted) and *ringnī* juāri or linseed as winter crops, and the produce of the vegetable gardens finds a ready sale in the weekly bazar at all seasons. There are about 100 houses of Kurumwārs (Canarese shepherds) who tend their flocks on the fields and uplands near the village, and manufacture woollen blankets. The weavers who made Garbori famous for its silk *sāris* a generation ago, appear to have migrated here, for there are about 100 households of Koshtīs who weave silk and *kosā* cloth and a superior class of *sāris*, *dhotīs* and *uparnās*. A large new school is being built. The school attendance is small in proportion to the population, partly owing to the large Canarese population who do not send their children to school, and partly owing to the village being divided into two during the rains. The village contains a post office and a police outpost.

Neri.—A large and most flourishing village in the Warorā tahsīl, situated on a tributary of the Andhāri river six miles south-east of Chimūr and 39 miles from Warorā town. The place has two forts in ruins and is divided into the old town and the new town, with an extensive stretch of rice cultivation between. The population of the village was 3362 in 1901, as against 3556 in 1891. There is an old temple of no small size and beauty, the pillars and carving of which resemble those met with in the cave temples at Ajantā. Of more modern construction are some graceful Panchāl tombs in which husband and wife sleep side by side. The old temple is being rapidly undermined by water from the tank and has been recently taken under Government conservation. The village contains some families of Panchāls and Koshtīs who manufacture brass and copper vessels and cotton cloths. A weekly market is held on Saturdays, there being a considerable trade in these goods and also in rice, which is largely grown here. Neri is also the headquarters of several Brāhman money-lending firms, notably the Bhegres ; it shares with Chimūr the honour of being the favourite residential quarter of this half of the Warorā tahsīl. There is a branch post office and a primary school. The village has been brought under the Mukaddam rules, and a sum of Rs. 650 is annually raised by a cess on the residents and expended on sanitation. The proprietor is a Brāhman widow of the Fadnavīs family and lives at Nāgpur. She is deeply indebted.

Pai-Muranda Zamindari.—See **Zamindaris.**

Palasgarh Zamindari.—See **Zamindaris.**

Panjurni. – Six miles north-west of Warorā, has a peculiarly shaped temple said to have been built on a site of a *satī*. In the centre of the building is seen a tomb with a figure

Bemrose, Collo., Derby.

OLD TEMPLE ON TANK FROM NORTH. NERI.

representing a woman kneeling on the funeral pile previous to its being fired.

Panori.—Two miles north-east of Deotek. Here are ruins of a small temple of laterite, similar to the one at Deotek; there are also several slabs precisely similar to the inscribed slab at Deotek; like it, they are grooved with a channel, but they are broken across and not inscribed. Several statues of Vishnu, Lakshmī, and Nandī, and some *lingas* lie scattered about. The ruins lie on a small mound about 15 feet in height and about 30 feet in diameter. There are no traditions bearing upon them, nor any inscriptions.

Phersagarh Hills.—This range runs parallel to the Chimūr hills and forms the eastern boundary of the Warorā tahsīl dividing it from Bramhapurī. The hills are 13 miles long and 6 miles broad with a height of 600 feet above the plain. They terminate on the south in a strikingly looking scarped cliff, which commands the surrounding country, and can be seen for 40 miles southward. This cliff, which gives its name to the range, is also called the 'Sāt-Bahini,' from seven sisters who are supposed to have lived in religious seclusion on its summit. Some of the glens have patches of rice cultivation, and on the western slopes is the famous Mugdai spring. On ascending this portion of the range a platform of rock is reached, and beyond it rises a smooth sheer precipice, a hundred feet in height, black from exposure, but in reality white sandstone. Over this in the rains forms a broad cascade, and in the driest weather a slender stream trickles from the foot of the precipice and falls into a cleft in the rocky platform, four feet long by one foot wide, where throughout the year is an unvarying depth of seven feet of water. A few yards from the crevice is a large shallow cavern, sacred to the Māna goddess 'Mugdai,' facing the precipice and having a deep rocky ravine on its left. During the ravages of the Pindāris this platform was the refuge of the neighbouring villages.

Pipalgaon Makta.—A village standing on the high bank of the Waingangā some four miles from Bramhapurī. The Waingangā here divides itself into two channels with the island of Lāduz between. The village, situated on the western channel, is liable to floods in the rains. Raghujī I granted this village to the queen of Mudhoji Bhonsla as personal allowance. On her death it came into the possession of Bakā Bai, who willed it to her adopted son Jānoji Bhonsla. The present mālguzār is Rājā Raghujī Rao of Nāgpur, the son of Jānoji. No bazar is held in the village, but there is a small vegetable market held weekly. The population of the village was 2228 in 1901 and mainly consists of Marāthās, Kunbīs and Mahārs. The village is entirely agricultural, and the chief crops are juāri and broadcast rice. A temple of Rāma some thirty years old is built in honour of a local saint called Adkuji Maharāj. An annual festival in honour of this saint takes place at Rām-Navamī, and considerable numbers of devotees assemble from neighbouring villages. The school is small for the size of the village, having only 75 pupils under the charge of two teachers.

Pombhurna.—A first-class rice village in the Chānda tahsīl with two excellent tanks, situated about 26 miles to the east of Chānda. The population in 1901 had declined to 1575 from 1827 in 1891. The area of the village is 3535 acres. It contains a small community of shop-keepers mostly of Telugu extraction, and a few houses of Panchāls who work in wood lacquered in different colours and make toys, fan-handles, chess, draughts, etc., of fine workmanship. Sugar-cane is an important crop of the village. A weekly bazar of little importance is held. There is a primary school for boys and a branch post office. The mālguzār was, until recently, the Brāhman proprietor of Chāmursi; but the village has now passed into the hands of a Komtī of Chāṇda in lieu of debt.

Potegaon Zamindari.—See **Zamindaris.**

Pranhita River.—(Lit. the giver of life.) This is the name given to the combined streams of the Wardhā and

Waingangā in their course from their confluence at Seonī until they join the river Godāvari near Sironchā and assume this name. Its course of 72 miles lies entirely along the western boundary of the Ahīri zamīndāri and the Sironchā tahsīl. In character it resembles the Godāvari and requires no separate description. Some distance below Ahīri occurs the Dewalmāri or Third Barrier of the Godāvari Navigation Scheme. Legend relates that once upon a time Brahmā cursed the Prānhita, saying that no one who bathed in it should be purified. The quarrel is said to have originated in an act of gross insubordination on the part of the river. Brahmā said to it, 'Why do you flow so fast?' to which the Prānhita retorted, 'Who are you to interfere?'. The god replied that he was Brahmā and that he had created the whole world, and that he hereby ordered the Prānhita not to flow so fast. To this the impious river rejoined by saying that no shrine would be established on its banks in honour of Brahmā, and it was in retribution for this conduct that Brahmā deprived the Prānhita of its purifying properties. Finally, however, the quarrel was made up and then Brahmā decreed that no worship of himself should be performed without the waters of the Prānhita.

Rajg rh—Is a fair-sized village in the Chānda tahsīl on the road, four miles south-east of Mūl. Population 585. Here is an old temple which, though small in size, is interesting for its details, as it is generally in very good preservation. The temple is dedicated to Mahādeo, whose *lingam* is enshrined inside. The style is the same as that of the Mārkanda temples, and the roof of the sanctum is a pyramid rising in steps like the pyramidal spires of the Das Avatāra temple at Mārkanda. Although surrounded by a tract of country closely studded with larger villages, Rājgarh is a place of importance, as it boasts the largest bazar in the interior of the District. This bazar is held every Tuesday, and is attended by some 2000 people: large numbers of agricultural stock change hands on these occasions, and there is also a big traffic in grain. The village has a primary school

Ramdighi Pool.—This lies at the foot of a precipice on the western slopes of the Chimūr hills, some ten miles north-north-east of Segaon. It is hollowed out of the rock, about 40 feet in diameter, and of unknown depth ; and into its basin falls during the rains a considerable stream from the precipice above. Tradition attributes the formation of the pool to Rāma when passing through the land. On an eminence above is an ancient temple, with two good carvings of a warrior with shield and straight sword. One of the warriors has fallen backwards, and the other is likely to topple down into the pool ere long.

Rangi Zamindari.—See Zamindaris.

Saoli.—A large village of the Chānda tahsīl, situated on the Mūl-Garhchirolī road, seven miles east of Mūl. The population consists largely of Telugus, and numbered 2548 souls at the last census. The mālguzārin is a resident Komtī widow, who owns three more villages in the vicinity. Saoli is one of the best protected rice villages in the Vīhar group : out of 800 acres under rice, 600 are irrigated, and there are two fine tanks as well as several *borīs.* Some twenty families of Koskātis are engaged in the tasar weaving industry, and are in a fairly flourishing condition : the only other local industry worthy of mention is the manufacture of slippers for which the place has a local reputation. The inhabitants do not appear to take much interest in education, as the primary board school has an average attendance of only 60 children. In 1894, a serious fire took place which burnt down most of the village. Eight hundred houses, including the school and sub-outpost, were reduced to ashes, and three persons lost their lives. There is a school, a post office and a Public Works Department inspection hut.

Sindewahi.—A village in the Bramhapurī tahsīl on the Mūl-Umrer road some fifteen miles to the north of Mūl. It is pleasantly situated on a wide wooded plain bordered by low hills. Groves of ancient mango and tamarind trees surround the village. The village is wholly agricultural and rice, transplanted and broadcast, and sugarcane are the chief *kharīf* crops, while *ringnī* juāri is the winter crop. Water for irrigation purposes is drawn from a large tank at Gadmausa, about two miles from the village. The population in 1901 was 2932, against 3951 in 1891. The cultivators belong mainly to the Kohlī and Gāndli castes The Gāndlis speak Telugu, the others are Marāthās. A small weaving community of the Sālewār (Telugu) caste, provide cotton *lugadās* and *dhotars*, but no silk is woven here. There is also an exceptionally large Mahār population. The village is said to have been gifted by Venkāji Bhonsla to his nephew Gujaba Dāda, whose heir is the present mālguzār Naoloji Rao[1] Gūjar of Nāgpur. Close by the public road stands the temple of the great local saint Someshwar Maharāj[2] founded 25 years ago. There are no shops of any note in the town, but two Gāndli *sāhukārs* conduct a fairly extensive business in the surrounding villages from here. The upper primary school has 150 pupils and a staff of five teachers; about 50 Mahār children attend the school. The sub-post-office is in charge of the headmaster who also looks after the cattle-pound. There is a police outpost with one head-constable and eight constables.

Sironcha Tahsil.—This is the most southerly tahsīl of the District situated between 17° 56′ and 20° 3′ N., and 79° 52′ and 80° 59′ E. It was formed in 1874 out of the Sironchā, Albāka, Nūgur and Cherlā tāluks of the Upper Godāvari District, which was simultaneously abolished. Until 1860, these tāluks had been included in Hyderābād territory, and the previous history and land revenue organisation of the tahsīl are thus entirely different from those of the rest of the District. Sironchā is usually known as the Upper Tāluk, and the other three as the Lower Tāluks. The Lower Tāluks are separated from the Upper Tāluk by a stretch of territory 20 miles in length belonging to the Bastar Feudatory State. The area as ascertained at the original settlement in 1868 was placed at 1053 square miles, but corrected measurements

[1] Now dead.

[2] See Section on Religion.

show a total area of 1085 square miles. In 1905, an area of 2603 square miles, consisting almost wholly of the Ahīri zamīndāri, was transferred from the Chānda to the Sironchā tahsīl, and in 1907 a small area of 13 square miles was transferred from Sironchā to Garhchirolī. The present area of the tahsīl is thus 3675 square miles. A proposal has been pending for some years to transfer the Lower Tāluks, chiefly on the ground of their inaccessibility, to the Madras Presidency, but up to the time of writing the final arrangements for transfer had not been concluded.[1] That portion of the tahsīl which consists of the Ahīri zamīndāri and Upper Tāluk is bounded on the north by the Chānda and Garhchirolī tahsīls of this District, on the west by the Sirpur, Tāndur and Yelgandal Districts of the Nizām's Dominions, on the east by the Bastar Feudatory State, and on the south by Yelgandal and Bastar. The Lower Tāluks are bounded on the north-east and east by Bastar, on the west and north-west by the Khamāmet District of the Nizām's Dominions, and on the south by the Godāvari District of the Madras Presidency. Down the whole of the west side of the tahsīl flows the river which above Sironchā is called the Prānhita, and below this the Godāvari. Along the east boundary of the Ahīri zamīndāri and the Upper Tāluk flows the Indrāvati, a mountain torrent on a large scale. This has one important affluent, the Bandia nullah, which drains a large tract in the east of Ahīri. Another considerable river, the Tālpir, flows into the Godāvari in the Cherlā tāluk. Except along the river banks, the country is practically one mass of dense forest, and is of an extremely broken character rising in places to peaks of considerable height. A large area in the east of the Ahīri zamīndāri consists of one vast maze of mountains attaining a height of some 2000 feet. The Sirkondā hills near Sironchā rise to some 1800 feet. The Gādulgutta hills cover the whole of the Lower Tāluks save for a broad strip along the bank of the Godāvari, and reach a height of over 3000 feet. Along the banks of the Godāvari

[1] The Lower Tāluks were transferred from the 1st July 1909.

occurs a rich belt of alluvial soil of varying breadth. In Ahīri this belt is extremely broken in character, owing to the encroachment of hills, but on reaching the Upper Tāluk it becomes continuous. It varies in breadth according to the distance of the hills from the river; around Sironchā Khās there is a fairly open plain: but except at this corner the strip of open land is rarely more than two miles across. It continues throughout the length of the Lower Tāluks. This alluvial belt is of great fertility being enriched yearly by deposits of silt from the river. Inland the soil is usually shallow and sandy, and villages are very scattered: in fact, the interior of the Lower Tāluks is entirely abandoned to Government forest very sparsely dotted with ryotwāri villages. Some fairly good soil is found along the bank of the Indrāvati, but this tract is not comparable with that bordering on the Godāvari, and the villages in it are much more isolated.

Population.

At the census of 1901 the ascertained population of the tahsīl was 75,154; of these 23,858 were inhabitants of the Ahīri zamīndāri, and 51,296 belonged to the *khālsa* portion of the tahsīl. As a full description of the Ahīri zamīndāri is given elsewhere in this Appendix, the remainder of this description of the tahsīl will relate to the *khālsa* area only. This *khālsa* area has shown a steady rise of population ever since the first census in 1866, the tract having experienced no great set back and coming off lightly in the famine of 1900. At the census of 1866, the population was 22,047, in 1881 it was 40,029, while in the decade 1881--1891 it increased by 4·8 per cent. and by 22 per cent. between 1891 and 1901. This rapid increase is due to the fertility of the tract, which encourages prolific reproduction and attracts immigrants from Hyderābād. The density of population works out at about 47 to the square mile: the distribution is, however, very different in areas. The vast majority of the population is found in the narrow strip along the banks of the Godāvari,

[1] From 1st October 1907, 16 villages with a population of 529 persons were transferred to Garhchirolī tahsīl.

while the mountains and forests of the interior are all but uninhabited. The riverain tract is one of the most thickly populated in the whole Province: each square mile of cultivated area supports 770 persons in the Upper and 930 in the Lower Tāluks as compared with 266 in Warorā. The prevailing language of the tahsīl is Telugu, and the population approximates far more closely to the Madrāsi than to the Marāthā type of the south of the Central Provinces. Gonds however inhabit the forest tracts, and Marāthā Kunbīs are also common in the Upper Tāluk. Many of the tenants of the Lower Tāluks are Gonds and Dhīmars who have entirely assimilated themselves to the Madras type, which is all pervading in this tāluk. The standard of comfort is low, but tenants of the Lower Tāluks are well enough off according to their lights, and can satisfy their simple wants with ease. In the Upper Tāluk, the natural conditions admit of similar well-being, but the tenants have, by a pernicious dependence on their *sāhukārs*, reduced themselves to a condition of practical serfdom, the *sāhukār* taking possession of their crops as soon as these are cut, and supplying all their wants from time to time at ruinous interest, so that they are never out of his debt.

Agriculture.

Excluding the Ahīri zamīndāri Sironchā, which is usually known as the Upper Tāluk, extends in a long narrow strip along the left bank of the Prānhita and Godāvari rivers and consists of a belt of rich alluvial soil. It is, however, to the river itself that the strip of land owes its extraordinary fertility. The soil is light coloured, as compared with the true black soil of the Wardhā valley. But it is exceptionally deep and the river floods, which occur almost every year, instead of scouring away the surface, manure it by depositing silt over it with great regularity, and even without this advantage the soil is very retentive and can produce bumper crops with very short rainfall. Outside this strip in the interior the soil is shallow and sandy except in isolated cases. In the tract known as the Lower Tāluks the river does not seem to enrich the soil to quite the same extent as it does in the Upper Tāluk, but the soil is generally fertile, and although it looks only moderate, it yields excellent crops with a light rainfall. There is less first-class soil but the lower class soils here are far more valuable than in the Upper Tāluk. The general fertility of the soil is attributed to the climatic conditions of the tract. On the whole, the Sironchā tahsīl soil is far better than in other tahsīls; 27 per cent of the cultivated area is *kanhār* against the District percentage of 9 per cent.; 31 per cent. *bersī* against 32 per cent; 26 per cent. *morand* against 40 per cent.; and only 14 per cent. is inferior to *morand*. Excluding about 130 square miles of forest acquired by Government in the Ahīri zamīndāri, the total Government forest area in the tahsīl is 880 square miles or about 82 per cent. of the total. At the time of the recent settlement the proportion of the village area occupied for cultivation was under 34 per cent. The increase in occupied area since the 30 years' settlement was 122 per cent., or much higher than in any of the other tahsīls. In 1906-07, the occupied area was about 31 per cent. of the village area and had increased by 10,608 acres since the recent settlement. One hundred and nine square miles or 40 per cent. of the village area, consist of forest or grass land. The following statement shows the statistics of cropping at recent settlement and during the years 1904—1906:—

Year.	Rice.	Juāri.	Gram.	Wheat.	Linseed.	Til.	Total cropped area
At Recent Settlement	6204	19.745	847	204	60	3386	37,679
1904-05 ...	9214	21,725	1161	1136	424	5039	44.096
1905 06 ...	7421	22,096	780	857	491	3812	40,794
1906-07 ...	8774	21,957	981	657	563	4938	43,091

Rice and juāri are the important crops in the tahsīl. The former is grown as an autumn crop and the latter as a spring crop. The juāri grown is apparently a *kharīf* juāri, which is sown rather late in order that it may get the full benefit of the Godāvari silt and at the same time suffer no damage if the river overflows in the middle of the rains. It is sown in September or the beginning of October and cut early in February or the end of January: another important crop grown in almost every village is maize; *bāris* are exceptionally large and are well manured and the *makai* is never known to fail; even the poorest tenants contrive to crop their *bāris*. The area under *bāri* is less than 3000 acres.

Land revenue.

[1]The land revenue demand at the 30 years' settlement in 1868 was Rs. 14,087, which fell at 61 per cent. of the estimated assets which amounted to Rs. 23,230. A summary settlement of this tahsīl was carried out in 1887-88, at which the revenue demand was raised to Rs. 23,075, which fell at about 63 per cent. of assets which amounted to Rs. 36,827. At the recent settlement the revenue demand was raised to Rs. 31,112, giving an increase of Rs. 8000 or about 35 per cent. on the figure of summary settlement and falling at nearly 61 per cent. of the assets which amounted to Rs. 51,475. The net demand for land revenue in 1906-07 was Rs. 25,199, the demand for cesses in the same year being Rs. 2408. A sum of Rs. 2000 is taken as *takolī* for the Ahīri zamīndāri which is included in this tahsīl. For assessment purposes the tahsīl has been divided into the five following groups, the number of villages contained by each being shown in brackets against it:—Sironchā (72), Sirkondā (43), Nūgur (76), Allbāka (31) and Cherlā (58). The most highly assessed group is Albāka of the Lower Tāluks with an acreage rate of R. 1-8-1. Then come Nūgur R. 1-7-4, Cherlā R. 1-4-4, Sironchā R. 1-3-10 and Sirkondā R. 0-9-9. The rental enhancement at this settlement was due largely to the extension of the occupied area which increased by 122 per cent., and also to the rise in prices of food-grains.

[1] The Chānda District was settled by Major Lucie Smith in 1867. The two tāluks now known as Sironchā tahsīl belonged to the Upper Godāvari District and were settled by Colonel Glasfurd in 1868. In 1874 the Upper Godāvari District was divided and these two tāluks under the name of the Sironchā tahsīl, were added to the Chānda District.

Miscellaneous.

The tahsīl has three police station-houses at Sironchā, Venkatāpur and Ahīri. It has three Revenue Inspectors' circles with head quarters at Ahīri, Sironchā and Venkatāpur and 25 patwāris' circles, of which 13 belong to the zamīndāri of Ahīri.

Sironcha Village—The headquarters of the tahsīl of that name, was formerly a place of much greater importance as being the headquarters of the old Upper Godāvari District. It is 112 miles to the south-east of Chānda. When in 1860 it was selected as the site of the *sadar* station it consisted merely of a few huts on the river bank, and the total population was under 500, but it rapidly grew till the inhabitants numbered 3500. The present population is 2813. The town is pleasantly situated on the left bank of the Prānhita, two miles above its confluence with the Godāvari, and 360 feet above sea-level. On a ridge overlooking the river stand the survivors of the old civil station buildings, most notable among which is the old Deputy Commissioner's bungalow which now forms a residence for the Tahsīldār. Two companies of Madras Native Infantry were quartered here until 1885, and their barracks and other military buildings are still to be seen. The old District jail, now reduced to the status of a subsidiary jail, is still kept up for the accommodation of local offenders. All these public buildings and the village itself stand on *nazūl* ground, which occupies 672 acres out of the total village area of 2316 acres. Sironchā once possessed a fort, which from an inscription on its principal gateway, appears to have been built in 1698 A. D. under the auspices of one Haidar Shāh Walī a short time before this part of the country came into the possession of the Velamā family. This fort bulks prominently in the later history of Sironchā, which has been recorded in Chapter II. When the District came under British rule, it was considered advisable to destroy this fort, and as anybody who cared to do so was allowed to take stone from it, the demolition was pretty thorough ; much of the stone was also used in the construction of the jail and of other public buildings. The founder of the fort, who is generally known as Walī Haidar Shā, was a holy man and is the patron saint of Sironchā, where he lies buried, and whither his tomb attracts many Muhammadans from the surrounding country. Sironchā also has sacred associations for the Hindus owing to its position close to the confluence of the Godāvari and Prānhita rivers, and pilgrims from all parts of India flock hither once in every twelve years. The town has a fair export trade in juāri and til, but there are no manufactures of any kind. The American Methodist Episcopal Church has established a mission here: the mission buildings stand on the site of the old barracks. There is a branch dispensary with accommodation for 15 in-patients, a post office, a police station-house, a second-grade middle school, a girls' school and a Public Works Department dâk bungalow.

Sirsundi Zamindari.—See **Zamindaris**.

Sonsari Zamindari.—See **Zamindaris**.

Surjagarh Hills.—This range is in the Ahīri zamindāri, and takes its name from a noble cliff of black ferruginous mica schist, which stands 1273 feet above the forests at its base. The ascent at first is by a narrow rift in the mountain, whose sides rise vertically on either hand six hundred feet in height, and then the path winds round the face of the cliff in natural steps formed by the weathering of the schist. The whole ascent has been carefully fortified by a series of stone breastworks, here thrown across the path, there perched on an overhanging ledge of rock, and if properly defended would be impracticable for troops without means of shelling. Within the keep on the summit[1] there used to be a small tank which has now disappeared. The gates of the fort are lying on the top and there is a stone platform, on which are images of horses and elephants sacred to the presiding deity, 'Thākur Deo.' Previous to the Gond conquest Surjāgarh was a noted

[1] The summit of the hill is now so covered with undergrowth and scrub jungle that only the platform is accessible.

Māna fortress, and about the end of the 17th century this position was occupied by two famous chieftains, Sadho Vuria and Mūla Vuria, who rebelled against the Chānda king, Rām Shāh, and, secure in their strong fastnesses, harried the low lands with impunity. At length Rām Shāh granted the tract to a relative named Kokshāh, who after some years of desultory warfare stormed the hill and put the insurgent leaders to the sword. Kokshāh then made Surjāgarh his citadel, and under its shadow his descendants, the present Ahīri family, have extended their possessions, east and west, and south and north, until nearly three thousand miles of country own them masters. The scenery of these hills is very wild, and the black glittering mass of Surjāgarh, streaked here and there with patches of bright green and red, stands out grandly against the sky. The upper cliffs have a beautiful shrub, with dark green leaves and clusters of lovely blue flowers.

Talodhi—Is six miles north-east of Dābha in the Chānda tahsīl and formed part of the grant made by Appā Sāhib to Rāmchandra Vyankatesh, father of the present mālguzār Anand Rao. It is now a village of 2494 inhabitants. The main road to Sironchā passes near this viilage and has, within the last two years, given a great impetus to its prosperity. A newly erected corrugated iron roof over the local opium shop, is the first outward and visible sign of the spirit of progress which is beginning to spread itself in this quiet little place. The village is mainly agricultural but has a growing trade in groceries and salt. The population is mainly Telugu, but there is a large colony of Kurumwārs, a caste of shepherds who support themselves by keeping large flocks of sheep and weaving *kambals*, the coarse woollen blankets which are eagerly bought by the labouring classes and Kunbīs. They speak a mongrel Canarese, and absolutely refuse to have their children educated. Talodhī has a school much smaller than it should be and a post office. The village is very straggling, and the houses mean and irregularly huddled together. The new houses that are being built are, however, larger and more commodious.

Talodhi Badge.—A village in the Bramhapurī tahsīl lying on the Mūl-Umrer road, some 22 miles from Bramhapurī. It probably derives its peculiar name from the mālguzār's family. The *abādi* consists of two villages Talodhī and Bamhni, both of which are shaded by mango and tamarind trees. The population in 1901 was 2727, about the same as in 1891. The inhabitants are of the Marār, Komtī, Dhīmar and Kāpewār castes, with small communities of Buruds and Sālewārs. All pursue their various caste occupations but the village is mainly agricultural. Rice is the staple crop but juāri and wheat are grown in the cold season. There are several shops dealing in cloth in the village. There is a police station-house with one Sub-Inspector, two head-constables and 12 constables. The school has a staff of five teachers and about 150 pupils and the post office and pound are in the charge of the head-master.

Talpir River.—Sometimes called the Tāl, rises in the hills of Bastar and falls into the Godāvari in the Cherlā tāluk after a course of 70 miles, the last fifteen of which only are through this District. Its bed is rocky, and it is a stream of no particular importance.

Thanegaon.—Four miles south of Armorī. Here are a small temple and a tank, the former being of about the same age as that of Armorī.

Tipagarh Hills.—This range is in the Muramgaon zamīndāri, and forms the highest portion of a wild mountain region 2000 feet above the sea, on the summit of which, encircled by chain upon chain of hills all covered with the densest forest, stands, far from human habitation, the old-world fortress of Tīpagarh. Its massive ramparts of huge undressed stone, flanked by bastions and entered through a winding gateway, are over two miles in circuit, and within is a tank of considerable size with stone embankment and steps along its water-face. This reservoir never fails, and is supposed to be of fabulous depth, forming the source of the Tīpagarhī, which flows from its western bank, and becomes in the rains a roaring mountain torrent. South of the tank, on lofty ground commanding the fortress and an immense expanse of country beyond, rises an inner fort or citadel, with lines of defence similar to those of the outer work, and having within it the remains of what was doubtless the dwelling of the lords of Tīpagarh. According to tradition the greatest of these was a Gond prince named Puram Rājā, who had a body-guard of 2000 fighting men, 5 elephants, and 25 horses, and held the whole Wairāgarh country under his sway. But those were days when princes only kept their own by doughty deeds in foughten field, and as his fame for wealth waxed great, so his peers of Chhattīsgarh swore more and more deeply to wrest the province from him. At length an invading army from Chhattīsgarh entered his dominions, and Puram Rājā advanced to bar its progress. The contending forces met at Kotgal, and from thence to Pāton, a distance of 8 miles, the battle raged among the hills during the whole long day. Wherever the fight was hottest there rode Puram Rājā, striking to the earth all foes within sweep of his sword, and as evening drew on the Chhattīsgarh troops began to fall back. But now one of the Prince's embroidered sandals dropped unnoticed to the ground, and, as the battle rolled northwards, was picked up by a laggard in the Tīpagarh ranks. This man fled with it to Tīpagarh, and, showing it to the Rānī, told that the day was lost and her lord among the slain. The Rānī shed no tear, but, placing the sandal in her bosom, decked herself in all her braveries of gems and silken robes, then mounting her ox-chariot, she drove to the bank of the little lake. Here she halted for a space, and raising her right hand, filled with til seed, to the heavens, thus prayed to Garh Bhawānī, who guards the fortress walls:—'Grant, dread goddess, that none in days to come may rule thy fort who hath not piled this bank with our foemen's heads as many as the til seed in my hand'; and then she forced the oxen down the steep slope in her front, and the waters closed above her loving head. In the meanwhile, the

Chhattīsgarh forces had been wholly broken, and Puram Rājā returned in triumph with roll of drum and cymbals' clash, but as he proudly rode through the arched gateway of his home he learnt what woe to him a coward's tale had wrought. Passing onwards he drew bridle on the spot where his wife had breathed her last prayer to heaven, and there, springing from the saddle, he plunged into the lake and was seen no more. From that day Tīpagarh became desolate and its kingdom passed away.

Waghnak.—Two miles south of Nāgri railway station. Contains a very old and peculiarly shaped temple, built of solid slabs without mortar.

Wainganga River.—(Lit. 'The Arrow of Water.') This river rises in 21°57′ N. latitude and 79°34′ E. longitude, 11 miles from the headquarters of the Seonī District. After a very circuitous route from the west to the east of that District it is diverted to the south, and emerging from the hills, which hem in its early course, pursues a southerly and south-westerly course through the rich rice lands of Bālāghāt and Bhandāra, receiving numerous affluents the chief of which are the Bāgh, the Kanhān and the Chūlband. Leaving Bhandāra, it strikes this District almost in the centre of its northern boundary, and, travelling in a general direction which is almost due south through the centre of the District, joins the Wardhā at Seonī on the south-west border of the District some miles to the east of Dābha. Its course to this point measures 360 miles of which 156 miles lie within this District. The confluence of the Wardhā and Waingangā rivers forms the Prānhita which, lower down in its course, receives the name of the Godāvari and empties itself into the Bay of Bengal near Cocanada in the Madras Presidency. The breadth of the Waingangā in this District is about 600 yards. Its volume during the rains is considerable, but ordinarily during the open season it flows quietly, long shallows alternating with stretches of deep water, and its broad and sandy bed interspersed with occasional barriers of rock. Some boat traffic goes on in the monsoon months; from the confluence of the Bāgh in Bālāghāt down to Garhchirolī navigation is easy, but below Garhchirolī until past Chinchgondī, where the river again becomes easy to navigate, boats cannot go without great difficulty or even danger The main affluents of the Waingangā during its course in this District are the Andhāri on the right bank and the Gārhvi, the Kophrāgarhī, the Katnī, the Porh and the Potpurī on the left; these are all more or less monsoon torrents, and have little or no continuous course in the open season. Until recently, the river was innocent of a bridge within the limits of this District, but it is now spanned by one on the narrow gauge Gondia-Chānda Railway at Wārsa.

The local legend about the Waingangā is that far away in the hills of the north it began to flow towards the holy Ganges, but losing its way in the windings of the valleys it was driven southward by fate; so it turns and winds ever seeking to flow northward, and ever failing. At Mārkanda near Chāmursi it gathers itself for a last effort and swings northward for some miles, but fate is ultimately too strong for it and hurries it away once more to the south.[1]

Wairagarh.—Lies some 80 miles north-east of Chānda at the confluence of the Kophrāgarhī and Sātnālas in the Garhchiroli tahsīl. It is a place of great antiquity and is supposed to have been founded in the Dwāpar Yuga by a king of the family of the moon, who called it Wairāgarh[2] after his own name Wairochan. On approaching historic times we find the city ruled by Māna chiefs, who about the 9th century fell before the Gonds, and a line of Gond princes then succeeded, holding in subjection to the Chānda kings the parganas of Wairāgarh with the zamīndāris attached

[1] For another legend accounting for the circuitous course of the Waingangā in its upper reaches, see the article on the river in the Seonī District Gazetteer.

[2] Mr. Hīra Lāl considers the name to be a corruption of 'Vajrākar' meaning 'Diamond mine.' The latter name is mentioned in Tamil inscriptions. For details of identification see Mr. Hīra Lāl's article in the *Epigraphia Indica*, Vol. X.

to it, and Garborī and Rājgarh. Forty years ago it was a village of 936 houses, but it has sunk steadily in importance and now only contains 326 houses with 1414 inhabitants, and altogether wears a very decayed appearance. The village is surrounded by groves of extremely fine and ancient trees, and is grouped around a large stone fortress in a fair state of preservation, which was erected about the beginning of the 17th century. It has a triple gateway with a deep and very filthy ditch: from the eastern bastions a fine view is obtained of the thickly wooded hills of the western zamīndāris. Within the forest is the tomb of the Gond prince Durga Shāh, not far from which is the grave of an unknown English girl, said to have been the daughter of the officer who commanded the garrison between 1818 and 1830 A.D. The surrounding forest contains numerous foundations of former buildings, and near the town are several temples, none of which however are very ancient. The oldest temple is that of Mahākāli, an unpretending structure probably built by one of the Gond Rājās: it overlooks a deep reach of the Kophrāgarhī, wherein is supposed to stand an old-world temple buried in the sand. Wairāgarh once possessed diamond mines, which are referred to in the Ain-i-Akbarī. On a hill, at the foot of which there used to be one of these mines, stands an old Muhammadan *idgāh* and a few Musalmān tombs. These probably belong to the period when Ahmad Shāh Bahmani made a raid on Wairāgarh about 1422 A.D. Wairāgarh is very unhealthy during a large part of the year, and its trade has consequently been almost wholly diverted to the neighbouring town of Armorī. It has a school for boys a post office, and a station-house.

Wardha River—This river rises in the Multai plateau of the Betūl District (at 21° 50′ N. and 78° 24′ E.) some 70 miles north-west of Nāgpur, and flowing south and south-east separates the Nāgpur, Wardhā and Chānda Districts of the Central Provinces from Berār and the Nizām's Dominions. It reaches this District at the angle made by the influx of the

Wunnā river and after a course of 290 miles, of which the last 103 miles constitute the western boundary of this District, it meets the Waingangā at Seonī some miles east of Dābha, and the united stream under the name of the Prānhita flows on to join the Godāvari. Soon after entering the District the Wardhā is opposed at Soit by a sheet of limestone stretching from bank to bank, over which it dashes in a waterfall of some size and considerable beauty. Below this point, the river flows peacefully and is well fitted for navigation, especially after its junction at Warhā near Chānda with the Pengangā, which doubles its volume, until just before its confluence with the Waingangā it meets a mighty upheaval of gneiss and granite which extends across the river, and is known as the Third Barrier. Here the river wanders through a tangle of rock and tiger-haunted bushes, in a thousand brawling streams and rapids quite impassable to boat traffic. The Godāvari Navigation Scheme of the sixties and seventies included the excavation of a channel through this barrier, but this part of the programme was abandoned in its most initial stage, and the river has consequently never been used except to float up a certain amount of timber from the Alāpalli forests. Major Lucie Smith also mentions a Government steamer of forty tons as plying in his day, but this has long ago disappeared into the limbo of things forgotten. The country on the Chānda bank of the Wardhā is eminently adapted to the growth of cotton and juāri, and as far south as Bhāndak consists of true black cotton soil. Underlying the same stretch of soil are the extensive coal-measures of the Wardhā Valley Coalfield. The principal tributaries of the Wardhā are the Wunnā and the Erai on the left bank and the Pengangā on the right. The Wunnā, as mentioned above, joins the Wardhā as it enters this District, while the Erai flows in a few miles below Chānda. There are different theories as to the origin of the name Wardhā; probably the word is *Var-dā* ' the giver of boons.'

Warha.—Ten miles east by south of Chānda. Has an

old temple with a broad flight of steps leading down to the Wardhā river. Here Bāji Rao's army was checked by Lieut.-Colonel Hopston Scott on the 2nd of April 1818, and the fall of Chānda assured.

Warora Tahsil—Occupies the north-western portion of the District. It was constituted in 1857, and comprises 1282 square miles: it is the only tahsīl of the District which has undergone no changes of area since its constitution. It is bounded on the north by the Wardhā, Nāgpur and Bhandāra Districts, on the east by the Bramhapurī tahsīl, on the south by Berār and the Chānda tahsīl, and on the west by Berār. It lies between 19°59′ and 20°44′ north latitude, and 78°48′ and 79°37′ east longitude. Its extreme length from north to south is 38 miles, and the breadth from east to west is 55 miles. Three hundred and seventy-three square miles of the tahsīl are included in Government forest. The tahsīl is traversed from north to south by a range of hills, known as the Chimūr hills some twenty miles in length, with an average breadth of six miles and an elevation of 450 feet above the surrounding plain. There is a gap of some five miles in the middle of the range south of which the hills become broader and lower, dwindling away near Moharli. The highest point of the range is named Lingā, and attains a height of 1341 feet above sea-level. Parallel to the Chimūr range and forming the eastern boundary of the tahsīl runs another range known as the Phersāgarh hills, 13 miles in length and 6 broad, with a height of 600 feet above the plain, terminating on the south in a bold scarped cliff known as 'Sāt Bahini' after seven sisters who are supposed to have lived in religious seclusion on the summit. This is only one of the confused legends that are attached to this hill but another legend says they are the seven Devis or "divine sisters" of the Telugus. The watershed of the Chimūr hills divides the tahsīl into two main basins, the valleys of the Wardhā and Waingangā rivers. The western portion is watered by the Wardhā and its tributaries, the Wunnā and Dahiwal, the Sir and the Erai. The greater part of the eastern portion is drained by three streams which unite to form the Gondarnadī, a branch of the Andhāri river, one of the chief affluents of the Waingangā. The trend of the course of all these streams is from north to south. The Wardhā river, which forms the south-western boundary of the tahsīl for some 40 miles, has a considerable volume of water throughout the year. The main valley of the Wardhā lies in the trap area, and a superstratum of black loam overlying the trap forms the true black cotton soil, well adapted for *rabi* crops and *bani* cotton. Further eastward comes a belt of light sandy loam and sandy soil, admirably adapted to tank construction and the cultivation of rice.

Population.

At the census of 1901 the tahsīl contained one town, Warorā, and 406 inhabited villages with an average of 70 houses each. The population numbered 134,547 with a density of 105 to the square mile; these figures exhibit a decrease of 10,000 or 6·9 per cent., as compared with the figures of the census of 1891. Between the first settlement in 1866 and 1891 the population appears to have increased by about 20 per cent., and the subsequent drop is wholly attributable to the bad seasons of recent years, which have affected the rice-growing tracts in the east of the tahsīl, although falling lightly on the cotton tract. The bulk of the population is dependent on agriculture and the chief cultivating castes are Kunbīs, Mānas, Marārs, Telis, Kohlīs, Pardeshīs, Dhangars and Gonds. The general condition of the tenants in the cotton tract is superior to that of other tenants of this District. Mālguzārs are as a rule substantial men, but are often non-resident. Besides the town of Warorā with a population of 10,626, the tahsīl has four villages, Chimūr, Bhāndak, Bhīsi and Neri with a population of over 3000 each. The Wardhā-Chānda-Ballālpur branch of the Great Indian Peninsula Railway runs through the entire length of the tahsīl having three stations within its limits at Nāgri, Warorā and Bhāndak. Until the beginning of the current year, 1908, this line had been carried no further than Warorā, which thus formed the main gate of the external traffic of the District. It is the presence of the railway that has led to the wide cultivation of cotton which is peculiar to this tahsīl.

Agriculture.

The greater part of the tahsīl is an open black soil tract in the valley of the Wardhā river bearing spring crops and thus differing considerably from the rest of Chānda which is mainly a rice District and resembling rather the adjoining District of Wardhā. According to the classification, the commonest soil in the tahsīl is what is known as *bersī*, which is less cohesive and less retentive of moisture than *kanhār* or *kāli*, easier to plough and benefited by good winter rains. It covers 47 per cent. of the cultivated area, as against the District figure of 32 per cent. The *kāli* or *kanhār*, rich black soil containing little or no grit and retentive of moisture, is found in a few villages only near the Wardhā river. This soil grows *bani* cotton, wheat and other first-class crops and covers 12 per cent. of the cultivated area. The yellow soil suited for rice and sugarcane is generally found in the eastern parts of the tahsīl and there is very little of it. An area of 373 square miles or 29 per cent. of the total area of the tahsīl consists of Government forest. At the time of settlement the occupied area was 67 per cent. of the village area of the tahsīl and the cultivated area 48 per cent. The cropped area was 67 per cent. of the occupied area. The increase in the occupied area since the 30 years' settlement was 14 per cent. In 1906-07 the occupied area was 73 per cent. of the village area and had increased by about 66,000 acres since settlement. One hundred and ninety three square miles or 20 per cent. of the village area, consists of forest or grass land in private hands. To sum up, the tahsīl is open, well cultivated, and well drained. In the western portion there is good black soil growing *rabi* crops. Rice, which is the most paying crop, is not much grown as the soil is suitable neither for the growing of the crop nor for the construction of tanks, being too apt to split and leak. As we travel east we come to light sandy loam and sandy soil excellent for rice growing and for tank construction. The following statement shows the statistics of cropping at settlement and during the years 1904 and 1906 :—

Year.	Rice.	Juāri.	Gram.	Wheat.	Linseed.	Til.	Total cropped area.
At Settlement.	30,403	53,357	5142	33,526	32,976	36,617	258,071
1904-05 ...	20,314	91,006	6052	38,447	36,013	28,192	305,172
1905-06 ...	15,877	78,298	6035	48,431	47,641	21,450	312,323
1906-07 ...	19,971	72,807	6172	52,476	57,580	20,762	314,965

The cropped area has increased since the settlement by about 57,000 acres, chiefly due to the reduction of fallows. The principal crops of the tahsīl are juārī, til, wheat and linseed, covering respectively 23, 7, 17 and 19 per cent. of the cropped area in 1906-07. Til and linseed have been regularly and largely exported, and the other grains both imported and exported according to the circumstances of the year.

Land Revenue.

The land revenue demand at the 30 years' settlement, was Rs. 90,795 which fell at 70 per cent. of the estimated assets. At the time of the recent settlement the land revenue demand of the tahsīl was found to be Rs. 94,707, and during this settlement it was proposed to enhance the demand to Rs. 1,23,918 giving an increase of Rs. 33,123 or 36 per cent. on the figure of 30 years' settlement, and falling at 60 per cent. of the revised assets which amounted to Rs. 2,04,833. The land revenue fixed at settlement according to the *kistbandī* was Rs. 1,10,385, and cesses Rs. 6840. The net demand for land revenue in 1906-07 was Rs. 1,11,855, the demand for cesses in the same year being Rs. 6832. At the 30 years' settlement the tahsīl comprised the Warorā, Bhāndak and Chimūr parganas. At the recent settlement these parganas have been formed into the eleven following assessment groups, the number of villages contained by each being shown in brackets against it, Nāgri

Lonhāra (35), Warorā (61), Bhāndak (46), Khemjai (46), Shegaon Yensā (73), Chandankherā (50, Shedegaon (48), Chimūr (70), Shankarpur (360), Neri (43) and Jāmbulghāta (42). The average rent-rate of the tahsīl was R. 0-8-3 against an average of R. 0-5-10 at 30 years' settlement, or an increase of about 42 per cent. The incidence of the revised revenue per acre in cultivation would be 7 annas and one pie; a moderate rate, having regard to the varied and valuable character of the cropping and the facilities for irrigation enjoyed by a portion of the tahsīl. The reason why the revenue incidence approximates so closely to R. 0-8-3, the revised rent-rate, is due primarily to the fact that more than one-fourth of the occupied area is old fallow, but partly to the existence of *mālik-makbūzas* (85 per cent. of whose payments are taken as revenue), and in a measure to the circumstance that *siwai*, which accrues mainly from waste and unoccupied areas, contributes about one anna in the rupee of the total mālguzāri income. Neri was the most highly assessed group in the tahsīl with an acreage rate of R. 0-11-8. Next to this comes Warorā R. 0-8-9. The lowest assessed group is Shegaon Yensā with an acreage rate of R. 0-4-9.

Miscellaneous.

The tahsīl has three police station-houses at Warorā, Shegaon and Chimūr. It has three Revenue Inspectors' circles with headquarters at Nandori, Shegaon and Chimūr and 53 patwāris circles.

Warora Town.—The headquarters town of the Warorā tahsīl, is the second largest town in the District, and the only other municipality besides Chānda. It is situated in 20° 14′ N. and 79° 1′ E. 28 miles north-west of the latter city, with which it is connected by a good metalled road and also by rail. Prior to the current year (1908), the road was he only means of communication with Chānda, and Warorā derived much importance from its position as the terminus of the Wardhā-Warorā extension: the merchandise not only of the western half of this District but also of a large part of the Wūn District of Berār and part of the Edlābād District of the Nizām's Dominions all passed through Warorā to and from the outside world. Most of the traffic was naturally with Bombay *viâ* Wardhā. The extension of the railway to Ballālpur has of course materially affected the position of Warorā, but it nevertheless continues to be an important trading centre, and is likely to remain so. The important cotton market of Hinganghāt lies on the rail only 26 miles north-west of Warorā. Primarily the town owes its importance to the colliery which formerly existed here, as it was simply the existence of the coal-measures which led to the construction of the Wardhā-Warorā extension. The history of the Warorā Colliery has been fully detailed in Chapter VI, and it is sufficient to say here that it was closed down in 1906 owing to a subsidence, after a life of 35 years during which the output of coal amounted to rather over three million tons. In connection with the colliery a brick industry was carried on, but this had to be discontinued when the mine stopped working. The closing down of the colliery has naturally been a great set-back to the prosperity of the town, involving the departure not only of the numerous colliery workers and their dependants but also of many persons who made a livelihood out of furnishing supplies to the colliery staff. The population of the town at the census of 1901 was 10,626, but it has now probably sunk by at least 3000. Warorā will, however, always retain a fair measure of importance from its position in the centre of a rich cotton tract, and of late years there has been considerable activity on the part of various firms in erecting gins and presses in the town. There are at present two gins and four presses, most of which have been constructed very recently. A good deal of trade is also carried on in oilseeds and grain.

Warorā was constituted a municipality in 1867, and the average municipal receipts for the ten years ending 1901 were Rs. 22,000. In 1903-04 the income had increased to

Rs 32,000 being principally derived from octroi. In 1906-07 the income was Rs. 31,000. The municipal limits, which have recently been re-adjusted, include two villages, Ekarjunā and Khanji, in addition to the town itself. The mālguzārs of Warorā and Ekarjunā are Deshpāndes: an account of this family has been given in the section on 'Leading families.' The mālguzār of Khanji, Ragho Atmārām, belongs to the peculiar caste known as Kalankīs (spotted): these are Marāthā Brāhmans who some sixty years ago adopted heterodox modes of ritual and worship and were consequently outcasted by their fellows: their present mode of living is exactly the same as that of the ordinary Brāhman, but they are not allowed to dine or marry outside their own Kalankī community.

The town has the usual tahsīl buildings: there is also a first-grade middle school with two branch schools belonging to the municipality, and a Government girls' school. The Chānda Mission has an out-station and a school here. Formerly there used to be two dispensaries, the Government town dispensary and also one at the colliery, but the latter has been closed. Libraries also formerly numbered two, one of which was attached to the colliery: the other, which now alone survives, is called the Native Library, but it suffers from lack of funds and the general public evinces but little interest in it. A dâk bungalow singularly distinguished for dirt and discomfort, and a municipal *sarai* stand within 200 yards of the railway station, and there is another *sarai* within the town itself which is about a mile distant from the station. The town itself is very congested and unattractive to look upon: its striving after more pleasant externals is practically limited to a moated garden which has been formed out of a tank reclaimed by Government at considerable expense during the famine of 1900. Every year, however, something is done to improve the appearance of the town by the construction of new roads and drains as funds permit. Of buildings presenting any antiquarian or artistic interest there are absolutely none.

One of the greatest problems of municipal administration is the lack of an adequate water-supply. During the hot weather months, water has to be obtained by pipes from the colliery. Popular opinion accounts for the dearth of water by the theory that the colliery workings have diverted the springs which formerly ran into the town wells. Most of the wells in the town only hold water for some eight months in the year. In spite of water difficulties and the extreme heat of the hot weather, Warorā is one of the healthiest places in the District.

A few words may be added on the subject of 'The Servants' Mutual Benefit Fund Shrī Gajānan Company, Limited, Warorā.' This is a kind of friendly society which was instituted in 1896. It is composed of members who are servants either of Government, the railway company, local bodies or registered companies. The object of the company is to pay a bonus with profit, if any, to its members or their heirs on their retirement from service for any cause. The minimum sum payable on retirement is equal to the amount of subscriptions paid in by the person retiring. There are three classes of subscribers, the first class paying an annual contribution of Rs. 2-4-0, the second R. 1-11-0 and the third R. 1-2-0. The members of the society are hardly sufficient to compass its objects satisfactorily.

General description. Area and position.

Zamindaris.—The zamīndāri estates of the Chānda District are sixteen in number and comprise an area of slightly under 4000 square miles; of this more than three-fifths is included within the limits of the Ahīri zamīndāri, while the other estates range in size from 262 to 17 square miles. Prior to the transfer of four of the zamīndāris to the Drug District in 1907, the number of the zamīndāris was twenty and their area some 4800 square miles. They are all grouped together in a large block which forms the eastern half of the District.

Nature of tenure.

In origin the estates appear to have been feudal grants made with the object of settling and keeping some sort of order in parts too remote and difficult for the ready exercise of the sovereign's direct authority. No documents survive to show the terms of the original grants, and the traditions of the ruling families are singularly meagre. It seems evident that neither the Gond nor the Marāthā sovereigns recognised any proprietary title to the soil on the part of the zamīndār, and Major Lucie Smith quotes instances to show that even as late as the end of the 18th century zamīndārs were made and unmade at the pleasure of the Rājā. Each zamīndār was assessed to a small tribute or *takoli* and was bound to furnish a contingent of men-at-arms when required, and, if he complied with these conditions, he was doubtless left pretty much to his own devices. There is a popular belief that at one time all the zamīndāris except Ahīri were united under one chief. In this connection a somewhat discursive story is told which is reproduced below with a few verbal alterations from a version kindly supplied by Mr. J. T. Chamberlain, I.C.S., who was in charge of the recent settlement operations in the northern zamīndāris; he in turn had it from a local Brāhman. 'Once upon a time, many hundred years 'ago, there was a chieftain who had a fortress on the borders 'of Bastar, and eked out his livelihood by taking toll of mer'chants and others, who passed by his castle. In the pursuit 'of this avocation, he happened to murder the son of a king 'who was passing with a small retinue northwards to per'form a marriage ceremony in Raipur. In revenge for this, 'the bereaved father laid siege to the castle and massacred 'the garrison. The sole survivor was the wife of the robber 'chief, who escaped by hiding on an island in the middle of a 'neighbouring lake, and eventually fell in with a band of 'Manjīs who gave her shelter until she died in the act of 'delivering a posthumous son. The boy lived with these 'wanderers till he was about fifteen, being brought up in 'knightly accomplishments. Then came a famine, and 'being hard pressed for food, the youth determined to offer 'his services to a Rājā who had been beleaguering the city 'of Chānda for two years without success. So he rode to 'Chānda, adopting the somewhat curious means of locomo-'tion of a *nīlgai* which he steered by means of ropes attached 'to its tail as to the rudder of a boat. Arrived at Chānda, 'the youth and his companions quickly attracted the notice 'of the besieging Rājā, who promised them any guerdon 'they might choose to ask if they succeeded in carrying the 'city. Hereupon the youth charged up to the city wall, and 'the defenders moved by panic took to their heels. The 'victorious Rājā, mindful of his promise, asked the youth 'to name his reward, upon which the latter proferred an 'apparently modest request for nineteen mango trees. The 'Rājā was surprised at the moderation of the demand until 'his wazīr explained that the language used was figurative, 'and that the youth was really asking for the nineteen zamīn-'dāris (*i.e.*, all the zamīndāris except Ahīri). The Rājā com-'plied readily with this request, the more so that the zamīn-'dāris were not his to give but were in the possession of 'various chiefs. So the youth united all the zamīndāris under 'his single rule, but, as time went on, by sale, gift and mort-'gage they have gradually become subdivided again until 'they are once more nineteen in number.' Pānābaras, added the recounter of this legend, was the first and foremost of the zamīndāris. The legend is given for what it is worth; it hardly seems convincing, and the coincidence of the number of mango trees asked for with the number of zamīndāris now existing appears to involve a somewhat violent *hysteron proteron.*

When the District came under British rule, it was held that, as the zamīndāris had no absolute right in the soil, it rested with Government to confer that right, attaching such conditions to its exercise as might be deemed fitting, and it was determined at the original settlement to embody these conditions in a patent of proprietary right based on the ancient usages actually found in existence at the time. The main conditions laid down in this patent, the Magna Charta of the zamīndāris, were that tenures should be indivisible and untransferable save to the nearest male heir, and then only subject to the approval of the Chief Commissioner: that the estate should be held by one person, the zamīndār for the time being, and subject to the conditions of loyalty, good police administration, and the improvement and cultivation of the estate. Succession was to devolve ordinarily upon the eldest son, or in default of a son by birth or adoption, upon the nearest male kinsman of the zamīndār, but Government reserved to itself the right to set aside unfit persons in favour of the nearest male heir duly qualified, and also to remove zamīndārs in event of gross misconduct. The zamīndārs were originally allowed to enjoy the revenue from land, forest, excise, *pāndhri*, ferries and pounds, but of late years, the right to the four last named sources of income has been resumed by Government, due compensation being made to the zamīndārs. The management of the police of the zamīndārs has also been taken over by Government; when under the zamīndārs themselves, the police force included men who carried out miscellaneous duties in addition to their police functions, some being even employed as cooks, and was chiefly valuable as a dumping-ground and convenient means of support for the zamīndārs' relatives. The present dignities and privileges of a zamīndār are much curtailed; he is exempt from the Arms Act because the zamīndāris are included in the scheduled Districts; he is a *darbāri*, and he has a hereditary status among his tenants which an ordinary mālguzār can seldom or never hope to rival. But as far as his recognised rights as a landlord are concerned he is now in a position little superior to that of the mālguzār of the *khālsa*. His estate is probably a good deal larger, it is far more lightly assessed, and it is by statute impossible for him to contract himself out of it. But most of the zamīndārs are the illiterate Gonds, prone to the vices and pleasures of the aboriginal, and it needs a somewhat generous imagination to invest them with the romantic interest of a decayed nobility. There are, however, one or two notable exceptions, and even apart from these the visitor to the zamīndāri tract cannot but carry away a kindly, if in some respects, compassionate impression of both the chiefs and their people.

General description of the zamīndāris.

Physically regarded the zamīndāris present a welter of hill and forest, watered by numerous rivers and streams but containing no rivers which are of any importance to them as means of communication or trade. Communications, in fact, are poor throughout, and so far comprise but some 40 miles of metalled roads, while trade is practically confined to exports of rice and forest produce, and to such simple imports as an aboriginal population requires. At the recent settlement the occupied area formed only 8 per cent. of the total area of the zamīndāris, and as by far the best developed and most open estate, Ambāgarh Chaukī, has since been transferred to Drug, the percentage is now probably even smaller. The forests, though extensive, contain with the single exception of those of Ahīri, little beyond ordinary kinds of timber, and have been denuded by extravagant cutting, so that the main source of the zamīndārs' incomes under this head is minor forest produce. The staple crop is rice, and this is supplemented mainly by smaller millets which give a crop with a minimum of attention and which have been supplanting rice to a considerable extent in the recent bad years; the primitive method of *khamori* cultivation is also commonly practised. At the first settlement, it was roughly estimated that about 100,000 acres of land were cropped in the zamīndāris as a whole. In 1904-05, this figure had risen to over 174,000 acres. No statistics are available for 1899, but there can be no doubt that the area then under cultivation was much larger, probably by 50 per cent. than it is now. The decline is due not merely to want of seed, but to loss of population. Between 1868 and 1891, the population of the zamīndāris rose from 86,594 to 137,501, but by 1901 it had declined to 106,079, out of which number only 58,651 belonged to the estates now included in the District. During the decade 1891—1901, four zamīndāris lost over 50 per cent. of their population, and in four only was the loss under 10 per cent. Gonds form the vast majority of the population, Mārias prevailing towards the south. A large part of the zamīndāris consists of vast tracts of forest which have never been surveyed. Even in the village areas which have been surveyed, cultivation is often of a very unstable character, and not only fields but whole villages come under cultivation or fall out of it year by year. The land record staff is weak and ill-trained and too remotely situated for close supervision. Statistics must therefore, when they are obtainable, be accepted with a good deal of reserve. The total *takolī* payable by all the zamīndāris amounts to only Rs. 4275 or little more than R. 1 for each square mile of their whole area. In addition to this Rs. 1890-9-0 are levied on account of cesses, but this is all the revenue derived by Government from this huge area. With these preliminary general remarks, we may now proceed to a brief account of each zamīndāri :—

Boundaries and physical features.

Ahiri Zamindari.—The Ahīri zamīndāri is a huge estate having an area which greatly exceeds that of all the other zamīndāris combined. The total area of the zamīndāri proper is 2545 square miles, but the estate also owns 77 villages in the Garhchirolī tahsīl in mālguzāri right; these villages cover 55 square miles and bring the area of the estate up to 2600 square miles. The zamīndāri is bounded on the north by the Jharāpāpra, Potegaon, Khutgaon and Pai-Murandā zamīndāris, on the east by the Bastar Feudatory State, on the south by the *khālsa* tracts of the Sironchā tahsīl and on the west by the Prānhita river, Dīna nullah and the *khālsa* tract of the Garhchirolī tahsīl. The mālguzāri villages all fall within the limits of the Amgaon and Ghot parganas of Garhchirolī tahsīl. The estate is drained by the Waingangā, Prānhita and Indrāvati rivers and their tributaries, the principal of which are the Denā flowing into the Prānhita and the Bāndia, Palmāgotam and Paralkot flowing into the Indrāvati. Almost the whole estate consists of one unbroken range of forests. On the extreme east stretches a simple maze of hills of considerable height, which fill almost the whole of the large tract east of the junction of the Palmāgotam, Paralkot and Indrāvati rivers at Bhāmrāgarh. These hills attain a height of from 2000 to 3000 feet and are absolutely inaccessible to any kind of vehicle. Some distance south of Ahīri itself are situated the Bhīmaram and the Dewalmāri hills, and to the east of these lies another range of hills known locally as the Mallanāguttā range. The greatest length and breadth of the estate are each about 80 miles, and with the exception of Government forests of an area of about 82,000 acres which have been acquired in its interior, it is altogether uninterrupted by other properties.

Historical notice.

The zamīndāri is said to have been granted six centuries ago to Mānsu Bāpu an ancestor of the present zamīndār, by one of the Gond Rājās of Chānda, on condition of reclaiming land, extending cultivation, and maintaining security of life and property particularly against inroads of dacoits from what is now the Nizām's Dominions. But there is absolutely no documentary or other evidence to fix the date of the acquisition. The authentic history of the estate and the lineage of its proprietor cannot be traced further back than to the days of Kokshā who held the zamīndārship from 1703 to 1769, and fought for the last of the Gond line of Chānda against the Marāthā invaders. He was a relative of the Gond King Rām Shāh (1672-1735 A.D.) from whom he received a grant of the zamīndāri on condition of expelling the rebel chiefs Sadho and Mula Vuria, who had established themselves in the fortress of Surjāgarh. This after some years of warfare he succeeded in doing. His successor Bhīmrao or Venkatrao (there appears to be a doubt as to which name is correct) who held the zamīndāri from 1770 to 1818, espoused the cause of Mudhojī in the internecine conflicts of the Marāthās in 1773. On this occasion, according to Major Lucie Smith, he and his brother Mohanshā, who were military governors of Chānda city, together with a third brother Vishwāsrao, then in charge of the Mānikgarh fortress, distinguished themselves by attacking a party of Poona troops who had captured the ladies of Mudhojī's family and succeeded in rescuing the prisoners. Bhīmrao left a great name behind him; he preserved complete order in the territories under his control, and appears to have collected various petty landholders of the neighbourhood around his standard. It was in his day that the zamīndāri is supposed to have expanded to its present limits. Bhīmrao's successor Musammāt Daryā Bai, only survived him by six months, and was then succeeded by Bhujangrao, whose tenure commenced at a stirring crisis. The seizure of Appa Sāhib by Mr. Jenkins was the signal for a general revolt, and Bhujangrao, true to the tradition of his house to support the reigning sovereign, threw himself into Chānda and participated in the valiant but unsuccessful defence of that city against the British. After the sack of Chānda, Bhujangrao continued to hold his zamīndāri undisturbed until his death in 1847, when he was succeeded by his son Venkateshwarrao, who died in 1851. The next proprietor was Lakshmī Bai, the widow of Bhīmrao who ruled the estate firmly and well until her death on the 21st June 1861. This lady distinguished herself by her loyalty to the British Government during the Mutiny. In March 1858, Bāburao, a petty chief of Mollampallī, began plundering in the Rājgarh pargana and was shortly afterwards joined by Venkatrao, the zamīndār of Ghot-Arpallī, the two finally declaring open rebellion against the British Rāj. The crowning act of these marauders was the murder of Messrs. Gartland and Hall of the Indian Telegraphs at Chinchgondī on the Prānhita. It was owing to the loyal activity of Lakshmī Bai that the capture of Bāburao was effected, and for this service she was rewarded with 67 villages of the confiscated Ghot-Arpallī zamīndāri, which still belong to the estate. Since the Mutiny and the advent of general peace the history of the estate has been marked by few events worthy of being chronicled. Three proprietors span the interval between Lakshmī Bai and the present zamīndār, Mengarao (1861—1866), Sāvitri Bai (1866—1871), and Dharmarao (1871—1893). During this time the succession was much chequered, and in 1869 Major Lucie Smith wrote of the family, 'Of late 'the curse of childlessness has fastened to their house, and 'Sāvitri Bai has seen three generations of chieftains die; has 'seen the line twice renewed by adoption, and twice fail of 'lineal heirs.' On the death of the latter in 1893, the estate descended to the present zamīndār Bhujangrao. Bhujangrao is unfortunately a man of stunted intellect, given to periodical drinking orgies, and he speedily fell a prey to parasites and involved the estate deeply in debt, at the same time allowing contractors to play havoc among the teak forests of the estate. In January 1902, the zamīndār was declared incapable of managing his own affairs, and the estate was taken under management by the Court of Wards, its indebtedness having by then accumulated to over a lakh. The assumption of the estate was marked by a somewhat unusual incident. Some six months after management had been assumed, the zamīndār under the promptings of mischief-mongers became possessed of the idea that whereas Government had only intended to assume management temporarily the manager of his own motion intended to usurp the zamīndāri in perpetuity. Accordingly, he summoned his followers to arms and concerted a kind of comic opera revolution, seizing the treasury and ejecting the manager from Ahīri by threatening to shoot him if he showed his face anywhere in the vicinity. As soon as the matter was firmly dealt with, this miniature rebellion collapsed. The zamīndār was brought into Chānda by the District Superintendent of Police, and was for a time kept under surveillance there. When his followers had been disarmed, his arms confiscated, and a clean sweep made of all the bad advisers who were at the bottom of the trouble, he was allowed to return to Ahīri. Since then, thanks to the firm hand kept on him by the new manager, he has been fairly amenable to reason, but even now at times indulges in frenzied drinking bouts during which nothing can be done with him. When not in his cups, he relapses into absolute lethargy, and all attempts to arouse his interest either in cultivation or in sport are found to be useless; he is, accordingly, perforce left to his own devices, and appears during these intervals to live a merely vegetable life. Until 1907, although the father of one or two illegitimate children, he remained without an heir and the house appeared doomed to a recurrence of its 'curse of childlessness,' but at length on the 21st March 1907 the elder of his two wives Pāpa Bai gave birth to a son who has been named Dharmarao, and the succession is thus for the present assured.

Details of the estate and subordinate tenures.

The estate now consists of 528 villages, 451 of which are zamīndāri and 77 mālguzāri. Three hundred and sixty-five of the zamīndāri and 60 of the mālguzāri villages are inhabited, and the rest are waste. Almost all these villages are directly managed, but a few are held by *thekādārs* or privileged holders. Two blocks of villages, known as the Jarawandi and Mollampallī tāluks, form estates which are held on subordinate tenure. The former, which comprised 17 villages, was granted in 1858 by the zamīndārs of Ahīri to one Jagarao Gond and his heirs for ever, originally on an annual rental of Rs. 100 in connection with a marriage settlement. This tāluk now consists of 23 villages and is held on a rental of Rs. 112 in *mālik-makbūza* right. The Mollampallī tāluk is the escheated estate of the rebel Bāburao. When this was conferred upon the zamīndārin Lakshmī Bai, she in turn made it over to the zamīndār of Bhopālpatnam, giving him full rights on an annual *takolī* of Rs. 101. This estate now consists of 23 villages paying a *takolī* of Rs. 172. This is held on a simple so-called *maktā* tenure, conferring no proprietary right.[1] Prior to the assumption of management by the Court of Wards, many of the villages, supposed to be held directly by the zamīndār, were very largely in the hands of headmen called *Gaitās* or Bhumias,[2] who appropriated large areas of rent-free land and diverted a goodly proportion of the rents into their own pockets. Great distances and lax supervision had given these men a very strong position, and their tenants depended upon them so absolutely that it was frequently found at settlement that large prosperous villages with stable rice cultivation had reverted into waste land simply because of the desertion of the Bhumia.

Population, trade and communications.

The population of the zamīndāri amounted in 1901 to 23,858 souls; this figure represents a density of 9 persons to the square mile and a decline of 10 per cent. from the returns of 1891. Ahīri has more natural advantages

[1] These various subordinate tenures have recently been settled on the basis of inferior proprietary right and assessed to revenue and *mālikāna*.

[2] The following note on Bhumias and *Gaitās* has been kindly furnished by Mr. Langhorne, Manager of the Ahiri zamīndāri. The Bhumia is a Māria institution. He is the man responsible for all the religious ceremonies of the village; all the arrangements for their observance are framed by him, but the actual ceremony cannot be carried out without the help of the *pujāri* of the village. In return for his services he is paid dues in grain and mahuā from every tenant in the village. The office used to be hereditary and was transferable either by sale or gift. The Bhumia was generally a man of great influence and no village was founded or could hope to thrive without his formal permission. He was very much the headman of the village and the office is even now highly prized. The Bhumia is not necessarily always a headman or *Gaitā* of a village; sometimes the office of Bhumia and *Gaitā* are separate; this separation usually is due to poverty or loss of influence on the part of the Bhumia which necessitates the appointment of a man in a stronger position to manage the village though the Bhumia still continues to draw his dues so long as he has not sold or transferred his right. *Gaitā* is the term in general use for headman or patel. Before the estate came under the Court of Wards the Bhumia and *Gaitā* were a power in the land and it lay with them to make or mar a village and the zamīndār very seldom if ever received his full dues; the Bhumia and *Gaitā* paid for one plough and cultivated five or six and in many cases also appropriated the rents of tenants who took up land in the village. This has now all changed since the estate came under Court of Wards and the position of the Bhumia and *Gaitā* have been clearly defined at settlement. The former is now purely and simply considered a religious official, and has no connection with land whatever; the office is heritable but not transferable and the original appointment of a Bhumia to a waste village rests with the zamīndār. The *Gaitā* is now simply a headman or patel, who is paid a commission of R. 0-2-0 on rentals and R. 0-1-0 on *siwāi* income as remuneration for his services.

than other zamīndāris in respect of soil and rainfall, and has therefore offered a better resistance to famine. The bulk of the population consists of aboriginals, Rāj-Gonds, Mārias and Koyās with a sprinkling of other castes. Telis and Marārs are fairly numerous in the parts adjacent to the *khālsa* in the north, and Kāpewārs on the border of Sironchā. Komtīs have also been attracted in some numbers by the trade in forest produce. Most of the inhabitants are true children of the jungle, and are content merely to raise so much food-grain as will suffice to supplement edible roots and fruits. Having an extremely low standard of comfort they are usually able to satisfy it without effort, and having no credit to speak of, they are generally able to get through life without incurring much debt. Imports are confined to salt, cloth and glass beads which are exchanged by petty traders for rice, a very fine quality of which is produced. Dhers and Mahārs bring in bales of home-made cloths and blankets which they exchange for bullocks. There are only two weekly bazars which are located at Ahīri and Alāpalli. Until quite recently the whole zamīndāri has been innocent of any communications worth speaking of, but roads are now being made linking Alāpalli with Sironchā and Chānda, and to the north-east with Muramgaon. Until the former road is completed development will necessarily be greatly handicapped.

Agriculture.

In respect of agricultural conditions, the greater part of the estate more or less closely resembles part of the Sironchā tahsīl, although owing to the encroachment of hills it possesses no broad belt of alluvial soils along the rivers. Nevertheless a fair amount of high class soil is found along the Prānhita, while in the hills of the interior numerous small perennial springs give the Māria every facility for his favourite *gattā* cultivation. In the north and west the physical characteristics are not unlike those of the neighbouring zamīndāris and the Ghot pargana. The tract probably gets more rain than other parts of the District owing to its dense forests and high hill ranges, and this, combined with the superiority of the average soil in cultivation, has made its cropping more secure than that of the other zamīndāris. Rice is the principal crop sown, and, as said above, is of particularly fine quality. At the last settlement it occupied over 14,000 acres out of 24,000 acres cropped. It is generally cultivated on the *jwālapod* and *gattā* systems, but the former method is now being confined within narrow limits by the Court of Wards. Sugarcane cultivation is now becoming fashionable. This is mainly due to the Court of Wards, which has spared no pains, both by demonstration and advice, to convince tenants of its value; but, as far as the aboriginal tenants are concerned, these efforts have been thrown away, as they never care to extend their cultivation beyond what they require for their own food. Kodon-kutkī, juār, mūng, urad and *kulthā* are the other chief crops. Also almost every tenant has a *bāri* in which he grows a little maize and tobacco. The area under crop has extended from 15,416 acres (probably a very conjectural figure) in 1868 to 30,622 acres in 1902 and to 35,480 acres in 1905-06. What extension there has been since the assumption of management is mainly due to immigrants from Hyderābād and Paralkot. In the *khālsa* area of the estate, the limit of cultivation has almost been reached in the inhabited villages, but efforts are being made to expand the occupied area by effecting an exchange of waste villages surrounded by Government forest for land lying along the Waingangā belonging to Government forest. The statistics of cultivation and rentals for the whole estate since it came under management are shown below:—

Year.	Area under cultivation.	Rental.
	Acres.	Rs.
1902-03	41,360	11,503
1903-04	43,158	11,898
1904-05	44,619	12,078
1905-06	46,513	13,521
1906-07	47,958	13,607

It will be seen that there has been a decided increase which is solely due to better management.

Forests.

The cultivation of the estate is however of minor importance in comparison with its forests. For an account of these the reader is referred to Chapter VI *supra* where the subject has been fully dealt with. The development of these forests on sylvicultural principles is the most remarkable achievement of the Court of Wards.

Receipt and expenditure.

Below are tabulated the receipts and expenditure under their main heads since assumption, the heads of the suspense account being excluded:—

RECEIPTS.

	1901-02.[1]	1902-03.	1903-04.	1904-05.	1905-06.	1906-07.
Rents, thekājamās, etc.	10,468	6513	11,573	11,595	12,931	13,607
Receipts from sīr ...	189	72	315	230	238	424
Forest receipts ...	11,362	28,694	31,780	47,689	38,457	43,024
Sīr and manorial dues	4667	5588	2932	2706	5196	...
Interest ...	...	2	5	39	101	154
Miscellaneous ..	6715	3322	10	...	21	4043
Total ..	33,401	44,191	46,615	62,259	56,944	61,252

EXPENDITURE.

	1901-02.[1]	1902-03.	1903-04.	1904-05.	1905-06.	1906-07.
Government revenue and cesses.	5837	1766	4094	4087	4819	6126
Village servants ...	2025	1282	702	819	...	833
Cost of management	5375	10,293	12,556	13,465	14,600	15,401
Interest on debts ...	...	40	284	1210	469	498
Personal expenses	1804	4,463	3995	4469	4344	4869
Education ...	54	91	102	...	...	...
Miscellaneous ...	4643	6154	5858	6025	11,437	6681
Total ...	19,738	24,090	27,591	30,075	35,669	34,408

[1] Figures for 1901-02 are for 8 months only.

The liabilities of the estate upon assumption were calculated at a total of 1·04 lakhs, but if the full figure subsequently claimed by the chief creditor be entered, this amount should have been shown as 1·30 lakhs. Rs. 31,073 of these claims were reduced by compromise with the creditors. The balance was paid off from savings out of current income as follows:—

Year.			Rs.
1901-02	...	...	404
1902-03	...	...	8050
1903-04	...	...	37,319
1904-05	...	...	4578
1905-06	...	...	38,667
1906-07	...	...	10,000
	Total	...	99,018

The estate has thus been fully cleared of its debts within about six years from its assumption, although it had been anticipated that at least ten years would be required to extricate it. It has now a clear field before it; an ample surplus may be expected every year, and owing to the tender age of the heir, it is not likely to be relinquished for many years to come. Hitherto, dictates of economy have circumscribed the scope for effecting improvements, but ample funds will in future be available.

Improvements.

But even with the limited means hitherto at command, it is safe to say that the estate has made almost as much progress in the last six years as in the whole of the previous six hundred years of its existence. *Pakkā* wells have been provided in some 20 villages, extensive repairs have been carried out on numerous tanks, substantial store buildings, office and quarters have been erected at Ahīri and *muram* tracks have been annually extended which will ultimately link up Ahīri and Dewalmāri and connect it with the Chānda-Sironchā road. The sums so far spent upon improvements are—1901-02, Rs. 140; 1902-03, Rs. 1321; 1903-04, Rs. 1130; 1904-05, Rs. 2523; 1905-06, Rs. [illegible]; and 1906-07, Rs. 4681.

Establishment.

The statement below shows the establishment which was employed by the zamīndār and also that now employed under the régime of the Court of Wards:—

ESTABLISHMENT EMPLOYED.

By Zamindar.		By Court of Wards.	
Particulars.	Cost.	Particulars.	Cost.
	Rs.		Rs.
Office establishment ...	1586	Manager	4800
Private servants of zamīndār	1998	Office establishment ...	1728
Revenue peons ...	1278	Local staff	2485
Kāmdārs and chuprassis ...	1482	Forest staff	1740
Forest staff	960	Miscellaneous staff ...	730
Pensioners	144	Chānda Sadar staff ...	192
Remuneration to Kotwārs	543	Remuneration to Kotwārs	648
Remuneration to Mukaddams.	147	Remuneration to Mukaddams.	748
Total ...	8138	Total ...	13,071

It will be seen that the staff has been considerably increased since assumption of management and the servants are sure of their pay and are paid regularly every month, whereas during the régime of the zamīndār the establishment were never sure of their pay, and for the greater part of the year they were obliged to live on the tenants. The zamīndār himself is given an allowance of Rs. 200 a month, and ample allowances are also made to his wives and a few other relatives. The policy of the Court of Wards is to keep the majority of villages under direct control, the collections being made by patels and *Gaitās* of villages who receive as remuneration for and stimulus to their services a commission of 2 annas in the rupee on rentals and 1 anna in the rupee on *siwai* income collected by them. The *thekādāri* system is only resorted to in villages which are deteriorating or in deserted villages, when one formed village, together with two or three which are deserted, are given to lessees on easy terms for a period of three years, renewable to five years if the villages are improved and new tenants brought in. In order to attract new tenants to the zamīndāris, lands are given for three years free of rent and, in addition, the new tenants do not pay any other dues for this period. After the expiry of three years the tenants are assessed full rentals on lands in their possession and are also called on to pay all the other ordinary dues paid by tenants and residents of the zamīndāri in accordance with the terms of the *wajib-ul-arz*. These tenants are bound down in a stamped bond to reside in the zamīndāris for ten years, failing which they are bound to pay up full rentals and other dues for the whole period since their settlement in the zamīndāris. The *takolī* payable to Government is Rs. 2000, and a further sum of Rs. 830-8-0 is payable on account of cesses.

Chandala Zamindari—With an area of 17 square miles is the smallest of all the zamīndāris. Although the zamīndāri itself is probably of ancient date, the ancestors of the present holder only obtained it as recently as 1820. During the troubles of 1818, the then zamīndār Bhauji Thākur deserted Chānda and went to Pānābaras where he died. In 1820, Captain Crawfurd conferred the zamīndārship upon one Indra Shā, in no way related to the former incumbent, setting forth in the patent that the new zamīndār should cause the estate to be inhabited, prevent robbery, extend cultivation, collect the rents and enjoy the proceeds of the zamīndāri from generation to generation. The present family is related to the Pānābaras zamīndārs. The zamīndāri is surrounded by the *khālsa* area of the Garhchirolī tahsīl on all sides save to the east where it adjoins the Khutgaon zamīndāri. Its northern and western borders lie only a few miles east of the Waingangā and south-east of the village of Garchirolī. Of the eleven villages constituting the zamīndāri only seven are inhabited. The soil is mostly *retāri*, and rice is the only crop of any importance, absorbing five-sixths of the cropped area. The area under cultivation had sunk from 768 acres in 1868 to 448 acres at the recent settlement, but has now expanded to 600 acres. Nearly 60 per cent. of the cultivated area is irrigated; this is due to the immigration of Marārs and Kunbīs from the *khālsa* who have taken villages and constructed tanks. The zamīndār himself with a home-farm of over 20 acres is the largest cultivator in the zamīndāri. Between 1891 and 1901, the population dwindled from 858 to 386; it is composed of Mārias, Golkars, and Kalārs. The succession of bad harvests has been too much for the zamīndār who in spite of careful and frugal management is heavily involved in debt. The family are Rāj-Gonds: the present representative is Nājuk Rao, a man between 65 and 70 years of age. Assets were taken at Rs. 548 at the recent settlement; the *takolī* was fixed at Rs. 30 while Rs. 16-8-0 are also payable on account of cesses. The income of the estate is something quite insignificant, probably not more than Rs. 400 or Rs. 500, and is insufficient to meet the expenses of the zamīndār.

Dhanora Zamindari—An estate with an area of 91 square miles, surrounded on all sides by other zamīndāris, having Rāngi to the north, Rāngi and Dūdhmāla to the west, Jharāpāpra to the south, and Muramgaon and the Aundhī zamīndāri of Drug to the east. Out of the 32 villages which are included in the estate only 17 are inhabited, and 52 square miles of the total area are unsurveyed hill and forest; some of the estate, however, consists of fairly open land. The Katni river runs from east to west across the estate Communications are provided for by the Garhchirolī-Dhanorā road, the earthwork of which has been carried eastward as far as Muramgaon. A few villages known as the Lekhā tāluk and at one time incorrectly styled the Lekhā zamīndāri are held in inferior proprietorship by the descendants of a Musalmān Jemādār of chuprassis, who used to be stationed at Wairāgarh about a hundred years ago, and who, after getting the villages mortgaged to him, took advantage of the ignorance which prevailed regarding the tract and styled himself zamīndār of Lekhā. The Dhanorā zamīndāri suffered very acutely during the late famines, its population sinking from 4432 to 2204 between 1891 and 1901. The area under cultivation sank *pari passu* and now stands at about 2000 acres only, of which 1500 acres are under rice. The forests used once to contain fair teak and *shīsham*, but at the recent settlement the forest income was calculated to be only Rs. 470 which works out at less than 3 pies per acre. The total assessable assets came to Rs. 2055 only; the *takolī* assessed is Rs. 120, while cesses amount to Rs. 60-8-0. The zamīndāri family are Rāj-Gonds; there are no documents to show how they came by their title, nor have they any legends of interest. The present zamīndār, Hanmant Rao, succeeded in 1905 and is aged about 35. Like his father before him, he is somewhat apathetic and leaves the management of the estate to a relative, in this case his younger brother Ambarshā Bābu. Dhanorā, the capital of the zamīndāri, possesses a very fine tank, and there are three other tanks in the estate. The income of the estate is probably about Rs. 1600 and its expenditure Rs. 1400.

Dudhmala Zamindari.—Dūdhmāla is a small zamīndāri on the extreme west of the zamīndāri area, lying in about the same parallel as the headquarters of the Garhchirolī tahsīl and to the south of the Rāngi zamīndāri. The Dhanorā zamīndāri lies to the east and the Khutgaon zamīndāri to the south. Out of a total area of 33 square miles, only 19 miles are included in village areas, the balance being unsurveyed hills and forests. The total number of villages is 15 of which 6 are uninhabited, and the area under cultivation which at the first settlement stood at 938 acres had shrunk to 549 acres when proposals for reassessment were framed. Soils and cultivation are of the usual zamīndāri type. Although well served by the Garhchirolī-Dhanorā road which runs through its centre, the zamīndāri is in a very depressed condition having been extremely hard hit by famine. The population which in 1891 stood at 1162 had fallen to 844 in

1901, and consists mainly of Gonds in poor circumstances. The zamīndār Vishnu Rao is a Rāj-Gond; he is aged about 37 and is of weak intellect. The estate is managed by his younger brother. The family can only trace their lineage for four generations, but are supposed to have held the zamīndāri some 300 years. The assessable assets were placed at Rs. 429 at the recent settlement, and the *kāmil-jamā* at Rs. 225; the *takolī* demand is only Rs. 30, while Rs. 13-4-0 are payable as cesses. The total income probably does not exceed Rs. 700, nearly Rs. 500 of this being derived from forests; the expenditure reaches approximately the same figure.

Gewardha Zamindari—Is divided into the three parganas of Bedgaon, Rāmgarh and Gewardhā; of these Bedgaon and Rāmgarh lie in the extreme north-east of the District adjoining the Ambāgarh Chaukī zamīndāri lately transferred to Drug, while Gewardhā lies some way to the west on the fringe of the *khālsa;* Rāmgarh and Bedgaon form a compact area, but they are separated from Gewardhā by a solid wedge of Palāsgarh territory several miles in breadth. A large part of Bedgaon and Rāmgarh is covered with forest-clad hills, and the stretch of fourteen miles lying between the headquarters villages of these two parganas is one of the wildest and most desolate tracts in the whole District. It goes by the name of the Sātnāla hills, and is watered by the Sāt, which is the only considerable stream, though nothing more than a mountain torrent, in the zamīndāri. The Gewardhā pargana is comparatively open and resembles the adjoining *khālsa*. The zamīndāri comprises 77 villages, of which the most considerable are Bedgaon and Markākasā at which bazars are held. Its population in 1901 stood at 7715, a decrease of 7·8 per cent. on the figures of the previous census. Compared with most other zamīndāris, the estate has made a good recovery from the famines and is in a fairly stable condition. On the death in 1895 of the zamīndārin Madīna Bi, who left no heirs, it was placed under the management of the Court of

Wards, and after a protracted inquiry into many counter-claims, the present ward Abdul Hamīd, then a boy of 11 years of age, was declared heir. The estate was practically clear of debt when taken over; subsequently a land improvement loan of Rs. 5000 was taken from Government, Rs. 3000 of which were repaid and the balance remitted in 1900. The estate has always been in easy financial circumstances, and in 1906 was able to invest the sum of Rs. 8000 in Government securities; in addition to this it has a large cash balance and extensive grain investments. The annual gross receipts since assumption average Rs. 8312, the largest receipts of any one year being Rs. 10,220 in 1901-02 and the smallest Rs. 4877 in the famine year 1899-1900. The average annual expenditure during the same period has been Rs. 8525 but this sum includes large amounts on account of investments and improvements. The average income and expenditure during the three years 1904-07 are shown below:—

Receipts.		Expenditure.	
	Rs.		Rs.
Rent and cesses ...	3685	Government revenue and cesses.	695
Forests	3978	Cost of management ...	2592
Sīr and manorial dues ...	680	Personal expenses ...	2391
Interest	279	Education	540
Miscellaneous ...	773	Miscellaneous	511
		Investments	3433
		Improvements	493
Total ...	9393	Total ...	10,655

Cultivation is expanding steadily, and stood at 21,586 acres in 1905-06. Several improvements have been effected since the Court of Wards took over the estate, mainly in the direction of tank improvement and sinking wells; Bedgaon has also been provided with a school at the cost of the estate. Four tanks were constructed as relief works in the famine of 1900. The ward is an amiable and intelligent young man who has been studying at the Alīgarh College since 1905. He will soon be of age to administer the estate himself, and it remains to be seen whether he has sufficient strength of character to do so without being eaten out of house and home by numerous esurient relatives[1]. The zamīndāri is of comparatively recent date, having been founded by a Musalmān Dīwān of some of the northern zamīndāris, who obtained the transfer of the Bedgaon and Rāmgarh *ilākas* from Ambāgarh Chaukī and Palāsgarh respectively, and the grant of the Gewardhā group of villages from the Wairāgarh pargana. The arrangement appears to have been sanctioned by the Marāthā government, but there is no *sanad* extant; Musalmān influence was paramount in Wairāgarh at the time, and probably the whole arrangement was simply an act of spoliation on the part of the authorities there. As hereditary Dīwāns, the Gewardhā zamīndārs are said to have kept all the important documents of the Wairāgarh chiefs, but these have all long been lost. The *kāmil-jamā* of the estate was placed at the recent settlement at Rs 4500, the amount of *takolī* and cesses payable to Government being fixed at Rs. 872-8-0.

Gilgaon Zamindari.—This zamīndāri has an area of 60 square miles of which 34 square miles consist of unsurveyed hill and forest; it lies in the west of the zamīndāri area, being only separated from the Waingangā river by a narrow strip of *khālsa* territory. To the east it is bounded by Khutgaon and Potegaon and to the south by Pai-Murandā, while *khālsa* territory surrounds it to the north and west. Nothing is known as to the acquisition of the zamīndāri, but it is undoubtedly of ancient tenure and has probably suffered a good deal from encroachment at the hands of its powerful neighbour Ahīri. At present it consists of 22 villages, 15

[1] The young zamīndār has unfortunately since died, and the question of succession is again *sub-judice*.

Ja'far's putting him to death (IKhn). Marwān was called AlJa'dī [because he had learnt (IAth, MAB)] from [his preceptor and master (TKh)] AlJa'd Ibn Dirham (IAth, MAB, TKh) the doctrines of the Creation of the Ḳur'ān and of Predestination (IAth, MAB), etc. (IAth) : and he was known as AlḤimār because of his bravery, from the saying فُلَانٌ أَصْبَرُ مِنْ حِمَارٍ فِي ٱلْحَرْبِ *Such a one is more patient than a he-ass in war*; for he used not to flag in waging war upon the rebels against him, and was the bravest of the Banù Umayya (TKh). It is said that AlJa'd Ibn Dirham published his doctrine of the Creation of the Ḳur'ān in the days of Hishām Ibn 'Abd AlMalik, under whose order he was put to death by Khālid alḲasrī, governor of Al'Irāḳ (IAth). The Wāsiṭ of Al'Irāḳ was founded by AlḤajjāj Ibn Yūsuf athThaḳafī between AlKūfa and AlBaṣra; and for that reason was named Wāsiṭ, because it was *intermediate* between the 2 cities, [the distance from it to each being 50 parasangs (MI), i.e. leagues]: it was begun by him in 84, and finished in 86 (Mk)—*l.* 12. The 1st hemistich is

حَشَايَ عَلَى جَمْرٍ ذَكِيٍّ مِنَ ٱلْغَضَا

My heart in on glowing embers of the wood called غَضًا ; and the verse is from an ode by AlMutanabbi : W says (AKB), He says *My heart is on glowing embers from passion*, i.e. on account of their bidding farewell and their departing; *and mine eye is revelling* in the face of the beloved *in a garden of beauty* (W, AKB). مِنَ ٱلْهَوَى (W) for مِنَ ٱلْغَضَا .

P. 860, *ll.* 2-3. بَطْنُ عَاقِلٍ *The bottom,* or *low land, of 'Āḳil* is [a place (MI)] on the road of the pilgrims of AlBaṣra between Rāmatān and (Mk, MI) Āmirra (Mk) [or] Immara (MI)—*l.* 4. 'Āḳil is said to be a mountain (Bk, ZJ) that Ḥujr, the father of Imra alḲais, used to dwell in (Bk). The author of the Mk, after enumerating 8 places named 'Āḳil, the 2nd of which he describes as "a mountain that the "children of [Ḥujr (KA)] Ākil alMurār, the ancestor of Imra alḲais, "used to stop in", adds "But I do not find myself confident that they "are 8 [separate] places; and perhaps there is some intermixture in them"—*l.* 8. See Md. II. 182 and P. II. 598—*ll.* 16-17. The R (*vol.* II, *p.* 142, *l.l.*) has "either because repetition of the *v.* is made a "substitute for dualization of the *ag.*", which, though it occurs in all 3 *eds.*, I have ventured to invert—*ll.* 19-20. The 2 Indian *eds.* of the R. (*vol.* ii, *p.* 143, *l.* 2) have صاحبه *his companion*; but the Persian *ed.* has صاحبيه *his 2 companions.*

P. 861, *l.* 1. تَسْمِيَةُ جُزْءٍ بِاسْمِ كُلٍّ *naming a part by the name of a whole* (R), i.e., *putting a whole for a part*, as *penes* for *penis* and *testicles* for *two testicles* in the *exs.* given—*l.* 3. Read "*two testicles*" and "substitutions."